COURAGE ALONE

The Italian Air Force 1940-1943

Chris Dunning

HIKOKI
PUBLICATIONS

First published in Great Britain in 1998 by
Hikoki Publications Ltd
16 Newport Road, Aldershot, Hants, GU12 4PB
Tel: 01252 319935 Fax: 01252 655593
E.mail hikoki@dircon.co.uk
© 1998 Hikoki Publications

ISBN 1 902109 02 3

Edited by Barry Ketley
Artwork by Richard Caruana
Maps by Steve Longland
Design by Hikoki Publications
Printed in Great Britain by
Hillmans, Frome, Somerset

Distribution & Marketing by
Midland Publishing Ltd
24 The Hollow, Earl Shilton, Leicester LE9 7NA
Tel: 01455 233 747 Fax: 01455 233 737

ALSO AVAILABLE

Luftwaffe Emblems 1939-1945
by
Barry Ketley & Mark Rolfe
ISBN 0 9519899 7 9

Luftwaffe Fledglings 1935-1945
Luftwaffe Training Units & their Aircraft
by
Barry Ketley & Mark Rolfe
ISBN 0 9519899 2 8

The Secret Years
Flight Testing at Boscombe Down 1939-1945
by
Tim Mason
ISBN 0 951899 9 5

Forever Farnborough
Flying the Limits 1904-1996
by
Peter J. Cooper AMRAeS
ISBN 0 951899 3 6

Royal Naval Air Service 1912-1918
by
Brad King
ISBN 0 9519899 5 2

FORTHCOMING

Eyes for the Phoenix
Allied Photo-reconnaissance Operations
in South-east Asia in World War 2
by
Geoff Thomas
ISBN 0 951899 4 4

Stormbird
Flying through fire as a Luftwaffe ground-attack
pilot and Me 262 ace
by
Oberst (i. R.) Hermann Buchner
ISBN 1 902109 00 7

Shadows
Airlift and Airwar in Biafra and Nigeria
1967-1970
by
Michael I. Draper
ISBN 1 902109 63 5

Condor
The Luftwaffe in Spain 1936-1939
by
Patrick Laureau
ISBN 1 902109 10 4

Caption to title page: The unknown soldier—an unidentified Tenente Pilota of the 80ª Squadriglia, 17° Gruppo, 1° Stormo CT posing in front of his Macchi MC 202 Series I Folgore. These early models were delivered without the later ribbed tropical dust filter to the air intake, so the location is probably Campoformido in October 1941, shortly before the unit moved to Ciampino for fitment of the dust filters and a rapid transfer to North Africa. The aircraft is finished in the overall dark green 'continental' camouflage, which was rarely seen on the MC 202, and it has a name, 'Filippo', painted under the canopy. Not visible, but certainly soon to be applied on the white fuselage band, is the Stormo's famous octagonal archer emblem

DEDICATIONS

In honour of the Italian airmen of World War II, whom Allied propaganda has often treated in an unkind way. I hope I have done them justice

To the person who laid the foundation in my formative years that I may create such as this—my mother. As one grows older one appreciates more the too often unstated, so I also wish to acknowledge my sisters, Adrienne and Elizabeth

ACKNOWLEDGMENTS

Thank you to the following :

For their original helpful advice and encouragement, Elizabeth Kirby, now a bookseller in Chipping Norton; Ron Murray of ISO Publications in London; Dave Hatherell of The Aviation Bookshop in London; Chris Ellis and Simon Parry of Air Research Publications who produced the earlier edition of this work. An extra thank you to Simon Parry for introducing me to Barry Ketley, who helped me get over the hurdles which held up earlier release of this greatly revised and expanded book, and without whom this volume would not have been possible.

My family and friends for their warmth, enthusiasm, and support, with special mention of John Bishop, Phil Minter and John Ruffalo.

Most of all, my main source of raw material, the Imperial War Museum staff for their patience, courtesy, and help. In particular, Phil Reed and his staff from the Department of Documents, and Mary and Terry from the Department of Books.

I would also like to acknowledge the many letters received from the readers of the first edition. Further information was supplied and helpful advice received from, to name just a few, members of the 82 Gruppo Association, Gregory Alegi of Gruppo Amici Velvoli Storici, Roberto Gentilli, *Dott. Ing.* Tullio Marcon, *Dott. Ing.* Umberto Ucelli,

Arno Lehtonen, Jack Greene, Frank McMeiken, Prof. Jean Gaillard, Michael Starmer, Capt. Howard Christie, Andy Stewart, Paolo Rossi, Alessandro Ragatzu, Jim Davila, Ron Mazurkiewicz, and Paul Brown. Space does not allow a further list of participants, but they know who they are and my grateful thanks to all those who helped fill in the gaps in this history.

I am considering a supplemental volume detailing unit badges and more personal experiences of the aircrew involved. If any ex-aircrew or their families would like to contribute information and anecdotes towards this, fill in missing information, or provide constructive comments for future editions, please write to me via Hikoki Publications. Any contributions will, of course, be acknowledged in the new volume if used.

Publisher's note: First published in 1988 as a slim paperback volume outlining only the first eighty-two Gruppi, this is a new and greatly revised and expanded work which covers *all* the combat units (almost 400 squadrons) and experi-mental establishments of the Regia Aeronautica from 10 June 1940 until the Armistice of 8 September 1943. This book would not have been possible without the generous assistance of the following people who supplied photographs: Richard Caruana, Malcolm Passingham, Giorgio Apostolo, Giancarlo Garello, Achille Ghizzardi, Giorgio Giorgi, Achille Vigna, Bruce Robertson, Stato Maggiore Aeronautica, Bundesarchiv, Barry Ketley.

CONTENTS

INTRODUCTION

The intention behind this book is to provide the aviation enthusiast with comprehensive and extensive information concerning the Italian *Regia Aeronautica* (Royal Air Force)* from the Italian declaration of war on 10 June 1940 until the Armistice of 8 September 1943. It will also provide a ready reference source for historians, wargamers, and interested parties who may have been involved in the theatres of war shown. It is the only single volume account of all the unit movements and equipment to date.

Despite being perceived as one of the most powerful air forces of the 1930s, the Regia Aeronautica failed to live up to its potential in the 1940s. I believe the main reasons (not necessarily in this order) were :

● A lack of a cohesive financial policy in Italy for limited industrial and material resources.

● Entry into a war with what were, despite the propaganda, ill-prepared and ill-equipped armed forces. The Italians were not alone in suffering from the consequences—in the early stages of the war Britain, also, did not have the quality and quantity of resources needed to prevent defeats.

● The ambivalent attitude of many Italians to the entry of Italy into the war on the Axis side, the reasons for which had little relevance to the average Italian, but had much to do with adventurism and vanity on the part of Benito Mussolini.

● Lack of a clearly thought out strategic or tactical doctrine for the air force, exacerbated by equipment mediocrity. The loss of Italo Balbo in 1940 robbed the Regia Aeronautica of one of the few men within its ranks who may have had the necessary vision to salvage the situation.

● Reliance on ideas and tactics 'proven' in Albania, Ethiopia and Spain, where success against limited opposition gave an exaggerated picture of the Regia Aeronautica's capabilities.

● Badly structured aircrew training with an over-emphasis on technical flying skills, to the detriment of strategic and tactical understanding relating to use of the air weapon.

● Too many different aircraft types produced from limited resources, rather than standardisation on a select few.

● Obsolescent equipment, despite some good engineering ideas. In particular, the under development of an efficient radio communications system.

● Excellent airframes were handicapped by lack of development of more powerful aircraft engines, which resulted in reduced performance, weapon and load carrying capabilities.

● The lethargic control and organisation of the supply system.

● Misapprehensions and poor communication between all the Services concerning each others needs and capabilities.

● A lack of appreciation between higher and lower ranks.

● Highly effective Allied propaganda.

Despite all this, the Italians were among the first to experiment with radio-controlled aircraft, and they taught the Germans about torpedo-bombing. They practiced air-to-air bombing, and were quick to learn the inadequacies of high level bombing against shipping. With engines licence-built and bought from Germany, they produced aircraft equal to their opponents (but as in most wars—too few and too late).

Essentially, Italian frontline airmen and groundcrew of World War II were no different to the young men of other nations. They suffered from the same in-adequacies (possibly more so) in the systems meant to support them, learned to make do in most situations, fought, lived and died—but in so doing shared the comradeship only those involved can truly understand.

Claims stated in the text are those in Italian records —not necessarily the real outcome of the combats. It must be remembered that all Air Forces suffered differences between those aerial victories claimed and enemy aircraft actually shot down. One of the related problems was identification. Such was the reputation of the Spitfire that Italian aircrew were claiming to have encountered them all over the Mediterranean and Balkans, months before they actually arrived!

In the following pages I hope to show the extent of the Regia Aeronautica's commitment to the various theatres they were expected to cover.

Chris Dunning
London 1998

*Italy was nominally a monarchy until 16 June 1946 when Umberto, son of the weak-willed Victor Emmanuel III who had been on the throne from 1900 until 8 May 1946, abdicated following a referendum which demanded the establishment of a republic

CHRONOLOGY
The timetable for the Regia Aeronautica's war

In addition to the main events listed below, there were also constant coastal patrols, convoy escorts, rescue duties, home defence, reconnaissance and transport flights.

1940

10 June to 25 June
Operations against France

10 June to 10 January 1941
Operations against Malta: first stage

10 June to 31 August
Conquest of Somaliland, East Africa

22 June
First raid on Eastern Mediterranean: Egypt, Palestine, Cyprus

8 July to 15 July
Battaglia di Punta Stilo (Battle of Calabria): convoy battle

17 July
First raid on Gibraltar

1 Above: Single-finned Cant Z.1007 bombers of the 261ª Squadriglia unload their bombs on a target somewhere in the Mediterranean, possibly Malta

19 July
Combattimento di Capo Spada: attack on HMS *Sidney* and HMS *Havock*

1 September to 18 September
First North African Offensive: capture of Sidi Barrani

27 September to 15 April 1941
Operations against England in the Battle of Britain

28 October to 23 April 1941
Operations against Greece

9 November to 13 November
British attack on Taranto

27 November
Battaglia di Capo Teulada: attack on Force H

9 December to 6 February 1941
Withdrawal from Cirenaica, under British counter-offensive

1941

9 January to 11 January
Attack on Force H

10 January to 22 May
First offensive against Malta

10 January to 27 November
British offensive in East Africa

9 February
British bombard Genova

15 February to 15 April
Axis reconquest of Cirenaica

28 March
Battaglia di Gaudo e Matapan (Battle of Matapan): mostly naval

6 April to 17 April
Operations against Yugoslavia

28 April to 1 May
Occupation of Cefalonia, Corfu, and Zante-Ionian Islands

8 May to 10 May
Attack on Force H and convoy

May 41 to September 1943
Anti-partisan operations in Albania and Yugoslavia

20 May to 31 May
Assistance to German assault on Crete

1 June to 30 November
Second stage of operations against Malta

22 July to 25 July
Attacks on Force H and convoy

29 July to 30 November 1942
Expeditionary force to Russia: advance to the Don river

26 September to 28 September
Attacks on Royal Navy in western Mediterranean

18 November to 10 January 1942
Withdrawal from Cirenaica, under British counter-attack

1 December to 31 December
Third stage of operations against Malta

1942
January to April
Preparation for the invasion of Malta

18 January to April
Axis retake Cirenaica

13 February to 14 February
Attacks on convoys in eastern Mediterranean

10 March to 11 March
Attacks on Royal Navy in eastern Mediterranean

20 March to 10 May
Second offensive on Malta

21 March to 24 March
Battaglia della Sirte: attacks on convoys from eastern Mediterranean

25 May to 21 June
Axis capture Tobruk

13 June to 15 June
Battaglia di Mezzo Giugno: HARPOON and VIGOROUS convoys to Malta

22 June to 20 July
Axis advance on El Alamein

22 July to 31 July
First battle of El Alamein

11 August to 13 August
Battaglia di Mezzo Agosto: PEDESTAL convoy to Malta

30 August to 5 September
Second battle of El Alamein

10 October to 20 October
Third offensive on Malta

20 October to 22 January 1943
Third battle of El Alamein, and withdrawal to Tunisia

7 November to 13 May 1943
Defence against invasion of North Africa and Tunisia

1 December to 15 May 1943
Unit replacements, and then withdrawal from Russian front

1943
18 May to 11 June
Defence of Pantelleria

9 July to 17 August
Defence against invasion of Sicily

3 September to 7 September
Defence against invasion of southern Italy

8 September
Italy signs the Armistice

COMMAND STRUCTURE
Doctrine, Area Commands and Theatres

After the carnage of World War One, most people regarded another mass blood-letting as unthinkable. More sober-minded and less optimistic individuals, however, were working on theoretical concepts for future armed conflicts. Some of these would influence military thinkers far beyond their national borders, one of the most important in the aviation world being the Italian, Giulio Douhet.

Douhet was an army officer who had commanded the prewar Italian Air Corps, but had been court-martialled in 1916 for disagreeing with his superiors on the use of aircraft. By the end of the war he was working in aviation administration, and had been reinstated with the rank of General. By 1922 he had determined to concentrate on writing about the theories concerning the use of air power.

In 1927 he revised and reissued a book which became widely read and of seminal influence through-out the western world—'Command of the Air'. The main thrust of his argument was that future victory in war would go to the nation which could dominate the skies. Bombing of industries and cities would cause panic among the population who would force their government to

2 Above: *Fiat G.50 fighters of an unidentified fighter squadron violating the air space of the Republic of San Marino. The basic tactical combat formation of the Regia Aeronautica fighter units until well into the war was the 'sezione' of three aircraft as seen here by the right hand wingman*

surrender. Ground forces were considered as purely defensive. Fighter aircraft were dismissed, as bombers were to be self-defending and as fast or faster than the interceptors. At the time, this was a reasonable proposition, as the latest bomber types entering service in the late 1920s-1930s were capable of outflying any interceptors. A case in point being the Fairey Fox, which was faster than anything else in RAF service at the time of its debut. In fact, later experience was to prove that this was a false premise.

Douhet's ideas were taken up by Chief of Air Staff, Sir Hugh Trenchard, for the RAF, and Brigadier General William Mitchell for the USAAC. All agreed that the Air Force must be an independent serice, not a supplement to the army or navy. Ideas about the role of ground forces and fighter aircraft were modified, but the basic idea of the the bomber as the ultimate war-winner remained. The fear of this ("the bomber will always get through") misguided many politicians in the thirties and forties and left them vulnerable to the likes of Adolf Hitler who exploited this fear to the full.

During the 1930s another Italian developed and proved practical what was to become a major element in the forthcoming war—the long range mass aircraft formation. Marshal Italo Balbo developed Douhet's theories and suggested that "closely formed units of bombers could operate over large distances and successfully fight their way through defences and saturate targets." He assembled and trained large formations of flying boats and successfully navigated and flew them all over Europe, before leading them personally to America where they created a sensation, as never before had more than one or two aircraft achieved the transatlantic flight in one passage. Therein lay the foundations for the RAF and USAAF mass bomber formations of 1942-1945, and the opening of ideas for the future success of Ferry Command. Unfortunately for the Italians, the limited resources of their home industries prevented their own air forces from developing in the same degree.

In the prewar and early war periods any large bomber formation was often termed as a 'balbo'. Applications of the theories were carried out in the Spanish Civil War and Ethiopia (where they were more in the nature of aerial demonstrations on account of the complete lack of any aerial opposition). On 28 June 1940, Marshal Balbo, by then Governor of Libya, was conducting an inspection of troops around the Tobruk area when his aircraft was accidentally shot down by friendly fire. Consequently he was never to see practical applications of the theories of air superiority fully-fledged over Europe. With him also died much of the driving force of the Regia Aeronautica.

In World War Two the RA bomber arm was initially used on medium and high level operations, targets being assigned by their own commands, who received inputs from the army and navy through slow and inefficient command systems. Interservice rivalries impeded progress, even if many plans were thorough and well thought out.

Over land the immediate army support units quickly proved to be inadequately equipped and too few in number with the result that the bomber and fighter units were drawn into the ground battles at low level and out of their optimum environment. Modern defences, improved anti-aircraft artillery and fighter opposition claimed many aircraft, which were already in short supply for their intended role. Consequently the army support units were withdrawn to occupied Yugoslavia on anti-partisan duties, which proved to be a costly drain on already limited resources.

By early 1941 the Regia Aeronautica in Africa had been devastated, so new units were hastily formed to keep up the numbers. Gradually, older fighters were transferred to the fighter-bomber and ground attack roles, where their robust radial engines proved to be less vulnerable than their equivalents in the Allied camp which used mainly liquid-cooled engines.

As the war proceeded, special force were created for campaigns in Belgium, Greece and Russia. These were mobile commands containing their own bomber, fighter and reconnaissance units. East African operations were conducted on a small scale, bomber formations for example rarely being more than three aircraft. This theatre ceased to exist once supply routes from the mother country were cut off. Paradoxically, some of the most successful units were to be found here, principally on account of the opposition being in nearly as bad a state as the Italians.

Over the sea the medium and high level formations were being driven out of effective range by ever-improving defences. This resulted in a concentration on low level torpedo-bombing which proved very successful, albeit often fatal for the crews.

By the start of 1942 resources were being concentrated on reconnaissance, torpedo-bomber, fighter and fighter-bomber roles. Bombers were being switched to night attacks. Throughout the war reconnaissance units, especially those equipped with flying boats, played a highly effective part. Behind the lines obsolete aircraft were used on local defence, sea and land patrols, transport and liasion duties, thereby releasing more modern aircraft for frontline use.

By late 1942, however, although still hamstrung by its lack of support elements, the Regia Aeronautica had learned the same lessons as all the participants, and had effectively become a purely tactical air force, similar in use and composition to the Luftwaffe.

Commands

The operational commands of the Regia Aeronautica were divided into areas known as either Zona Aerea Territoriale, Squadra, Comando of the named area, or the title of the Expeditionary Force if they entered non-Italian zones of influence. The first of these was a pre-war allocation which was soon discarded.

The abbreviations shown in brackets after the command title are the author's and consequently unofficial, but have been used for convenience in the 'Zone' column in the movement charts for the different operational units. These commands were the approximate equivalent to the German 'Luftflotte', British 'Group', or American 'Division', and could use a mixture of aircraft types. The following descriptions give an outline of their duties:

Squadra 1 (SQA1): HQ Milan

This command was responsible for the protection of northern Italy, where most of the home industries were located. It was also a training area for the other commands. In the early weeks units participated in attacks on southern France and Corsica, thereafter patrolling the French coastline and escorting the navy until September 1943. They also provided units for occupied France.

Squadra 2 (SQA2): HQ Palermo

Initially based in Sicily for operations against Tunisia, Algeria, and Malta, it also controlled the sea between France and French West Africa, blocked the Sicilian Canal, and carried out anti-shipping operations in the central Mediterranean. On 23 December 1940 it moved to Italy (HQ Padova) and from 6 April joined operations against Yugoslavia, supporting Squadra 4 and Aeronautica dell'Albania with supplies, equipment and back-up operations, until 17 April. Thereafter, it remained on home defence duties until 1943, when many of its units were disbanded.

Squadra 3 (SQA3): HQ Rome

This command controlled the sea between Corsica and the French coast and conducted operations in the western Mediterranean. Attacks were made in June 1940 on France and Corsica. It turned to home defence duties until November 1942, when several units were passed to Aeronautica della Sardegna and Aeronautica della Sicilia for anti-invasion operations. From July to August 1943 it helped defend Sicily, resuming home defence duties until September.

Squadra 4 (SQA4): HQ Bari

This command covered the central and eastern Mediterranean, the Adriatic Sea, and watched the Balkan countries. From 28 October 1940 to 23 April 1941, with HQ now at Brindisi, replacing 4 ZAT on 30 December, they operated against Greece. The Yugoslavia campaign was entered from 6 to 17 April 1941. Then from 28 April to 1 May they covered the occupation of Corfu, Cefalonia, and Zante Islands. HQ was moved to Bari on 10 May 1941. They then supported Aeronautica dell'Albania through to 1943. Some units were then passed to the defending commands of Sardinia and Sicily and the rest helped defend Sicily in July and August 1943. Home defence duties continued until the armistice.

Squadra 5 (SQA5): HQ Tripoli

Originally Aeronautica della Libia until 15 July 1940, when this split into Settore Ovest (Tripoli) and Settore Est (Tobruk) to ease administration problems over such a vast area of North Africa. Operations were carried out on Egypt and Tunisia, mainly border patrols at first, and attacks on shipping in the central and eastern Mediterranean.

On 1 September 1940 they supported the advance on Sidi Barrani, losing heavily during the subsequent retreat from 9 December to 6 February. A lack of proper ground attack aircraft meant committing even ordinary bombers to attacks at ground level where small arms fire was deadliest.

With German assistance they returned to the attack on 15 February 1941, only to retreat again in November. Once again there were heavy losses, nearly 250 unserviceable aircraft being captured on bases in Cirenaica by the advancing British. The Germans lost almost as many. Hundreds of other aircraft had been shot down, or were found in aircraft graveyards in the open desert. A counter-attack was launched in January 1942, ending in the conquest of Tobruk in June and the advance to Alamein by July.

On account of the comparatively lower combat capabilities of the Italian aircraft, combined with a low level of supply, the Germans agreed in 1941-1942 that Italian aircrew in Africa would be responsible for the protection of ports, supply lines and escort duties. The Luftwaffe would shoulder the front-line activities, calling on the large numbers of Italian aircraft only when a major offensive was launched. This doctrine was modified when the MC 202s arrived in numbers, allowing the MC 200s, G 50s and CR 42s to switch to fighter-bomber roles. A Settore Centrale was added on 15 July 1942 to cover Cirenaica.

A build-up of resources culminated in the Alamein battles which reached a pitch in October 1942, ending in a retreat from Egypt and Libya by January 1943. On 15 February the command took over the Tunisian area until withdrawn from Africa in May, when the Squadra ceased to exist.

Aeronautica della Sardegna (ASAR): HQ Cagliari

This command covered the central Mediterranean, Tunisia, Algeria, and helped block the Sicilian Canal. Operations were made on French shipping between France and Africa in June 1940. They were very active against the Malta-bound convoys and were thrown against the invasion forces, reinforced by Squadras 3 and 4, from November 1942 to May 1943. They then assisted in the defence of Sicily, relying on self-defence in the last weeks before the armistice. When Corsica was occupied in 1943 they commanded that area too.

Aeronautica dell'Egeo (AEGE): HQ Rodi

This controlled the Aegean Islands and later Greece. (Aeronautica della Grecia [AGRE] was not operational until 15 August 1941: HQ Athens). The main duties were escorting convoys from Greece to Libya, anti-shipping operations in the eastern Mediterranean and armed reconnaissance of Egypt, Turkey, Palestine, Syria, and Cyprus. They supported the campaigns against Greece, then Crete (20 to 31 May 1941).

Aeronautica dell'Albania (AALB): HQ Tirana

This command controlled the Adriatic Sea, watched the Balkans and joined the Greek (28 October 1940 to 23 April 1941), and Yugoslav (6 to 17 April 1941) campaigns. Following the Balkan surrender the area was split into German and Italian occupation zones. On 7 May 1942 the area was sub-divided into air commands for Albania and Slovenia-Dalmazia, for anti-partisan operations until September 1943.

Aeronautica della Sicilia (ASIC): HQ Palermo

From 23 December 1940 they took over from Squadra 2, with operations against Malta, blocking the Sicilian Canal and anti-shipping sorties in the central Mediterranean. They were heavily involved in the campaign to reduce Malta and from November 1942, operated against the invasion forces in French West Africa and protected the sea and air convoys en route to and from Tunisia. It was virtually wiped out in July and August 1943, trying to defend itself and Pantelleria.

Aeronautica della Tunisia (ATUN): HQ Tunis

This command was formed in November 1942 for the control of supply routes between Sicily and Tunisia, and for the protection of the main ports in Tunisia. These were Tunis, Bizerte, Sousse, and Sfax. Units from the Sicilian command were used until 15 February 1943, when the area was absorbed by Squadra 5 and the command ceased.

Aeronautica della Provence (APRO): HQ Salon

The Italians moved into southern France on 9 November 1942, at the same time occupying Corsica and moving into Tunisia. The air command was set up on 15 April 1943, using mainly close support units. Later, it became a training ground for the remnants of the bomber force until ousted by the Germans in September.

Africa Orientale Italiana (AOI): HQ Addis Abeba

Limited in resources and reliant on supplies via Libya, this area covered Eritrea, Ethiopia and Somaliland, and was widely fought over from June 1940 to November 1941. The command was split into north, east, west, and south areas. They patrolled the Sudanese, Kenyan, French and British Somaliland borders and watched for activities in the Red Sea, Indian Ocean, and at Aden. Attacks were launched on British Somaliland and southern Sudan. Many battles were fought with antiquated and sparse numbers of aircraft on both sides. The area was unusual in that its bomber units, for the most part, had duplicate numbers with those in other command areas.

Corpo Aereo Italiano (CAI): HQ Brussels

Mussolini decided to join Hitler's subjugation of England and formed this expeditionary force on 10th September 1940. However, the units proved relatively ineffective in the aerial campaign due to outdated aircraft and tactics. They were withdrawn by 15 April 1941, having made a few coastal raids and local fighter patrols.

Corpo di Spedizione Italiano in Russia (CSIR): HQ Tudora

The Comando Aviazione for this expeditionary force was formed on 25 July 1941. They were to support the Italian 8th Army in its advance to the River Don and operations in southern Russia. Where necessary, they also assisted the Germans, receiving commendations from General Messe and the local German commanders for covering the assault over the Don. After the retreat from Stalingrad began, the air contingent withdrew to Italy in January 1943. In 17 months the two fighter Gruppi had flown over 6,000 sorties, claiming 88 kills for the loss of 19.

Regia Marina (RM)

This was a similar organisation to RAF Coastal Command and was equipped with squadriglie using Cant Z501, Z506B, and later Fiat RS14B flying boats and seaplanes. Two individual commands covered the different areas. The Adriatic, Ionian and Tyrrhenian Seas were all under Comandi Dipartimenti Marittimi, while Sardinia, Sicily, and the Aegean islands were under Comandi Militari Marittimi. Shortly after the start of hostilities, the two commands were reformed into the Comandi Aviazione for easier administration. The squadriglie carried out anti-shipping, anti-submarine, convoy escort, air-sea-rescue, and maritime reconnaissance duties. The Z506Bs flying boats were initially used to bomb land targets too.

On 10 June 1940 the commands also controlled several coastal sections which were all equipped with Z501s, and were based as follows:

1 Sezione Costiera at Cadimare. Became 140 Sq from 1 August 1942

2 Sezione Costiera at Messina? Became 138 Sq from 1 August 1942

3 Sezione Costiera at Taranto. Became 139 Sq from 1 August 1942

4 Sezione Costiera at Pola. Became 149 Sq from 1st August 1942

5 Sezione Costiera at Olbia. Became 193 Sq from 3rd March 1941.

By November 1942 the Regia Marina had 190 out of 290 aircraft serviceable. On 20 May 1943 eleven 'Sezioni Aerei di Soccorso' replaced all ASR units.

Supermarina

Rather like the Royal Navy in the between-war years, the Italian Admiralty had no airforce of its own but did directly control all shipborne aircraft. Sections of these aircraft, Ro 43s and Ro 44s, were allocated to each of the naval divisions, initially in the Squadra 1 and 2 areas. They performed armed reconnaissance, spotting, and escort duties, and were administratively placed in three naval squadriglie, which collectively became 1 Gruppo FF.NN from April 1943.

Light cruisers used two aircraft, heavy cruisers used two to three each, and battleships three. For further aerial support for merchant and warships the Admiralty had to apply for land-based cover through the Air Ministry (Superaereo) which was a slow process, even in an emergency.

Servizi Aerei Speciali (SAS)

This was the Transport Command, which was split in two sections based on the old airlines structure (Nucleo LATI and Nucleo Ala Littoria). The SAS itself was equipped with military aircraft, based in various areas of Italy, according to the current support requirements. The second section was the Nuclei Communicazioni, which by and large used commandeered civil aircraft, older transport and light communications types. Where possible and relatively safe, they used the pre-war civil routes to keep in touch with the Italian Empire and its Allies. Both sections ferried supplies, men, and mail to and from the war zones. The excellent SM 82 could carry a complete fighter and was important to continued operations in East Africa. Most aircraft ferrying was done by front-line units at rest, or those due to use them. Heavy losses were suffered during the Tunisian campaign.

Aviazione per il Regia Esercito (AVRE)

This was the Army Co-operation Command and the individual Gruppi and Squadriglie were attached directly to various Army Commands. By late 1942 these units were only operating in the Balkans where there was less threat of annihilation for their vulnerable aircraft. Although giving good support in the early stages of the war, they were later a great drain on the already limited resources of the RA, despite the excellent work by the crews. The emphasis was by then on fighter defence and anti-shipping strikes.

Tactical Units & Aircraft Establishment

The basic tactical unit was the Stormo. This consisted of two or three Gruppi and normally had one type of aircraft. Each Gruppo comprised two (bomber, reconnaissance and naval) or three (fighter) Squadriglie, which in turn had from six to twelve aircraft each. These are shown in tabular form below. There was also sometimes a Nucleo, which was in effect a Staff Section. There were also many independent (Autonomo) Gruppi and Squadriglie which were directly responsible to their area command. These usually had slightly more aircraft and crews on strength. An example would be the CSIR which had four fighter squadriglie each to the 21° and 22° Gruppi Autonomo, while the 61° Gruppo OA had a third squadriglia.

Each unit was supplied with replacement aircraft and crews from its own Gruppo Complementare (Training Unit) which was based in Italy. A transport Stormo was intended to have 54 aircraft, plus four more as support machines.

Needless to say, the numbers of aircraft given were the ideal peacetime establishment. Once in combat, losses and shortage of replacements quickly conspired to ensure that these were very much theoretical paper strengths.

As related in the chapter on airmen, individual fighter units were left to evolve their own tactics. These mainly depended upon the preferences of the unit commander. To their Allied opponents this made them unpredictable, which often did little for the Italians' lethality, although

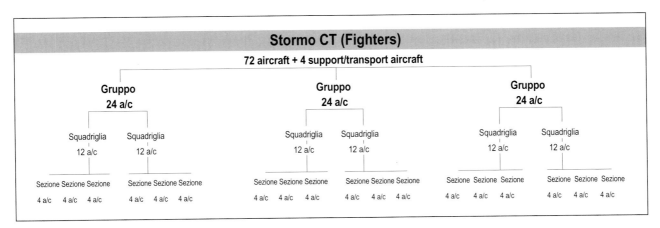

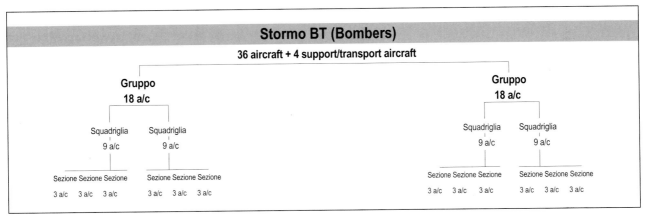

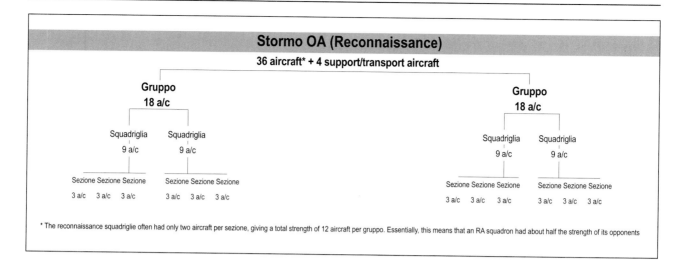

Stormo OA (Reconnaissance)

36 aircraft* + 4 support/transport aircraft

Gruppo — 18 a/c
Squadriglia — 9 a/c
Sezione 3 a/c, Sezione 3 a/c, Sezione 3 a/c

* The reconnaissance squadriglie often had only two aircraft per sezione, giving a total strength of 12 aircraft per gruppo. Essentially, this means that an RA squadron had about half the strength of its opponents

it did assist their survival against increasingly unfavourable odds. Initially the RA fighter pilots flew in flights (sezione) of three, usually with only the commander's aircraft fitted with radio. In later years, they adopted the conventional leader/wingman pair formation.

Contemporary Italian documents use several terms referring to the cessation of active service. The most common are 'scioglie' (dissolved), and 'quadro' (suspended). For simplicity these terms have all been translated as 'disbanded'.

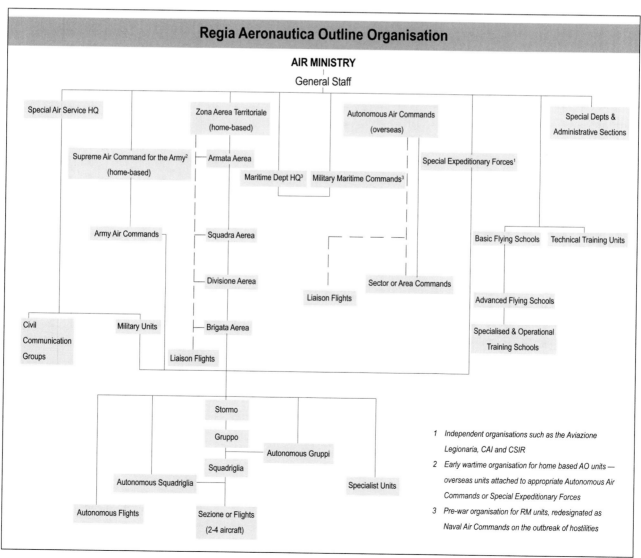

Regia Aeronautica Outline Organisation

1 Independent organisations such as the Aviazione Legionaria, CAI and CSIR

2 Early wartime organisation for home based AO units — overseas units attached to appropriate Autonomous Air Commands or Special Expeditionary Forces

3 Pre-war organisation for RM units, redesignated as Naval Air Commands on the outbreak of hostilities

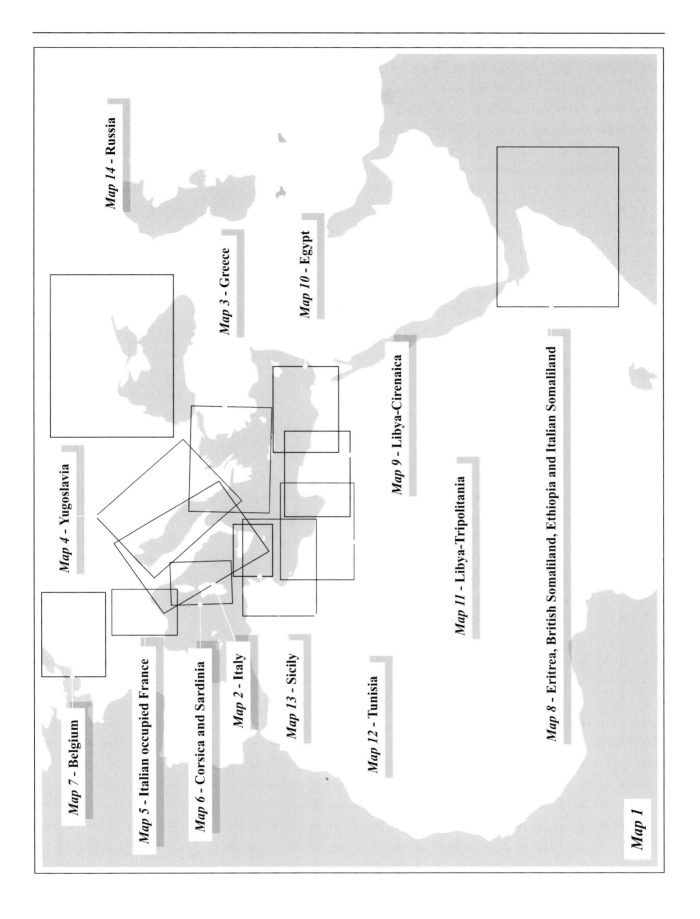

Map 14 - Russia

Map 4 - Yugoslavia

Map 3 - Greece

Map 10 - Egypt

Map 9 - Libya-Cirenaica

Map 11 - Libya-Tripolitania

Map 8 - Eritrea, British Somaliland, Ethiopia and Italian Somaliland

Map 7 - Belgium

Map 5 - Italian occupied France

Map 6 - Corsica and Sardinia

Map 2 - Italy

Map 13 - Sicily

Map 12 - Tunisia

Map 1

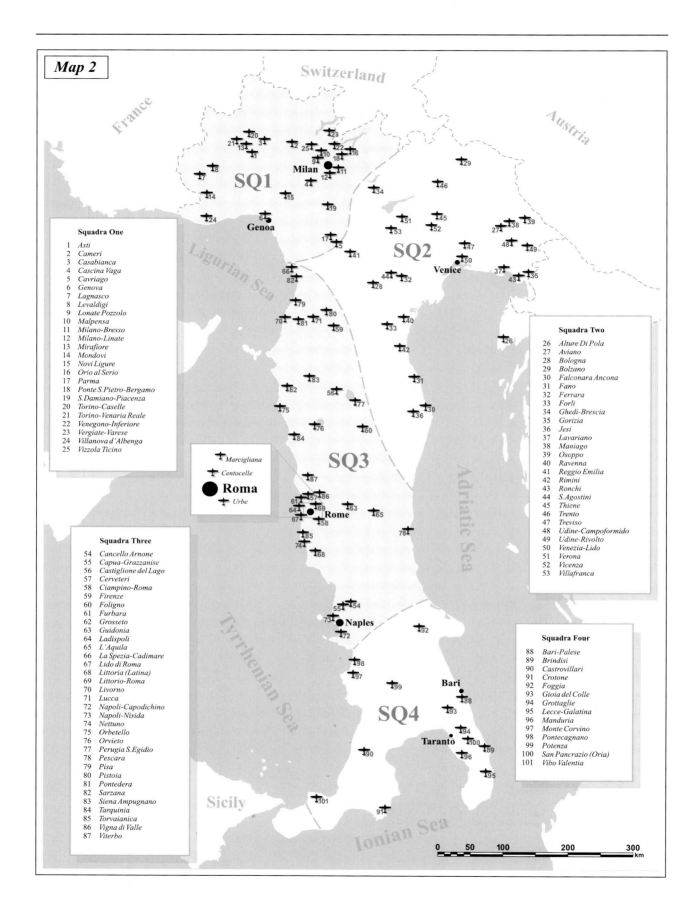

Map 2

Squadra One

1. Asti
2. Cameri
3. Casabianca
4. Cascina Vaga
5. Cavriago
6. Genova
7. Lagnasco
8. Levaldigi
9. Lonate Pozzolo
10. Malpensa
11. Milano-Bresso
12. Milano-Linate
13. Mirafiore
14. Mondovi
15. Novi Ligure
16. Orio al Serio
17. Parma
18. Ponte S.Pietro-Bergamo
19. S.Damiano-Piacenza
20. Torino-Caselle
21. Torino-Venaria Reale
22. Venegono-Inferiore
23. Vergiate-Varese
24. Villanova d'Albenga
25. Vizzola Ticino

Squadra Two

26. Alture Di Pola
27. Aviano
28. Bologna
29. Bolzano
30. Falconara Ancona
31. Fano
32. Ferrara
33. Forli
34. Ghedi-Brescia
35. Gorizia
36. Jesi
37. Lavariano
38. Maniago
39. Osoppo
40. Ravenna
41. Reggio Emilia
42. Rimini
43. Ronchi
44. S.Agostini
45. Thiene
46. Trento
47. Treviso
48. Udine-Campoformido
49. Udine-Rivolto
50. Venezia-Lido
51. Verona
52. Vicenza
53. Villafranca

Marcigliana
Centocelle
Roma
Urbe

Squadra Three

54. Cancello Arnone
55. Capua-Grazzanise
56. Castiglione del Lago
57. Cerveteri
58. Ciampino-Roma
59. Firenze
60. Foligno
61. Furbara
62. Grosseto
63. Guidonia
64. Ladispoli
65. L'Aquila
66. La Spezia-Cadimare
67. Lido di Roma
68. Littoria (Latina)
69. Littorio-Roma
70. Livorno
71. Lucca
72. Napoli-Capodichino
73. Napoli-Nisida
74. Nettuno
75. Orbetello
76. Orvieto
77. Perugia S.Egidio
78. Pescara
79. Pisa
80. Pistoia
81. Pontedera
82. Sarzana
83. Siena Ampugnano
84. Tarquinia
85. Torvaianica
86. Vigna di Valle
87. Viterbo

Squadra Four

88. Bari-Palese
89. Brindisi
90. Castrovillari
91. Crotone
92. Foggia
93. Gioia del Colle
94. Grottaglie
95. Lecce-Galatina
96. Manduria
97. Monte Corvino
98. Pontecagnano
99. Potenza
100. San Pancrazio (Oria)
101. Vibo Valentia

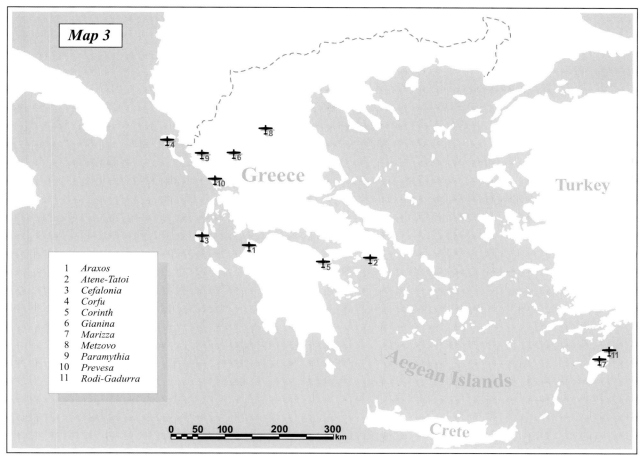

Map 3

1 *Araxos*
2 *Atene-Tatoi*
3 *Cefalonia*
4 *Corfu*
5 *Corinth*
6 *Gianina*
7 *Marizza*
8 *Metzovo*
9 *Paramythia*
10 *Prevesa*
11 *Rodi-Gadurra*

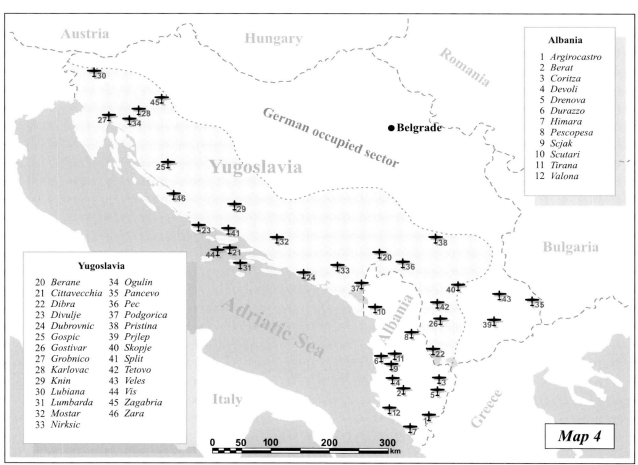

Map 4

Albania

1 *Argirocastro*
2 *Berat*
3 *Coritza*
4 *Devoli*
5 *Drenova*
6 *Durazzo*
7 *Himara*
8 *Pescopesa*
9 *Scjak*
10 *Scutari*
11 *Tirana*
12 *Valona*

Yugoslavia

20	*Berane*	34	*Ogulin*
21	*Cittavecchia*	35	*Pancevo*
22	*Dibra*	36	*Pec*
23	*Divulje*	37	*Podgorica*
24	*Dubrovnic*	38	*Pristina*
25	*Gospic*	39	*Prjlep*
26	*Gostivar*	40	*Skopje*
27	*Grobnico*	41	*Split*
28	*Karlovac*	42	*Tetovo*
29	*Knin*	43	*Veles*
30	*Lubiana*	44	*Vis*
31	*Lumbarda*	45	*Zagabria*
32	*Mostar*	46	*Zara*
33	*Nirksic*		

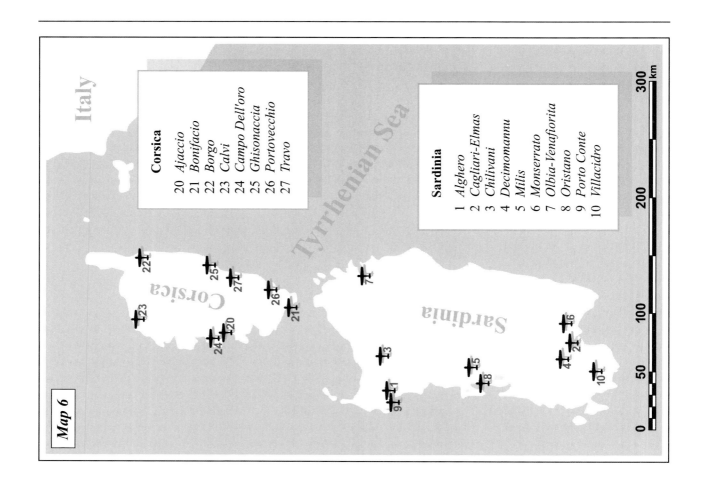

Map 6

Corsica

20 Ajaccio
21 Bonifacio
22 Borgo
23 Calvi
24 Campo Dell'oro
25 Ghisonaccia
26 Portovecchio
27 Travo

Sardinia

1 Alghero
2 Cagliari-Elmas
3 Chilivani
4 Decimomannu
5 Milis
6 Monserrato
7 Olbia-Venafiorita
8 Oristano
9 Porto Conte
10 Villacidro

Italy

Tyrrhenian Sea

Corsica

Sardinia

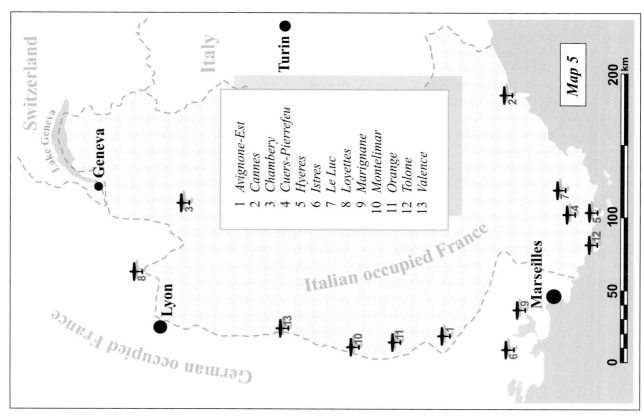

Map 5

Switzerland

Italy

Turin

Geneva

Lake Geneva

German occupied France

Italian occupied France

Lyon

Marseilles

1 Avignone-Est
2 Cannes
3 Chambery
4 Cuers-Pierrefeu
5 Hyeres
6 Istres
7 Le Luc
8 Loyettes
9 Marignane
10 Montelimar
11 Orange
12 Tolone
13 Valence

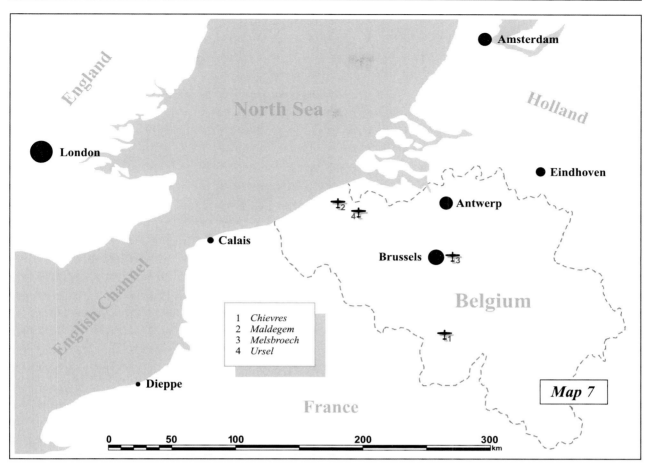

1 Chievres
2 Maldegem
3 Melsbroech
4 Ursel

Map 7

0   50   100   200   300
km

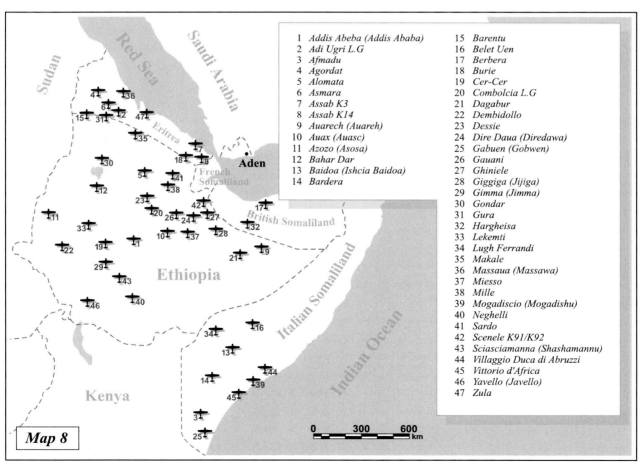

1 Addis Abeba (Addis Ababa)
2 Adi Ugri L.G
3 Afmadu
4 Agordat
5 Alomata
6 Asmara
7 Assab K3
8 Assab K14
9 Auarech (Auareh)
10 Auax (Auasc)
11 Azozo (Asosa)
12 Bahar Dar
13 Baidoa (Ishcia Baidoa)
14 Bardera
15 Barentu
16 Belet Uen
17 Berbera
18 Burie
19 Cer-Cer
20 Combolcia L.G
21 Dagabur
22 Dembidollo
23 Dessie
24 Dire Daua (Diredawa)
25 Gabuen (Gobwen)
26 Gauani
27 Ghiniele
28 Giggiga (Jijiga)
29 Gimma (Jimma)
30 Gondar
31 Gura
32 Hargheisa
33 Lekemti
34 Lugh Ferrandi
35 Makale
36 Massaua (Massawa)
37 Miesso
38 Mille
39 Mogadiscio (Mogadishu)
40 Neghelli
41 Sardo
42 Scenele K91/K92
43 Sciasciamanna (Shashamannu)
44 Villaggio Duca di Abruzzi
45 Vittorio d'Africa
46 Yavello (Javello)
47 Zula

Map 8

0   300   600
km

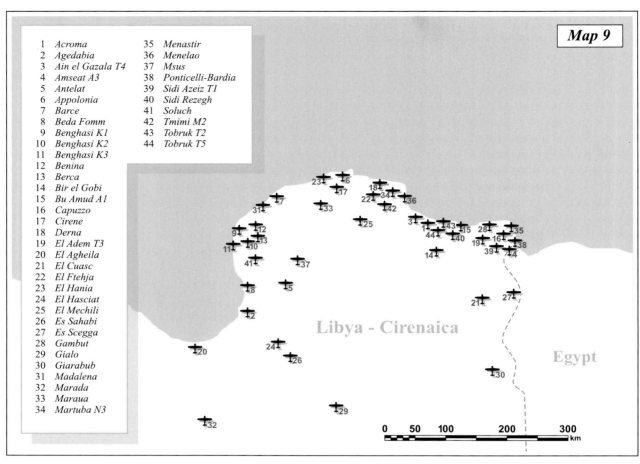

Map 9

1	Acroma	35	Menastir
2	Agedabia	36	Menelao
3	Ain el Gazala T4	37	Msus
4	Amseat A3	38	Ponticelli-Bardia
5	Antelat	39	Sidi Azeiz T1
6	Appolonia	40	Sidi Rezegh
7	Barce	41	Soluch
8	Beda Fomm	42	Tmimi M2
9	Benghasi K1	43	Tobruk T2
10	Benghasi K2	44	Tobruk T5
11	Benghasi K3		
12	Benina		
13	Berca		
14	Bir el Gobi		
15	Bu Amud A1		
16	Capuzzo		
17	Cirene		
18	Derna		
19	El Adem T3		
20	El Agheila		
21	El Cuasc		
22	El Ftehja		
23	El Hania		
24	El Hasciat		
25	El Mechili		
26	Es Sahabi		
27	Es Scegga		
28	Gambut		
29	Gialo		
30	Giarabub		
31	Madalena		
32	Marada		
33	Maraua		
34	Martuba N3		

Libya - Cirenaica

Egypt

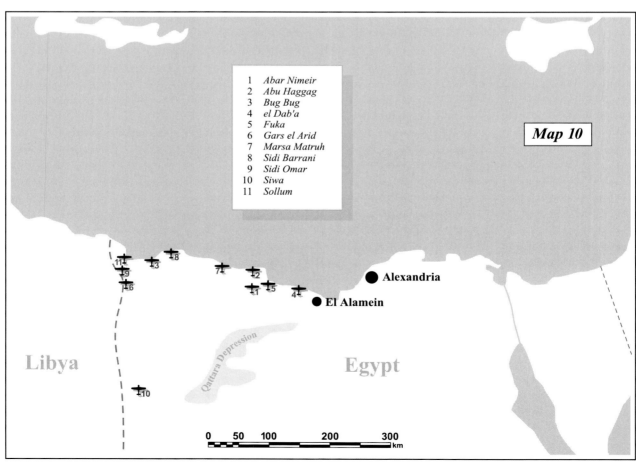

Map 10

1	Abar Nimeir
2	Abu Haggag
3	Bug Bug
4	el Dab'a
5	Fuka
6	Gars el Arid
7	Marsa Matruh
8	Sidi Barrani
9	Sidi Omar
10	Siwa
11	Sollum

● **Alexandria**

● **El Alamein**

Libya

Egypt

Qattara Depression

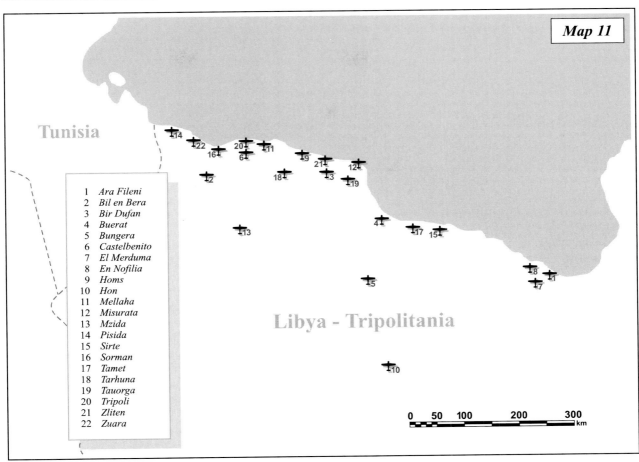

Map 11

Tunisia

Libya - Tripolitania

1 Ara Fileni
2 Bil en Bera
3 Bir Dufan
4 Buerat
5 Bungera
6 Castelbenito
7 El Merduma
8 En Nofilia
9 Homs
10 Hon
11 Mellaha
12 Misurata
13 Mzida
14 Pisida
15 Sirte
16 Sorman
17 Tamet
18 Tarhuna
19 Tauorga
20 Tripoli
21 Zliten
22 Zuara

0   50   100   200   300
                                 km

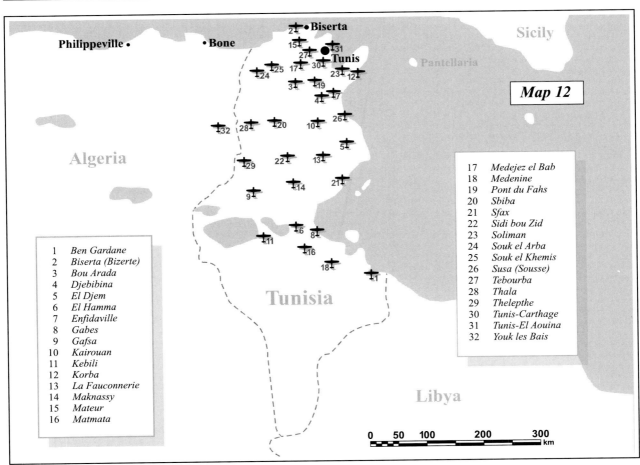

Philippeville •

• Bone

• Biserta

Sicily

Pantellaria

Tunis

Map 12

Algeria

Tunisia

Libya

17 Medejez el Bab
18 Medenine
19 Pont du Fahs
20 Sbiba
21 Sfax
22 Sidi bou Zid
23 Soliman
24 Souk el Arba
25 Souk el Khemis
26 Susa (Sousse)
27 Tebourba
28 Thala
29 Thelepthe
30 Tunis-Carthage
31 Tunis-El Aouina
32 Youk les Bais

1 Ben Gardane
2 Biserta (Bizerte)
3 Bou Arada
4 Djebibina
5 El Djem
6 El Hamma
7 Enfidaville
8 Gabes
9 Gafsa
10 Kairouan
11 Kebili
12 Korba
13 La Fauconnerie
14 Maknassy
15 Mateur
16 Matmata

0   50   100   200   300
                                 km

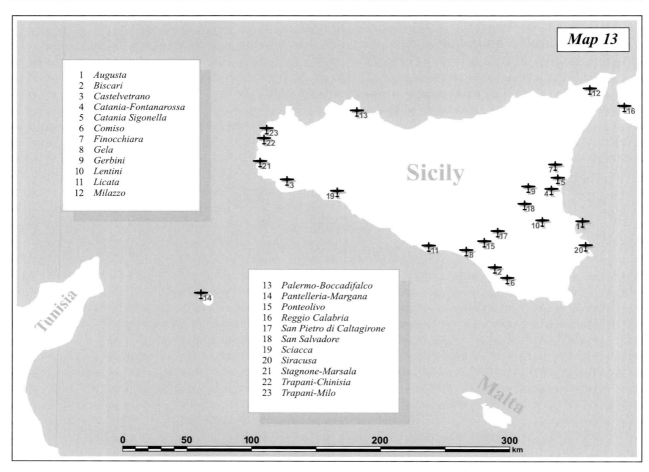

Map 13

1 Augusta
2 Biscari
3 Castelvetrano
4 Catania-Fontanarossa
5 Catania Sigonella
6 Comiso
7 Finocchiara
8 Gela
9 Gerbini
10 Lentini
11 Licata
12 Milazzo

13 Palermo-Boccadifalco
14 Pantelleria-Margana
15 Ponteolivo
16 Reggio Calabria
17 San Pietro di Caltagirone
18 San Salvadore
19 Sciacca
20 Siracusa
21 Stagnone-Marsala
22 Trapani-Chinisia
23 Trapani-Milo

Sicily

Tunisia

Malta

0   50   100   200   300
km

1 Beneasa
2 Borvenkvo
3 Bucharest
4 Kalinovskaja
5 Kantemirovka
6 Kirovograd
7 Krivoi-Rog
8 Makejevka
9 Millerovo
10 Oblivskaja
11 Odessa
12 Otopeni
13 Stalino
14 Tazinskaja
15 Tudora
16 Voroscilovgrad
17 Zaporoshje

Poland

Russia

● Kursk

R.Don

● Kiev

R. Donetz

● Stalingrad

This lake is a feature
on modern maps only

R. Dnieper

● Rostov

Sea of Azov

Romania

Crimea

Black Sea

0 50 100   200   300
km

Map 14

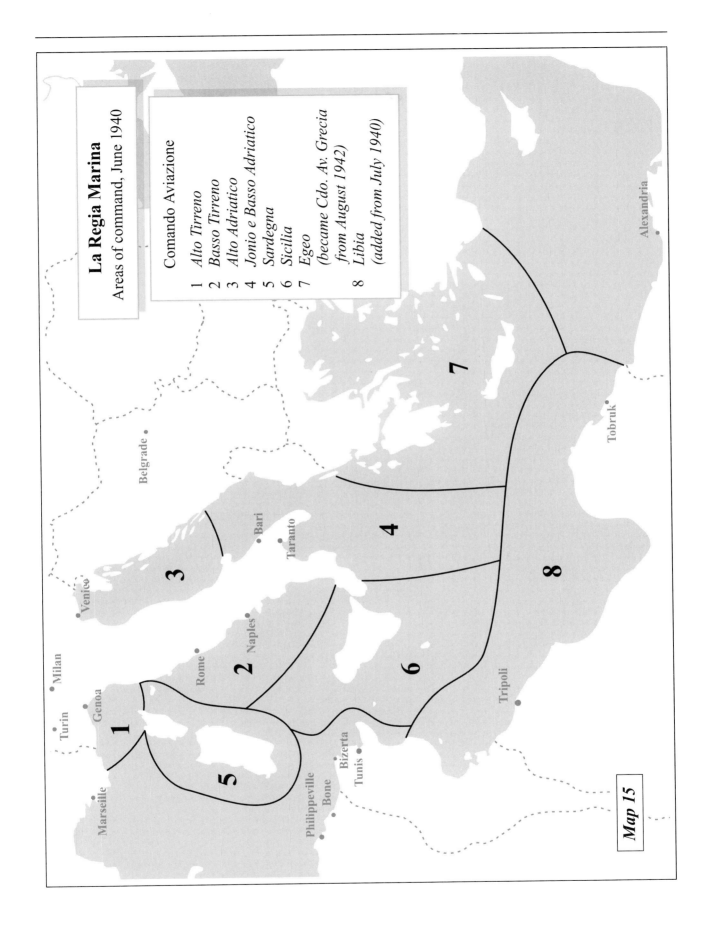

La Regia Marina
Areas of command, June 1940

Comando Aviazione

1 Alto Tirreno
2 Basso Tirreno
3 Alto Adriatico
4 Jonio e Basso Adriatico
5 Sardegna
6 Sicilia
7 Egeo
   (became Cdo. Av. Grecia
   from August 1942)
8 Libia
   (added from July 1940)

Map 15

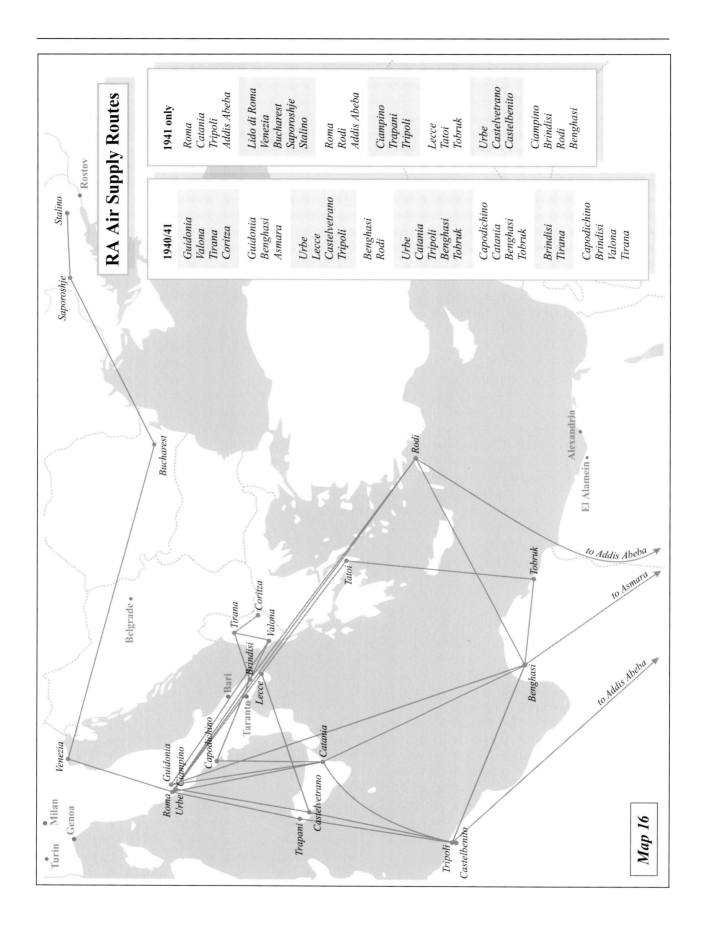

RA Air Supply Routes

1940/41

Guidonia
Valona
Tirana
Coritza

Guidonia
Benghasi
Asmara

Urbe
Lecce
Castelvetrano
Tripoli

Benghasi
Rodi

Urbe
Catania
Tripoli
Benghasi
Tobruk

Capodichino
Catania
Benghasi
Tobruk

Brindisi
Tirana

Capodichino
Brindisi
Valona
Tirana

1941 only

Roma
Catania
Tripoli
Addis Abeba

Lido di Roma
Venezia
Bucharest
Saporoshje
Stalino

Roma
Rodi
Addis Abeba

Ciampino
Trapani
Tripoli

Lecce
Tatoi
Tobruk

Urbe
Castelvetrano
Castelbenito

Ciampino
Brindisi
Rodi
Benghasi

Map 16

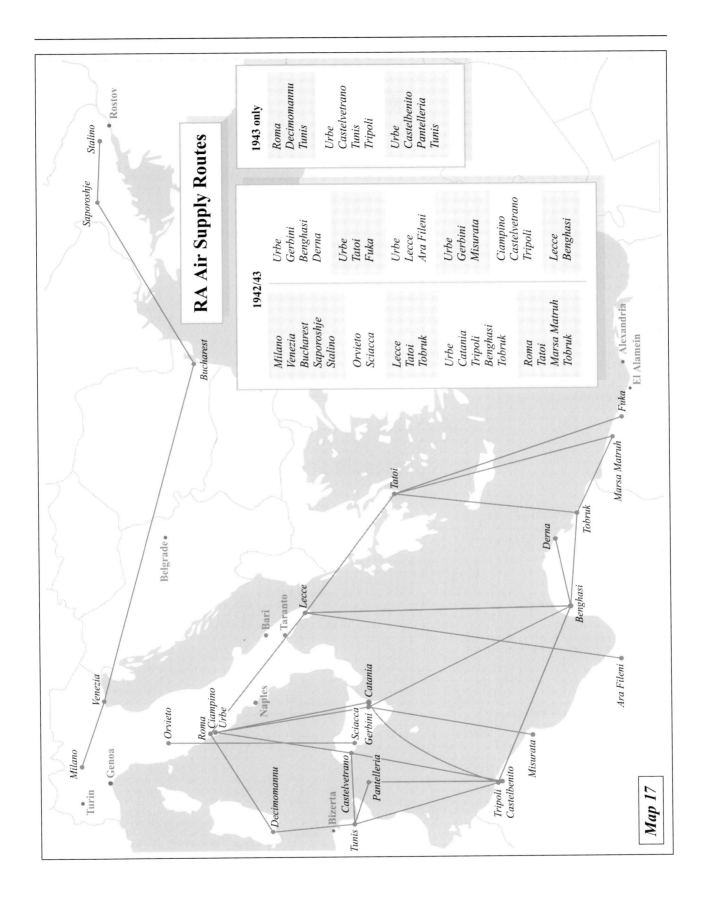

RA Air Supply Routes

1943 only

Roma	*Urbe*
Decimomannu	*Castelvetrano*
Tunis	*Tunis*
	Tripoli
Urbe	
Castelbenito	
Pantelleria	
Tunis	

1942/43

Milano	*Urbe*	*Ciampino*
Venezia	*Gerbini*	*Castelvetrano*
Bucharest	*Benghasi*	*Tripoli*
Saporoshje	*Derna*	
Stalino		*Lecce*
	Urbe	*Benghasi*
Orvieto	*Tatoi*	
Sciacca	*Fuka*	
Lecce	*Urbe*	
Tatoi	*Lecce*	
Tobruk	*Ara Fileni*	
Urbe	*Urbe*	
Catania	*Gerbini*	
Tripoli	*Misurata*	
Benghasi		
Tobruk		
Roma		
Tatoi		
Marsa Matruh		
Tobruk		

Map 17

COMBAT UNITS
Gruppo movements and operations

As can be seen from the organisation chart on page 14, the Regia Aeronautica had many more links in the chain of command as compared to, say, the RAF. This fragmentary approach to the means of control is fairly symptomatic of Mussolini's Italy. Needless to say, the system did not lend itself to swift and incisive decision-making, with consequent effects upon the conduct of operations. This chapter concentrates upon the Gruppo, the most important tactical unit of the RA. The attachments of particular Squadriglie are covered in Chapters 5 and 6 which chart the various parent units they moved through.

Notes to the section headings:

The status and squadriglie shown are those on 10 June 1940, or when the unit formed. Subsequent changes are detailed up to 8 September 1943, where known, in the text.

Arrival: Earliest known day or month the unit used the base.

Zone: Command area or Expeditionary Force. Again, note that the abbreviations are the author's own and are not official. See Glossary for full title.

Base: The most used at the time, although the aircraft may have also been scattered to subsidiary bases.

Duties: The most common during the time at that base, in the order of importance or chronology. See glossary for a full explanation of initials.

1 GRUPPO APC
Squadriglie   12, 89, 104

Arrival	Zone	Base	Country	Aircraft	Duties
10 Jun 40	ALIB	Tripoli-Mellaha	Tripolitania	Ca 309 Ca 164	
				Fi156C	AR
Jan 43	Sqa 5	Zuara	Tripolitania	Ca 309	IT
20 Jan 43	Sqa 3	Capua-Grazzanise	Italy	Ca 313 Ca 314	TG

The Aviazione Presidio Coloniale (APC) was formed to patrol the vast desert areas of Libya; surveying, mapping, liaising with the garrison forts and keeping an eye on natives and bordering countries. Despite limited maintenance and fuel facilities, which were even more pronounced when war began, the APC units continued these duties with much success. They also carried out many desert rescues with which the Ca 309 coped well. Although fragile by military standards, it proved quite capable of withstanding the desert conditions.

This unit began its war by patrolling the Tunisian border as well as the oases and western desert area of Libya. They had 12 aircraft available; an SM 75 arrived in

3 Above: Fiat CR 42, MM 5668, of the 83ª Squadriglia, 18° Gruppo. The aircraft was built between March-August 1940, and is seen in Tripolitania soon after the unit arrived there in early 1941. The camouflage appears to be of the C1 or C1B type. Note the ornate shadowing to the yellow code numbers, a characteristic of this unit

August, followed by a Fi 156C in September. On 22 November a rarely seen Cant Z509 (MM351) joined the Gruppo and was used to escort S 75s around Libya. Two Ca 164s were received for local liaison duties from January 1941. Sometime after that 89 Sq left the unit.

103 Sq was one of the Squadriglie Aviazione Sahariana which carried out similar duties to the APC, but on a more local basis. They were at Hon in December 1941, with SM 81s, and joined 1 Gruppo in June 1942. Their aircraft were passed to the Battaglione Sahariana.

On 8 January 1942 a Ca 133S arrived at Sirte, followed by another on 16 February, for ambulance duties in Libya. On 23 May 12 Sq moved to Agedabia, maintaining sections at Mellaha, Derna, and Gialo. In July 103 Sq was detached to Misurata. 104 Sq stayed at Mellaha. On 15 August 12 Sq with five Ca 309s went to Siwa, from where they helped to halt an enemy attack on Gialo oasis between 16 and 22 September 1942. On the 20 103 Sq had 8 Ca 309s serviceable at Misurata and 104 Sq had 5 serviceable at Mellaha. 12 Sq then returned to Agedabia on 9 November, then to Sirte on 20, joining 103 Sq at Misurata on the same day. Sections were still kept at Mersa Matruh, Derna, and Gialo. 12 Sq disbanded on 10 December, passing its aircraft and crews to 103 Sq. 104 Sq was still at Mellaha.

103 Sq meanwhile was acting with 102 Sq Aviazione Sahariana to protect against further attacks on Gialo in December. This latter unit was equipped with eleven ex-torpedo-bomber SM 79s of 133 Gruppo and was formed on 1 December for the aforesaid purpose at Castelbenito. It left for Italy by 20 January with five remaining SM 79s.

As the Allies advanced across Libya the Gruppo, together with 102 Sq, retired to Mellaha, then withdrew to Italy in January 1943 with 13 Ca 309s. On 1 March 1 Gruppo APC became 1 Gruppo OA with 103 and 104 Sq and joined 20 Stormo. 103 Sq left the same day for 69 Gruppo and 36 Sq took its place. 104 Sq left in April, also for 69 Gruppo. 102 Sq disbanded on 15 March. By 28 July the unit had 30 aircraft at Grazzanise.

1 GRUPPO FF.NN
Squadriglie   1, 2, 3

Arrival	Zone	Base	Country	Aircraft	Duties
April 43		Sarzana	Italy	Re 2000 Ro 43 Ro 44	AR CE

This unit consisted of three naval squadriglie which used floatplanes aboard warships for reconnaissance, gunnery spotting, and escort duties. The aircraft were allocated between the nine naval divisions in two Naval Squadra.

On 10 June 1940, 2 and 3 Squadriglie had 49 Ro 43s and Ro 44s embarked, of which 42 were serviceable. The

Ro 44s were gradually relegated to training duties. No confirmed reference to the status of 1 Squadriglia at this time has been found, although it appears to have operated some Ro 43s by 1941.

During the Battle of Cape Matapan in March 1941, the Ro 43 launched from the battleship *Vittorio Veneto* carried out constant reconnaissance sightings of the British naval forces. Unfortunately for the Italian naval commander, Admiral Iachino, the aircraft could not be recovered due to the design of his ship. Therefore, when fuel ran low the Ro 43 had to make for Rodi, thus depriving the Italians of a useful pair of eyes.

The squadriglie were noticeably active in the Central and Eastern Mediterranean areas until the second half of 1942. In March of that year an Italian Admiral praised the crews for more accurate reconnaissance patrols than their land-based air force partners. After that, these vulnerable aircraft were only used around the Sicilian, Sardinian, Aegean, and Tirrenean waters.

During late 1941 and early 1942 experiments were started at Guidonia and Reggio Emilia with the Re 2000 fighter as a catapultable fighter. The test pilots were very critical of the poor quality of the catapult gear, which delayed trials for several months while it was redesigned. These trials continued almost to the end of the war, as the Admiralty became wary of sending their ships to sea if the weather was too rough or if they expected heavy opposition. Consequently, the catapult trials had to be made statically or within port for the most part. From May 1942 they used a test catapult platform on the support vessel *Miraglia* at Taranto, as this was cheaper than converting a warship just for tests.

Eventually, it was agreed that 1 Sq would be equipped with the Re 2000 for the defence of the naval bases, and for embarking on board the major warships. After launch the fighters were to fly to the nearest land-base, which was not a problem for them, as they were equipped with larger fuel tanks than the land-based version. 1 Sq may also have received some MC 200s and G 50s for comparison trials and local defence. It certainly used CR 42s, forming at Grottaglie, then moving to Taranto to work with the Naval Squadra there, then on to Capodichino when the Naval Squadra transferred to Naples. Finally it settled in Sarzana from January 1943, to cover La Spezia naval base.

On 1 August 1942 there were 28 Ro 43 and Ro 44 aircraft embarked, with 23 being serviceable.

By 1 January 1943 the battleships *Littorio* and *Vittorio Veneto* each had a single Re 2000 on board. During the summer three more were received, the latter ship getting one and the *Roma* getting the other two. It appears there may have been only one operational sortie, with an armed reconnaissance from *Vittorio Veneto* on 26 August 1943.

The fighter landed safely back at Sarzana.

In April 1943 the three squadriglie were united as a Gruppo, with 1 Sq (Re 2000s, CR 42s) at Sarzana, 2 Sq (Ro 43s) at Grottaglie, and 3 Sq (Ro 43s) at La Spezia Cadimare. By 7 September 18 Ro 43s out of 28 were embarked, and the Gruppo still had the following aircraft disembarked :

1 Sq:	0 serviceable Re 2000 out of 2
2 Sq:	0 serviceable Ro 43 out of 11
	2 serviceable Ro 44 out of 3
3 Sq:	4 serviceable Ro 43 out of 9
	3 serviceable Ro 44 out of 3.

1 GRUPPO OA
Squadriglie 27, 121
Stormo 20

Arrival	Zone	Base	Country	Aircraft	Duties
10 Jun 40	Sqa 1	Arezzo	Italy	Ro 37	IT
11 Jun 40	Sqa 3	Lucca	Italy	Ro 37	AR
13 Jun 40	Sqa 1	Airasca	Italy	Ro 37	AR

This unit began the war under the command of Alto Comando Regio Esercito with ten aircraft. Operations against France started on 11 June, with 27 Sq detached to Casabianca. Two days later the unit transferred to the control of IV Corpo d'Armata.

27 Sq disbanded on 25 February 1942. The 1 Gruppo OA was disbanded on 1 April, reforming from 1 Gruppo APC on 1 March 1943 (see above). 121 Sq had meanwhile become autonomo on 20 March 1942 and was now under the control of 2 Armata.

2 GRUPPO APC
Squadriglie 16,23

Arrival	Zone	Base	Country	Aircraft	Duties
10 Jun 40	ALIB	El Adem	Cirenaica	Ca 309	AR
Jun 1940	ALIB	Benghasi	Cirenaica	Ca 309 S 81S	AR

This unit began its war by patrolling the Egyptian border as well as the oases and eastern desert of Libya. They had seven aircraft available.

In June they received five S 81s modified as ambulance aircraft, which were then used by 16 Sq. Due, however, to the shortage of transport aircraft, these eventually left for units such as 145 Gruppo in early 1941. Five Ca 309s of 23 Sq joined in the advance on Sidi Barrani.

After the British counter-offensive swept through their territory, this unit remained based in the Benghasi area until it was disbanded in August 1942. Desert missions were carried out to the south and south-east, but the unit was constantly under strength and limited in its use.

2 GRUPPO CT
Squadriglie 150, 151, 152
Stormo 6

Arrival	Zone	Base	Country	Aircraft	Duties
1 Jun 40	4 ZAT	Grottaglie	Italy	CR 32 G 50	DF,TG, AE
21 Dec 40	Sqa 5	Castelbenito	Tripolitania	G 50	DF
1 Jan 41	Sqa 5	Maraua	Cirenaica	G 50	DF,GA, AE
1 Feb 41	Sqa 5	Castelbenito	Tripolitania	G 50AS	TG
Mar 41	Sqa 5	El Ftehja	Cirenaica	G 50AS	AE
22 Jul 41	Sqa 2	Treviso ?	Italy	G 50	TG
Mar 42	Sqa 3	Ciampino	Italy	Re 2001	TG
4 May 42	ASIC	Caltagirone	Sicily	Re 2001	DF, AE, AN, AR
14 Jun 42	ASIC	Castelvetrano	Sicily	Re 2001	AE
15 Jun 42	ASIC	Pantelleria	Sicily	Re 2001	AR, AE, AN
Jul 42	ASIC	Castelvetrano	Sicily	Re 2001	AE, AN, AR
13 Aug 42	ASIC	Chinisia	Sicily	Re 2001	AE, AN,CE
Jan 43	Sqa 2	Treviso	Italy	Re 2001	DF, NF
15 May 43	Sqa 3	Sarzana	Italy	Re 2001	DF, NF
23 May 43	Sqa 1	Genova	Italy	Re 2001 CR 42CN	
				D 520	DF, NF

From June to November 1940 the unit patrolled the lower Ionian Sea and Italian coastline. This did not bring much excitement, but enabled the pilots to gain valuable flying experience as the CR 32s were gradually exchanged for the more modern G 50s. On 20 September the Gruppo became autonomo. The first action came between 8 and 14 July, in the battle of Punta Stilo. Orders arrived in December for a move to Africa, taking 18 of the new G 50s. 151 Sq was left in Italy and subsequently joined 20 Gruppo in April. Being the first monoplane fighter unit to serve in Africa, they were reinforced on 16 December by 358 Sq with 9 G 50s and a Ca 133.

From 21 to 23 December 18 G 50s arrived at Castelbenito. Like most transferring Italian units they began suffering from sand in the engines and lubricants. Even so, they defended Tripoli port and its surrounding area during December.

After moving to Maraua, they began more offensive duties such as ground strafing, escorting such units as 50 Stormo Assalto, as well as intercepts. February 1941 found them equipping their G 50s with sand filters, which only partly cured the wear and tear problems.

March through to June saw bomber escort duties to

98 Gruppo's BR 20s and Ju 87s of Italian and German units. These missions flew over the Tobruk, Sollum, and Sidi Barrani areas. They also flew cover for the Savona Division in the Acroma area during June. Derna was used as a forward base on 11 July. The last mission was an escort to Tobruk and back on 16 July. On the 22nd they returned to Italy.

After several months in limbo, 152 Sq was sent to Gorizia to train on the Re 2001 in January 1942. They rejoined the Gruppo in April, where it had reformed in March in Ciampino. 151 Sq disbanded from January. 150 and 358 Sq also disbanded in January, but reformed in March. The pilots of 152 Sq then introduced them to their new aircraft.

After numerous delays the unit finally moved to Sicily with 18 Re 2001s. It was the first unit to use these aircraft in combat, making its debut over Malta. A busy time was had with bomber escorts, intercepts and fighter sweeps over and around Malta. For example, on 14 June 17 Re 2001s escorting SM 79s against the HARPOON convoy, bound for Malta, claimed seven intercepting Hurricanes. 150 Sq used Monserrato from July to August, and 358 Sq was detached to Pantelleria from July to November. By 13 August 150 and 152 Sq still had 19 Re 2001s when they reunited at Chinisia on that date.

On 14 August a mission gave credibility to the fact that German bomber crews often liked to have Italian fighter escorts. Eighteen Re 2001s of this Gruppo, from Pantelleria, with four German Bf 109s, escorted three He 111 torpedo-bombers against the PEDESTAL convoy. When attacked by Spitfires, three Re 2001s defended the bombers and were all downed. The bombers escaped unharmed. The fighter commander, *Maggiore* Pier Luigi Scarpetta, received a posthumous *Medaglia d'Oro*.

150 Sq was detached to Monserrato in July and on return to Chinisia in August, was disbanded the next month. In August 362 Sq temporarily joined 2 Gruppo, flying in from 22 Gruppo where it had been detached to Monserrato. By 1 November only 21 out of 31 aircraft were serviceable. 358 Sq was detached from July to November to Pantelleria, then was temporarily disbanded on 11 November, along with the rest of the Gruppo.

In the spring of 1943 the Gruppo reassembled with its HQ at Genova, becoming 2 Gruppo Intercettori with about 15 Re 2001s and CR 42s. On 9 May 156 Sq Intercettori was formed, and on 1 July replaced the now disbanded 358 Sq at Albenga. It was then renumbered as 358 Squadriglia. The crews of the old 358 Sq were spread through the other Squadra 1 Intercettori units and the aircraft went to 160 Gruppo.

During May the Gruppo collaborated with 8 Gruppo in aerial bombing trials. On 26 May 152 Sq was detached to Sarzana, and 358 Sq to Albenga, to defend the La Spezia and Genova areas. They replaced the Sezione Intercettori which were disbanded at those bases on 23 May. Between 21 June and 11 July 358 Sq was at Sarzana. 152 sq received four cannon-armed Re 2001s in June.

By July the unit also used Venegono, and 358 Sq had received five D 520s to help in day and night defence. At this time the Gruppo also had six Re 2001s and thirteen CR 42s operational. By 1 September there were only six Re 2001s and eleven CR 42s on strength.

3 GRUPPO CT

| Squadriglie | 153, 154, 155 |
| Stormo | 6 |

Arrival	Zone	Base	Country	Aircraft	Duties
1 Jun 40	ASAR	Monserrato	Sardinia	CR 32 CR 42	DF, TG, AE, CE
24 Jul 41	Sqa 5	Sorman	Tripolitania	CR 42	CE, DF, NF GA
Dec 41	Sqa 5	Ara Fileni	Tripolitania	CR 42	DF, GA
Jan 42	Sqa 5	El Merduma	Tripolitania	CR 42	DF, GA
29 Jan 42	Sqa 5	Sidi Omar	Egypt	CR 42	DF, GA
Feb 42	Sqa 5	Benghasi K2	Cirenaica	CR 42	CE, NF, DF GA
May 42	Sqa 5	Benghasi K3	Cirenaica	CR 42	DF
10 May 42	Sqa 5	Martuba 5	Cirenaica	CR 42	GA, DF
14 Jun 42	Sqa 3	Ciampino	Italy	MC 200	TG
Sep 42	Sqa 4	Lecce	Italy	MC 200	CE
11 Nov 42	ASIC	Chinisia	Sicily	MC 200	CE, AE, DF
May 43	ASIC	Caltagirone	Sicily	Bf 109G-6	TG
12 Jun 43	ASIC	Comiso	Sicily	Bf 109G-6	TG, DF
16 Jul 43	ASIC	Palermo	Sicily	Bf 109G-6	IT
16 Jul 43	Sqa 3	Littoria	Italy	Bf 109G-6	TG
22 Jul 43	Sqa 1	Torino Caselle	Italy	Bf 109G-6	DF

From 1 June 1940 155 Sq was detached to Alghero under training, and also to defend Cagliari port and escort 19 Gruppo on sea reconnaissance. The first operation was on 16 June, escorting Breda 88s to Corsica. At this time 3 Gruppo had 28 CR 32s and 3 Ca 133s. On 9 August two pilots of 153 Sq downed a French LeOH 470 flying boat. In November the Gruppo joined in the battle of Capo Teulada, escorting bombers and ships, and making day intercepts. It was also involved in training with the Regia Marina units.

From January 1941 the CR 32 was gradually replaced by the CR 42. The older aircraft ceased operations around April. A G 50B two-seat trainer arrived that month, with the intention of converting the pilots to the G 50bis. Lack of available numbers of the latter type meant that the unit remained on CR 42s. On 7 May they escorted bombers attacking the convoy from Gibraltar.

On 25 May 155 Sq left Alghero for Roma-Lecce-Rodi-Aleppo-Mossul to help the Iraqi revolt. On 6 June it returned to Rodi and was renumbered as 164 Sq.

With a new 155 Sq formed on 14 July the Gruppo moved ten days later to the Libyan front, having left its aircraft to 24 Gruppo in Sardinia. On arrival they received 12 CR 42s from 150 Gruppo who were returning to Italy. There followed a period of ground strafing, night fighting, convoy escorts, and the defence of Tripoli port. 153 Sq used Misurata in August and September. Six CR 42s from this squadriglia formed a Nucleo d'Assalto on 1 September. On 28 December Ara Fileni and Bir El Merduma were used to help protect German forces from approaching Allied units. 154 Sq moved to Martuba in March, followed in May by the rest of the Gruppo. They carried out night attacks on the Gazala area, ceasing operations on 28 May.

On 3 June 1942 the unit returned to Italy to rest and re-equip with MC 200s and replacement pilots after eleven months of operations. In September 153 Sq was detached to Reggio Calabria. The whole unit now began escorting convoys in the central Mediterranean.

Reuniting in November at Chinisia, they escorted ships and aerial transports reinforcing Tunisia. Bases in Pantelleria and Tunisia were used in shuttle fashion. In January 154 Sq went to Reggio Calabria for convoy escort duties off Calabria.

After the Axis withdrawal from Africa, the unit received 40 Bf 109G-6s in June, having lost many aircraft to Allied bombing in May. The Germans also supplied technicians to assist with the conversion, but after an initial briefing these left the Italian pilots to their own devices. Each pilot flew several missions a day, but with more losses in the air and on the ground, the unit retired to Italy to re-equip with new Bf 109s. On 7 September they still awaited full equipment.

4 GRUPPO BT

Squadriglie	14, 15
Stormo	7

Arrival	Zone	Base	Country	Aircraft	Duties
10 Jun 40	Sqa 1	Lonate Pozzolo	Italy	BR 20	DB
Jul 41	Sqa 1	Cameri	Italy	SM 84	TG
30 Apr 42	ASIC	Sciacca	Sicily	SM 84	DB, AN
Aug 42	ASIC	Castelvetrano	Sicily	SM 84	NB, DB, AN
Oct 42	Sqa 1	Lonate Pozzolo	Italy	SM 84	TG

This unit received the BR 20 in 1936. After a tour in Africa they returned home before the war started. BR 20Ms arrived in the spring of 1940. On 12 June they began attacks on southern France. The next day they were intercepted by the D.520s of GC III/6 over Toulon. The CR 42 escort defended the Fiat bombers well, who escaped without loss.

By 29 July 1941 the Gruppo was re-equipping at Cameri with SM 84s. These new aircraft were difficult to train on. However, the unit was declared operational in April 1942 and moved to Sicily.

Operations began against Malta and its shipping routes. On 7 May the unit became part of the Aerosilurante, but did not use the Savoias as torpedo-bombers. They reverted to the Bombardamento Terrestre title on 1 October. From July to August they made high-level escorted raids over Malta, as well as operations against ships supplying Malta.

Returning to Italy the unit remained in training until disbanded on 15 June 1943.

4 bis GRUPPO BT

Squadriglie	14bis, 15bis
Stormo	Autonomo

Arrival	Zone	Base	Country	Aircraft	Duties
10 Jun 40	AOI	Scenele K91	Ethiopia	SM 81	DB
Jul 40	AOI	Ghiniele	Ethiopia	SM 81	DB
Aug 40	AOI	Dire Daua	Ethiopia	SM 81 SM 79	DB, NB
Mar 41	AOI	Addis Abeba	Ethiopia	SM 79	DB

The war started on 13 June with four out of twelve SM 81s raiding Aden. One was shot down by four Gladiators of 94 Squadron RAF, one by AA, and one crashed from technical trouble. Not a good start ! On 20 July the remaining nine aircraft were at Ghiniele for operations against British Somaliland. A month later they were switched from Dire Daua to Sciasciamanna.

On 18 November 15 Sq was detached to Giggiga for night bombing sorties over Aden. Four days later 14 Sq converted to SM 79s, passing its surviving SM 81s to 15 Sq. On 3 December two SM 79s moved to Gura for operations in the north. By 30 March 1941 the situation had so worsened that the unit disbanded and its remaining aircraft went to 44 bis Gruppo.

5 GRUPPO OA

Squadriglie	31, 39, 40
Stormo	19

Arrival	Zone	Base	Country	Aircraft	Duties
10 Jun 40	Sqa 1	Venaria Reale	Italy	Ro 37	TG, AR
Oct 40	4 ZAT	Bari Palese	Italy	Ro 37	TG
15 Jan 41	AALB	Devoli	Albania	Ro 37	AR
Apr 41	AALB	Berat	Albania	Ro 37	AR
21 May 41	AALB	Scutari	Albania	Ro 37	AG

Arrival	Zone	Base	Country	Aircraft	Duties
Jul 42	AALB	Zara	Yugoslavia	Ro 37 Fizir Ca 111	AG
1 Sep 42	Sqa 3	Lucca	Italy	Ca 311 Ca 314	TG
Sep 42	AALB	Mostar	Yugoslavia	Ca 311 Ca 314	
Sep 42	AALB	Mostar	Yugoslavia	Ca 111bis Ca 164	AG

The squadriglie began the war under the command of 6 Armata (31 Sq), I Corpo d'Armata (39 Sq), and IV Corpo d'Armata (40 Sq). The next day 31 and 40 Sq joined 39 Sq under I Corpo for operations against France. On 24 June 31 Sq was temporarily assigned to 71 Sq Gruppo with the Corpo d'Armata Alpino.

31 and 39 Sq moved to Bari for action over the Greek front. 40 Sq remained at Venaria Reale, becoming Autonomo and transferring to Sicily. Moving forward to Devoli with 18 Ro 37s, the Gruppo began operations on 20 January 1941. Their reconnaissance missions were often escorted by the G 50s of 154 Gruppo.

In April they moved base again, to cover the ground forces advancing into Yugoslavia. From July, still with 17 Ro 37s, they carried out anti-partisan duties in the Montenegro area. During the summer of 1942 they added some ex-Yugoslavian Rogozarski *Fizir* biplanes to their operational strength. 31 Sq was replaced by 36 Sq, but the latter left to join 20 Stormo on 26 August. A Ca 111 was attached in July.

39 Sq passed to 70 Gruppo on 1 September and the Gruppo was repatriated to Italy, retraining on the Ca 311 and Ca 314. Some of these types may have been used from July. On 2 September the unit came under 21 Stormo and received 121 Sq, followed by 120 Sq in February. Each squadriglia had a Ca 164 and a Ca 111bis for liaison duties. 128 Sq joined in March 1943, at Zara, followed by 33 Sq at Mostar in early June.

120 Sq was at Mostar until early July then moved to Ronchi, with a section at Ghedi. They then went to Lavariano by 23 July and disbanded on 16 August. 121 and 128 Sq were at Zara. The former left for 68 Gruppo in late August. By 7 September the Gruppo had three Ca 311s and twelve Ca 314s operational.

6 GRUPPO CT

Squadriglie	79,81,88
Stormo	Autonomo

Arrival	Zone	Base	Country	Aircraft	Duties
3 Jun 40	Sqa 2	Fontanarossa	Sicily	MC 200	TG, DF, AE
21 Jun 41	Sqa 2	Campoformido	Italy	MC 202	TG
25 Nov 41	Sqa 5	Martuba	Cirenaica	MC 202	DF
12 Dec 41	Sqa 5	Derna	Cirenaica	MC 202	DF
18 Dec 41	Sqa 5	Sidi Magrum	Cirenaica	MC 202	DF
20 Dec 41	Sqa 5	El Merduma	Tripolitania	MC 202	DF
22 Dec 41	Sqa 5	Tamet	Tripolitania	MC 202	DF

Arrival	Zone	Base	Country	Aircraft	Duties
Jan 42	Sqa 5	Ara Fileni	Tripolitania	MC 202	DF, AR
29 Jan 42	Sqa 5	Agedabia	Cirenaica	MC 202	DF
Feb 42	Sqa 5	Benghasi K3	Cirenaica	MC 202	TG DF
Mar 42	Sqa 5	Martuba	Cirenaica	MC 202	AE, DF, AR
Jun 42	Sqa 2	Campoformido	Italy	MC 202	TG
Dec 42	ASIC	Margana-Pantelleria	Sicily	MC 202	DF, AE, CE GA, AN
Jan 43	ASIC	Sciacca	Sicily	MC 202 MC 205V	DF
24 Jan 43	ATUN	Sfax	Tunisia	MC 202	DF, AE
5 Mar 43	Sqa 5	Gabes	Tunisia	MC 202	DF, AE
Mar 43	Sqa 1	Lonate Pozzolo	Italy	MC 205V	TG
Apr 43	ASIC	Pantelleria	Sicily	MC 205V	DF, CE, AE
May 43	ASIC	Catania	Sicily	MC 205V	DF
25 Jun 43	Sqa 1	Torino Caselle	Italy	MC 205V	DF
2 Jul 43	Sqa 2	Osoppo	Italy	MC 205V	DF
30 Jul 143	Sqa 2	Ronchi	Italy	MC 205V	DF

This was the first unit to receive the MC 200 Saetta, taking 29 on charge by 1 November 1939. After two fatal crashes and numerous technical problems with the Series 1, they were all grounded for inspection. Thus the unit did not begin full operations until September 1940. At the end of July they joined 1 Stormo, carrying out their first operation on 15 September, with later series aircraft escorting Ju 87s of 96 Gruppo over Malta. On 1 November two Macchis of 88 Sq downed a Sunderland flying boat from 228 Squadron RAF near Augusta. In the winter a section was detached to Reggio Calabria for armed reconnaissance over the Messina Straits.

In early 1941 the unit was involved in medium and high level sweeps over Malta. They tried out at least one Re 2000 in March at Catania. The comparative comments with the MC 200 were not officially recorded. Returning to Italy to re-equip with MC 202s, six being received on 15 October, they prepared for the Libyan front. Tropical filters were added to the new fighters before departure.

After acclimatizing the unit began fighter sweeps in January 1942, using the latest Series 3 aircraft. Withdrawing in the spring to Benghasi for a rest and local defence duties, they were soon launched back into the fight. By March they were flying escorts, sweeps and intercepts over the Gambut, Tobruk and Bir Hacheim areas until they were recalled to Italy in June.

With the campaign for Tunisia under way the Gruppo was sent to Pantelleria, with two squadriglie detached to Sfax in northern Tunisia. Operations were carried out, strafing the invasion fleets off the Tunisian coast, and escorting the sea and air traffic between Sicily and Tunisia. By 21 February 1943 the unit was split between Sfax (79 Sq) Achichina (81 Sq) and Gammart (88 Sq). The latter squadriglia flew in to that base on 3 February with nine fighters, retiring to Pantelleria on 30 March. On 6 March six aircraft were detached from Sfax to Gabes for AR duties.

The first MC 205 Veltro fighters were received in Italy

during this period, when 79 Sq arrived at Sciacca. At the end of March the Gruppo returned to Italy to fully equip with the potent new fighter. They rejoined 1 Stormo.

On rejoining the fray over Pantelleria they were the main defence unit, maintaining air superiority through April and May. On 20 April 32 Veltros of 1 Stormo claimed 18 out of 80 Spitfires and P-38s for the loss of one !

By June they were back in the homeland defending northern Italy with their few remaining airworthy fighters. On 7 September they had no serviceable aircraft left.

7 GRUPPO Comb

| Squadriglie | 76, 86, 98 |
| Stormo | 5 |

Arrival	Zone	Base	Country	Aircraft	Duties
10 Jun 40	Sqa 3	Campiglia Marrittima	Italy	Breda 88	IT
19 Jun 40	Sqa 1	Lonate Pozzolo	Italy	Breda 88	GA
Aug 40	Sqa 2	Castelvetrano	Sicily	Breda 88	IT
9 Aug 40	Sqa 5	Castelbenito	Tripolitania	Breda 88	GA
Sep 40	Sqa 5	Derna	Cirenaica	Breda 88	GA
Sep 40	Sqa 5	Benina	Cirenaica	Breda 88	DF
16 Nov 40	Sqa 2	Treviso	Italy	MC 200	TG, DF, AE
25 May 41	ASIC	Comiso	Sicily	MC 200	DF
Jun 41	ASIC	Catania	Sicily	MC 200	DF AE
Jun 41	ASIC	Pantelleria	Sicily	MC 200	AE,CE, AN
Jun 42	ASIC	Reggio Calabria	Italy	MC 200	AE, CE
Jul 42	ASIC	Pantelleria	Sicily	MC 200	CE
Jul 42	AGRE	Araxos	Greece	MC 200 CR 42CN	CE, DF, AE NF
Sep 42	Sqa 4	Crotone	Italy	MC 202	TG, DF
25 Mar 43	Sqa 5	El Hamma	Tunisia	MC 202	DF, AE, GA
6 Apr 43	Sqa 5	La Fauconnerie	Tunisia	MC 202	DF, AE
10 Apr 43	Sqa 5	Enfidaville	Tunisia	MC 202	AE
5 May 43	Sqa 5	Soliman	Tunisia	MC 202	AE
6 May 43	Sqa 5	Korba	Tunisia	MC 202	DF
10 May 43	ASIC	Castelvetrano	Sicily	MC 202	DF

On 6 May 1939 5 Stormo received the Breda 88 at Lonate Pozzolo. On 11 June 1940 this Gruppo became Autonomo, moving to Squadra 1 control for operations over the French Alps. They rejoined 5 Stormo on 13 July, after flying in the final phase of the French campaign.

On 9 August they left the Stormo again and moved to Libya to support the advance on Sidi Barrani. The sand filters added to the 32 Bredas slowed them down and caused engine overheating, thus handicapping further an already underpowered aircraft. By the 11 only 13 aircraft were still serviceable. The unit did operate over the Sidi Barrani area, but with limited results. They were seconded to local defence duties by mid-September. 76 Sq was at Derna N1, 86 Sq at Benina, and 98 Sq at T2. On 14 October only 10 Bredas were flyable out of 29 on charge. When the Gruppo returned to Italy the Bredas were left behind

as decoys on various bases—some aircrew claiming that that was their most effective use !

In March 1941 the unit joined 54 Stormo, re-equipping with the MC 200 fighter. They then became involved in operations against Yugoslavia. Two months later they were in Sicily, protecting shipping, escorting bombers over Malta and on local defence duties.

In early 1942 a detachment was sent to Palermo. In June the Gruppo was escorting bombers over Malta again, followed by convoy escorts in July. 76 Sq stayed in Pantelleria until early August on escort duties.

Moving to Greece and adding some CR 42 night fighter variants, they resumed escorting ships and bombers, together with local defence patrols. 76 Sq was still at Pantelleria and acquired some MC 202s and CR 42s by August.

The enthusiasm of 76 Sq for the MC 202 sped up the re-equipment of the Gruppo with this fighter in Italy. From March 1943 they were thrown into action in Tunisia. Detachments were sent to K34 and K41 Landing Grounds. These were the last Italian units to leave the African continent. Fourteen Macchis, taking off from Soliman, ended up dogfighting P-40s near Capo Bon on 6 May in the last Regia Aeronautica action from Tunisia. They then joined 16 Gruppo at Korba. By 18 May they had no aircraft or crews left and were disbanded on the 27th.

8 GRUPPO CT

| Squadriglie | 92,93,94 |
| Stormo | 2 |

Arrival	Zone	Base	Country	Aircraft	Duties
3 Jun 40	ALIB	Tobruk T2	Cirenaica	CR 32 CR 42	DF, CE, AE
22 Jul 40	Sqa 5	Berka	Cirenaica	CR 42	TG
20 Aug 40	Sqa 5	Derna	Cirenaica	CR 42	DF
6 Sep 40	Sqa 5	Gambut	Cirenaica	CR 42	DF, AR
12 Sep 40	Sqa 5	El Adem	Cirenaica	CR 42	DF
19 Sep 40	Sqa 5	Uadi el Menastir	Cirenaica	CR 42	DF, AE
15 Dec 40	Sqa 5	Berka	Cirenaica	CR 42	IT
20 Dec 40	Sqa 1	Mirafiori	Italy	CR 42	TG
20 Jan 41	Sqa 1	Torino Caselle	Italy	CR 42 MC 200	TG, DF, NF
Apr 41	Sqa 4	Oria Manduria	Italy	CR 42 MC 200	DF, NF
May 41	Sqa 1	Torino Caselle	Italy	MC 200 CR 42 MC 202	DF, NF, CE
25 Nov 41	Sqa 5	Benghasi K3	Cirenaica	MC 200	DF, AR
20 Dec 41	Sqa 5	Agedabia	Cirenaica	MC 200	DF
25 Dec 41	Sqa 5	En Nofilia	Tripolitania	MC 200	DF, AR
Jan 42	Sqa 5	Agheila	Cirenaica	MC 200	DF
Feb 42	Sqa 5	Benghasi K3	Cirenaica	MC 200	DF, CE
11 May 42	Sqa 5	Martuba 5	Cirenaica	MC 200	AE, AR, GA, DF
24 Jun 42	Sqa 5	Ain el Gazala	Cirenaica	MC 200	TG,CE, AE
15 Jul 42	Sqa 5	Abu Haggag	Egypt	MC 200	AE,CE,DF,GA

4: *Even in World War II Walt Disney knew no frontiers—the Donald Duck insignia of 1ª Squadriglia BT on the port tailfin of one of the unit's Fiat BR 20 bombers*

5: *A Fiat BR 20M of the 3ª Sq BT displaying both the unit emblem of Peg-leg Pete, another Walt Disney character, known to the RA as 'La Torbida' and, most unusually, an operations log. Number 6 was based at Pugli, southern Italy, during April 1941 prior to moving to North Africa. The aircraft had already carried out eight missions over England as part of the CAI, and six daylight raids over Greece*

6: *Another Fiat BR 20M of the 3ª Squadriglia, 43° Gruppo, 13° Stormo BT, carrying a small diagonally divided emblem just below the extended dorsal turret. MM 22256 earlier served with the CAI in Belgium, since when it has acquired a white fuselage band and yellow engine cowlings. It is seen here near Cascina Vega. Camouflage is the classic 'Continental' type*

7: A sezione of Breda 88s from the 7° Gruppo Autonomo Combattimento. The dark camouflage scheme and lack of white bands suggests that the period is summr 1940, when the unit was still based in Italy and carried out raids on France (Achille Vigna via MP)

8: One of the first production version Fiat BR 20s of 9ᵃ Squadriglia, 25° Gruppo, 7° Stormo BT. It is seen here in June 1940 while based at Ghemme in Italy. Note the open ventral gunner's trapdoor and the retracted dorsal turret

9: An SM 84 of the 14ᵃ Squadriglia, 4° Gruppo BT seen in its dispersal pen. Location is probably Sicily in 1942. Typically, refuelling is being done by hand from fuel drums. The lack of suitable bowsers created major difficulties for the ground crews, with a consequent effect upon time on the ground between sorties

Arrival	Zone	Base	Country	Aircraft	Duties
15 Oct 42	Sqa 5	Bu Amud	Cirenaica	MC 200	CE, DF
5 Nov 42	Sqa 5	Benghasi K3	Cirenaica	MC 200	CE, DF
15 Nov 42	Sqa 5	En Nofilia	Tripolitania	MC 200	CE,DF, GA
17 Nov 42	Sqa 5	Ghindel	Tripolitania	MC 200	GA
7 Dec 42	Sqa 5	Tauorga	Tripolitania	MC 200	IT
7 Dec 42	Sqa 5	Misurata	Tripolitania	MC 200	IT
10 Dec 42	Sqa 2	Campoformido	Italy	MC 200	DF
26 May 43	Sqa 3	Sarzana	Italy	MC 200	DF, CE
5 Aug 43	Sqa 3	Capua	Italy	MC 200	DF
7 Aug 43	Sqa 3	Sarzana	Italy	MC 200	DF, CE
Sep 43	Sqa 3	Littoria	Italy	MC 200	DF, CE

The first operation occurred on 11 June 1940 when three CR 32s scrambled over base to 4000 metres. One Blenheim was claimed during a scramble by CR 42s in the afternoon of the 10th but this has not been verified. Poor maintenance and supply meant limited use could be made of Tobruk T2. It was, however, useful for protecting the port and T3 base. Two Blenheims were claimed over T3 on the 11th. The Gruppo made 96 sorties that day. On 14 June six CR 32s escorted SM 81 bombers over the front and claimed three intercepting Gladiators for the loss of one CR 32. During this period the unit was active over Sidi Barrani, Mersa Bagush, and coastal areas. A Sunderland was downed on 21 June.

The next day the first nine CR 42s arrived from Tripoli and joined 94 Sq. By late June sand was causing many engine and weapon problems. On 2 July the CR 32s ceased operations when more CR 42s arrived. The latter claimed another Sunderland on 3 July near Bardia. Escorts to Ro 37s began over the Sollum area. Four CR 42s were lost in a dogfight over Menastir with six Gladiators on 4 July. By 7 July all aircraft were non-operational for maintenance work, resuming action two days later.

On 22 July eight aircraft were passed to 13 Gruppo and the remaining eleven moved to Berka for modernisation. Sand filters were applied in late August.

A section was detached to Derna and Tobruk T4 for local defence. During the advance on Sidi Barrani the unit patrolled over the Italian ground troops. Three fighters were detached to Tmimi on 18 September, claiming five out of nine Blenheims in one incoming raid. Two days later the Gruppo claimed a Sunderland and a Blenheim, as well as successfully escorting SM 79s over Mersa Matruh. October saw intercepts and bomber escorts in the Sollum area. A Lysander and a Wellington were claimed in the month. November found the unit protecting the supply routes and frontline troops in the Sidi Barrani area. On 7 December they strafed Bir Quatrani during a sandstorm. Operations were reduced while the storm blew itself out after two days. The first Hurricanes were met on 11 December—one CR 42 was lost. By the 14th only one fighter was still serviceable, so it was passed to 13 Gruppo and the unit returned to Italy.

Picking up replacement crews at Mirafiori, on 25 January 1941 they received CR 42s from 157 Gruppo for the day and night defence of Milano, Torino, and Genova. The first MC 200s arrived on 23 February and sections were detached to Albenga, Piacenza, and Novi Ligure.

During April the unit carried out defensive patrols in support of the Yugoslav campaign. The following month sections were sent to Novi Ligure for naval escort and local defence. On 21 August pilots went to Venegono to convert to the MC 202. The first was received on 7 October. It was, however, passed to 1 Stormo on 15 October and 8 Gruppo became fully equipped with MC 200s.

Resuming operations in Africa on 18 December, they protected the retiring troops and defended Benghasi port and its shipping. In May 1942 they began supporting the new offensive with armed reconnaissance, ground strafing, bomber escorts, and local defence. Apart from 6 and 7 June, when sandstorms curtailed operations, life was hectic. On 24 June the unit moved to Gazala for a rest and refit, detaching sections to Derna, Benghasi, and El Ftehja for bomber and convoy escorts. On 29 June they escorted the Cape Governor during his tour. On 7 July 8 new MC 200s arrived at Abu Haggag from Derna. In late July individual squadriglia, operating from Sidi Barrani, protected convoys traveling between there and Mersa Matruh. Strafing sorties were also carried out in the Fuka and Qattara areas.

In August the aircraft received bomb racks. There were several fights with Beaufighters attacking ships in the Tobruk area at this time. On 4 September the Macchis were first used as fighter-bombers, in a night action against 10 Indian Division and New Zealand Division west of El Mreir. On 20 they had 26 Macchis on charge. By 1 October there were 16 out of 21 MC 200s serviceable. Clashes with Beaufighters, Marylands, Bostons, and Halifaxes occurred in the sea area off Tobruk. The Gruppo claimed one of each of the latter three types on the 26th.

On 4 November the unit passed its aircraft to 13 Gruppo and collected more from 150 Gruppo at Benghasi. 94 Sq was detached to Sidi Barrani between 1 and 6 November. The Gruppo protected Benghasi port against heavy bomber raids, then carried out fighter-bomber sorties in the Agedabia and El Amar areas. By 3 December only three aircraft were serviceable out of 26! Four days later they were passed to 13 Gruppo and the crews flew to Italy in an SM 82.

New MC 200s arrived in January 1943 for the defence of the Valle Padana area. 92 and 94 Sq moved to Caselle and 93 Sq to Albenga. 92 Sq joined 93 Sq on 15 February. During January and February the pilots were employed ferrying D.520s from France to Italy. In March they experimented with air to air bombing. By May it was fully realised that the MC 200 was proving inadequate for bringing down four-engined bombers due to poor armament, low speed advantage and low numbers intercepting.

On 26 May the Gruppo reunited at Sarzana and protected La Spezia naval base and its shipping. Some Re 2001s may have been used at this time. Battles were fought with B-24s, B-17s, Baltimores, and Beaufighters. A B-17 was claimed west of Capo Corso on 5 June, and a Beaufighter near Gorgona on the 28th. The Re 2001s and D.520s were not as effective as hoped, due to poor radio communications and lack of training. In July 94 Sq was detached to Metato with 12 MC 200s for the defence of Livorno, followed by naval escort duties.

2 Stormo disbanded on 10 August and the Gruppo became Autonomo. On the 21st a section of four Macchis went to Grottaglie to defend Taranto. The Gruppo's last operation was on 3 September, when a B-17 was claimed over Pisa.

9 GRUPPO CT

Squadriglie	73, 96, 97
Stormo	4

Arrival	Zone	Base	Country	Aircraft	Duties
10 Jun 40	Sqa 2	Gorizia	Italy	CR 42	TG
Jun 40	Sqa 1	Torino Mirafiori	Italy	CR 42	AE, AR
1 Jul 40	Sqa 2	Comiso	Sicily	CR 42	AE, AR
11 Jul 40	ALIB	Berka	Cirenaica	CR 42	TG
Aug 40	Sqa 5	Benghasi	Cirenaica	CR 42	DF
Sep 40	Sqa 5	El Adem	Cirenaica	CR 42	DF, AE
25 Dec 40	Sqa 2	Gorizia	Italy	MC 200	TG
1 Mar 41	Sqa 4	Brindisi	Italy	MC 200	AR, AE
Apr 41	Sqa 2	Gorizia	Italy	MC 200	AR, AE
Apr 41	Sqa 4	Bari	Italy	MC 200	IT
Jul 41	Sqa 2	Gorizia	Italy	MC 202	TG
24 Sep 41	Sqa 3	Ciampino	Italy	MC 202	DF
29 Sep 41	ASIC	Comiso	Sicily	MC 202	AR, AE, GA
25 Nov 41	Sqa 5	Martuba	Cirenaica	MC 202	DF
12 Dec 41	Sqa 5	Barce	Cirenaica	MC 202	DF
20 Dec 41	Sqa 5	El Merduma	Tripolitania	MC 202	DF
22 Dec 41	Sqa 5	Tamet	Tripolitania	MC 202	DF
Dec 41	Sqa 2	Gorizia	Italy	MC 202	TG
15 Apr 42	ASIC	Castelvetrano	Sicily	MC 202	AR, AE
Apr 42	Sqa 2	Campoformido	Italy	MC 202	TG
22 May 42	Sqa 5	Tripoli	Tripolitania	MC 202	IT
24 May 42	Sqa 5	Martuba 4	Cirenaica	MC 202	DF, AR
24 Jun 42	Sqa 5	Sidi Barrani	Egypt	MC 202	AR
30 Jun 42	Sqa 5	Fuka Sud	Egypt	MC 202	DF, AR, GA AE
30 Oct 42	Sqa 5	Abu Smeit	Egypt	MC 202	IT
1 Nov 42	Sqa 5	Martuba 4	Cirenaica	MC 202	TG. DF
13 Nov 42	Sqa 5	Benghasi K3	Cirenaica	MC 202	DF
15 Nov 42	Sqa 5	Ara Fileni	Tripolitania	MC 202	AE, AR, DF
6 Dec 42	Sqa 5	Misurata	Tripolitania	MC 202	IT
6 Dec 42	Sqa 5	Castelbenito	Tripolitania	MC 202	DF, AE, CE

Arrival	Zone	Base	Country	Aircraft	Duties
16 Jan 43	Sqa 1	Milano Bresso	Italy	MC 202	TG, CE
May 43	Sqa 3	Ciampino Sud	Italy	MC 202 MC 205V	DF
Jun 43	Sqa 3	Furbara	Italy	MC 202	DF
9 Jun 43	Sqa 3	Ciampino Sud	Italy	MC 202	DF
Jun 43	ASIC	Gerbini	Sicily	MC 202 Bf 109G	TG, DF
21 Jun 43	ASIC	Catania	Sicily	MC 202	DF
10 Jul 43	ASIC	Palermo	Sicily	MC 202	IT
14 Jul 43	Sqa 4	Crotone	Italy	MC 202	DF
16 Jul 43	Sqa 4	Castrovillari	Italy	MC 205V	TG, DF
27 Aug 143	Sqa 4	Gioia del Colle	Italy	MC 205V	DF

Although the first unit to receive the new MC 200 in 1940, the pilots preferred their CR 42 biplanes. So they swapped (!) with 1 Stormo, who were delighted to accept the latest aircraft. The Gruppo moved to Mirafiori shortly before war broke out and began operations against France by patrolling the Alpine border.

After the French surrender they flew escort to bombers over Malta, then moved on to the Libyan front. During the British counter-offensive in late 1940 this unit suffered heavy losses to action and environment. By the end of the year they were re-equipping in Italy, with the once-rejected MC 200. In March 73 Sq moved to Brindisi to support the Greek campaign. The following month all three squadriglie joined operations against Yugoslavia, one being detached to Alture di Pola.

By July they were re-equipping again, this time with the excellent MC 202. In late September the unit was testing their new aircraft in the skies over Malta. On 25 November, 96 and 97 Sq transferred to Libya to check out their non-tropical fighters in desert conditions. 73 Sq remained in Sicily and began a career of photo-reconnaissance. Its MC 202s were given Avia cameras, but kept their weapons, and were known to dogfight as much as their fellow squadriglie. The other two squadriglie returned to Sicily, having passed their aircraft to 1 Stormo. Then the whole Gruppo retired to Italy to receive new MC 202s with sand filters.

On 26 May 1942 the freshly equipped unit left for a second tour of the desert. With air superiority their main role, they effectively supported the advance to El Alamein. In the period leading to the Allied onslaught, the unit suffered many losses to ground-strafing fighters and the bombing of their bases. Even so, by 20 September they still had 27 MC 202s on charge.

In late October they passed their ten surviving Macchis to 3 Stormo at Abu Smeit. Picking up 28 brand new aircraft at Martuba, they returned to the front once more. By December, however, they were back at Castelbenito defending Tripoli port. Bad weather and lack of fuel reduced the number of sorties. The next month they once again handed their aircraft to 3 Stormo and left for Italy.

With no new fighters immediately available, the pilots

were used to ferry aircraft to operational units. Consideration was given to re-equipping with the D.520. During May 1943 some MC 205Vs joined the trickle of MC 202s arriving at the unit. They defended Rome for the next two months, having 21 MC 202s on strength by 9 June. The replacements arrived from Furbara and Cerveteri.

By late June they were retraining with 18 Bf 109G-4s and G-6s. The pilots were, however, more impressed with the newer MC 205Vs. They transferred to Sicily, conducting operations over the surrounding waters. Finocchiara and San Salvadore were used as forward strips during this time. 73 Sq was detached to Reggio Calabria with six MC 202s and two borrowed MC 205Vs, moving on to Sigonella in July. The latter aircraft may have received cameras for reconnaissance work at this time, although this is still unconfirmed.

After vainly trying to stem the Allied advance on Sicily, the unit returned to Italy where they received the latest MC 205Vs. A section was detached to Pescara in Mid-August. By 7 September the Gruppo had only nine fighters left on operations.

10 GRUPPO CT

| Squadriglie | 84, 90, 91 |
| Stormo | 4 |

Arrival	Zone	Base	Country	Aircraft	Duties
10 Jun 40	ALIB	Tobruk T2	Cirenaica	CR 42	DF
Jun 40	ALIB	Benina	Cirenaica	CR 42	DF
Jun 40	ALIB	Berka	Cirenaica	CR 42	DF
Aug 40	Sqa 5	Bir el Gobi	Cirenaica	CR 42	DF
Sep 40	Sqa 5	El Adem	Cirenaica	CR 42	DF AE
Sep 40	Sqa 5	Berka	Cirenaica	CR 42	DF AE
6 Jan 41	Sqa 2	Gorizia	Italy	MC 200	TG
Apr 41	Sqa 2	Ronchi	Italy	MC 200	AE AR
16 Jun 41	ASIC	Trapani	Sicily	MC 200	IT
Sep 41	ASIC	Comiso	Sicily	MC 200	AE GA AR
Nov 41	ASIC	Chinisia	Sicily	MC 200	DF
Dec 41	Sqa 2	Gorizia	Italy	MC 202	TG
15 Apr 1942	ASIC	Sciacca	Sicily	MC 202	AE AR
Apr 42	Sqa 2	Campoformido	Italy	MC 202	TG DF
22 May 42	Sqa 5	Tripoli	Tripolitania	MC 202	IT
24 May 42	Sqa 5	Martuba 4	Cirenaica	MC 202	DF AR
28 Jun 42	Sqa 5	Sidi Barrani	Egypt	MC 202	AR DF
30 Jun 42	Sqa 5	Fuka Nord	Egypt	MC 202	DF AR GA AE
3 Jul 42	Sqa 5	Mumin Busak	Egypt	MC 202	DF
15 Jul 42	Sqa 5	Fuka Sud	Egypt	MC 202	DF
30 Oct 42	Sqa 5	Abu Smeit	Egypt	MC 202	IT
1 Nov 42	Sqa 5	Martuba 4	Cirenaica	MC 202	TG DF
13 Nov 42	Sqa 5	Benghasi K3	Cirenaica	MC 202	DF
15 Nov 42	Sqa 5	Ara Fileni	Tripolitania	MC 202	AE AR DF
10 Dec 42	Sqa 3	Ciampino	Italy	MC 202	AE DF
May 43	Sqa 3	Furbara	Italy	MC 202 MC 205V	TG DF

Arrival	Zone	Base	Country	Aircraft	Duties
4 Jun 43	Sqa 3	Cerveteri	Italy	MC 202 MC 205V	
				Bf 109G	DF
9 Jun 43	Sqa 3	Ciampino	Italy	MC 202 MC 205V	DF
21 Jun 43	ASIC	Catania Sigonella	Sicily	MC 202 MC 205V	DF
9 Jul 43	ASIC	Palermo	Sicily	MC 202 MC 205V	IT
14 Jul 43	Sqa 4	Crotone	Italy	MC 205V	DF
24 Jul 43	Sqa 3	Ciampino	Italy	MC 205V	TG DF
Aug 43	Sqa 4	Castrovillari	Italy	MC 205V	DF

This unit had used the CR 42 since September 1939 and were very fond of it. So when the new MC 200 arrived in 1940 the pilots decided, along with their soulmates in 9 Gruppo, to retain the biplane, passing the monoplane to 1 Stormo.

The unit maintained patrols on the Egyptian border and then moved to support the advance on Sidi Barrani in September. During the British counter-offensive in late 1940 they received heavy losses, both from enemy action and the lack of protection from the environment. However, they did have moments of glory. On 6 August three CR 42s attacked a Sunderland flying boat of 228 Squadron RAF. Within fifteen minutes they had knocked out the gun positions, the starboard inner engine, set the main fuel tank on fire, and wounded several crew members. The pilot landed the plane on the water, and the crew were rescued by an Italian destroyer summoned by their victors. By early January the Gruppo were back in Italy re-equipping again with the MC 200.

Operations were carried out against Yugoslavia in April, with 23 aircraft on strength. Two months later the unit was in Sicily, operating over Malta and the Sicilian Canal. 91 Sq was initially detached to Palermo. By the end of 1941 the Gruppo had re-equipped with MC 202s and returned to Sicily for two weeks in April.

Having tested their new aircraft in action they returned to Italy to modify the fighters with sand filters, and on 26 May 1942 they left for a second tour of desert operations. They supported the advance to El Alamein, maintaining air superiority alongside the Luftwaffe units. Damage to their bases reduced their response to enemy attacks, and they suffered many losses to ground strafing fighters. Nevertheless their fighter sweeps caused the Allies some problems. By 20 September there were still 27 Macchis on charge. In late October they passed their surviving Macchis to 3 Stormo at Abu Smeit. Brand new fighters were picked up at Martuba, and were flown to the front in time to cover the retreat. In December they handed their aircraft to 9 Gruppo and returned to Italy.

While waiting for replacement aircraft the pilots were employed ferrying aircraft to operational units. By April 1943 some MC 205Vs were added to the MC 202s, followed by a few Bf 109Gs in May. 90Sq defended Naples from Capua in April and May. 91Sq was detached to Furbara with eight MC 202s until the end of June, when it moved to Sigonella. The other squadriglie had 12 MC 202s and 2 Bf 109Gs operational at Ciampino. On the 23rd ten MC 202s were detached to Reggio Calabria.

By late June the whole unit moved to Sicily to carry out defensive operations over the island. The Bf 109Gs were passed to 9 Gruppo. 84Sq was at Catania by the 25th. After suffering losses during the Allied invasion they returned to the mainland. A section was detached to Pescara in August. By 7th September the Gruppo had only eight MC 205Vs left on operations.

11 GRUPPO BT

Squadriglie	1, 4	
Stormo	13	

Arrival	Zone	Base	Country	Aircraft	Duties
10 Jun 40	Sqa 1	Piacenza	Italy	BR 20	DB, TG
27 Sep 40	CAI	Melsbroech	Belgium	BR 20	NB
10 Jan 41	Sqa 1	Piacenza	Italy	BR 20	TG
8 Apr 41	Sqa 4	Gioia del Colle	Italy	BR 20	DB, AR
27 Apr 41	Sqa 1	Piacenza	Italy	BR 20	TG
22 Jul 41	Sqa 5	Derna	Cirenaica	BR 20	DB, AN
7 Dec 41	Sqa 5	Barce	Cirenaica	BR 20	DB
14 Dec 41	Sqa 5	Misurata	Tripolitania	BR 20	DB
Mar 42	Sqa 5	Bir Dufan	Tripolitania	BR 20	DB
8 Apr 42	Sqa 1	Piacenza	Italy	Ca 314	TG
Jun 42	Sqa 2	Reggio Emilia	Italy	Ca 314 Ca 313	TG
Jun 42	Sqa 4	Manduria	Italy	Ca 314	CE
Jan 43	Sqa 2	Treviso	Italy	CR 42CN	TG

The BR 20 was received in December 1936 and, when the BR 20M arrived, training began with the crews of 7 Stormo at Cameri in 1940. This base and San Damiano Piacenza were used for training.

After operating over southern France they became part of the expedition to Belgium, for operations over England. The first mission was on 24 October against Harwich. Sixteen BR 20Ms from both 13 and 4 Stormo participated, losing two aircraft in the bad weather over Belgium. Night raids were carried out by this Gruppo on Harwich and Ipswich when weather permitted. In January they returned to Italy, via Monaco and Bolzano, One squadriglia flew direct to Piacenza.

They then joined in the end of the Greek campaign and the Yugoslav offensive. After a rest and more training they moved to Libya for operations over Tobruk. Low serviceability resulted from sand affecting engine, weapon, and hydraulic parts.

On 8 April the unit returned to Italy for retraining in the maritime escort role. Moving to Manduria they patrolled the sea lanes between Italy and Greece. The unit changed roles from Combattimento to Intercettori when 13 Stormo disbanded on 10 January 1943. The

Gruppo disbanded on 28 August.

12 GRUPPO ASSALTO

Squadriglie	159, 160	
Stormo	50	

Arrival	Zone	Base	Country	Aircraft	Duties
10 Jun 40	ALIB	Sorman	Tripolitania	Ca 310 CR 32	
				Breda 65	GA
30 Jun 40	ALIB	El Adem	Cirenaica	CR 32 Breda 65	GA
Sep 40	Sqa 5	Tobruk T2	Cirenaica	CR 32 Breda 65	
				Ro41	GA
1 Dec 40	Sqa 5	Benina	Cirenaica	CR 32 Breda 65	
				Ro41	GA
Dec 40	Sqa 5	El Adem	Cirenaica	CR 32 Breda 65	GA
Jan 41	Sqa 5	Benghasi	Cirenaica	CR 32 Breda 65	GA
7 Jan 41	Sqa 5	Derna	Cirenaica	CR 32 Breda 65	GA
Feb 41	Sqa 5	Zuara	Tripolitania	CR 32 Breda 65	IT
1 Feb 41	Sqa		Italy	G 50	TG
Dec 41	Sqa 5	Castelbenito	Tripolitania	G 50bis	GA, DF, CE
42	Sqa 5	Sirtica	Cirenaica	G 50bis	GA
42	Sqa 5	Castelbenito	Tripolitania	G 50bis	GA
Aug 42			Italy		TG
May 43	ASIC	Sciacca	Sicily	MC 200	DF, CE, AR
21 May 43	ASIC	Castelvetrano	Sicily	MC 200 MC 202	
				CR 42	DF, CE, AR

Starting with 24 ex-Hungarian order Ca 310s it was realised that these were inadequate for the approaching offensive. They were passed to 16 Gruppo on 17 June. Consequently, from the 21st of the month, 159 Sq received Breda 65 A80s and 160 Sq received CR 32s. The former were not much better but were all the industry could immediately offer as an assault plane. The fighters were fitted with bomb racks to increase their effectiveness.

On 11 June 159 Sq was detached to Tobruk T2 with seven Ca 310s for ground strafing and reconnaissance duties. On the afternoon of the 13th, 3 aircraft of 159 Sq carried out the Regia Aeronautica's first offensive operation in Africa, with a bombing attack on enemy transport near Scegga. They strafed enemy troops and armoured vehicles over the next few days, but the aircraft suffered heavily from return fire, the sand and the weather. On 20 July 159 Sq had 7 Bredas and 160 Sq had 10 Fiats at the T.2 base. By October the whole unit was at Tobruk, having covered the advance to Sidi Barrani. Four Ro 41s were used by 159 Sq for local day and night defence from 10 August. The Gruppo became Autonomo at the end of December, and 160 Sq received some CR 32s from 16 Gruppo.

From 1 January they flew Bredas and Fiats against armoured units in the Sidi Barrani and Sidi Rezegh areas. At the start they had only 3 out of 6 Fiats and 3 out of 4 Bredas serviceable. By 30 January all aircraft were unserviceable. The unit had retired to Benghasi in

10: *Caproni Ca 313 R.P.B.2 of the 20ª Squadriglia, 46° Gruppo, 15° Stormo somewhere over Italy in 1941. The unit later re-equipped with the CR 42*

11: *Fiat CR 42 fighter-bomber of the 20ª Squadriglia, 46° Gruppo, 15° Stormo in November 1942, shortly before El Alamein. The camouflage scheme is a recent innovation by Fiat known as a 'lizard' finish. Individual aircraft number '10' is probably red*

12: *A poor but rare picture of a Caproni Ca 111 of the 39ª Squadriglia, 5° Gruppo OA in June 1940. The finish is probably the typical Caproni colonial scheme of light cream with red or blue contrasting panels*

13: *IMAM Ro 37 with a Fiat A.30bis in-line engine of the 39ª Squadriglia OA somewhere near Scutari in 1942. Note the yellow nose and the missing wheel spats*

14: *Caproni Ca 314 of the 40ª Squadriglia, 5° Gruppo, probably somewhere over Italy in 1942 when the unit was converting to the type prior to a move to Yugoslavia on anti-partisan duties. In this view the aircraft has a marked similarity to the Avro Anson*

15: *Not even the RA wanted the porcine Piaggio P.32, examples from the 47ª Squadriglia being featured here in 1938 at Aviano. A typically unlovely design of the 30s, Italian airmen were fortunately not called upon to take the aircraft into combat, those built being relegated to use as ground targets*

16: *A Fiat BR 20 of the 48a Squadriglia, 37° Gruppo, 18° Stormo. Note how the early black and white under wing markings overlap the wing leading edge*

17: *An SM 79, 58-2, of the 32° Gruppo preparing to takeoff, probably from Sciacca for an attack on a Malta-bound convoy on June 14 1942. The machine carries its individual number on the wing leading edge and the camouflage on the engines appears to wrap right round the cowling*

18 **Above:** A twin-finned Cant Z1007 of the 62ª Squadriglia, 29° Gruppo, 9° Stormo. The unit was heavily involved in raids on Malta from June 1941

19 **Right:** An unidentified pilot posing by the tail of his Macchi MC 200. The archer emblem is that of the 1° Stormo and according to the original caption the aircraft belonged to the 79ª Squadriglia, 6° Gruppo, the first unit to operate the Saetta. The fuselage code is that of the 72ª Squadriglia, but is explained by the fact that the aircraft were transferred in May 1940. During winter 1940 the unit was based in Sicily—but do they get snow there?

20: Fiat CR 42, 75-12, of the 23° Gruppo on convoy escort duty somewhere between Pantelleria, where the unit was based, and Tripoli in mid-summer 1941. At least one aircraft from the unit was shot down by friendly naval fire during such activities. With good cause, all air forces had reason to be wary of their own naval gunfire which was often indiscriminate

21: *A closer view of another CR 42, MM 7613, of the 75ᵃ Squad-riglia, somewhere over the Mediterranean in summer 1941. As the aircraft was part of a batch of 100 built between March and September that year it is obviously brand new. The yellow engine cowling and white fuselage band were typical Axis recognition markings for the period*

22: *One of the earliest production versions of the Macchi MC 200 with an enclosed cockpit. The very dark camouflage finish is typical for the early months of the war, as here where a pilot of the 81ᵃ Squadriglia, 6° Gruppo, prepares to takeoff on a convoy escort from Catania Fontanarossa in June 1940. Emblem is that of the 1° Stormo*

23: *A later model MC 200 from the 81ᵃ Squadriglia, 6° Gruppo, probably at Campoformido in late 1941 shortly before the unit began refitting with the MC 202. Note how the white cross has been extended to cover the tail cone*

February, after being decimated in the retreat. In eight months the Gruppo had flown 542 operations, losing 2 Ca 310s, 6 Ba 65s, 6 CR 32s, and one SM 81 to the enemy, plus 7 Ba 65s and 6 CR 32s to other causes. The last operation of this tour was flown on the 28th, with four Fiats of 160 Sq and one Breda of 159 Sq attacking Allied ground forces east of Umasi Selinas.

Converting to the ground attack version of the G 50, and joined by 165 Sq, they operated over Libya for a second tour. By 25 December 1941 they were the only such type of unit left in Libya, with 35 G 50bisAS. They were switched to local defence and convoy escorts. In August 1942 the Gruppo was made Autonomo. They had 18 G 50bisASs at Castelbenito, which they passed to 160 Gruppo before returning to Italy in the middle of the month.

By 20 April 1943 they were using MC 200s and MC 202s to escort Ju 52s and SM 82s between Sicily and Tunisia. In May 1943 they were still operating around Sicily, sometimes with the MC 202s of 53 Stormo. The unit disbanded on 26 June.

13 GRUPPO CT

Squadriglie	77, 78, 82
Stormo	2

Arrival	Zone	Base	Country	Aircraft	Duties
10 Jun 40	ALIB	Castelbenito	Tripolitania	CR 42 CR 32	TG
19 Jun 40	ALIB	Tobruk T2	Cirenaica	CR 42	DF, AE, GA
8 Aug 40	Sqa 5	Berka	Cirenaica	CR 42	DF
16 Sep 40	Sqa 5	Gambut	Cirenaica	CR 42	DF, AE, GA
18 Sep 40	Sqa 5	Tmimi	Cirenaica	CR 42	DF, AE, GA
Feb 41	Sqa 2	Jesi	Italy	CR 42	DF
Jun 41	Sqa 1	Genova	Italy	CR 42	AN, AR
Oct 41	Sqa 1	Torino Caselle	Italy	MC 200	TG
Jan 42	Sqa 3	Ciampino Sud	Italy	MC 200	DF
Feb 42	Sqa 5	Castelbenito	Tripolitania	MC 200	DF
Mar 42	Sqa 5	Misurata	Tripolitania	MC 200	CE
Apr 42	Sqa 5	Benghasi K3	Cirenaica	MC 200	DF
7 May 42	Sqa 5	Martuba 5	Cirenaica	MC 200	DF, AE
24 Jun 42	Sqa 5	Ain El Gazala	Cirenaica	MC 200	DF
15 Jul 42	Sqa 5	Bu Amud	Cirenaica	MC 200 MC 202	
				CR 42CN	DF, CE
Jul 42	Sqa 5	Abu Haggag	Egypt	MC 200	GA
Sep 42	Sqa 5	Bu Amud	Cirenaica	MC 200	DF
9 Nov 42	Sqa 5	Benghasi K3	Cirenaica	MC 200	DF, GA
13 Nov 42	Sqa 5	En Nofilia	Tripolitania	MC 200	DF, GA
17 Nov 42	Sqa 5	Ghindel	Tripolitania	MC 200	DF, GA
30 Nov 42	Sqa 5	Tauorga	Tripolitania	MC 200 MC 202	GA
17 Jan 43	Sqa 5	Sorman	Tripolitania	MC 200	DF, GA
22 Jan 43	ATUN	Gabes Est	Tunisia	MC 200 MC 202	GA, DF
31 Jan 43	Sqa 1	Torino Caselle	Italy	MC 200	TG
1 Feb 43	Sqa 5	El Hamma	Tunisia	MC 200	GA
26 Feb 43	ASIC	Palermo	Sicily	MC 200	GA
May 43	Sqa 1	Torino Caselle	Italy	MC 202 D.520	DF
Jun 43	Sqa 3	Ciampino	Italy	MC 202	TG
12 Jul 43	Sqa 3	Furbara	Italy	MC 202	TG, DF
Jul 43	Sqa 1	Lonate Pozzolo	Italy	MC 202 D.520	TG
Jul 43	Sqa 3	Metato	Italy	MC 202 D.520	DF, TG

On the eve of war this unit had 11 CR 32s and 28 CR 42s. The older fighters were passed to 50 Stormo in June, when the Gruppo was fully proficient on the CR 42. For the rest of the year the unit supported operations against Egyptian targets, being especially active over Tobruk. 78 Sq remained in defence of Benghasi in June.

The new year found the unit split into local defence sections around the industrial cities of northern Italy. From June 1941 they tackled units of the Royal Navy operating in the Ligurian Sea.

Re-equipping in October they returned to the African front the following February. They assisted the Axis offensives with ground attacks, intercepts, bombing, and troop protection. From Bu Amud they protected Tobruk, using a day section of MC 202s and a night section of CR 42s, as well as their usual MC 200s. On 14 September aircraft from 82 Sq sank the destroyer *Zulu* and set fire to four MTBs off Tobruk. On this day the unit had 9 out of 17 MC 200s serviceable, one out two MC 202s, and 5 out of 6 CR 42s, at Bu Amud. 82 Sq was detached in November to Castelbenito for local defence duties. By 7 January 1943 this squadriglia was using Misurata Sud for fighter-bomber missions in the Sirte area.

Leaving Libya in January 1943, they fought on in southern Tunisia mainly with ground attacks on pursuing Allied troops. 77 and 78 Sq used MC 202s, while 82 Sq remained on MC 200s. After heavy losses they passed their surviving aircraft to 3 Stormo and returned to Italy.

With the situation getting more desperate they were sent back to Tunisia in February for more ground attack sorties. By the 26 only the Nucleo was operational, the main unit having retired with no aircraft left.

During March the pilots ferried aircraft from the factories to operational units. This held up training and prevented a much needed rest. Eventually re-equipping with MC 202s, they joined the interceptor defences of Italy. The D.520s being used by 358 Sq on local defence duties were passed to 13 Gruppo on 20 July.

At the end of July 78 and 82 Sq moved to Metato with 12 D.520s and a few MC 202s. On 10 August the Gruppo became Autonomo when 2 Stormo disbanded. By 7 September 82 Sq was detached to Venafiorita with six out of ten Macchis serviceable, while the rest of the Gruppo was still at Metato with only a few Macchis operational.

15 GRUPPO OA

Squadriglie	32, 125
Stormo	22

Arrival	Zone	Base	Country	Aircraft	Duties
10 Jun 40	Sqa 1	Udine	Italy	Ca 311	AR
17 Jun 40	Sqa 1	Mirafiori	Italy	Ca 311	AR

This unit began the war under 2 Armata control, with twelve aircraft. Seven days later they transferred to 4 Armata for operations against France. 114 Sq was at Mirafiori and was temporarily attached to the Gruppo for action before the French Armistice.

The Gruppo and its two squadriglie were disbanded on 25 February 1942.

16 GRUPPO ASSALTO

Squadriglie	167, 168
Stormo	50

Arrival	Zone	Base	Country	Aircraft	Duties
10 Jun 40	ALIB	Sorman	Tripolitania	Ca 310 CR 32	
				Breda 65	GA
30 Jun 40	ALIB	Tobruk T2	Cirenaica	Ca 310 CR 32	
				Breda 65	GA
Oct 40	ALIB	Bir el Cuasc	Cirenaica	CR 32 Breda 65	GA
Dec 40	Sqa 5	Derna	Cirenaica	CR 32	GA
16 Dec 40	Sqa 5	Benina N1	Cirenaica	CR 32	GA
Dec 40	Sqa 5	El Adem	Cirenaica	CR 32 Breda 65	GA
Jan 41	Sqa 5	Benghasi K1	Cirenaica	CR 32 Breda 65	GA
Jan 41	Sqa		Italy	MC 200	TG
Apr 41	Sqa 2	Ravenna	Italy	MC 200	DF, AE, AR
12 Jun 41	ASIC	Gela	Sicily	MC 200	DF, AE
Jul 41	ASIC	Gerbini	Sicily	MC 200	DF, AN, CE
13 Jun 42	ASAR	Monserrato	Sardinia	MC 200	DF, AN, CE
Jul 42	ASIC	Castelvetrano	Sicily	MC 200	CE, DF
1 Aug 42	Sqa 4	Crotone	Italy	MC 200 MC 202	
				CR 42	DF, NF, CE
Feb 43	Sqa 5	K41 LG	Tunisia	MC 202	DF, GA
21 Feb 43	Sqa 5	K34 LG	Tunisia	MC 202	DF, GA
24 Feb 43	ATUN	Medenine	Tunisia	MC 202	DF, GA
5 May 43	Sqa 5	Korba	Tunisia	MC 202	AE
10 May 43	ASIC	Castelvetrano	Sicily	MC 202	DF

167 Sq received CR 32s and 168 Sq received Breda 65 K14s from 2 Stormo, and proceeded to support the advance on Sidi Barrani in September 1940. The CR 32s were given bombracks to assist the assault planes. Both types were poorly equipped for the work required. The Ca 310s were briefly re-used in July after heavy losses by the unit. Ain El Gazala was used as a forward base in June. On 20 July 167 Sq had 10 CR 32s and 168 Sq had 5 Ba 65s at Tobruk T2. By 18 October both squadriglie were using Bir el Cuasc. From early 1941 the remnants of the unit were back in Benghasi. They left 50 Stormo on 15 January.

Converting to the MC 200 they joined 54 Stormo as a Caccia Terrestre Gruppo in March. 169 Sq had joined them by then. The following month they had two squadriglie at Ravenna and one detached to Udine for operations against Yugoslavia. Only 11 of the 22 Macchis were serviceable at this time.

After the Balkan experience they began sorties over Malta, both escorting bombers and sweeps, followed by a long tour of shipping escort in the surrounding waters.

With the Allied invasion of North Africa the unit was ordered to Tunisia in December 1942, having received the more modern MC 202s in the meantime. On their first operation, on 25 February 1943, they escorted German aircraft to attack Ben Gardane, then carried out strafing sweeps. Fighting continued until May with many dogfights. For example, on 7 March, 17 Macchis claimed nine Spitfires and a P-38 for the loss of two of their own. Nine new MC 202s were received at K41 on the 20th to replace those lost to Allied bombing in the previous days. On the 30th the Gruppo joined the reformed 54 Stormo. By mid-April only this Stormo remained in Tunisia.

Withdrawing to Sicily for a rest before the next round, they helped defend that island and southern Italy through the Spring. With no aircraft or crews left by 18 May, the unit was disbanded on the 27th.

17 GRUPPO CT

Squadriglie	71, 72, 80
Stormo	1

Arrival	Zone	Base	Country	Aircraft	Duties
10 Jun 40	Sqa 2	Boccadifalco	Sicily	CR 32	DF
Sep 40	Sqa 2	Trapani Milo	Sicily	MC 200	TG, AE, AR
					DF
21 Jun 41	Sqa 2	Campoformido	Italy	MC 202	TG
Nov 41	Sqa 3	Ciampino	Italy	MC 202	TG
18 Nov 41	ASIC	Comiso	Sicily	MC 202	IT DF
25 Nov 41	Sqa 5	Martuba	Cirenaica	MC 202	DF
Nov 41	Sqa 5	Benina	Cirenaica	MC 202	DF
12 Dec 41	Sqa 5	Benghasi K2	Cirenaica	MC 202	DF
Dec 41	Sqa 5	Sidi Magrum	Cirenaica	MC 202	DF
20 Dec 41	Sqa 5	Bir el Merduma	Tripolitania	MC 202	DF
21 Dec 41	Sqa 5	Ara Fileni	Tripolitania	MC 202	DF
22 Dec 41	Sqa 5	Tamet	Tripolitania	MC 202	DF, AR
Jan 42	Sqa 5	Benghasi K3	Cirenaica	MC 202	DF
16 Mar 42	Sqa 5	Martuba 4	Cirenaica	MC 202	DF, AR
24 Jun 42	Sqa 5	Sidi Barrani	Egypt	MC 202	IT DF
26 Jun 42	Sqa 2	Campoformido	Italy	MC 202	TG
Nov 42	ASIC	Pantelleria	Sicily	MC 202	GA, AE, AN, DF
Nov 42	Sqa 3	Pontedera	Italy	MC 202	TG
6 Nov 42	ASAR	Decimomannu	Sardinia	MC 202	GA, AN
Jan 43	Sqa 3	Capodichino	Italy	MC 202	DF, CE
Jan 43	Sqa 1	Lonate Pozzolo	Italy	MC 205V	TG

Arrival	Zone	Base	Country	Aircraft	Duties
Feb 43	ASIC	Sciacca	Sicily	MC 205V	TG
Apr 43	ASIC	Pantelleria	Sicily	MC 205V	CE,AE, DF

Arrival	Zone	Base	Country	Aircraft	Duties
14 May 43	ASIC	Chinisia	Sicily	MC 205V	AE, DF
21 May 43	ASIC	Finocchiara	Sicily	MC 205V	AE, DF
26 Jun 43	Sqa 1	Torino Caselle	Italy	MC 205V	DF
Jul 43	Sqa 2	Osoppo	Italy	MC 205V	DF
17 Jul 43	Sqa 2	Ronchi	Italy	MC 205V	DF

In May 1940 this unit passed its MC 200s to 6 Gruppo, returning provisionally to the CR 32. Easier logistics demanded this action. So, on the eve of war there were 26 of these older fighters in readiness. Moving to Trapani and receiving new MC 200s, operations began on 15 September when they escorted Ju 87s of 96 Gruppo to Malta. For the rest of that year they used Castelvetrano and Pantelleria as forward bases. 72 Sq went to Comiso in August, escorting bombers and reconnaissance aircraft over Malta. The Gruppo transport was provided by three Ca 133s.

In early 1941 fighter sweeps were flown over Malta, and a section was sent to Pantelleria for local defence during the winter period. 80 Sq used Fontanarossa in January.

From June to October 1941 the unit trained in Italy on the new MC 202, being only the second unit to receive them. The aircraft were taken to Ciampino where they were fitted with sand filters and prepared for Africa.

The first ten Macchis of 71 Sq left for Africa on 18 November. By the 23rd 71 and 72 Sq were at Castelbenito, proceeding on to Tamet, then Martuba. With the brief stop in Sicily, the unit arrived in Cirenaica doing much to reduce the RAF's dominance there. In December, at Martuba, they additionally received 9 Gruppo's old Macchis. Fighter sweeps were carried out from Tamet, and Benghasi port was defended. During May 1942 sweeps and intercepts were made in the Tobruk and Bir Hacheim areas. The following month the unit returned to Italy for a rest and refit.

Due to the poor production supply the unit was without aircraft for several weeks. Eventually it went to Pantelleria where it operated against the Allied fleet at Bone, escorting bombers, strafing and making intercepts. Moving to Sardinia with 33 fighters, it dealt with targets on or near the Algerian coast, being among the few units capable of surviving such missions.

Retiring briefly to escort warships and defend Italian cities from the increasing Allied bomber raids, it was re-equipped with the superb MC 205V *Veltro* and sent back to Sicily. Communications problems caused the navy to be attacked four times in January before the fighters could intervene. The inter-service wrangles did not help!

Hastily completing its training, operations recommenced at the end of April 1943 in support of the evacuation of Tunisia. Protection was given to the air and sea transports plodding between Tunisia and Sicily. Moving to Chinisia, with Finocchiara as a forward landing ground, they continued their intercepts and escorted torpedo-bombers who still tried to break the Allied flow. With few aircraft left they retreated at the end of June to Italy where further equipment was awaited.

18 GRUPPO CT

Squadriglie	83, 85, 95
Stormo	3

Arrival	Zone	Base	Country	Aircraft	Duties
3 Jun 40	Sqa 1	Novi Ligure	Italy	CR 42	GA,AE,AR
9 Jul 40	Sqa 1	Mirafiori	Italy	CR 42	TG
6 Oct 40	CAI	Monaco	Monaco	CR 42	IT
17 Oct 40	CAI	Darmstadt	Germany	CR 42	IT
19 Oct 40	CAI	Ursel	Belgium	CR 42	AE, AR
10 Jan 41	CAI	Frankfurt	Germany	CR 42	IT
13 Jan 41	Sqa 3	Pisa	Italy	CR 42	TG
29 Jan 41	Sqa 5	Sorman	Tripolitania	CR 42	CE
30 Jan 41	Sqa 5	Mellaha	Tripolitania	CR 42	CE
12 Feb 41	Sqa 5	Tamet	Tripolitania	CR 42	DF
7 Apr 41	Sqa 5	Benghasi K2	Cirenaica	CR 42	DF
10 Aug 41	Sqa 5	Tamet	Tripolitania	CR 42	IT
10 Aug 41	Sqa 5	Sorman	Tripolitania	CR 42	IT
12 Aug 41	Sqa 1	Torino Caselle	Italy	G 50	TG
12 Oct 41	Sqa 1	Mirafiori	Italy	MC 200	TG
20 Oct 41	Sqa 3	Ciampino Sud	Italy	MC 200	TG
10 Dec 41	Sqa 3	Lecce	Italy	MC 200	IT
11 Dec 41	AGRE	Araxos	Greece	MC 200	TG, CE
1 May 42	Sqa 1	Mirafiori	Italy	MC 200	TG
16 Jul 42	Sqa 3	Ciampino Sud	Italy	MC 200	TG
18 Jul 42	ASIC	Pantelleria	Sicily	MC 200	IT
18 Jul 42	Sqa 5	Tripoli	Tripolitania	MC 200	IT
21 Jul 42	Sqa 5	Tamet	Tripolitania	MC 200	IT
22 Jul 42	Sqa 5	K3	Cirenaica	MC 200	IT
22 Jul 42	Sqa 5	Derna	Cirenaica	MC 200	IT
23 Jul 42	Sqa 5	Abu Haggag	Egypt	MC 200	AR, DF, CE, GA
22 Oct 42	Sqa 5	Abu Smeit	Egypt	MC 200 MC 202	TG
3 Nov 42	Sqa 5	Bir el Astas	Egypt	MC 200 MC 202	DF, GA
6 Nov 42	Sqa 5	Bu Amud	Cirenaica	MC 200 MC 202	DF, GA
10 Nov 42	Sqa 5	Benghasi	Cirenaica	MC 200 MC 202	DF, GA
12 Nov 42	Sqa 5	En Nofilia	Tripolitania	MC 200 MC 202	DF GA
16 Nov 42	Sqa 5	Tauorga	Tripolitania	MC 200 MC 202	DF, GA
15 Jan 43	Sqa 5	Castelbenito	Tripolitania	MC 200 MC 202	DF, TG
19 Jan 43	ATUN	Medenine	Tunisia	MC 200? MC 202	DF, GA
22 Jan 43	ATUN	El Hamma	Tunisia	MC 200? MC 202	DF, GA
Feb 43	ATUN	Achichina	Tunisia	MC 202	DF, GA
Feb 43	Sqa 5	El Hamma	Tunisia	MC 202	DF, GA
Mar 43	Sqa 5	Gabes	Tunisia	MC 202	DF, GA
26 Mar 43	Sqa 5	Achichina	Tunisia	MC 202	DF, GA
16 Apr 43	Sqa 1	Torino Caselle	Italy	MC 202	TG
11 Jun 43	Sqa 3	Ciampino Sud	Italy	MC 202	DF

85 Sq was detached to Villanova d'Albenga on 6 June 1940. At the outbreak of war the Gruppo carried out strafing attacks on bases in southern France and escorted bombers. The unit opened its score with 3 Bloch 151s of Aeronavale AC3 being claimed on the 15th for the loss of two Fiats. From 9 August the pilots were occupied in ferrying 30 CR 42s to Castelbenito, via Pantelleria, Ciampino, Reggio Calabria, Trapani, Pantelleria, and Zuara, returning in the Gruppo's Ca 133s on the 14th. They had six of these on strength.

The unit temporarily transferred to 56 Stormo for operations over the English Channel, receiving new aircraft and new grey-blue uniforms. Bad weather hampered their transfer to Belgium. The first mission was on 27 October escorting BR 20s of 43 Stormo to Ramsgate, repeating this on the 29th. On 11 November, on a similar mission, they fought a desperate battle with the RAF over Harwich. Ten BR 20s of 242 and 243 Sq were escorted by forty CR 42s of 18 Gruppo. Thirty Hurricanes from 17, 46, and 257 Squadrons intercepted, claiming eight bombers and five fighters. Actual losses were three of each type, with a further eight fighters damaged on landing back at base due to unfamiliarity with the weather. The pilots felt that reducing the two 12.7mm guns to one 12.7mm and one 7.7mm in order to save weight and increase manouevrability had not helped. In return they claimed nine fighters, but in fact the RAF lost none.

After this, they were restricted in offensive sorties although sweeps were flown over the Channel, eventually ceasing on 3 January 1941. During this time pilots checked out the Bf 109E in a neighbouring German unit, JG51. From 18 November two CR 42s were detached to Vlissingen on night fighter and reconnaissance duties. On 23rd the Gruppo fought with Spitfires of 603 Sqn RAF, claiming 5, while losing 2. Some of these claims were shared with JG26. It appears only one Spitfire was actually damaged. The Gruppo was known to the Germans as 18./ JG 56.

After a brief rest in Italy they moved to Libya for the first half of 1941, stepping through Capodichino (27th January), Regia Calabria (28th), Pantelleria (28th), and Castelbenito (29th). More CR 42s were then received, from 23 Gruppo at Sorman, on 1 March to replace losses. The faithful old Ca 133s were still in attendance.

In February Sirte was used as a forward base and 83 Sq and 95 Sq were detached to Tauorga on the 12th. 85 Sq replaced 95 Sq at Tamet on the 25th. 83 Sq then moved to Hon (9 March), Mellaha (23 April), Benghazi K2 (17 May) and Derna (22 May), reuniting with the Gruppo at K2 on 15 July. Meanwhile, 85 and 95 Sq had moved to

Bengazi K2 on 7 April, for both training and intercept duties. On 14th of that month 151 Gruppo handed them CR 42 fighter-bombers and detachments were sent to Derna during May. In August they left their aircraft at Sorman, and returned to Italy in SAS SM 81s. After the first Libyan tour there may have followed a short spell of escort duty in Sicily.

After training on G 50s back in Italy, then re-equipping with MC 200s, they transferred to Greece for convoy protection duties. 95Sq was detached to Grottaglie on 16 December, then to Lecce, then to Tatoi on 6 January for the defence of Athens, returning to Lecce and Mirafiori on 15 April. The other squadriglie left their aircraft at Araxos, and were flown back to Mirafiori on 1 May.

Rejoining 3 Stormo on 15 May 1942, with 30 MC 200s, the Gruppo moved to Ciampino where 21 aircraft were fitted with bomb racks and they began ground attack training. They then flew to Libya. By July they were 60% operational and preparing for the Alamein battles. On the night of 12 August seven pilots were killed on the ground by raiding Swordfish and Albacores—this was a great blow to the Gruppo. Further losses on the ground and in the air reduced their effectiveness, but in the retreat across Libya they still managed to hinder the Allied advance with fighter-bomber attacks under the escort of 23 Gruppo. By 20 August they still had 15 MC 200AS on charge. On 9 September two MC 200s defended a convoy against Blenheims of 15 Squadron SAAF and Beaufighters of 272 Squadron RAF. The Gruppo also had to deter Wellingtons, Beauforts, and Hudsons during this period. On 27 October they received 12 of 4 Stormo's old MC 202s in place of 13 MC 200s lost to bombing on the 21st. They were followed by more from 13 Gruppo on 31 December. 83 Sq was detached to Castelbenito on 20 November. On 10 December the Gruppo went to Tamet to cover a convoy, returning to Tauorga the next day.

Further MC 202s were transferred from 4 Stormo, at Castelbenito on 8 January 1943. 83 Sq moved from there to Medenine on the 20th, sharing with 70 Sq of 23 Gruppo the role of last Italian air unit to leave Libya. On the 26th 95Sq was detached to Gabes, to pick up more MC 202s from 13 Gruppo. They rejoined the mother unit at EL Hamma on the 8 February. The number of MC 200s used declined rapidly during the Tunisian battles, as more MC 202s were received. By 16 February 13 MC 202s out of 29 were still serviceable. At the end of March the unit withdrew to Italy, having no serviceable aircraft left.

The pilots were then used to ferry French D.520 fighters from France to Italy before re-equipping at Caselle with new MC 202s. They then moved south for the defence of Rome. Six MC 205V Series III and between three and six SAI 207 fighters arrived at the end of July and joined in the bomber intercepts. The latter prototypes were tried out by 83 Sq who thought the lightweight fighters were very competent at low and medium altitudes.

They were passed to 161 Gruppo in August for further assessment.

Brief detachments to Sicily ended with a mauling which caused a quick return to Cerveteri. They then successfully fought against the incoming B-17s and B-24s with their Macchis. On 19 July the Gruppo downed 3 B-24s and one P-38 over Rome, while two more B-24s and another P-38 were claimed later that day. By 7 September there were two MC 205Vs and nine MC 202s still operational.

19 GRUPPO Comb

Squadriglie 100, 101, 102
Stormo 5

Arrival	Zone	Base	Country	Aircraft	Duties
10 Jun 40	ASAR	Alghero	Sardinia	Breda 88	GA
Jul 40	Sqa 1	Lonate Pozzolo	Italy	Breda 88	TG

On 6 May 1939, 5 Stormo received the Breda 88 at Lonate Pozzolo. On 11 June 1940 the Gruppo became Autonomo. On 16 and 19 June raids were carried out on Corsican targets, but the 13 aircraft were found to be grossly underpowered for war operations. The unit rejoined 5 Stormo on 13 July, moving back to Italy, where it finally disbanded on 1 December 1940.

20 GRUPPO CT

Squadriglie 351, 352, 353
Stormo 51

Arrival	Zone	Base	Country	Aircraft	Duties
10 Jun 40	Sqa 3	Ciampino Sud	Italy	CR 32 G 50	NF, DF
19 Oct 40	CAI	Ursel	Belgium	G 50	AE, DF
10 Jan 41	CAI	Maldegem	Belgium	G 50	DF
Mar 41	CAI	Desvres	France	G 50	DF
Apr 41	Sqa 3	Ciampino	Italy	G 50	TG
Apr 41	Sqa 5	Castelbenito	Tripolitania	G 50	DF
May 41	Sqa 5	Misurata	Tripolitania	G 50	DF, CE
May 41	Sqa 5	El Ftehja	Cirenaica	G 50	DF, CE, GA
Jun 41	Sqa 5	Martuba	Cirenaica	G 50	DF, GA, AE
Aug 41	Sqa 5	Gambut	Cirenaica	G 50	AR, AE
18 Nov 41	Sqa 5	Sidi Rezegh	Cirenaica	G 50	DF AE
12 Dec 41	Sqa 5	Derna	Cirenaica	G 50	TG, DF, AE
14 Dec 41	Sqa 5	Agedabia	Cirenaica	G 50	DF, AE
Dec 41	Sqa 5	El Merduma	Tripolitania	G 50	DF, AE
20 Dec 41	Sqa 3	Ciampino	Italy	MC 202	TG
May 42	ASIC	Chinisia	Sicily	MC 202	AE, AR
30 Jun 42	ASIC	Gela	Sicily	MC 202	AE, AR
Nov 42	ASIC	Castelvetrano	Sicily	MC 202	CE, DF
Dec 42	Sqa 3	Ciampino Sud	Italy	MC 202	TG
Mar 43	Sqa 3	Ciampino	Italy	MC 202 G55	TG
May 43	ASIC	Chinisia	Sicily	MC 202 G55	DF
16 May 43	ASAR	Capoterra	Sardinia	MC 202 G55	DF
Jul 43	ASAR	Casa Zeppera	Sardinia	MC 202 G55	DF
31 Jul 43	Sqa 3	Foligno	Italy	MC 202 G55	DF
23 Aug 43	ASAR	Milis	Sardinia	MC 202	DF
27 Aug 43	Sqa 3	Foligno	Italy	MC 202 G55 MC 205V	DF

As part of the Rome defences this unit had four CR 32s as interim nightfighters, plus 25 G 50s for day sorties. On 13 June 1940 the CR 32s were detached to Guidonia. From September the unit joined 56 Stormo, and took 45 G 50s and 6 Ca 133s to Belgium.

Low range capability and lack of radios kept them from being more active in this theatre, and several pilots suffered from severe frostbite due to the lack of cockpit heating. Escorts and sweeps were, however, carried out over Ramsgate and Harwich, but without much opposition. 24 G 50s escorted 5 Z1007bis to Great Yarmouth on 11 November. The main sweeps were made over Margate and Folkestone by the CR 42s of 18 Gruppo, especially on 23 November. After the main CAI units had left for Italy, 352 and 353 Sq remained for patrols along the Dutch, Belgian and French coasts as far as Calais, until 15 April 1941.

The Germans referred to the Gruppo as 20./JG 56. Some of the unit's pilots were allowed to fly the Bf 109Es of JG51's training unit, based at Cazaux, France. The pilots were so impressed with the German fighters that they asked their commanders to order 100 for the Regia Aeronautica. The Germans declined to supply this amount due to the need for all aircraft for the coming invasion of Russia. They did offer to equip one Gruppo, however, but this was rejected by the Italian higher command.

With the Italian forces under pressure in Libya the Gruppo was rushed straight to the front there. It was about this time 351 Sq went to 155 Gruppo and was replaced by 151 Sq. During the Spring of 1941 they protected the troops and supply columns, and made local intercepts. Operations were concentrated around the Sidi Barrani area in June. For example, on 4 July five G 50s of 151 Sq took off from Martuba and claimed two Hurricanes destroyed on the ground at Sidi Barrani. The commanding officer, *Capitano* Montefusco, was badly wounded during a second run and crashed 10 km from the target, despite attempts by his wingman to guide him back to base. He was awarded the *Medaglia D'Oro*. Like most units the Gruppo's aircraft suffered from the sand until intake filters could be fitted. In July they escorted 209 Sq in attacks on Tobruk.

For the remainder of 1941 the unit made many armed reconnaissance and escorted dive-bombers, sometimes jointly with the Germans. On 19 November a British commando raid on Sidi Rezegh cost them 18 G 50s, and five more on 22 December at Agedabia. With virtually no aircraft left, they returned to Italy in the new year, having flown over 4,000 hours in more than eight months of desert operations.

They now rejoined 51 Stormo, which had been disbanded from September 1940 until 1 January 1942. The MC 202 arrived in March, and the unit was ordered to Sicily for operations around Malta, starting in June. Then they returned to Italy in December.

On 21 March 1943 they received the third prototype G55 for operational trials. The unit moved to Sardinia in May, where the G55 successfully fought in several dogfights. During March the crews complained that the new Macchis needed much modification to make them combat ready. Poor petrol quality and excessive oil loss caused problems. Hydraulic, pneumatic and electrical systems often caught fire—and still the aircraft lacked radios...

Meanwhile, nine pre-production Series 0 G55s were taken on at Ciampino Sud. In June 11 G55 Series Is arrived, and together with the G55/0s, were used by 353 Sq for the defence of Rome. The other squadriglie were now at Foligno. On 5th August several aircraft and pilots were passed to 155 Gruppo.

On 23 August 151 and 352 Sq went to Milis for interceptor duties, scoring well against USAAF P-40s. They were soon back at Foligno, where the unit also received a few MC 205Vs. They were hoping to fully equip with G55s, but no more arrived before the Armistice. 353 Sq was still detached at Ciampino, with 12 G55s on 7th September.

21 GRUPPO CT

Squadriglie 354, 355
Stormo 51

Arrival	Zone	Base	Country	Aircraft	Duties
10 Jun 40	Sqa 3	Ciampino Sud	Italy	CR 32	NF, DF
4 Aug 40	Sqa 3	Capodichino	Italy	CR 32 G 50 MC 200	NF, DF
12 Apr 41	Sqa 4	Bari	Italy	MC 200	DF
4 May 42	CSIR	Otopeni	Romania	MC 200	IT
4 May 42	CSIR	Stalino	Russia	MC 200	AR, AE, DF
Jul 42	CSIR	Voroscilovgrad	Russia	MC 200	AR, DF, GA
9 Jul 42	CSIR	Makejevka	Russia	MC 200	AR DF
24 Jul 42	CSIR	Voroscilovgrad	Russia	MC 200 MC 202	AE, DF, GA
22 Jan 43	CSIR	Stalino	Russia	MC 200 MC 202	DF, GA
Jan 43	CSIR	Saporoshje	Russia	MC 200 MC 202	DF
Feb 43	CSIR	Odessa	Russia	MC 200 MC 202	IT
May 43	CSIR	Zagabria	Yugoslavia	MC 200 MC 202	IT
15 May 43	Sqa 3	Firenze	Italy	MC 202	TG
Jun 43	Sqa 3	Capua	Italy	MC 202	DF
23 Jun 43	ASIC	Chinisia	Sicily	MC 202	DF
15 Jul 43	ASIC	Palermo	Sicily	MC 202	IT
16 Jul 43	Sqa 4	Manduria	Italy	MC 202	DF
24 Jul 43	Sqa 2	Pescara	Italy	MC 202	DF
6 Aug 43	Sqa 4	Gioia del Colle	Italy	MC 202	DF

356 Sq became Autonomo on 3 June 1940, but rejoined the Gruppo on 4 August. On 13 June the CR 32s were detached to Guidonia as a nightfighter section. The Gruppo transferred from 51 to 52 Stormo on 11 September. 354 and 355 Sq became Autonomo and moved to the Greek-Albanian front on 28 October. Three CR 32qtr nightfighters were assigned to 356Sq on 7 November, to add to their G 50s. By December, however, the unit was training on 17 new MC 200s, as well as a few G 50s.

382 and 386 Sq now joined 356 Sq. In April they moved to Bari for operations in the Yugoslav campaign. They may have been on convoy escort duties between Tunisia and Sardinia in August. While preparing for anti-partisan operations they received orders to transfer for the Russian front.

Between March and July 1942 the unit personnel moved to Stalino, replacing 22 Gruppo as the fighter component of the Russian Expeditionary Force. They received that unit's surviving aircraft in addition to the ten new MC 200s they had brought with them. In early June 361 Sq arrived from the Aegean.

On 27 June two squadriglie were detached to Borvenkovo to cover the crossing of the River Don at Izyum, carrying out fighter sweeps and ground strafing. Using Voroscilovgrad as their main base, squadriglie were detached where needed most. Two went to Tazinskaja as escorts to German Ju 87Ds from 24 July, and two then went to Oblivskaja four days later. In August two were on intercept duties at Millerovo and one was at Kantamirovka until 18 December when it moved to Starobelsk.

It was on 12 December that Tenente Walter Benedetti led seven MC 200s of 361 Sq from Kantamirovka to attack Russian troops attempting to surround units of the Italian 8th Army, who were defending the approaches to Stalingrad. It seems that the officer was downed by anti-aircraft fire, but it is known that the Yak 9s of the 586th Regiment, under Commander T. Kazarinova, were making their first appearances in the area and so may have caused the loss of this highly experienced and decorated pilot. The weather was icy cold and a freezing mist covered the low altitude. The superb view from the open cockpit Macchi may have been countered by the icy blast and poor weather, and allowed one or more Yaks to attack unnoticed while the Italians concentrated on strafing the troops below.

Reunited back at Voroscilovgrad by the end of December, the last operation was carried out on 17 January 1943 over the Millerovo area. Five days later they retired to Stalino, ready for the return journey home. Fifteen unserviceable aircraft were left behind.

During September they had received 12 MC 202s, and

later two photo-reconnaissance versions had arrived. Bad weather hindered operations and the MC 202s only managed 17 sorties with no losses or claims. The MC 200s claimed 88 Russian aircraft for the loss of the 15 write-offs. A creditable performance for an open-cockpit fighter in the Russian autumn and winter. In February, at Odessa, the unit had 24 MC 200s and 9 MC 202s left.

Fully equipping with MC 202 Series VIII on return home, they were sent to Sicily after two months in training. 382 Sq left the Gruppo at this time. By August the Gruppo was back in Italy with only a few serviceable aircraft left.

22 GRUPPO CT

| Squadriglie | 357, 358, 359 |
| Stormo | 52 |

Arrival	Zone	Base	Country	Aircraft	Duties
10 Jun 40	Sqa 3	Pontedera	Italy	G 50	AE
21 Jun 40	Sqa 1	Liguria	Italy	G 50	AE
Jun 40	Sqa 1	Piemonte	Italy	G 50	AE
Jun 40	Sqa 3	Ciampino	Italy	G 50 MC 200	TG, DF, AE
6 Mar 41	AALB	Tirana	Albania	MC 200	DF, AG
12 Aug 41	CSIR	Beneasa	Romania	MC 200	IT
12 Aug 41	CSIR	Tudora	Russia	MC 200	DF
26 Aug 41	CSIR	Krivoi Rog	Russia	MC 200	DF, AE
20 Oct 41	CSIR	Saporoshje	Russia	MC 200	DF, AE, GA
7 May 42	CSIR	Otopeni	Romania	none	IT
7 May 42	Sqa 3	Ciampino	Italy	Re 2001	TG
Jul 42	ASAR	Elmas	Sardinia	Re 2001	AN
Sep 42	ASIC	Gela	Sicily	Re 2001	GA, AR, AE
7 Nov 42	ASAR	Monserrato	Sardinia	Re 2001	AN, GA, AR
26 Dec 42	Sqa 3	Capodichino	Italy	Re 2001 D.520	
				Re2005 FC20bis	TG, DF
10 Jul 43	ASIC	Pantelleria	Sicily	Re 2001	AN, DF, CE
Jul 43	Sqa 3	Capodichino	Italy	Re 2001 Re2005	
				MC 202	DF

The war began for this unit during a transfer to bases closer to the front, because of the poor range of their 28 G 50s. The first operation was on 15 June, escorting SM 79s of 9, 41 and 46 Stormi to Calvi port in Corsica. For operations against the French mainland they moved to Ligure and Piemonte, with 357 and 358 Sq detached to Torino Caselle. 358 Sq left for Libya and 2 Gruppo on 23 December, the first G 50 unit to arrive in that theatre.

On 24 October 360 Sq reformed and joined the Gruppo, which also received its first three MC200s that month. During December 362 Sq left 24 Gruppo to defend La Spezia naval base from Sarzana. They subsequently joined 22 Gruppo at Ciampino for the defence of Rome. 369 Sq also joined in December. By this time the Gruppo had 37 MC 200s and a few G 50s.

In March 1941, with 36 MC200s, the unit moved to Albania, taking 359, 362, and 369 Sq. For the next three

months they carried out intercepts over the Greek and Yugoslav fronts. On 8 May the pilots ferried fresh aircraft from Niksic to Scutari and Tirana, being brought back to their unit by the Gruppo SM 81. From June they became involved in anti-partisan operations, becoming Autonomo in August.

They then headed for their next assignment, flying through Romania to what was to be a relatively successful campaign, despite the bitter weather and harsh conditions. For this, the Russian front, they received an additional squadriglia, 371 from 157 Gruppo. The numbers of unit aircraft sent were 51 MC 200s, 2 SM 81s, and 3 Ca 133s. The latter joined at Krivoi Rog on the 26th then they moved to Stalino. Two were lost by March 1942, and were not replaced as they were found to be inferior to the companion SM 81s and newly arrived SM 73s.

In the first combat, on 27 August, the Gruppo claimed six SB-2 bombers and two I-16 fighters. Intercepts and escorts for reconnaissance aircraft were the early duties. Bad weather restricted the number of sorties and by October they were ordered to give direct support to the ground forces as well.

On 9 November 371 Sq was detached to Stalino, exchanging with 359 Sq on 1 December. They in turn were replaced by 369 Sq on the 28th. On 18 February 1942 362 Sq replaced them, followed by 371 Sq again on 24 March. Between September 1941 and March 1942 the unit downed 14 Russian fighters plus several bombers, for no loss.

In December 1941 371 Sq issued a report to command headquarters explaining some of the reasons for reduced effectiveness, namely :

1. Inadequate protective covers for the aircraft against the weather

2. Freezing of oil in engine parts, leading to seizures and cracked bearings

3. Freezing of oil in hydraulics system, leading to some severe undercarriage problems

4. Freezing up of hydraulics system

5. Necessity of warming up engines by lighting fires underneath to unfreeze working parts

6. Reduced visibility of pilot's goggles, permanently dimmed by constant freezing over

7. Mechanics working in open air in temperatures as low as -30°C

8. Pilots living in open air in low temperatures, which decreases their efficiency and increases chances of frostbite

Between 5 March and 3 May the Gruppo joined the German *Nahkampfführer Stalino* to escort German aircraft, mainly Ju 87s, over the Don front. Fighter sweeps and ground strafing were also undertaken. The unit earned a German commendation for their assistance in this area. However, the crews were by now showing signs of strain from their constant battles with the elements and the enemy, so they were recalled to Italy on 7 May. Their aircraft were passed to the incoming 21 Gruppo.

Recuperating at Ciampino, the unit was re-equipped with Re 2001 fighter-bombers. 371 Sq left the Gruppo at this time. In late July the unit moved to Sardinia for operations against the Allied convoys.

Three specially equipped Re 2001s flew in from Furbara to join the Gruppo, and on 12 August two of them took off with an escort for an eventful mission. The British aircraft carrier, HMS *Victorious,* was sighted and the Italians entered the landing circuit. Looking similar to the Fleet Air Arm Sea Hurricanes, they managed to avoid the anti-aircraft guns and fighter patrols and planted their 640kg bombs on the carrier deck. Fortunately for the Royal Navy one bomb bounced harmlessly off the deck into the sea, and the other disintegrated killing four crewmen without penetrating the armoured surface. The Re 2001s both returned to Elmas to a celebration, tempered only by the loss of some of their escort. Some sources state only 100kg bombs were used due to technical hitches with the larger experimental bombs. Even so it was an audacious attack.

In early September the special Re 2001s followed the Gruppo to Sicily, and were possibly converted to photo-reconnaissance aircraft.

362 Sq had been detached to Monserrato in mid-August and now temporarily joined 2 Gruppo at that base. On 27 September 22 Gruppo sent nine aircraft to Palermo for convoy escort duties. The main unit now turned from anti-shipping to fighter-bomber attacks on Malta. Its experience was useful during the last major blitz on the Maltese defences. However, the Allied invasion of North West Africa meant a recall to Sardinia for more anti-shipping sorties from 7 November. The first eight fighter-bombers had arrived at Elmas on the previous day. 23 Re 2001s operated against Bone and Bougie from the 7th. By 24 November the Gruppo still had 16 out of 20 aircraft serviceable.

With only ten serviceable aircraft left by 26 December the Gruppo withdrew to Capodichino, intending to re-equip with MC 202s. They were also suffering from radio problems at this time, as diad most of the units on home defence. The supply situation was such that they never fully re-equipped. Various types were received with varying results. On 15 January 1943 371 Sq temporarily joined the Gruppo. For bomber intercepts D.520s arrived in February, while the unit was still overseas. The pilots

appreciated the reliable and potent Hispano cannon in the coming battles. In April they tried out the new FC20bis twin-engined fighter from Capua against B-24 raids near Rome, but without success.

From 10 May to 24 June the Gruppo joined 42 Stormo Intercettori. 362 Sq had rejoined the unit in June at Capodichino, and had received the first prototype and ten pre-production models of the Re 2005. They were used for the defence of Rome and Naples, operating from Metato and Guidonia in June. The Gruppo carried out radio training at Littoria from the 28th. On 10 July eight Re 2005s of 362 Sq went to Catania-Sigonella. By 14 July the two survivors were passed to 371 Sq, when 362 Sq returned to Italy. Ten more of these potent fighters were received at Capua on 31 July.

The Gruppo was briefly sent to Pantelleria in July, joining 8 and 160 Gruppi on convoy escorts. 369 Sq was detached to Littoria and an SM 81 radio plane was used to improve liaison control between the escorts and the shipping.

The unit spent the rest of 1943 defending the homeland. 150 Sq joined at Capua in May. From mid-July 359 and 369 Sq were at Capodichino, while 150 and 362 Sq were at Capua. By 7 September the only aircraft still flying were nine MC 202s.

23 GRUPPO CT

| Squadriglie | 70, 74, 75 |
| Stormo | 3 |

Arrival	Zone	Base	Country	Aircraft	Duties
9 Jun 40	Sqa 1	Cervere	Italy	CR 42	GA, AE, DF
21 Jun 40	Sqa 1	Torino Mirafiori	Italy	CR 42	IT
22 Jun 40	Sqa 1	Villanova d'Albenga	Italy	CR 42	DF
25 Jun 40	Sqa 1	Torino Mirafiori	Italy	CR 42 Ca 133	TG
9 Jul 40	Sqa 1	Campiglia	Italy	CR 42	IT
9 Jul 40	Sqa 3	Capodichino	Italy	CR 42	IT
10 Jul 40	ASIC	Reggio Calabria	Italy	CR 42	IT
11 Jul 40	Sqa 2	Comiso	Sicily	CR 42	AE, DF, AR
16 Dec 40	Sqa 5	Castelbenito	Tripolitania	CR 42	IT
19 Dec 40	Sqa 5	Ain el Gazala	Cirenaica	CR 42	IT
20 Dec 40	Sqa 5	Derna	Cirenaica	CR 42	DF, AE
1 Jan 41	Sqa 5	Ain el Gazala	Cirenaica	CR 42	DF, AE
5 Jan 41	Sqa 5	Tmimi	Cirenaica	CR 42	AE
6 Jan 41	Sqa 5	Derna	Cirenaica	CR 42	AE
7 Jan 41	Sqa 5	Berka	Cirenaica	CR 42	AE, DF
9 Jan 41	Sqa 5	Benghasi K2	Cirenaica	CR 42	DF
4 Feb 41	Sqa 5	Tamet	Tripolitania	CR 42	DF
7 Feb 41	Sqa 5	Sorman	Tripolitania	CR 42	DF
1 Mar 41	ASIC	Comiso	Sicily	CR 42 Re 2000	DF, AE, AR
19 Apr 41	ASIC	Pantelleria	Sicily	CR 42	CE
21 Jun 41	ASIC	Boccadifalco	Sicily	CR 42 MC 200	
				Re 2000	DF, NF, TG
12 Dec 41	Sqa 5	Castelbenito	Tripolitania	CR 42 MC 200	DF

24 Above: *An MC 202 Series 12, MM 91815, of the 84ª Squadriglia, 10° Gruppo lies derelict at Catania in Sicily in 1942. Probably wrecked by an explosive charge in the cockpit, the breeches of the fuselage-mounted machine guns are clearly visible. In the background is a German Gotha Go 242 glider*

25 Right: *86-5, a Macchi MC 200 of the 86ª Squadriglia, 7° Gruppo, 54° Stormo, possibly at Comiso. Note how the aircraft number is repeated on a black disc on the wheel door. Tiger head badge is that of the Stormo*

26: *Specialisti rearming an early model MC 200 of 88ª Squadriglia during June 1940. Location is Catania Fontanarossa. This is a good example of the early C10 type of dense mottle finish. The white octagon on the fuselage is the unfinished 1° Stormo archer insigne*

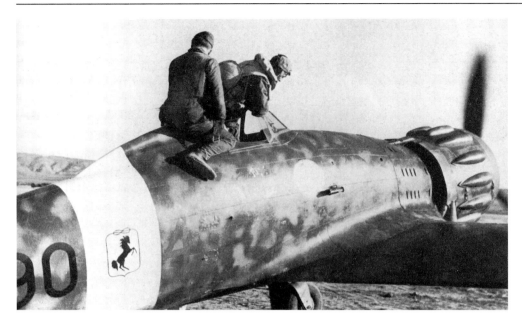

27: *The pilot of a 90ª Squadriglia, 10° Gruppo MC 200 is assisted into the cockpit. Probably seen in November 1941 at Trapani-Chinisia, the typically bulbous Italian back parachute clearly hinders access into the machine. The 'Cavallino Rampante' emblem is that of the 4° Stormo*

28: *Two IMAM Ro 37bis of the 120ª Squadriglia, 72° Gruppo OA somewhere over the hills of Grammos in Greece in November 1940. The nearest aircraft is serial MM 10821. At this time the squadron had only just joined the Gruppo, being based at Argirocastro, moving in December to Valona in Albania*

29: *An IMAM Ro 63, the Italian answer to the Fieseler Storch, by which it was clearly inspired. Very few found their way into service before the Armistice. This one belongs to the 132ª Squadriglia, 76° Gruppo OA, in Libya in 1942. The pilot, Capitano Aldo Gasperi, wears a natty white flying suit*

30: *One for the album as an unidentified* Capitano *poses in front of a lineup of Cant Z.501s of the 141ᵃ Squadriglia R.M., based at Brindisi. All the aircraft have been modified by the addition of an enclosed bow position*

31: *A Cant Z.501, 141-8, of the 141ᵃ Squadriglia R.M. being hoisted from the water, complete with 100kg bomb on the strut rack, for shore maintenance at Brindisi. Note the typical marine light silver-grey uppersurfaces and black anti-fouling undersides to the hull. Unusually the white fuselage band has black outlines*

32: *Cant Z.501 of the 146ᵃ Squadriglia R.M. in flight somewhere over the sea around Sardinia in summer 1940. At the time the unit was principally occupied with ASR duties, being based at Cagliari-Elmas. The cross on the rudder appears to have been created by the simple expedient of painting the horizontal white bar over the earlier red and green stripes*

33 Above: *A fine study of a Cant Z.501 (MM 35574) of the 141ᵃ Squadriglia R.M. at Brindisi in summer 1942. The tail cross now appears on a dark green ground*

34 Left: *Fiat-CMASA RS 14, 148-10, of the 148ᵃ Squadriglia R.M. in the dark and light blue-grey finish adopted from 1941 by maritime aircraft. Note how the rudder is still finished in dark green with a white cross. Vigna de Valle 1943*

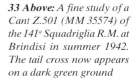

35: *Clearly marked as belonging to the 149ᵃ Squadriglia, this Fiat G 50 is something of a mystery as the unit operated autonomously throughout its existence from August 1942 until the Armistice—but as a maritime reconnaissance unit equipped with Z.501 flying boats and Z.506 float planes. Possibly the G 50 served as a unit hack. Note the pilot's white summer flying helmet*

Arrival	Zone	Base	Country	Aircraft	Duties
13 Dec 41	Sqa 5	Misurata	Tripolitania	CR 42 MC 200	CE
24 Dec 41	ASIC	Trapani Milo	Sicily	CR 42 MC 200	DF
27 Dec 41	Sqa 1	Torino Mirafiori	Italy	MC 200 G 50bis	
				MC 202	TG
14 Jul 42	Sqa 3	Ciampino	Italy	MC 202	IT
14 Jul 42	Sqa 3	Capodichino	Italy	MC 202	IT
14 Jul 42	ASIC	Gerbini	Sicily	MC 202	IT
15 Jul 42	ASIC	Gela	Sicily	MC 202	IT
15 Jul 42	ASIC	Pantelleria	Sicily	MC 202	IT
15 Jul 42	Sqa 5	Castelbenito	Tripolitania	MC 202	IT
16 Jul 42	Sqa 5	Abu Haggag	Egypt	MC 202	GA, DF, AE
22 Oct 42	Sqa 5	Abu Nimeir	Egypt	MC 202	DF
1 Nov 42	Sqa 5	Abu Smeit	Egypt	MC 202	DF
5 Nov 42	Sqa 5	Bir el Astas	Egypt	MC 202	IT
6 Nov 42	Sqa 5	Bu Amud	Cirenaica	MC 202	DF
10 Nov 42	Sqa 5	Benghasi	Cirenaica	MC 202	IT
11 Nov 42	Sqa 5	En Nofilia	Tripolitania	MC 202	GA
16 Nov 42	Sqa 5	Tauorga	Tripolitania	MC 202	DF
17 Jan 43	Sqa 5	Castelbenito	Tripolitania	MC 202	DF
19 Jan 43	ATUN	Medenine	Tunisia	MC 202	DF, AE, GA
2 Feb 43	ATUN	El Hamma	Tunisia	MC 202	DF, AR
26 Mar 43	Sqa 5	Achichina	Tunisia	MC 202	DF
30 Mar 43	ASIC	Castelvetrano	Sicily	MC 202	IT
Apr 43	Sqa 1	Torino Caselle	Italy	MC 202	DF
18 Jun 43	Sqa 1	Milano Bresso	Italy	MC 202	DF
28 Jun 43	Sqa 3	Ciampino Sud	Italy	MC 202	DF
1 Jul 43	Sqa 3	Cerveteri	Italy	MC 202 MC 205V	
				Bf 109G-6	DF, TG

At the start of the war the Gruppo carried out strafing attacks on bases in southern France and escorted bombers. Bad weather hindered early operations, making Cervere particularly impractical. Combats were fought with French fighters, notably on 15 June with GC III/6 who claimed four CR 42s and three BR 20s for the loss of two D.520s. The Italian losses appear to have been one fighter and two bombers although some sources state five fighters and one bomber (which may include some of 18 Gruppo's losses for the same day).

Border patrols were flown in the latter stages of the campaign. After the Armistice a detachment was sent to Bresso to form a Sezione Caccia Noturne, for the night defence of Milano.

On 9 July the Gruppo became Autonomo and moved to Sicily. They made their first raid on Malta on 12 July, claiming a Hurricane. They escorted SM 79s, Z1007bis, and Ju 87s on bombing and reconnaissance missions, and Z506B rescue planes around Maltese waters. At this time claims were made by both sides that aircraft with 'Red Cross' insignia were being shot at and/or used for non-rescue-evacuation purposes. Both allegations were probably without foundation. Several fighter sweeps and reconnaissance escorts were made over Malta.

In August they moved to the African front to counter the British offensive with their Fiats and attendant Capronis. They left behind a small Nucleo of pilots and aircraft, which evolved into 156 Gruppo on 20 January 1941. Some fighters used base Z1, near Gazala, for strafing sorties on 17 December. Three days later the Gruppo was at Derna, where they received the aircraft of 9 and 10 Gruppi who were returning to Italy. Their first big operation was on Christmas Day escorting 15 Stormo over Sollum port. On 11 January 75 Sq was detached to Maraua until the 20th. On 1 March two SM 79s of the SAS transferred personnel and crews from Sorman to Comiso. The CR 42s were left to 18 Gruppo and part of 151 Gruppo.

After a rest the men rejoined the unit on 1 April, and took over the equipment of 156 Gruppo which disbanded on the 8th. That month some of the Gruppo pilots were formed into a Sezione Sperimentale with six Re 2000 Series I fighters. Although potentially a better aircraft than the MC 200, it lost the major production contract and only a limited number were built for the Italian forces. (It did serve well with the Hungarian Air Force however). The Sezione was attached to 23 Gruppo, and had 9 Re 2000 at Trapani Milo, on convoy escort duties.

Meanwhile, on 19 April, 75 and part of 74 Sq moved to Pantelleria for convoy escorts between Naples and Tripoli. The unit was spread between Pantelleria (74 and 75 Sq convoy escort), Trapani Milo (70 Sq defence) for the next four months. The Sezione Sperimentale left Comiso for Trapani Milo on 19 June, then on to Palermo two days later. It became 377 Sq CT on 1 August, then leaving to become Autonomo on 28 December.

On 27 September a CR 42 was shot down by Italian naval anti-aircraft fire while on convoy escort. This raised the usual inter-service arguments which the leaders never seemed to resolve. That same month the unit received some MC 200s. These were used on day and night training at Boccadifalco.

On 12 December the unit took 14 CR 42s and 7 MC 200s to Libya, leaving the Re 2000s and a CR 42 at Milo with 377 Sq. Twelve days later, after coastal defence work, they returned to Sicily. SM 82s were used at this time for personnel transport.

Reuniting in Italy they received five G 50bis for training. Some pilots went to Bresso, using MC 200s to defend Milano from February to May 1942. The rest of the unit underwent intensive training. On 15th May they rejoined a reformed 3 Stormo under Squadra 1, along with 18 Gruppo. By this time they had 12 G 50bis and one MC 200. The pilots were also called on to ferry these types to Libya during this period. The first MC 202 was now received, being passed from 20 Gruppo to 70 Sq on 22 May. The Gruppo was intended to join operations over Malta but the African front was in more urgent need of fighters. So, on 8 July, leaving the G 50bis at Mirafiori, 75 Sq moved south picking up new MC 202s at Ciampino and Capodichino along the way. They then flew to Derna, via Tamet and Benghazi K3. On the 11th and 14th 74 and 70 Sq followed a similar route. 74 Sq joined 75 Sq at Derna on the 13th, then both went to Abu Haggag on the 16th.

A P-40 was claimed during their first sorties the next day. The new fighters were set to escorting the CR 42s of 50 Stormo and the MC 200s of 18 Gruppo on fighter-bomber raids. From 25 July the aircraft were flown to Abu Smeit each night to escape RAF night bombing, and returned to Abu Haggag in the day. They had operated under 4 Stormo until 25 July then returned to 3 Stormo control. For the next two months there were many dogfights with P-40s, Spitfires, Martlets, and Hurricanes. The CO of Squadra 5 sent them congratulations on 31 July for five claims without loss. The MC 202s were having problems with the sandy conditions, ten being forced down at Derna on 31 August during a sandstorm. The aircraft had been rushed to the frontline before sand filters could be installed. This had to be remedied under operational conditions, despite the heavy involvement in the Alamein battles.

During the second battle (30 August to 5 September) the unit managed a 60% serviceability rate, claiming 18 aircraft for the loss of 3 in 175 sorties. On 20 September they still had 20 MC 202s on charge. One of the pilots went to the assistance of a Luftwaffe pilot who was cornered in a dogfight. The German was none other than Hans-Joachim Marseille, the 'Star of Africa' and the top-scoring ace of the desert war with 157 claims. In gratitude his unit, I./JG 27, sent the Gruppo a crate of champagne.

Heavy rain now made the bases less efficient, and night bombing raids caused casualties. Between 15 and 17 October the desert winds reduced visibility and made breathing difficult, which meant cancellation of operations. Many aircraft were destroyed and damaged by bombing on 21 October, the unit being forced to move the next day. Serviceability was now down to 40%, with a daily average of 12 to 15 aircraft available. On 30 October 4 Stormo passed 12 MC 202s to this Gruppo.

On 5 November the unit, one of the last to pull out of the forward area, withdrew to Bir el Astas, 40 km from Mersa Matruh. The ground staff went straight to Bu Amud, joined by the surviving aircraft and pilots the next day. The unit helped delay the Allied advance across Libya by constantly strafing the forward troops.

On 3 December 70 Sq was detached to Castelbenito for the defence of Tripoli. The rest of the Gruppo joined them on 17 January 1943. 4 Stormo left for Italy, passing its remaining MC 202s to 18 and 23 Gruppi. On 19 January 74 and 75 Sq moved into Tunisia. 70 Sq, and 83 Sq of 18 Gruppo, followed the next day, being the last Italian air units in Libya.

During the Tunisian phase P-38s and P-39s were met for the first time. The former initially proved easier to shoot down than other fighter types. 70 Sq was known to use an FN 305 liaison aircraft at this time. 75 Sq was detached to Sfax during January and February. German General Seideman arrived on 11 February to present the Iron Cross Second Class to several pilots of 18 and 23 Gruppi. By the end of March the personnel flew to Sicily in SM 82s, leaving their aircraft to 54 Stormo.

For a time the pilots were employed in ferrying D.520s from France to Italy, then re-equipped, and with further training on new MC 202s in Italy, they sent sections to Bresso and Lonate Pozzolo for local defence duties. From 28 June the unit reunited at Ciampino for the defence of Rome.

About 15 Bf 109G-6s and a Bf 109F-4 arrived early in July from 9 Gruppo, and joined 70 Sq who trained on the Bf 109G-6s, using these for bomber intercepts during July to September. There were rarely more than two of these aircraft serviceable.

On 9 August half a dozen MC 205V Series III were also received by the Gruppo. All serviceable fighters were now used on bomber intercepts, mainly against the B-17s and B-24s. The unit was meant to move to Sardinia on 21 August, but the chaotic situation prevented this. On 7 September they had eight MC 202s and two MC 205Vs operational.

24 GRUPPO CT

Squadriglie	361, 362
Stormo	52

Arrival	Zone	Base	Country	Aircraft	Duties
10 Jun 40	Sqa 3	Sarzana	Italy	CR 32	DF
Oct 40	AALB	Tirana	Albania	G 50	TG
Oct 40	AALB	Berat	Albania	G 50	AE
Nov 40	AALB	Devoli	Albania	G 50	AE, DF
5 Jan 41	AALB	Durazzo	Albania	G 50	AE
Mar 41	AALB	Tirana	Albania	G 50	AE, DF
Jun 41	Sqa 4	Grottaglie	Italy	G 50	DF
19 Jul 41	ASAR	Monserrato	Sardinia	G 50 CR 42	DF, AE
Aug 42	ASAR	Elmas	Sardinia	G 50 CR 42	DF, AE, AS, CE
14 May 43	ASAR	Olbia Venafiorita	Sardinia	MC 202 MC 205V D.520	TG, DF
27 Aug 43	Sqa 3	Metato	Italy	MC 202 D.520	DF

Originally, the unit had 360 Sq as well, but this disbanded on 28 May 1940. The two squadriglie defended Sardinian naval ports until October when the Gruppo became Autonomo.

On transferring to Albania they received G 50 fighters for escorting bombers and transport aircraft. 354 Sq joined them in October 1940, bringing its own G 50s and a Ca

111bis transport plane. Twenty-four G 50s operated from Devoli, for missions over Yugoslavia. 361Sq went to 154 Gruppo in October and 362 Sq joined 22 Gruppo in December. 355 Sq, which operated from Tirana against the Greeks, joined the Gruppo in March or April.

After the Yugoslav surrender, 361 Sq returned, also bringing 395 Sq from 154 Gruppo, to help defend the Puglie area. 354 and 355 Sq were at Grottaglie, 361 Sq was at Lecce, and 395 Sq was at Brindisi. In addition, 370 Sq joined in April.

The Gruppo was sent in July 1941 to Sardinia to escort SM 79 and SM 84 torpedo-bombers. The Fiat G 50 lacked the range, however, so some CR 42s were acquired for the longer missions. 361 and 395 Sq became Autonomo at this time. This still left three squadriglie attached. After the occupation of Corsica a mixed section was sent to Ajaccio.

Throughout the summer of 1941 the unit flew escort missions from Sardinia. By 1 August 1942, 354 and 370 Sq were at Elmas and 355 Sq was at Alghero. They had 19 CR 42s and 16 G 50s on strength. As the Allied bombing raids increased the Gruppo found they did not have enough warning to take off and attack in strength. Usually they flew into action during the bombing. Always outnumbered, they claimed nine victories from three escorted raids in February 1943. In March they made 28 scrambles. Three B-17s were claimed over Cagliari on the 31st, out of 18 aircraft that were hit—thus underlining the inadequacy of their aircraft's firepower.

On 30 April a section was detached to Venafiorita to check out the MC 205V. The rest of the unit followed on 14 May, but due to the shortage of supply of these potent aircraft, they received mainly MC 202s. This was still a great improvement on the G 50.

Some bomber intercepts were made while still training. One squadriglia was detached to Alghero from May to August, then to Foligno. To assist the cannon-armed fighters, D.520s were received from 2 Stormo when that unit disbanded on 13 August. The Gruppo reunited at Metato and defended the home skies until the Armistice.

25 GRUPPO BT

Squadriglie   8, 9
Stormo   7

Arrival	Zone	Base	Country	Aircraft	Duties
10 Jun 40	Sqa 1	Ghemme	Italy	BR 20	DB
Apr 1941	Sqa 2	Forli	Italy	BR 20	DB, AR
Jul 41	Sqa 1	Cameri	Italy	SM 84	TG
1 Jul 42	ASIC	Sciacca	Sicily	SM 84	DB, AN
Jul 42	ASIC	Castelvetrano	Sicily	SM 84	DB, AN, NB
1 Oct 42	Sqa 1	Lonate Pozzolo	Italy	SM 84	TG

This unit received the BR 20 in 1936. After a tour in Africa they returned home before the war started. Updated BR 20Ms arrived in the spring of 1940. On 12 June they began attacks on southern France. The next day they were intercepted by D.520s of GC III/6 over the Toulon area, who claimed two bombers, but were in turn attacked by the escorting CR 42s.

Fifteen bombers were moved to Forli for operations over Yugoslavia. The bad weather reduced the effectiveness of this and other units in the area. By 29 July 1941 they were exchanging their BR 20s for SM 84s. The new aircraft were found difficult to train on. Even so, the unit was declared operational in April 1942.

On 7 May the unit became part of the Aerosilurante, but did not use its Savoias as torpedo-bombers and eventually reverted to the Bombardamento Terrestre title on 1 October. Having earlier moved to Sicily on 1 July with 24 SM 84s, operations began against Malta and its shipping routes. In July and August the unit carried out high level escorted raids on Malta, as well as anti-shipping sorties.

Returning to Italy they remained in training until disbanded on 15 June 1943.

25bis GRUPPO BT

Squadriglie   8, 9
Stormo   Auto

Arrival	Zone	Base	Country	Aircraft	Duties
10 Jun 40	AOI	Gabuen	Ethiopia	Ca 133	DB
Dec 40	AOI	Vittoria d'Africa	Ethiopia	Ca 133	DB
Jan 41	AOI	Gabuen	Ethiopia	Ca 133	DB
Mar 41	AOI	Dire Daua	Ethiopia	Ca 133	DB
Mar 41	AOI	Alomata	Ethiopia	Ca 133	DB, TR

On the outbreak of war, 9 Sq was detached immediately to Lugh Ferrandi with six Ca 133s. They moved to Belet Uen ten days later for operations over Kenya and the Indian Ocean, returning to Lugh Ferrandi by 11 July. In August they went to Baidoa, moving to Vittoria d'Africa on 16 September for better dispersal. Three 9 Sq aircraft left for Bardera on 18 December for sorties over the British offensive from Kenya.

By 16 June a section of 8 Sq was at Afmadu, returning to Gabuen in September. 8 Sq then moved in December to support 9 Sq over Kenya.

On 17 January 1941 the unit had just seven aircraft left. These old types were now suffering severely from the increasing numbers of Hurricane and Gladiator opposition, and from four years of constant use. Only large escorts of CR 42s could help, but there were not enough of them available.

On 16 March two Capronis flew from Dire Daua to Dessie for operations over the Cheren area during the British northern offensive. All remaining aircraft then went to Alomata, turning to supply drops during April. The unit had ceased to exist by July.

26 GRUPPO BT

| Squadriglie | 11, 13 |
| Stormo | 9 |

Arrival	Zone	Base	Country	Aircraft	Duties
10 Jun 40	Sqa 3	Viterbo	Italy	SM 79	DB
11 Sep 40	Sqa 5	Castelbenito	Tripolitania	SM 79	DB
Sep 40	Sqa 5	Derna	Cirenaica	SM 79	DB
12 Jan 41	Sqa 3	Viterbo	Italy	SM 79	TG
Sep 41	ASIC	?	Sicily	Z1007bis	NB, AR
42	Sqa 3	Viterbo	Italy	Z1007bis	TG
Aug 42	ASIC	?	Sicily	Z1007bis	NB

In June 1940 bombing operations were carried out over Corsica. In July and August 11Sq was detached to Sardinia for reconnaissance and bombing sorties in the Baleari Islands. The Gruppo was subsequently transferred to Libya to support the advance on Sidi Barrani, from Derna up to 18 September. Close support sorties and bombing of Egyptian targets were carried out for the rest of the year.

The unit was nearly always understrength because of a lack of spares and the use of an aircraft not designed for the ground support role. In January they returned to Italy, abandoning many SM 79s that could not be repaired. The Stormo was disbanded on 15 January.

In September 1941 the Gruppo appeared in Sicily with Z1007bis for operations against Malta, using single aircraft at night. Returning to Viterbo for new crews and retraining, they returned to Sicily in August 1942 for further night operations.

26bis GRUPPO BT

| Squadriglie | 11, 13 |
| Stormo | Auto |

Arrival	Zone	Base	Country	Aircraft	Duties
10 Jun 40	AOI	Gondar	Ethiopia	Ca 133 SM 81	AR TG

This unit carried out reconnaissance over the Sudan during June 1940. 11 Sq was at Gondar with six Ca 133s and 13 Sq was at Bahar Dar, converting to SM 81s. It was intended that the whole Gruppo should replace the older Capronis as they became unserviceable, however, due to lack of aircraft and crews, the unit appears to have been disbanded and dispersed to other units by July 1940.

27 GRUPPO BT

| Squadriglie | 18, 52 |
| Stormo | 8 |

Arrival	Zone	Base	Country	Aircraft	Duties
10 Jun 40	ASAR	Villacidro	Sardinia	SM 79	DB, AN
4 Apr 41	Sqa 5	Castelbenito	Tripolitania	SM 79	DB, AR
Nov 41	Sqa 5	Barce	Cirenaica	SM 79	DB
14 Dec 41	Sqa 5	Misurata	Tripolitania	SM 79	DB
27 Dec 41	Sqa 3	Viterbo	Italy	Z1007bis	TG
May 43	Sqa 4	Manduria	Italy	Z1007bis	NB
Jul 43	Sqa 2	Bologna	Italy	Z1007bis	NB

From January 1938 to June 1939 this unit and its crews fought in Spain. This experience was put to good use in operations over Corsica and Tunisia, although many of the veterans had moved on. The unit remained in Sardinia until April 1941, continuing in action against Allied shipping after the French surrender. They were especially active on 9 July and 1 August 1940 against Force H from Gibraltar. The Royal Navy aircraft carrier, HMS *Ark Royal,* was claimed as damaged on the former date although the propaganda ministry had wanted to announce that it was sunk.

The unit was transferred to the Libyan front for the rest of 1941, supporting the ground forces. They returned to Italy at the end of the year, and had converted to the Z1007bis by August 1942.

By July 1943 they were using ten aircraft from Manduria for night operations.

27bis GRUPPO BT

| Squadriglie | 18, 52, 118 |
| Stormo | Auto |

Arrival	Zone	Base	Country	Aircraft	Duties
10 Jun 40	AOI	Assab K14	Eritrea	Ca 133	DB
15 Jun 40	AOI	Dessie	Ethiopia	Ca 133	DB
Arrival	Zone	Base	Country	Aircraft	Duties
Jul 40	AOI	Assab	Eritrea	Ca 133	DB
Aug 40	AOI	Scenele LG	Ethiopia	Ca 133	DB
Jan 41	AOI	Assab K14	Eritrea	Ca 133	DB
Mar 41	AOI	Dessie	Ethiopia	Ca 133	DB

This was the only three squadriglie bomber unit, with 18 Ca 133s. 118 Sq was detached to Sardo when the unit was moved to Dessie for operations over French Somaliland and Aden. 118 Sq began converting to SM 81s, leaving the Gruppo soon after.

The rest of the unit operated over British Somaliland, losing several aircraft on the ground to Blenheims from Aden. Reinforced with spare aircraft from Asmara, the Gruppo operated over the Sudan taking part in the conquest of Kassala. In July raids were made on Jibuti airbase in French Somaliland. 18 Sq, with six Capronis, moved to Scenele on 30 July, followed by 52 Sq in August. Dagabur and Combolcia were used as dispersal bases during the raids on British Somaliland.

In case of a British counter-attack the unit sent three Ca 133s to Miesso, four to Dessie, and two to Giggiga. Another aircraft returned from Hargheisa to Dire Daua. With the threat of retaliation decreasing the unit was used to fly reinforcements and mailbags between Asmara and Addis Abeba.

From 6 to 9 November the unit assisted in halting the British offensive in Eritrea and northern Ethiopia. By January 1941 they were back in Assab, with every operation becoming more dangerous with the increasing quality of the opposition.

During the battle of Cheren the unit flew from Dessie. By 31 March they had only four serviceable aircraft left. Shortly afterwards the last was destroyed by a bombing raid. Four pilots and two mechanics escaped in a SM 81 from Combolcia to Gondar. The remaining personnel helped to defend Dessie, surrendering on 26 April 1941.

28 GRUPPO BT

Squadriglie	10, 19				
Stormo	8				
Arrival	Zone	Base	Country	Aircraft	Duties
10 Jun 40	ASAR	Villacidro	Sardinia	SM 79	DB, AN
30 Apr 41	Sqa 5	Castelbenito	Tripolitania	SM 79	DB, AR
Jun 41	Sqa 5	Benghasi K1	Cirenaica	SM 79	DB, AR
Nov 41	Sqa 5	Barce	Cirenaica	SM 79	DB
14 Dec 41	Sqa 5	Misurata	Tripolitania	SM 79	DB
27 Dec 41	Sqa 3	Viterbo	Italy	Z1007bis	TG
May 43	ASIC	Gela	Sicily	Z1007bis	NB
May 43	ASIC	Castelvetrano	Sicily	Z1007bis	NB
May 43	Sqa 4	Manduria	Italy	Z1007bis	NB
4 Jun 43	Sqa 3	Perugia	Italy	Z1007bis Z1007ter	NB

From November 1937 to June 1939 this unit fought in Spain. A year later they were attacking Corsica and Tunisia. Following the French surrender they were active against shipping in the Mediterranean, especially against Force H from Gibraltar in July and August. They joined 27 Gruppo in attacks on the aircraft carrier HMS *Ark Royal* on 9 July.

19 Sq moved to Libya on 30 April, followed by 10 Sq in May. They supported the major operations in that theatre until the end of the year.

After converting to the Z1007bis by August 1942, they carried out a series of night raids against Allied forces in North Africa, intensifying this in May 1943 as the Allies closed in. In June they joined the Raggruppamento Bombardamento at Perugia, where they also received some uprated Z1007ters.

28bis GRUPPO BT

Squadriglie	10, 19				
Stormo	Auto				
Arrival	Zone	Base	Country	Aircraft	Duties
10 Jun 40	AOI	Zula	Eritrea	SM 81 SM 79	AR, NB
Aug 40	AOI	Gura	Eritrea	SM 79	AN, DB, NB
Apr 41	AOI	Sciasciamanna	Ethiopia	SM 79	DB

From the start this unit patrolled the Red Sea for British shipping and carried out night raids over southern Sudan. 10 Sq moved to Gura in July, from where the whole unit converted to SM 79s in August. These new aircraft were received straight from Italy, via Libya. On 17 August three were sent to Addis Abeba returning five days later. Operations were carried out over Aden and the Gulf of Aden to stem the British supply system. By January 1941 the Savoias were being escorted by 412 Sq. Three aircraft were detached to Dessie on 16 March for operations against the offensive on Cheren. The following month the unit appears to have been disbanded at Sciasciamanna.

29 GRUPPO BT

Squadriglie	62, 63				
Stormo	9				
Arrival	Zone	Base	Country	Aircraft	Duties
10 Jun 40	Sqa 3	Viterbo	Italy	SM 79	DB
11 Sep 40	Sqa 5	Castelbenito	Tripolitania	SM 79	DB
Sep 40	Sqa 5	Martuba	Cirenaica	SM 79	DB
Dec 40	Sqa 3	Viterbo	Italy	SM 79 Z1007bis	TG
Jun 41	ASIC	Chinisia	Sicily	Z1007bis	DB
Jan 42	Sqa 3	Viterbo	Italy	Z1007bis	TG
13 Jun 42	ASAR	Villacidro	Sardinia	Z1007bis	AN
18 Jun 42	ASIC	Chinisia	Sicily	Z1007bis	AN, DB, NB
May 43	Sqa 3	Viterbo	Italy	Z1007bis Ju88A-4	TG

Operations were carried out over Corsica during June 1940. Three months later the unit transferred to Libya to support the advance on Sidi Barrani. The aircraft were called on for tactical close support and suffered severe losses due to lack of spares and improper use of the aircraft type. On 16 December they were unfortunate in losing the leaders of 63 Sq, 29 Gruppo, and 9 Stormo—all in one attack on Sidi Omar. Some ordinary level bombing was made on Egyptian targets before the unit returned to Italy.

The 9 Stormo disbanded on 15 January, reforming on 10 May 1941. The unit converted to the Z1007bis. Operations began against Malta in June and continued until January 1942. On 5 January four aircraft were detached to Castelvetrano for anti-shipping and reconnaissance operations. The whole unit returned to Sicily, after a rest, in June. They continued their attacks on Malta and its shipping lanes, day and night.

By July 1943 they had only two serviceable aircraft left and training had begun on the imported German Ju88A. The unit was still non-operational on 7 September.

29bis GRUPPO BT

Squadriglie	62, 63
Stormo	Auto

Arrival	Zone	Base	Country	Aircraft	Duties
10 Jun 40	AOI	Assab K3	Eritrea	SM 81	DB, NB
15 Jun 40	AOI	Mille	Ethiopia	SM 81	DB, NB
1 Jul 40	AOI	Dessie	Ethiopia	SM 81	DB, NB
20 Jul 40	AOI	Sciasciamanna	Ethiopia	SM 81	DB
Oct 40	AOI	Yavello	Ethiopia	SM 81	DB
19 Dec 40	AOI	Bardera	Ethiopia	SM 81	DB

For the first few weeks of the war the unit flew their twelve SM 81s over Aden and the Sudan, switching to support the offensive against British Somaliland from Sciasciamanna in July. 63 Sq was detached to Scenele, receiving three replacement aircraft on 13 August and again on 16 August.

In late October 65 Sq with Ca 133s joined 29 Gruppo, although it stayed at Yavello for the time being. The Gruppo lost three SM 81s to two Hurricanes over Lodwar while operating from Yavello. On 16 December 65 Sq left for 49 Gruppo and the surviving four SM 81s of 62 and 63 Sq returned from Scenele to Sciascimanna. Three days later the unit moved to Bardera for operations over El Wak. By March 1941 the unit was non-operational.

30 GRUPPO BT

Squadriglie	55, 56
Stormo	10

Arrival	Zone	Base	Country	Aircraft	Duties
10 Jun 40	ALIB	Benina	Cirenaica	SM 79	DB, AR
8 Jul 40	ALIB	Derna N1	Cirenaica	SM 79	AR, AN
19 Sep 40	ASIC	Catania	Sicily	SM 79	IT
20 Sep 40	Sqa 3	Viterbo	Italy	SM 79	TG
25 Apr 41	ASIC	Sciacca	Sicily	SM 79	AN
Jun 42	ASIC	Boccadifalco	Sicily	SM 79	AN, AR
Aug 42	ASIC	Sciacca	Sicily	SM 79	AN CE
1 Nov 42	ASIC	Boccadifalco	Sicily	SM 79 SM 84	TG, AR, DB, AN
May 43	Sqa 2	Villafranca	Italy	Ca 314	TG, CE
28 May 43	Sqa 2	Jesi	Italy	Ca 314	CE
25 Jun 43	Sqa 1	Milano Bresso	Italy	Ca 314	CE

The SM 79 Sparviero bomber was received in 1939 and operations began in June 1940 against shipping in the Mediterranean, east of Malta. A detachment used Tobruk T2 on 12 June, then El Adem T3 on the following day. Several combats were fought with RAF Gladiators and FAA Sea Gladiators. By September the unit was re-

equipping in Italy with updated SM 79s.

From 13 December the crews flew SM 79 reinforcements to Libya, delivering the aircraft to Benina by the 15th, and returning in SM 82s of the SAS. On 9 February the crews unsuccessfully searched for the Royal Navy warships that had been attacking Genova. From 12 to 14 March 56 Sq carried out night training, flying to Alghero and back.

The Gruppo began to move to Sciacca in Sicily on 21 April 41. 15 aircraft were on strength at this time. They carried out patrols and convoy escort duties mixed with bombing strikes. The Germans then took over most of the Sicilian bases, and thus restricted Italian means of operation. By November 1942 the unit was exchanging the old SM 79s for SM 84s which were used in the anti-shipping, reconnaissance and bombing roles. In January 1943 the unit lost 17 SM 84s at Palermo Boccadifalco to bombardments.

By May they were back in Italy re-equipped with Ca 314s for convoy escort duties. The Gruppo had now joined 13 Stormo Combattimento. On 7 September under Squadra 1 they had seven out of twenty-one aircraft operational.

31 GRUPPO BT

Squadriglie	65, 66
Stormo	18

Arrival	Zone	Base	Country	Aircraft	Duties
10 Jun 40	Sqa 1	Aviano	Italy	BR 20	DB, AR
9 Jun 41	ASIC	Fontanarossa	Sicily	BR 20/M	NB
Oct 41	Sqa 4	Lecce Galatina	Italy	BR 20M	IT
Oct 41	Sqa 1	Milano Bresso	Italy	BR 20M	TG

The BR 20 bomber was received in 1938 and was used by this unit over France in June 1940. Missions were carried out over the Mediterranean approaches to southern France, then over the Alpine border in the latter stages of the campaign.

Remaining at Aviano, now under Squadra 2, they began operations against the Sebenico area of Yugoslavia. The BR 20M arrived to back up the older model.

On 9 June 1941, 18 BR 20Ms joined 99 Gruppo of 43 Stormo in night operations over Malta. Losses were suffered from the Hurricanes of the Malta Night Fighter Unit. 18 Stormo was disbanded from May 1941 to 15 October 1941, reforming as a transport wing, but without 31 Gruppo. Due to losses and inefficient technical aids, despite a stable and relatively robust aircraft, this unit was recalled to Italy in October. It was withdrawn from operations and disbanded on 21 January 42.

31bis GRUPPO BT

Squadriglie	65, 66
Stormo	Auto

Arrival	Zone	Base	Country	Aircraft	Duties
10 Jun 40	AOI	Yavello	Ethiopia	Ca 133	AR, DB

This unit carried out reconnaissance duties during June 1940, switching to day bombing in August. 65 Sq was at Neghelli from 10 June, joining 66 Sq at Yavello on 12 August. In late October 66 Sq disbanded, passing its crews to 65 Sq. They were then transferred to 29 Gruppo at Sciasciamanna, then to 49 Gruppo at Gimma on 16 December 1940.

32 GRUPPO BT

Squadriglie	57, 58
Stormo	10

Arrival	Zone	Base	Country	Aircraft	Duties
10 Jun 40	ALIB	Benina	Cirenaica	SM 79	AR, DB
6 Jul 40	ALIB	Derna N1	Cirenaica	SM 79	AR, AN
19 Sep 40	ASIC	Catania	Sicily	SM 79	IT
20 Sep 40	Sqa 3	Viterbo	Italy	SM 79	TG
29 Apr 41	ASIC	Chinisia	Sicily	SM 79	AN
Jun 42	ASIC	Boccadifalco	Sicily	SM 79	AN
Oct 42	ASIC	Palermo	Sicily	Ca 314	TG,CE, AR
May 43	Sqa 2	Villafranca	Italy	Ca 314	CE
21 May 43	Sqa 1	Milano Linate	Italy	Ca 314	TG
28 May 43	Sqa 2	Jesi	Italy	Ca 314	CE

This unit had flown the SM 79 since 1939, and operated over the shipping lanes in the eastern Mediterranean from June to September 1940. Tobruk T2 and El Adem were used as forward bases in June. When the crews moved to Derna they were not pleased with the lack of facilities and war preparations at that base. They used Ain el Gazala as a forward base from 12 July. As well as fighting RAF Gladiators in this period, they also met the only Hurricane then in Africa, losing 3 aircraft to it on 17 August.

During late November and early December 57 Sq supported the Greek campaign with armed reconnaissance and photo reconnaissance operations in the Corfu area, which proved useful practical experience for trainee crews. From 15 December six crews delivered new SM 79s to Benina in Libya, then returned in SM 82s of the SAS. 57 Sq resumed photo reconnaissance operations over Greece through December and January.

While continuing training for day and night missions, the Gruppo was involved in searching for and attacking the Royal Navy warships who had attacked Genova. Their escorts, MC 200s of 362 Sq from Sarzana, were tardy and the formation had to return to Pisa for refueling. Subsequently they only found a Vichy French convoy on its way to Tunisia. Royal Navy radar had picked up the

aircraft on its screens, causing an air alert, but the Gruppo flew by without seeing the ships. There were several more complaints and discussions between the Regia Marina and Regia Aeronautica about co-operation procedures after this.

In April 1941 they transferred to Sicily operating from that island for the next two years. Force H from Gibraltar was attacked on 23 July, and another notable mission was on 14 June 1942 when five SM 79s were detached to Sciacca for operations against the Malta-bound *Harpoon* convoy.

Two Ca 314s arrived on 21 October 1942 and the unit began to convert to escort duties. There were 18 of the new type operational by 1 November. Four days later they carried out their first convoy escort. By the following January they had added maritime reconnaissance to their roles.

10 Stormo moved to Jesi shortly after with few, if any, aircraft. They awaited re-equipment with Ju 88As which never arrived.

33 GRUPPO BT

Squadriglie	59, 60
Stormo	11

Arrival	Zone	Base	Country	Aircraft	Duties
3 Jun 40	Sqa 2	Comiso	Sicily	SM 79	AN
Jul 40	ALIB	Castelbenito	Tripolitania	SM 79	AN
Aug 40	ALIB	Benina	Cirenaica	SM 79	AN, DB
Sep 40	ALIB	Z1	Cirenaica	SM 79	DB
Dec 40	Sqa 3	Viterbo	Italy	Z1007bis SM 79	TG
Jun 41	ASIC	Trapani Milo	Sicily	Z1007bis	AN
29 Aug 41	ASIC	Chinisia	Sicily	Z1007bis	AN
Jan 42	Sqa 3	Viterbo	Italy	Z1007bis	TG
25 May 42	ASIC	Chinisia	Sicily	Z1007bis	AN
13 Jun 42	ASAR	Villacidro	Sardinia	Z1007bis	AN
18 Jun 42	ASIC	Chinisia	Sicily	Z1007bis	AN
Sep 42	ASIC	Castelvetrano	Sicily	Z1007bis	DB, AR
Nov 42	Sqa 3	Viterbo	Italy	Z1007bis	TG
25 Jun 43	Sqa 2	Jesi	Italy	Z1007bis	TG

The SM 79 was used by this unit in 1939 as a high speed transport, ferrying troops to Albania during the invasion. From the outbreak of the war in 1940 they operated against shipping in the western and central Mediterranean. In July they were very active around the eastern approaches to Malta.

The demands of the desert offensive caused the unit to move to Libya in July with 16 SM 79s. They continued anti-shipping operations, this time along the African coastline. In September they supported the advance on Sidi Barrani.

Returning to Italy at the end of the year they were rested. On the reformation of 9 Stormo they joined on 10 May 1941 with new Z1007bis bombers. After a month's training they moved to Sicily for operations around Malta. Re-equipping in January 1942 with Z1007bis Series VIII they returned for more anti-shipping strikes from Sardinia and Sicily. From September to November they diverted their efforts to bombing Malta, and then to the Allied invasion forces in North West Africa.

By 7 September 1943 they were attached to 10 Stormo at Jesi, awaiting re-equipment with Ju88As.

34 GRUPPO BT

Squadriglie   67, 68
Stormo   11

Arrival	Zone	Base	Country	Aircraft	Duties
3 Jun 40	Sqa 2	Comiso	Sicily	SM 79	AN
Jul 40	AEGE	Rodi Gadurra	Aegean	SM 79	NB, AN, DB

This unit used the SM 79 in 1939 to transport troops to Albania, and from June 1940 operated against shipping in the Mediterranean. On 4 July they made their first night sorties against Alexandria, repeating this on 27 July with four aircraft and on 5 October with six. In mid-July they were very busy against shipping off Malta, especially during the operations of 19 July known to the Italians as as the 'Battaglia de Capo Spada'.

In November four torpedo-bombing SM 79s were attached to the unit for trials. Between 31 January and 21 March 1941 the crews were rushed to operate around Crete, without much formal training. As a result they scored no hits and were mauled by the defences, but did claim one enemy fighter north of Crete on the latter day. The following day they began combining level bombing with torpedo attacks, sometimes with 281 Sq. As the results were promising, on 20 April 1941 the unit became Aerosilurante. At this time 279 and 281 Sq replaced 67 and 68 Sq. The outgoing squadriglie were disbanded.

279 Sq was sent to Cirenaica on 7 May, operating from Berka by 17 November. On 15 May 1941 the Gruppo disbanded, both squadriglie becoming Autonomo. One was in Libya and the other was in the Aegean.

35 Gruppo BT

Squadriglie   43, 44
Stormo   33

Arrival	Zone	Base	Country	Aircraft	Duties
10 Jun 40	ALIB	Bir el Bhera	Tripolitania	SM 79	AR, DB, GA
Sep 40	ALIB	Benina	Cirenaica	SM 79	DB, GA
21 Oct 40	Sqa		Italy	SM 79	TG

This unit maintained patrols along the Tunisian coastline in June 1940. In July they joined anti-shipping operations against Malta-bound vessels. On 11 July they attacked the aircraft carrier HMS *Eagle* and its convoy, repeating the attacks the next day. This was followed by ground attack and low level bombing missions during the eastward offensive against Sidi Barrani. Following heavy losses, on 21 October the unit was withdrawn to Italy.

36 GRUPPO BT

Squadriglie   45, 46
Stormo   33

Arrival	Zone	Base	Country	Aircraft	Duties
10 Jun 40	ALIB	Bir el Bhera	Tripolitania	SM 79	AR, DB, AN
Sep 40	ALIB	Benina	Cirenaica	SM 79	DB, GA
21 Oct 40	Sqa		Italy	SM 79	TG

This unit worked with 35 Gruppo on the same operations and suffered the same fate.

37 GRUPPO BT

Squadriglie   47, 48
Stormo   18

Arrival	Zone	Base	Country	Aircraft	Duties
10 Jun 40	Sqa 1	Aviano	Italy	BR 20	TG
6 Dec 40	4 ZAT	Grottaglie	Italy	BR 20/M	DB, NB
1 Apr 41	Sqa 2	Aviano	Italy	BR 20/M SM82	DB, TG
5 Oct 41	Sqa 3	Viterbo	Italy	SM82	TG
13 Oct 41	ASIC	Trapani	Sicily	SM82	TR
21 Nov 41	Sqa 4	Lecce	Italy	SM82	TR
27 Dec 41	Sqa 3	Viterbo	Italy	SM82	TG
Nov 42	ASIC	Castelvetrano	Sicily	SM82	TR

Moving to Grottaglie in December 1940, this unit gave tactical support over the Greek front to the end of March. They then tried night bombing, which was not common at that time. Bad weather over the Balkans hindered most operations anyway.

Rejoining 18 Stormo at Aviano, now under Squadra 2, the unit operated against the Serbenico area of Yugoslavia. The improved BR 20M had been received in December but an enforced cessation of operations still took place on 12 April due to losses and inefficient equipment. The Stormo temporarily disbanded.

On 10 April a 'Sezione Speciale Bombardamento' formed at Ciampino with seven SM 82s. From 16 May they made bombing raids from Gadurra to Alexandria. In July they switched to transport duties only, assisting the supply runs to Cirenaica from Lecce by October. On 1 January 1942 the Sezione disbanded and the aircraft and crews were passed to 37 Gruppo.

36: *Groundcrew manhandle a Reggiane Re 2001 of the 152ª Squadriglia, 2° Gruppo CT. According to the original caption the scene is San Pietro-Caltagirone in Sicily in 1943. However, the very dark, possibly all-black, finish to the aircraft strongly suggests that it is being used as a night fighter from Sarzana in Italy during May that year. The unit emblem, a machine gun carrying parrot, can be made out on the fin. Alternatively, the airfield could be Caltagirone, in which case the date is most likely to be May 1942*

37: *Captured Fiat G 50bis, once on the strength of the 151a Squadriglia, 20° Gruppo, 51° Stormo, some where in Libya in 1941. The aircraft has a very soft mottle finish and a rather crude representation of the cat insigne of the Stormo on the fin*

38: *Servicing a Breda 65 of the 159ª Squadriglia, 12° Gruppo Assalto, 50° Stormo, somewhere in Cirenaica, possibly Tobruk, in autumn 1940. Sand in the engines proved to be nearly as big a danger as enemy fire to the Bredas, all of which had been lost by the end of February 1941. The unit consequently refitted with ground attack versions of the Fiat G 50*

39: *Fiat CR 42s from the 162ª Squadriglia, 161° Gruppo Autonomo, over the Aegean Sea during a convoy protection flight from Rodi Marizza. As the unit converted to the MC 200 in May 1942, having first formed in June 1941, the date of the picture is probably late in 1941. The hyphen between the unit code and the individual aircraft number '4' appears to be in the red/white/green Italian colours*

40: *This elderly Fiat CR 32 is a most unusual type to see in the markings of the 163ª Squadriglia, 161° Gruppo, as the unit did not exist before June 1941 and the CR 32 was not official equipment. Presumably it was retained for training purposes. Just visible on the fuselage is a red devil's head, the emblem of the 6° Stormo, who were probably the previous owners*

41: *Groundcrew refuelling an MC 200 of 165ª Squadriglia the old-fashioned way. Seen on a Sicilian airfield sometime in spring 1941, the aircraft wears a C2 camouflage scheme consisting of a yellow overspray to create green blotches*

42 Right: A lineup of IMAM RO 44s, still in 166ᵃ Squadriglia markings, although at the time this picture was taken in autumn 1940 they had been transferred to the Scuola Idrovolanti at Pola-Puntisella

43 Below: RAF airmen sleeping in the shelter of an abandoned Macchi MC 202 of 168ᵃ Squadriglia, 16° Gruppo, at La Souka near Tunis, 1943. Surprisingly, nobody has looted the rudder crest. Camouflage is the typical Macchi D3 type

44 Right: A Sicilian-based Macchi MC 200 of the 168ᵃ Squadriglia, 16° Gruppo, in late 1941. At the time the unit was heavily involved in operations against Malta. The attractive tiger's head badge of the 54° Stormo is clearly visible under the cockpit. In the foreground can be seen the lower port wing of a Fiat CR 42 fighter-bomber with a parachute lying on it. Underneath can be seen a light bomb rack

45 Left: *Fiat CMASA RS 14 of the 170ª Squadriglia R.M. flying out from Augusta in Sicily in July 1943 just before disbandment. It is fitted with a ventral weapons pannier*

46 Below: *Another RS 14 from 170ª Squadriglia, 83° Gruppo R.M.. Location is almost certainly Augusta in July 1943. Note how the dark grey uppersurface camouflage wraps around the wing leading edge*

47 Left: *A Fiat CR 25bis, MM 3654, of the 173ª Squadriglia RST, preparing for take-off, probably from Boccadifalco in Sicily in 1942. The engine cowlings have been given a solid coat of green paint*

Reformed at Aviano in July 1941, under 18 Stormo Trasporto, 37 Gruppo received three armed and five unarmed SM 82s by September. Moving to Sicily the following month, with ten SM 82s and two Ca 164s, they began ferrying troops and evacuating wounded between Castelvetrano-Tripoli-Castelbenito. Despite delays by engine changes to most of the aircraft, this busy unit carried out its duties very successfully. In November they delivered enough fuel to Derna to help the ground units beat off several Allied attacks. By the 21st of that month seven SM 82s were still serviceable, flying engines, spares and fuel to Tripoli, Benghasi and Martuba. In December the aircraft were withdrawn for a complete overhaul.

On 10 March 1942 the unit replaced 148 Gruppo in 45 Stormo. On 1 April three SM 82s of 47 Sq were detached to Villacidro for a bombing raid on Gibraltar. In May the unit practiced paratroop drops for the intended invasion of Malta. This did not proceed so the Gruppo, with four others, transferred the Folgore Division to Fuka, only a few days before the battles of El Alamein.

From November to March they switched to sending men and materials to Tunisia, suffering heavy losses on the new routes. For example, on 12 November, four SM 82s of 47 Sq were lost to six Beaufighters flying between Tripoli and Castelvetrano.

The Gruppo may have returned to Italy, or have been disbanded in Sicily by April.

38 GRUPPO BT

| Squadriglie | 49, 50 |
| Stormo | 32 |

Arrival	Zone	Base	Country	Aircraft	Duties
3 Jun 40	ASAR	Decimomannu	Sardinia	SM 79 SM82	DB, AN
Sep 41	Sqa 2	Bologna	Italy	SM 84	TG
28 May 42	Sqa 4	Gioia del Colle	Italy	SM 84	AN
Aug 42	ASAR	Villacidro	Sardinia	SM 84	AN
Aug 42	Sqa 4	Gioia del Colle	Italy	SM 84	TG
6 Nov 42	ASAR	Alghero	Sardinia	SM 84	AN
30 Nov 42	Sqa 4	Gioia del Colle	Italy	SM 84	TG
11 Jan 43	Sqa 4	Lecce	Italy	SM 84bis	AN
Mar 43	Sqa 4	Manduria	Italy	SM 84bis	TG

The SM 79 was received in 1939. This was the first unit to operate against Tunisia, bombing Bizerte on 12 June. The unit then turned to anti-shipping operations in July and August, including attacks on Force H from Gibraltar. Three SM 82s arrived in August for 49 Sq and were used from March for long range attacks on Gibraltar. One was lost to anti-aircraft fire and the other two returned to Ciampino in July 1941.

Meanwhile, on 9 November 1940, 19 SM 79s of 32 Stormo hit shipping north of Cap de Fer. Losses were

taken during attacks on coastal convoys in January. More attacks were sent from Sardinia on 8 and 10 May, 23 and 25 July. These were the more notable efforts.

The need to rest and re-equip sent the unit to Bologna, where SM 84s arrived on 17 October. On 1 May 1942 the 32 Stormo became Aerosilurante. However, 38 Gruppo remained as B.T., but accompanied their fellow 89 Gruppo on shipping raids. They occasionally used the special motorised bombs, known as FF. (See the chapter on weapons for more information). Crews were sent to Gorizia for instruction on radio-guided torpedoes.

On 12 August ten SM 84s, each with two of these weapons, attacked shipping in the *Pedestal* convoy. The results did not seem to be any more successful than with ordinary torpedoes. Several aircraft used Milis during November for attacks on the Allied invasion fleets. On 1 December the unit made a rare day raid overland, sending ten SM 84s to Bone. Due to bad weather the bombers missed their MC 202 and Re 2001 escorts. They ran into waiting USAAF and RAF Spitfires which downed three of the bombers, caused another three to crash on landing and badly damaged the rest. 89 Gruppo handed over its SM 84s to replenish the unit and changed to SM 79s.

On 11 January 1943 the unit received the updated SM 84bis and became Autonomo on the 27th. By April they ceased to operate these aircraft and disbanded on 15 June.

39 GRUPPO BT

| Squadriglie | 51, 69 |
| Stormo | 38 |

Arrival	Zone	Base	Country	Aircraft	Duties
10 Jun 40	AALB	Tirana	Albania	SM 81	TR
Oct 40	AALB	Valona	Albania	SM 81	TR
Oct 40	AALB	Scutari	Albania	SM 81	TR, DB
Feb 41	Sqa 4	Gioia del Colle	Italy	BR 20	TG
14 Apr 41	Sqa 4	Foggia	Italy	BR 20	DB, CE, AR
Jun 41	AALB	Tirana	Albania	BR 20	AG
20 Jan 42	AALB	Mostar	Yugoslavia	BR 20 Fi156C	AG, AR, DB

The SM 81 bomber-transport was received on 7 April 1939 when 38 Stormo was formed. Operations were immediately carried out over Albania and they stayed in that theatre throughout World War 2.

So that fighter and reconnaissance units could use the more suitable base at Valona, the Gruppo moved to Scutari for the Greek campaign. The SM 81s were occasionally used for tactical bombing, but were mostly utilised to ferry reinforcements and materials to the Julia Division. BR 20s were gradually introduced in February and March 1941, sixteen of these operating from Foggia over the Yugoslavian front. Three quarters of the sorties were in tactical support of the Italian ground forces, while the remainder were on reconnaissance, convoy escort and strategic raids.

By June they were preparing for anti-partisan operations which would be their duties until hostilities ceased. 51 Sq was detached to Zara on 19 July 1942. During that summer the CO of 69 Sq used a Fiesler Storch for liaison and reconnaissance duties. On 15 February 1943 the Gruppo left 38 Stormo, becoming Autonomo then disbanding on 4 June. The squadriglie became Autonomo. 69 Sq moved from Mostar to Scutari on 27 August. By 7 September 51 Sq was still at Mostar and 69 Sq at Scutari.

40 GRUPPO BT

| Squadriglie | 202, 203 |
| Stormo | 38 |

Arrival	Zone	Base	Country	Aircraft	Duties
10 Jun 40	4 ZAT	Lecce Galatina	Italy	SM 81	TR
Oct 40	AALB	Valona	Albania	SM 81	TR
Oct 40	AALB	Scutari	Albania	SM 81	TR, DB
Feb 41	Sqa 4	Gioia del Colle	Italy	BR 20	TG
14 Apr 41	Sqa 4	Foggia	Italy	BR 20	DB, CE, AR
Jun 41	AALB	Tirana	Albania	BR 20	AG
Nov 41	ASIC	Fontanarossa	Sicily	BR 20M	NB
Nov 41	AALB	Tirana	Albania	BR 20M	AG

This unit accompanied their sister unit, 39 Gruppo, throughout the war. However, they were used in anti-shipping attacks on 12 July in the Battaglia de Punta Stilo. In November the unit briefly operated at night over Malta, losing one aircraft on both 20th and 21st, the only two active nights. After that it was back to the Balkans.

In late 1942 or early 1943 ten aircraft of 202 Sq were detached to Sicily for reconnaissance and escort duties. On 14 May 1943 203 Sq was detached to Scutari, returning to Tirana on 18 June. A section was sent to Manduria from 30 July to 6 August. 202 Sq then went to Gioia del Colle that day. On 7 September there were 18 BR 20Ms available at the two bases.

41 GRUPPO BT

| Squadriglie | 204, 205 |
| Stormo | 12 |

Arrival	Zone	Base	Country	Aircraft	Duties
10 Jun 40	Sqa 3	Ciampino Nord	Italy	SM 79	DB
6 Jul 40	AEGE	Rodi	Aegean	SM 79	DB, AR, AN
7 Aug 40	Sqa 3	Ciampino	Italy	Z1007bis SM82	TG
25 Sep 40	AEGE	Gadurra	Aegean	Z1007bis SM82	DB, AR
5 Nov 40	4 ZAT	Brindisi	Italy	Z1007bis	DB
20 Jan 41	Sqa 3	Littoria	Italy	SM 84	TG
5 May 41	Sqa 3	Capua	Italy	SM 84	IT
May 41	Sqa 4	Lecce	Italy	SM 84	IT

Arrival	Zone	Base	Country	Aircraft	Duties
May 41	AEGE	Gadurra	Aegean	SM 84 SM 79	AN, AR, DB
9 Feb 42	Sqa 3	Ciampino	Italy	SM 79	AN, TG
2 Aug 42	Sqa 3	Pisa San Giusto	Italy	SM 79	TG
Apr 43	ASAR	Decimomannu	Sardinia	SM 79	AN
May 43	Sqa 2	Gorizia	Italy	SM 79	AN
1 Jul 43	Sqa 3	Siena Ampugnano	Italy	SM 79	AN
16 Jul 43	Sqa 4	Lecce	Italy	SM 79	TG
30 Jul 43	Sqa 3	Siena	Italy	SM 79	AN
13 Aug 43	Sqa 4	Gioia del Colle	Italy	SM 79	TG
27 Aug 43	Sqa 3	Siena	Italy	SM 79	AN

The crews from this unit had flown the SM 79 in Spain and had then used the aircraft as a high speed transport during the invasion of Albania in 1939. Briefly operating against France, with an attack on Ghisonaccia on 19 June 1940, they then moved to the Aegean theatre. Attacks were carried out on convoys and land targets in the eastern Mediterranean.

In June an SM 83, the transport version of the SM 79, was used for reconnaissance duties over Gibraltar, using the Spanish base of Cartegena. It was intended that the SM 79s used that base for bombing the Royal Navy around Gibraltar, but Spain would not allow this. The SM 83 eventually rejoined the unit at Gadurra.

The unit continued operations, now equipped with the Z1007bis, against Haifa, Palestine and Tel Aviv. For longer range operations they received six SM 82s. Three of these arrived at Ciampino on 11 August. They moved to Gadurra on 2 September where they were damaged by enemy bombardment two days later. On 13 October five SM 82s joined the Gruppo, and on the 18th operated against the Bahrain oil refineries, flying on to Zula in East Africa. The two remaining SM 82s were passed to 92 Gruppo on 5 November.

A lack of strategic bombers meant a transfer to the Greek front. With a greater need for tactical support, however, they were returned to Italy with no aircraft left on strength. On 31 October the SM 83 moved to Brindisi to support the Greek campaign, moving to Littoria via Ciampino on 8 January 1941.

In February the Gruppo was the first to receive the new SM 84. By May they were partially trained in torpedo-bombing and were hastened back to the Aegean with 12 SM 84s. On the way they stopped at Capua to pick up torpedoes and at Lecce for additional crews. The SM 83 rejoined the unit at Gadurra in May but was shot down by a Beaufighter near Amorgos on 3 July. The Gruppo CO was lost in this aircraft.

From 20 to 28 May the SM 84s carried out operations on and around Crete, bombing, torpedoing and reconnoitering. On the 21st three aircraft attacked ships south of Caso Canal, in conjunction with bombers from 30 Gruppo, resulting in the sinking of the destroyer, HMS

Juno. On the 23rd two crews became lost on returning from Alexandria and made emergency landings on the Turkish coast. They were interned, with one crew returning to Italy a year later.

282 Sq was attached for the month of July. During the year the SM 84 was found to be inadequate for the anti-shipping role. On 19 January 1942 the unit re-equipped with the SM 79, receiving aircraft and crews from the now disbanded 281 Sq. The SM 84 was no longer used after 1 February. Since May 1941 the unit had had an average of seven SM 84s on strength, with only three operational.

With the additional experienced crews the level of competence rose sharply. On 15 February three aircraft of 205 Sq attacked a *Jervis* class destroyer, claiming a defending Beaufighter which damaged all three bombers. Two more SM 79s arrived and one was shot down by P-40s. The crew were later rescued by German U-boat (U-311). In March the unit operated over the bay of Sollum. On 9 June they sank the neutral Swedish ship, *Stureborg*, in error. Between 13 and 15 June they struck heavily against shipping from Alexandria to Malta. The Gruppo had by now left 12 Stormo, possibly from January. It was certainly Autonomo in June 1942. Withdrawing to Pisa in August, they received new SM 79s, made by Reggiane, in November.

205 Sq went to Decimomannu in April 1943, and 204 Sq left for Siena on 25 May to join Raggruppamento Aerosilurante when that unit formed on 1 June. By 5 April 205 Sq had only two serviceable aircraft. 205 Sq joined 204 Sq at Siena on 2 July, retaining an emergency section at Milis on a ten day relay. On 25 June two aircraft of 204 Sq used Gerbini for a night operation over Capo Bon, returning to Siena the next day. On 9 July 205 Sq had four serviceable aircraft at Milis.

42 GRUPPO BT

Squadriglie	206, 207
Stormo	12

Arrival	Zone	Base	Country	Aircraft	Duties
10 Jun 40	Sqa 3	Orvieto	Italy	SM 79	DB, AN
27 Nov 40	4 ZAT	Grottaglie	Italy	SM 79	DB
Feb 43	AALB	Tirana	Albania	BR 20M	AG
15 May 43	AALB	Scjak	Albania	BR 20M	AG

The crews of this Gruppo had already received combat experience in Spain and Albania when they began anti-shipping operations in June 1940. An attack was made on Ghisonaccia on 19 June, before the resumption of attacks on shipping. They participated in the Battaglia de Capo Spada on 19 July.

Fourteen SM 79s were taken to Grottaglie but after only two weeks the unit disbanded. On 12 December the

aircraft and crews were transferred to Libya to reinforce 41 Stormo.

Reforming in February 1943, the unit moved to Albania to replace 39 Gruppo as part of 38 Stormo. It began anti-partisan operations, bombing and reconnoitering until the armistice. In May it completed a night training course and moved to Scjak. On 7 September it had thirteen serviceable aircraft.

43 GRUPPO BT

Squadriglie	3, 5
Stormo	13

Arrival	Zone	Base	Country	Aircraft	Duties
10 Jun 40	Sqa 1	Cascina Vaga Pavia	Italy	BR 20	DB
27 Sep 40	CAI	Melsbroech	Belgium	BR 20	DB, NB
12 Jan 41	CAI	Monaco	Monaco	BR 20	IT
Jan 41	Sqa 1	Zavente	Italy	BR 20	IT
Jan 41	Sqa 2	Bolzano	Italy	BR 20	TG
8 Apr 41	Sqa 4	Gioia del Colle	Italy	BR 20	DB, AR
27 Apr 41	Sqa 1	Piacenza	Italy	BR 20	TG
Jun 41	Sqa 1	Rovasenda	Italy	BR 20	TG
Jul 41	Sqa 1	San Damiano/ Piacenza	Italy	BR 20	TG
Jul 41	Sqa 5	Barce	Cirenaica	BR 20	DB, AN
Nov 41	Sqa 5	Martuba	Cirenaica	BR 20	DB
7 Dec 41	Sqa 5	Barce	Cirenaica	BR 20	DB
14 Dec 41	Sqa 5	Misurata	Tripolitania	BR 20	DB
Jan 42	Sqa 5	Bir Dufan	Tripolitania	BR 20	DB
2 Mar 42	Sqa 5	Barce	Cirenaica	BR 20	DB
15 Mar 42	Sqa 2	Reggio Emilia	Italy	Ca 313 Ca 314	TG
Jul 42	Sqa 4	Manduria	Italy	Ca 314	CE
Jan 43	AALB	Tirana	Albania	Ca 314	TG
27 Jan 43	AALB	Devoli	Albania	Ca 314	AG, TG
May 43	AALB	Scjak	Albania	Ca 314	AG
15 May 43	AALB	Devoli	Albania	Ca 314	TG, AG

The BR 20 was received in 1936 and first used in action against southern France in June 1940. In the autumn the unit joined Mussolini's expeditionary force to help the Germans defeat the RAF over England. Operations began with a night raid on 24 October against Harwich. The first daylight raid was on the 29th of that month, against Ramsgate. Neither raid caused much damage and opposition was minimal. Several night raids were then undertaken against Ipswich and Harwich. Local newspapers unkindly reported that the bombers sounded like 'rattling tin cans' when they found out that Italians were responsible for keeping them awake. The remaining day raids were left to 43 Stormo.

They returned to Italy in January via Monaco, Neubiberg, Zavente, and Bolzano, where the unit was rested and re-equipped. It then took part in the last phase of the Greek campaign, and made reconnaissance and bombing missions over Yugoslavia.

After a further period of retraining, they left for Africa beginning sorties against Tobruk in July 1941. Technical problems arose from sand erosion so anti-shipping operations were flown from November.

In March 1942 they received replacement aircraft from 11 Gruppo who were returning to Italy. On 15 March the Gruppo was also ordered home, to convert to the Ca 314 for the maritime combat and escort role. They commenced convoy escort duties between Italy and Greece while based in Manduria. 13 Stormo disbanded on 10 January 1943 and the Gruppo passed to 32 Stormo, which subsequently also disbanded on 27 January. During that month the Gruppo limited its flying because of the need to refit and improve its radio communications.

The unit now went to Albania as 43 Gruppo Combattimento, completing night training at Tirana. They settled in to Devoli in May, with a section detached to Scutari until June. Five pilots were sent to Italy to learn to fly the Ju88A. The Gruppo continued training in July.

44 GRUPPO BT
Squadriglie	6, 7
Stormo	14

Arrival	Zone	Base	Country	Aircraft	Duties
10 Jun 40	ALIB	El Adem	Cirenaica	SM 79	DB, AN
Sep 40	Sqa 5	Tmimi	Cirenaica	SM 79	DB
Dec 40	Sqa		Italy	SM 79	TG

This unit had been in Libya since 1936. The eleven SM 79s were unarmed versions which had previously been prepared for use as bomber-transports in East Africa. The unit operated against shipping in the eastern Mediterranean in June and July 1940. They then supported the advance on Sidi Barrani in September.

The surviving SM 79s then went to East Africa for operations against Port Sudan and Aden. Six were lost on the ground, three were shot down, and the rest were captured in that theatre.

44bis GRUPPO BT
Squadriglie	6, 7
Stormo	Auto

Arrival	Zone	Base	Country	Aircraft	Duties
10 Jun 40	AOI	Ghiniele K92	Ethiopia	SM 79	DB, AN, AR
20 Jul 40	AOI	Addis Abeba	Ethiopia	SM 79	DB, AR
15 Dec 40	AOI	Gura	Eritrea	SM 79	DB, AR, AN
19 Dec 40	AOI	Addis Abeba	Ethiopia	SM 79	DB, AR
Apr 41	AOI	Combolcia	Ethiopia	SM 79	DB, AR
Arrival	Zone	Base	Country	Aircraft	Duties
22 Apr 41	AOI	Gimma	Ethiopia	SM 79	DB

Arrival	Zone	Base	Country	Aircraft	Duties
Apr 41	AOI	Cer-Cer	Ethiopia	SM 79	DB

This was the only modern bomber unit in the theatre when war was declared. The main targets were naval ports and airbases, for which large numbers of small bombs were carried. They were thought more likely to hit the target, besides which there was a scarcity of the heavier bombs. Poor navigational skills and lack of radio communications hindered success.

Five SM 79s of 7 Sq went to Addis Abeba on 15 June 1940, moving on to Gura on 28th. The whole unit rejoined at Addis Abeba on 20 July with eleven aircraft, beginning operations against British Somaliland two days later. They took part in all actions in the central sectors until February 1941.

On 27 July 1940 three SM 79s were detached to Scenele for operations over Aden. During August various detachments were sent to Dire Daua to support the Italian offensive. In September they operated over Aden and the Gulf of Aden, watching for convoys from India and attacking ships, ports, and airbases when possible.

Three aircraft were sent to Yavello on 21 September for raids on SAAF units at Archers Post. They returned on 11 October. Five days later three machines from 6 Sq used Dire Daua for anti-shipping sorties. Ten aircraft from Gura then operated over Port Sudan area, with sections detached to Asmara. They returned to Addis Abeba four days later.

By 30 March 1941 they were the only bomber unit still operational. All remaining bombers were passed to its control. Supplies and replacements were virtually at a standstill. Two SM 79s, on this day, were raiding Giggiga. Three were sent to Dessie on 5 April, but by the 9th of the month only two were left serviceable in the whole unit. These were evacuated from Combolcia to Gimma on 22 April. A week later the last SM 79, flying from Cer-Cer to Sciasciamanna, was shot down by 3 Squadron, SAAF.

45 GRUPPO BT
Squadriglie	2, 22
Stormo	14

Arrival	Zone	Base	Country	Aircraft	Duties
10 Jun 40	ALIB	El Adem	Cirenaica	SM 81	AN
Sep 40	Sqa 5	Tmimi	Cirenaica	SM 81	DB
Jan 41	Sqa 5	Castelbenito	Tripolitania	SM 81	TR

This unit had operated in Libya since 1936. The 19 SM 81s on strength in June 1940 were used in anti-shipping operations. On 8 July they successfully a convoy in the eastern Mediterranean. In September they switched to supporting the advance on Sidi Barrani.

By January 1942 the surviving aircraft were passed to the newly formed 145 Gruppo Trasporto.

46 GRUPPO BT

Squadriglie	20, 21
Stormo	15

Arrival	Zone	Base	Country	Aircraft	Duties
10 Jun 40	ALIB	Tarhuna T18	Tripolitania	SM 79	DB
13 Jun 40	ALIB	Benina	Cirenaica	SM 79	DB, AN
Sep 40	Sqa 5	Maraua	Cirenaica	SM 79	DB
Apr 41	Sqa 2	Ferrara	Italy	Ca 313	TG
19 Apr 41	Sqa 2	Vicenza	Italy	Ca 313 CR 42	TG
28 Aug 42	Sqa 5	Benghasi K1	Cirenaica	CR 42	CE
Sep 42	Sqa 5	El Adem	Cirenaica	CR 42	GA
16 Sep 42	Sqa 5	Bu Amud	Cirenaica	CR 42	GA
1 Nov 42	Sqa 5	Benghasi K1	Cirenaica	CR 42	GA, DF
14 Nov 42	Sqa 5	Tamet	Tripolitania	CR 42	GA
18 Nov 42	Sqa 5	Sorman	Tripolitania	CR 42	GA
Jan 43	Sqa 5	Zuara	Tripolitania	CR 42	IT
19 Jan 43	Sqa 2	Vicenza	Italy	CR 42	TG
May 43	Sqa 3	Siena	Italy	CR 42	TG
21 May 43	ASAR	Capoterra	Sardinia	CR 42	CE, GA
16 Jul 43	Sqa 3	Pontedera	Italy	CR 42	GA
28 Jul 43	Sqa 3	Firenze Peretola	Italy	CR 42	TG

The unit had been in Libya since 1936. Tarhuna base may also have been known as Maraua. In July they made several attacks on shipping from Alexandria, notably on the 8th, 12-13th, and 19th. In September they supported Italy's first desert offensive, the advance on Sidi Barrani.

By April 1941 they were training in Italy, receiving the first Ca 313s on 11th. By 30 March 1942 they still had nine Ca 313s. Poor electrics and underpowered engines held up training, along with various crashes, some fatal. When the unit was officially declared Stormo Assalto in May it was decided to re-equip with the assault version of the CR 42. On 12 August they are mentioned as escorting units of the Regia Marina between Sicily and Libya, so may have reached Libya earlier than noted above.

In early September they transferred to the El Alamein front and gave good ground support in the face of much Allied fighter defence. By the 20th they still had 15 Fiats on charge. They withdrew in January 1942, with 27 CR 42s and 2 SM 79s still on strength.

Re-equipping in Italy, and supported by SM 75s of NuCom, they moved briefly to Sardinia in case of invasion there. One squadriglia went to Pontedera from 28 May to 25 June. There were 34 CR 42s on strength on 9 July. 20 Sq was detached to Palermo between 16 and 28 July. By September there were very few serviceable aircraft.

47 GRUPPO BT

Squadriglie	53, 54
Stormo	15

Arrival	Zone	Base	Country	Aircraft	Duties
10 Jun 40	ALIB	Tarhuna T18	Tripolitania	SM 81	DB
13 Jun 40	ALIB	Benina	Cirenaica	SM 79 SM 81	DB, AN
Sep 40	Sqa 5	Maraua	Cirenaica	SM 79 SM 81	DB
Apr 41	Sqa 2	Ferrara	Italy	Ca 313	TG
19 Apr 41	Sqa 2	Vicenza	Italy	Ca 313 CR 42	TG
28 Aug 42	Sqa 5	Benghasi K1	Cirenaica	CR 42	IT
7 Sep 42	Sqa 5	Bu Amud	Cirenaica	CR 42	CE
Sep 42	Sqa 5	Derna	Cirenaica	CR 42	CE
Sep 42	Sqa 5	Barce	Cirenaica	CR 42	CE, DF
9 Nov 42	Sqa 5	Agedabia	Cirenaica	CR 42	DF
13 Nov 42	Sqa 5	Tamet	Tripolitania	CR 42	GA, DF
25 Nov 42	Sqa 5	Sorman	Tripolitania	CR 42	GA, DF
Jan 43	Sqa 5	Zuara	Tripolitania	CR 42	IT
8 Jan 43	Sqa 2	Vicenza	Italy	CR 42	TG
21 May 43	ASAR	Oristano	Sardinia	CR 42	GA
16 Jul 43	Sqa 3	Pontedera	Italy	CR 42	GA
28 Jul 43	Sqa 3	Firenze Peretola	Italy	CR 42	TG

The unit had been in Libya for four years when they commenced operations against shipping in the eastern Mediterranean. Attacks were particularly effective in July. Two months later they were operating against Sidi Barrani. In January 1941 the surviving SM 81s were passed to the newly formed 145 Gruppo Trasporto and the unit carried on with its SM 79s.

By April they were re-equipping in Italy with the new Ca 313 light bomber. This aircraft was underpowered, causing several of the inexperienced crews to crash. In May 1942 they joined 15 Stormo Assalto and re-equipped with CR 42 fighter-bombers.

Five months later they were facing the Allied forces at El Alamein. 54 Sq had arrived at K1 on 6 September with 11 CR 42AS. The Gruppo carried out ground support, local defence, and reinforcement convoy escort duties during this hectic period. On 20 September they had 15 Fiats at Barce. By 13 November it was at Tamet intercepting ground forces who had broken through the Axis lines. In January 1943 they left Libya with 23 surviving CR 42s.

Re-equipped by May they moved to Sardinia in case that island was invaded. 53 Sq was detached to Palermo from 16 to 28 July. The unit then had 16 operational CR 42s, but there were none left serviceable by September.

49bis GRUPPO BT

Squadriglie	61, 64
Stormo	Auto

Arrival	Zone	Base	Country	Aircraft	Duties
10 Jun 40	AOI	Gimma	Ethiopia	Ca 133	AR, DB
Dec 40	AOI	Yavello	Ethiopia	Ca 133	DB, AR
16 Dec 40	AOI	Gimma	Ethiopia	Ca 133	DB, AR
Feb 41	AOI	Alomata	Ethiopia	Ca 133	DB
Mar 41	AOI	Dire Daua	Ethiopia	Ca 133	AR
Apr 41	AOI	Dessie	Ethiopia	Ca 133	AR
7 Apr 41	AOI	Alomata	Ethiopia	Ca 133	AR, TR
Jul 41	AOI	Gondar	Ethiopia	Ca 133	TR

This unit carried out armed reconnaissance during June to October 1940, turning to day bombing in November against the British attacks on Eritrea and northern Ethiopia. Three aircraft were detached to Neghelli on 30 June.

On 16 December 65 Sq joined the Gruppo and the unit moved that day to Gimma, leaving two Capronis behind. Operations restarted against the British in the north, with CR 42s escorts in January. It is possible this unit lost nine aircraft at Alomata on 6 February to two strafing Blenheim IVFs of 203 Squadron, RAF, flying from Aden. The survivors moved to Dire Daua then to Dessie. On 7 April the last four returned to Alomata, beginning supply-drops to troops on 19 April. Gimma and Lekemti were also used for this purpose. By 10 May only two aircraft were left, reducing to one at Gondar on 6 July. It used Azozo as a forward base until it was destroyed by fire on 21 September 1941.

50 GRUPPO BT

Squadriglie	210, 211
Stormo	16

Arrival	Zone	Base	Country	Aircraft	Duties
10 Jun 40	Sqa 1	Vicenza	Italy	Z1007 Z1007bis	TG
Oct 40	4 ZAT	Brindisi	Italy	Z1007bis	DB
14 Apr 41	AEGE	Marizza	Aegean	Z1007bis	DB, AN
6 Sep 41	Sqa 2	Vicenza	Italy	Z1007bis	TG
Feb 42	ASIC	Sciacca	Sicily	Z1007bis	AN, DB
Jun 42	Sqa 4	Manduria	Italy	Z1007bis	TG
29 Oct 42	ASAR	Alghero	Sardinia	Z1007bis	DB, AN
31 Jan 43	Sqa 3	Viterbo	Italy	Z1007bis	TG
May 43	Sqa 3	Pistoia	Italy	Z1007bis	TG
11 Jun 43	Sqa 1	Bresso	Italy	Z1007bis	TG, NB
30 Jul 43	Sqa 1	Cameri	Italy	Z1007bis	NB

This unit received the original Z1007 in May 1939. By June 1940 the 20 on strength were considered non-operational due to their poor characteristics. The much improved Z1007bis was issued and the unit moved to Brindisi for operations over Greece.

On 25 January 1941 they bombed Salonika, and on 6 April began operations against Yugoslavia with a raid on Mostar. Moving to the Aegean in mid-April they pursued the Allied forces with attacks around Crete and Tobruk

(12 May). Between 21 and 29 May they supported the German invasion of Crete with bombing and reconnaissance missions. This was followed by raids on Egypt and Palestine. One aircraft was lost over Alexandria harbour during a reconnaissance mission, being shot down by five Tomahawks of 250 Squadron, RAF, on 8 June.

After a rest and refit in Italy they were sent to Sicily for anti-shipping sorties and the bombing of Malta. The Gruppo was by now Autonomo and a daily average of 15 to 18 aircraft were used against Malta.

After another refit in Italy they were sent to Sardinia to take on the invasion fleets and ports of North West Africa. On 31 January 1943 they rejoined 16 Stormo. On 9 July they had six operational aircraft. By September there were none left serviceable.

51 GRUPPO BT

Squadriglie	212, 213
Stormo	16

Arrival	Zone	Base	Country	Aircraft	Duties
10 Jun 40	Sqa 1	Vicenza	Italy	Z1007 Z1007bis	TG
1 Mar 41	ASAR	Alghero	Sardinia	Z1007bis	AN
Jul 42	ASAR	Villacidro	Sardinia	Z1007bis	AN, NB, DB
12 Aug 42	ASAR	Alghero	Sardinia	Z1007bis	AR
15 Aug 42	ASAR	Villacidro	Sardinia	Z1007bis	AN, DB
Mar 43	Sqa 2	Bologna	Italy	LeO451	TG
25 Jun 43	Sqa 3	Littoria	Italy	LeO451 Ju88A	TG
2 Jul 43	Sqa 3	Viterbo	Italy	Ju88A	TG

This unit used the Z1007 from August 1939 but it was not considered up to operational standards. Therefore, the updated Z1007bis was delivered and training continued for the first few months of the war.

In March 1941 the unit moved to Sardinia for anti-shipping duties as it was felt that the Z1007bis would stand more chance of survival than other types. Although very sturdy and easy to fly, they too were found to suffer from inadequate defensive armament, a prerequisite for survival against an aggressive opponent.

In September the unit experimented with night attacks on shipping, but lacking radar and other "modern" equipment they returned to day raids. By this time the Gruppo was Autonomo. Seventeen aircraft from this unit were in action in the convoy battles of June 1942. In August thirteen were engaged in watching the convoys and subsequently informing the torpedo-bombing units.

By March 1943 the unit was re-equipping in Italy with ex-Vichy French LeO 45 bombers. It is possible that these were briefly used in Sardinia, but as the aircraft were apparently in poor condition this seems unlikely.

The crews moved in June to Littoria to learn day and night flying on the Ju88A-4. The Gruppo joined 9 Stormo and the following month the LeO 451s were passed to the Germans for transport duties.

Also in June six pilots from the Gruppo joined the reformed 172 Sq RST which was to train on the Ju88D. By 7 September neither unit was up to operational standard.

52 GRUPPO BT

Squadriglie 214, 215
Stormo 34

Arrival	Zone	Base	Country	Aircraft	Duties
10 Jun 40	Sqa 2	Fontanarossa	Sicily	SM 79	AN
Dec 40	Sqa 5		Cirenaica	SM 79	AN, DB

Originally equipped with SM 81s they operated as a transport unit during the occupation of Albania. The SM 79 was received in July 1939 and began operations in June 1940 with attacks on ships in the eastern Mediterranean and around Malta. The unit had previously been at Fontanarossa in 1937. On 11 July they attacked the aircraft carrier *Eagle* and its support ships, east of Malta.

By December the unit was in Libya covering the gains made in the advance on Sidi Barrani. It is assumed, like many other units, they ceased operations after the retreat in early 1941.

53 GRUPPO BT

Squadriglie 216, 217
Stormo 34

Arrival	Zone	Base	Country	Aircraft	Duties
3 Jun 40	Sqa 2	Fontanarossa	Sicily	SM 79	AN
Dec 40	Sqa 5		Cirenaica	SM 79	AN, DB

This Gruppo followed the same destiny and operations as its sister unit, 52 Gruppo.

54 GRUPPO BT

Squadriglie 218, 219
Stormo 37

Arrival	Zone	Base	Country	Aircraft	Duties
10 Jun 40	4 ZAT	Lecce	Italy	SM 81	TG
15 Jul 40	Sqa 5	Ain El Gazala	Cirenaica	SM 81	NB
40	Sqa 5	Barce	Cirenaica	SM 81	NB
41	Sqa 5	Martuba	Cirenaica	SM 81	NB
Mar 41	Sqa 5	Bir Dufan	Tripolitania	SM 81	NB

This unit was formed at Lecce in April 1939 for operations over Albania. In July 1940, after its first war operations in the so-called Battle di Punta Stilo, the unit became Autonomo and moved to Libya with 13 aircraft to commence night bombing. They then supported the offensive on Sidi Barrani with strafing and bombing missions around Bug Bug and Sollum in October. By the end of January the SM 81s were being passed to the newly formed 145 Gruppo Trasporto. The last operations were made in March, from Bir Dufan.

55 GRUPPO BT

Squadriglie 220, 221
Stormo 37

Arrival	Zone	Base	Country	Aircraft	Duties
10 Jun 40	4 ZAT	Lecce	Italy	SM 81 BR 20/M	TG, DB
11 May 41	ASIC	Gerbini	Sicily	BR 20M	NB, CE
17 Dec 41	Sqa 4	Lecce	Italy	BR 20M	TG
Apr 42	ASIC	Castelvetrano	Sicily	BR 20M	NB
2 Jun 42	Sqa 4	Lecce	Italy	BR 20M	TG, CE
Nov 42	Sqa 2	Reggio Emilia	Italy	BR 20M	IT
28 Nov 42	ASAR	Milis	Sardinia	BR 20M	NB, AR
20 Jan 43	ASAR	Villacidro	Sardinia	BR 20M	AR
15 Feb 43	ASAR	Decimomannu	Sardinia	Z1007bis	TG, AR
21 May 43	Sqa 3	Pistoia	Italy	Z1007bis	TG

After operating over Albania with SM 81s in 1939 the unit received BR 20 and BR 20M bombers in October 1940. Two months later 15 were operational over the Yugoslav frontier. Difficult terrain and bad weather reduced the effectiveness of this unit. It was also involved in covering the occupation of Corfu and Cefalonia.

In May they began night operations over Malta. After making room for German air units in December, they returned the following April to resume the night raids. This time they suffered heavy losses to the improved Maltese defences. 221 Sq was detached to Castelvetrano on 20 January 1942.

By June they began training and refitting again. 277 Sq had replaced 220 Sq on the 5th and the Allied invasion of North West Africa meant more action for this unit. The first operation, from Sardinia, was a night raid on 8 December against Philippeville in Algeria. In January and February 1943 they were switched to maritime reconnaissance, with an average of six to eight aircraft operational, receiving the Z1007bis bomber in February.

When the unit returned to Italy it was intended to re-equip with the Z1007ter, but was disbanded on 29 May, having been made Autonomo the day before. They had flown their last operation on 18 May.

56 GRUPPO BT

Squadriglie	222, 223				
Stormo	39				

Arrival	Zone	Base	Country	Aircraft	Duties
10 Jun 40	AEGE	Gadurra	Aegean	SM 81	AN DB NB
Nov 41	ASIC	Castelvetrano ?	Sicily	SM 81	TR
May 43	Sqa 3	Orvieto	Italy	SM 73 SM82 SM 83	
				SM 75 SM 75bis	TR

This unit formed at Marizza in November 1938 with SM 81s. During the early months of the war they were very active against convoys from Alexandria and targets on the Egyptian coastline.

On 8 July they joined in the Battaglia de Punta Stilo attacking shipping making its way from Malta to Alexandria. This latter port was a regular target, being attacked on 22 June, 7th, 16th and 25 July, 26 August, 8th and 21 September, and 5 October, with an average of 8 SM 81s from 39 Stormo. On 19 July they damaged the destroyer *Havock*. On 28 August they operated against Port Said, Suez, and El Qantara. From February to April 1941 the unit made several night attacks on Crete in support of the German invasion.

On 2 November 1941 the Gruppo transferred to 18 Stormo as a transport unit. Along with 37 Gruppo it ferried troops and materials to Libya, then Tunisia, continuing this task through 1942. Heavy losses were suffered from enemy air attacks, both in the air and on the ground.

In February 1943 two SM 83s were used for liaison trips between Italy and Albania. From May to July aircraft of both squadriglie, including armed SM 75bis of 223 Sq, were busy reinforcing units on the Orvieto-Manduria-Rodi run and evacuating civilians on the Castelvetrano-Palermo-Catania runs. They also flew a Orvieto-Decimomannu-Villacidro route, in case of an invasion of Sardinia. By 31 July the unit had five SM 75s, one SM 73, and about six SM 82s serviceable at Orvieto. The SM 73 was operating Roma-Orvieto-Pisa-Bastia.

The unit was still based at Orvieto in September.

57 GRUPPO T

Squadriglie	224, 225				
Stormo	Auto				

Arrival	Zone	Base	Country	Aircraft	Duties
10 Oct 41	ASIC	Castelvetrano ?	Sicily	SM 81	TR
Feb 43	Sqa 3	Orvieto	Italy	SM 73 SM82 SM 83	
				Ca 133S	TR

This unit was formed by 10 October 1941, possibly before. They were part of 18 Stormo from November,

transporting men and materials to Libya then Tunisia. This task became more vital during the Allied invasion a year later. However, enemy fighters began to deal severely with the old aircraft.

On 15 December 1942 an aerial convoy left Sciacca for Lampedusa, losing two SM 81s to fighters and another four badly damaged. Five more were destroyed on the ground. By February the unit was using SM 82s and two SM 83s at Orvieto. During that month the SM 83s were used for liaison trips between Italy, Albania and Yugoslavia.

By 31 July they had about ten SM 82s and one SM 73 at Orvieto, using that base until the Armistice. They were the last unit to use Ca 133S ambulance planes.

The above information is often quoted for 37 Gruppo, but due to lack of records this cannot be verified.

59 GRUPPO BT

Squadriglie	232, 233				
Stormo	41				

Arrival	Zone	Base	Country	Aircraft	Duties
10 Jun 40	Sqa 2	Gela	Sicily	SM 79	DB
21 Jun 40	Sqa 1	Milano Bresso	Italy	SM 79	DB
24 Jun 40	Sqa 2	Gela	Sicily	SM 79	AN, DB
21 Oct 40	Sqa 5	Benina	Cirenaica	SM 79	DB, AN
Apr 41	Sqa 2	Ferrara	Italy	Ca 313	TG
23 Dec 41	Sqa 2	Treviso	Italy	Ca 313 CR 42CN	
				Do 217J-1	TG, NF
Jan 43	Sqa 1	Torino Caselle	Italy	CR 42CN Do 217J-1	
				Re 2001CN	
				Beaufighter	TG, NF
21 May 43	Sqa 3	Metato	Italy	Re 2001CN	
				CR 42CN Do 217J-1	NF
10 Jul 43	Sqa 3	Ciampino	Italy	Re 2001CN	
				CR 42CN Do 217J-1	NF
16 Jul 43	Sqa 3	Littoria	Italy	Re 2001CN	
				CR 42CN Do 217J-1	NF
30 Jul 43	Sqa 1	Lagnasco	Italy	Re 2001CN	
				CR 42CN Do 217J-1	NF
7 Aug 43	Sqa 1	Venegono	Italy	Re 2001CN	
				CR 42CN Do 217J-1	NF

This unit formed on 1 July 1939 with veterans of the Spanish Civil War. SM 79s were received on 16 September, beginning operations on the 21 and 23 June 1940 with attacks from Bresso over the north east Alps. Poor weather defeated effective results. The unit returned to Sicily and switched to shipping attacks, especially in the 'Battaglia de Punta Stilo' on 10 and 11 July.

Severe losses by the air force in Libya during September meant a transfer for the Gruppo to desert operations. Twelve new SM 79s were received in

48: *Two Fiat CR 25 escort fighters from 173ª Squadriglia RST over Palermo, probably in 1943. Nearest to camera is MM 3652. It is believed that some, at least, of the aircraft were allocated the same individual number as their serial. Camouflage pattern is the attractive three-tone C1B variant consisting of Giallo Mimetico 1 or 3, Marrone Mimetico 1 or 2 and Verde Mimetico 3 with Grigio Mimetico undersides and overall dark green engine cowlings*

49: *Engine running on a Fiat-CMASA RS 14 of the 186ª Squadriglia, 83° Gruppo R.M. at Augusta, Sicily. This view shows the detachable under-fuselage weapons container capable of carrying a 400kg offensive load. Note the soft-edged demarcation line between the upper and lower camouflage colours on the float struts*

50: *Aircraft '7' of the 187ª Squadriglia R.M. seen from another Cant Z.501. The early silver-grey camouflage and white background to the underwing fasces insignia dates the pictures to about late 1940. Throughout its existence the unit was based at La Spezia-Cadimare, tasked with protecting the important Regia Marina base there*

51: *Close-in view of an SM 79 of the 192ª Squadriglia of the 87° Gruppo, 30° Stormo, seen in January 1941, probably over Italy. At the time they were involved in joint operations against Malta with the Luftwaffe, which may explain the early use of yellow engine cowlings, an Axis recognition device not in general use until the invasion of Yugoslavia in April that year*

52: *Another Savoia Marchetti SM 79 of the 192a Squadriglia showing a different camouflage pattern and different position of the white fuselage band*

53: *Four SM 79s from the 194ª Squadriglia, 90° Gruppo, in attack formation on the approach to a Maltese target. From September 1941 the unit relinquished its SM 79s in favour of the Cant Z1007*

54: *Another formation of SM 79s from the 194ª Squadriglia, 90° Gruppo, sometime in late 1940. Note the variety of camouflage patterns and that none of the dorsal positions are manned*

55: *A peaceful anchorage at Brindisi in early 1941 for these CRDA Cant Z.506Bs of the 191ª and 190ª Squadriglie of the 86° Gruppo B.M. Both are finished in the pre-war silvery grey finish applied to marine aircraft, modified by the overpainting of the rudder stripes with dark green and with the newly introduced white fuselage band. In May the Gruppo moved to Greece to take part in the campaign there and to gradually convert onto the Cant Z.1007 landplane bomber*

56 Right: *A Fiat CMASA RS 14, Series III, MM 35650, of the 197ª Squadriglia R.M. seen at Marsala-Stagnone in summer 1942 from where they were principally involved in ASR duties*

57 Below: *A Pipistrello lumbers overhead on a transport mission. The previous owners of this SM 81, the 201ª Squadriglia, 92° Gruppo, whose overpainted markings can be seen on the fuselage, disappeared at about the time of the German invasion of Crete in spring 1941. This presumably dates the picture to summer 1941*

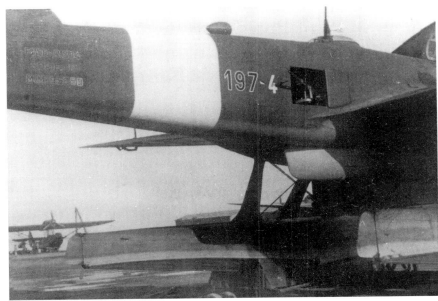

58: *Surrounded by the usual fuel drums, this is a Savoia Marchetti SM 84 of the 205ª Squadriglia, 41° Gruppo BT. The unit was the first to receive the type, which it operated from bases in Italy against Allied shipping off Crete and the Aegean for a year from January 1941 until February 1942. Operational experience proved the type to be unsatisfactory in its intended anti-shipping role and the unit re-equipped with the SM 79*

59: *The failure of the Italian aircraft industry to produce a viable attack aircraft led to use of the Junkers Ju 87 by the RA. Using Ju 87Bs, the 208ª Squadriglia, 101° Gruppo BaT was based at Lecce in March 1941, before it acquired longer-range Ju 87R models for use against Malta from Trapani. This may be the location of the scene here, although drop tanks are not visible on the aircraft in the background. For a while the unit used a system of black and white fuselage bands on the aircraft to distinguish different flights*

60: *A Junkers Ju 87R-2 of the 208ª Squadriglia banking into the landing pattern over Trapani-Milo in summer 1941. Note the black-white-black fuselage band*

December and strikes began against Mersa Matruh with close support duties as the main role. By mid-December the unit was worn out in the confusion of the retreat.

They re-equipped with Ca 313s in April 1941, but the crews only considered these as interim types. However, it was December before they received the assault and night-fighter versions of the CR 42. They began training intensively for the ground attack role. Following their move to Treviso it was realised there was no real night defence of Italy's industries against the increasing RAF raids. Therefore the Gruppo, along with 60 Gruppo, changed to the Intercettori role, protecting central and northern Italy. Through 1942 the crews were sent to Germany for night training on Dornier and Messerchmitt nightfighters.

By January 1943 the unit had mainly CR 42CNs, with some Do 217J-1s and a captured Beaufighter. The latter (unfortunately unidentified, but carrying day-fighter camouflage) had landed in error at Magnisi, Syracuse, on 7 January 1942. It was passed to 41 Stormo for trials, but on 29 January 1943 it was destroyed when an engine failed on the landing approach during training.

Bad winter weather reduced the number of flights in January. Even the activities of the recently attached FN305 liaison aircraft were restricted. There was also trouble with the local anti-aircraft units, who fired on anything that flew. The pilots were sent to Salon, France, to ferry in some MS 406s and D.520s while the anti-aircraft units improved their training.

Ten Re 2001CNs arrived in May and were used with the Fiats and Dorniers from Metato, with detachments to Littoria. Between 20 May and 21 June they made 26 scrambles and 19 patrols, but the enemy was only seen three times. A BR 20 was attached for night training, due to the limited hours available on the Dornier's engines. 233 and 234 Sq exchanged Gruppo between 21 May and 30 July then rejoined their original units.

The Gruppo was often split between several bases in an effort to cover all the night bombing. This reduced efficiency and by July they had only an overall average of seven serviceable aircraft. In early August they reunited at Venegono, now as a Gruppo Autonomo. 41 Stormo had disbanded on 24 June. By 7 September they had only four Re 2001CNs and two CR 42CNs operational.

60 GRUPPO BT

Squadriglie	234, 235
Stormo	41

Arrival	Zone	Base	Country	Aircraft	Duties
10 Jun 40	Sqa 2	Gela	Sicily	SM 79	DB, AN
21 Oct 40	Sqa 5	Benina	Cirenaica	SM 79	DB, AN

Arrival	Zone	Base	Country	Aircraft	Duties
Apr 41	Sqa 2	Ferrara	Italy	Ca 313	TG
23 Dec 41	Sqa 2	Treviso	Italy	Ca 313 CR 42CN	
				Bf 110C Do 217J-1	TG, NF
21 Oct 42	Sqa 1	Lonate Pozzolo	Italy	Do 217J-1 Bf 110C	
				Re 2001 Do 217J-2	
				CR 42CN	NF, DF
Apr 43	Sqa 1	Venegono	Italy	Re 2001CN D.520	
				Bf 110C Do 217J-1	
				Do 217J-2 CR 42CN	
				MC 205V BR 20M	NF, DF

This unit raided Biserta port in June 1940 then commenced operations against shipping, especially in the Battaglia de Punta Stilo. The Spanish Civil War veterans flew well, and as the Libyan situation deteriorated they were transferred to that front. Level bombing operations began against Mersa Matruh, but the ground forces requested more and more close support, having seen its effect during the German conquests in Europe. Consequently the unit was worn out by mid-December, using the aircraft for a purpose they were not designed for. Limited anti-shipping sorties were carried out in February 1941, then the unit was retired to Italy.

The Ca 313 was received as replacement to the trusty SM 79, and the crews trained on this until December when they re-equipped with CR 42s. Trained continued in the ground attack role, but then switched to night-fighting, to assist 59 Gruppo in defending the national industries against the growing RAF night raids. The new role began on 18 February 1942. The crews were sent to Germany for night training on the expected replacement aircraft, Dorniers and Messerscmitts.

On 21 October the unit moved to Lonate Pozzolo with the first, and it turned out only, three Bf 110Cs, together with twelve Do 217J-1s. Four days later they flew their first patrol, with two of each type over the Venegono area. Without radar they had limited ability.

In January 1943 the pilots were called on to ferry some D.520s and an MS 406 from France to Lonate Pozzolo. These aircraft were to boost the lack of cannon-armed aircraft defending southern Italy. Nine of the Dewoitines were allotted to the unit in April for day interceptions. Tests were made for their night use and the pilots considered the Dewoitine better than the CR 42 for night flying.

On 5 February the first Do 217J-2 arrived. This differed from the J-1 by having radar equipment fitted. Most of the German aircraft were given to 235 Sq. The Dorniers had few spares, troublesome undercarriages and, with poor crew training, operational numbers were low. Throughout February the crews were rotated to Germany for further training. Meanwhile, the Re 2001s were used on day intercepts, weather permitting.

On 16 July a Lancaster was claimed over Cislago by an Italian-flown Dornier. By now the unit was trying to cover the Liguria, Piemonte, Lombardia, and Emilia areas. This meant detaching sections all over Italy—which had been the dispersal problem since 1941. Re 2001CNs were received in May to help boost the numbers. Four BR 20Ms were assigned for training.

234 Sq used the Reggianes at Metato and Littoria between May and July, while it exchanged Gruppo with 233 Sq. The latter went to Caselle from 21 May to 9 July. The Gruppo became Autonomo when 41 Stormo disbanded on 24 June. In July 59 Gruppo supplied this unit with Re 2001s, three with cannon and two with machine-guns, for use at Lagnasco and Venegono.

German engineers were then asked to help repair the aging Dorniers. In August three MC 205Vs were received at Lonate Pozzolo for day intercepts. 234 Sq had been at Venegono since 9 July and 235 Sq at Lonate Pozzolo since the previous October. By 7 September the unit had two Bf 110Cs, two Do 217Js, two CR 42CNs, and seven Re 2001CNs operational.

61 GRUPPO OA

| Squadriglie | 34, 128 |
| Stormo | Auto |

Arrival	Zone	Base	Country	Aircraft	Duties
10 Jun 40	Sqa 1	Parma	Italy	Ro 37 Ca 311	AR
11 Jun 40	Sqa 1	Mondovi	Italy	Ro 37 Ca 311	AR
Apr 41	Sqa 2	Gorizia	Italy	Ca 311	AR
22 May 41	AALB	Mostar	Yugoslavia	Ca 311	AG
16 Aug 41	CSIR	Tudora	Russia	Ca 311	IT
31 Aug 41	CSIR	Krivoi Rog	Russia	Ca 311	AR
16 Nov 41	CSIR	Stalino	Russia	Ca 311	DB, AR
May 42	AALB	Valona	Albania	Ca 311	AG
Feb 43	Sqa 2	Gorizia	Italy	Ca 311	TG
1 Mar 43	AALB	Scutari	Albania	Ca 311 Ca 314	AG, AS
Jul 43	Sqa 2	Jesi	Italy	Ca 311 Ca 314	
				BR 20M	AS

At the start of the war 34 Sq had four Ro 37s and three Ca 311s, while 128 Sq had four Ca 311s under 4 Armata control. A day later they moved to Mondovi, under 6 Armata. 34 Sq left for 65 Gruppo at Cervere and 33 Sq, already at Mondovi, took its place. 129 Sq also arrived, from 72 Gruppo. Patrols were flown against French incursions and on 25 June the Gruppo passed to 1 Armata control. 33 Sq went to 67 Gruppo on 1 July and 34 Sq rejoined that month. 129 Sq left for 67 Gruppo in December.

From 6 to 15 April the unit's 15 Capronis operated over the Yugoslav front, continuing with anti-partisan duties from May. 34 and 128 Sq were now under 2 Armata. In July 119 Sq arrived and the following month the Gruppo took 32 Ca 311s and an SM 82 to Russia.

On 26 August 34 Sq moved to Krivoi Rog. The others followed five days later. In October 128 Sq used Saporoshje. On 16 November 119 Sq went to Stalino, closely followed by the others. They began bombing duties from here, in addition to the reconnaissance duties for the army. In the spring of 1942 the unit left its surviving Capronis to the incoming 71 Gruppo at Stalino. During their tour in Russia, between August 1941 and April 1942, they made 337 sorties in 686 hours and lost only four aircraft.

The Gruppo returned to anti-partisan duties in Albania, joining 21 Stormo from May 1942. Various bases were used, such as Valona, Scutari, Scjak, and Coritza. Two Fi 156C liaison aircraft were used from Coritza in October. On 25 November six Ca 314 were received by 119 Sq. This latter squadriglia also used two Ca 164s from February 1943.

34 Sq joined 68 Gruppo from December to June then rejoined 61 Gruppo. From March 1943 128 Sq was at Zara with Ca 314s under 5 Gruppo. In that same month 119 Sq had departed and 25 Sq had joined. The Gruppo then became Autonomo. Also in March, 39 Sq arrived and was based at Scutari until 28 May, subsequently moving to Jesi with sections at Pescara and Ghedi. 25 Sq was at Scjak until 30 July and then moved to Scutari. They also maintained a section at Coritza until September.

During July 1943 34 Sq temporarily used BR 20Ms from Jesi for anti-submarine duties in liaison with the Regia Marina. By 7 September the Gruppo had only three Ca 311s and three Ca 314s operational.

62 GRUPPO OA

| Squadriglie | 28, 29 |
| Stormo | Auto |

Arrival	Zone	Base	Country	Aircraft	Duties
10 Jun 40	Sqa 3	Lucca	Italy	Ro 37bis	AR

This unit transferred on 11 June 1940 from 8 Armata to 6 Armata control for operations against the French. 29 Sq was detached to Arezzo. 42 Sq replaced 28 Sq in 1941. The Gruppo was disbanded on 15 March 1942.

63 GRUPPO OA

| Squadriglie | 41, 113 |
| Stormo | 22 |

Arrival	Zone	Base	Country	Aircraft	Duties
10 Jun 40	Sqa 1	Udine	Italy	Ro 37	AR
Sep 40	Sqa 5		Cirenaica	Ro 37	AR
Jul 42	Sqa 2	Ronchi	Italy	BR 20	TG AG
Feb 43	AALB	Lubiana	Yugoslavia	Ca 314 BR 20	

Arrival	Zone	Base	Country	Aircraft	Duties
Feb 43	AALB	Lubiana	Yugoslavia	Ca 314 BR 20	
				Ca 164	AG

This unit began the war under II Gruppo Armata Est, with 16 Ro 37s. During September 1940 the Gruppo was transferred to Africa, searching for, and finding, enemy concentrations in the Cheigat-Brug area.

By 1 January 1941 three Ca 311s had joined the unit, now back in Italy. In April the unit began operations with the Ro 37s over Yugoslavia, with a very intensive period from 11 to 14 April, searching for frontline units for Squadra 2. The unit passed to 2 Armata control during the summer and began anti-partisan duties over Yugoslavia until the end of the war.

The Gruppo detached sections to various bases such as Alture di Pola, Zara, Lubiana, Grobnico, and Mostar. In July and November 1942 99 and 98 Gruppi passed their respective BR 20s to 63 Gruppo at Ronchi. In February 1943, 113 Sq was at Alture di Pola and 41 Sq was at Lubiana, both using some Ca 164s for liaison and local reconnaissance duties. 119 Sq joined in March and the Gruppo passed to 21 Stormo. By May, 41 and 113 Sq were at Lubiana and 119 Sq was at Alture di Pola where they remained until the Armistice.

64 GRUPPO OA
Squadriglie 122, 136
Stormo Auto

Arrival	Zone	Base	Country	Aircraft	Duties
10 Jun 40	ALIB	Mellaha	Tripolitania	Ro 37bis	AR
Mar 42	Sqa	Grottaglie	Italy	CR 42	TG
Jun 42	Sqa 1	Milano Bresso	Italy	Ca 313	TG
Oct 42	Sqa 3	Capua	Italy	Ca 313	IT
Oct 42	Sqa 5	Castelbenito	Tripolitania	Ca 313	IT
9 Oct 42	Sqa 5	Benghasi	Cirenaica	Ca 313 Ca 311	CE
20 Nov 42	Sqa 5	Zuara	Tripolitania	Ca 313 Ca 311	AR
Nov 42	Sqa 5	Sorman	Tripolitania	Ca 313 Ca 311	AR
Jan 43	Sqa 5	Zuara	Tripolitania	Ca 313 Ca 311	IT
8 Jan 43	Sqa 1	Venaria Reale	Italy	Ca 313	AR
Apr 43	APRO	Cuers Pierrefeu	France	Ca 313	AR

This unit had an exhausting tour on the African continent, starting with patrols along the Tunisian border under 5 Armata, while France was still a threat. On 12 June 1940 136 Sq was detached to Tobruk T5, replacing 127 Sq which had suffered badly from RAF ground attacks. On 1 September, following a disagreement with the Tobruk commander, the squadriglia moved to Gambut for reconnaissance and ground support duties. 129 Sq joined in December but may have been temporarily disbanded through 1941 due to lack of aircraft. In February the Gruppo received some Ca 311s.

By March 1942 they were in Italy experimenting with CR 42 fighter bombers using 2 x 50kg anti-submarine bombs. In June they were training on the Ca 313 and getting ready for the Russian front. Orders were, however, changed and consideration was given to re-equipping with BR 20s for a second tour of Africa. By October they were embroiled in the retreat from El Alamein, using Ca 311s from 66 and 68 Gruppi, as well as their own Ca 313s. The unit ended up split between Barce and Benghasi. On 5 November the Gruppo left 19 Stormo after only about a month, then rejoined it on 25 January 1943. Because of the worsening situation they left Libya with 12 Ca 313s in mid-month.

Three Ca 164s were received in February for liaison duties, and after a rest in Italy, the Gruppo moved to southern France. 122 Sq used Cuers Pierrefeu, while 136 Sq used Hyeres. On 7 September they were the only Italian unit based in occupied France. They had ten Ca 313s operational out of fourteen. These were all captured, with their crews, by the Germans.

65 GRUPPO OA
Squadriglie 36, 87
Stormo 21

Arrival	Zone	Base	Country	Aircraft	Duties
10 Jun 40	Sqa 1	Padova	Italy	Ca 311	AR
17 Jun 40	Sqa 1	Quarto D'Asti	Italy	Ca 311	AR
9 Jul 40	Sqa 1	Padova	Italy	Ca 311	TG
10 Apr 41	AALB	Tirana	Albania	Ca 311	AR
Jun 41	Sqa 4	Padova	Italy	Ca 311	AS
Aug 41	Sqa 2	Forli	Italy	Ca 311	IT
Aug 41	AALB	Mostar	Yugoslavia	Ca 311	AR
Jul 42	Sqa 5	Benghasi ?	Cirenaica	Ca 311	AR
Aug 42	ASAR	Alghero	Sardinia	Ro 37bis Ca312	
				Ca 313 Ca 314	AR, AN, AS
Sep 43	ASAR	Ajaccio	Corsica	Ca 313 Ca 314	AR, AN

At the outbreak of war this unit was attached to 4 Armata with seven Ca 311s. They quickly transferred to 6 Armata and also received 34 Sq from 61 Gruppo at Cervere on 17 June 1940. The latter squadriglia stayed detached at Cervere and returned to 61 Gruppo on 9 July when the main unit returned to Padova.

In April 1941 87 Sq went to Albania with the seven Ca 311s for operations against Yugoslavia. After the surrender the unit carried out anti-submarine duties over the Adriatic Sea. Two months later they returned to Yugoslavia for anti-partisan operations. 87 Sq joined 66 Gruppo in October. 36 Sq stayed on in the Balkans.

In July 1942 they reformed with 28 and 124 Sq and joined 66 Gruppo in Libya, possibly at Benghasi. It was decided that the OA units were too vulnerable there, so by 1 August they moved to Sardinia, becoming part of 20

Stormo OA.

The Gruppo then received some Ro 37bis followed by Ca 314s, undertaking anti-shipping and anti-submarine duties, with 28 Sq at Elmas and 124 Sq at Alghero. On 1 February 1943 a Ca 312 was delivered to 131 Sq which had joined the Gruppo the previous month. 28 Sq had left for Oristano, moving to Novi Ligure by 23 July. Also in February, 124 Sq became Autonomo, directly under 20 Stormo. Both 131 and 124 Sq were by now at Alghero, and by April used Ca 313 and Ca 314 aircraft. On 17 April and 14 May 131 Sq lost five aircraft to Allied bombing. On 23 July 131 Sq moved to Ajaccio. By 7 September the Gruppo had 14 Ca 314s operational out of 23, plus one Ca 313.

66 GRUPPO OA

Squadriglie 42, 131
Stormo 2

Arrival	Zone	Base	Country	Aircraft	Duties
10 Jun 40	Sqa 3	Capodichino	Italy	Ro 37bis	TG
1 Oct 41	Sqa 4	Bari Palese Macchie	Italy	Ca 311	TG
May 42	Sqa 3	Capodichino	Italy	Ca 311	TG
18 Jul 42	Sqa 5	Zuara	Tripolitania	Ca 311	IT
Jul 42	Sqa 5	Benghasi K3	Cirenaica	Ca 311	AR, AN, CE
Aug 42	Sqa 5	Zuara	Tripolitania	Ca 311	AR, CE
Sep 42	Sqa 5	Abu Nimeir	Egypt	Ca 311	AR, GA
Sep 42	Sqa 5	Barce	Cirenaica	Ca 311 Ro 63	AR
13 Nov 42	Sqa 5	Tamet	Tripolitania	Ca 311	AR
26 Nov 42	Sqa 5	Zuara	Tripolitania	Ca 311	IT
28 Nov 42	ASIC	Palermo	Sicily	Ca 311	AR, AS
Feb 43	ASIC	Gela	Sicily	Ca 312 Ca 313	
				Ca 314	AR, AS
May 43	ASIC	Gerbini	Sicily	Ca 313 Ca 314	AR, AS
16 Jul 43	Sqa 1	Novi Ligure	Italy	Ca 313 Ca 314	TG

At the start of the war, seven aircraft of 42 Sq were detached to Bari-Palese while six of 131 Sq remained at Capodichino. The Gruppo also had a Ca 111bis on liaison duties. After the French surrender they passed to 6 Armata control. On 25 October 42 Sq went to 72 Gruppo at Valona. 131 Sq became Autonomo and joined 30 Corps d'Armata, leaving the Gruppo without squadriglie for a year. On 1 October 1941 87 Sq joined at Bari, leaving for Africa ten months later.

Shortly after arrival in Africa 87 Sq was reunited with 131 Sq. They both then moved to Benghasi. 131 Sq had been detached to Barce in July 1942. By 1 August the unit had 12 Ca 311s at Zuara and moved to the frontline at El Alamein to undertake ground attacks, convoy escorts, and reconnaissance. An Ro 63 lightplane was used from Barce for crew rescue in the desert at this time. The Gruppo left 20 Stormo on 16 August. On 20 September they had four aircraft at Barce. 87 Sq was back at Benghasi K3 by 1 November.

After the retreat from Egypt the unit retired to Sicily and rejoined 20 Stormo. The surviving aircraft were passed to the incoming 64 Gruppo, and 66 Gruppo were then re-equipped with Ca 313 and Ca 314 aircraft. A Fi 156C went to 40 Sq who had replaced 131 Sq in December.

A Ca 312 trainer was used by 87 Sq at Gela in February 1943. 87 Sq moved from there to Gerbini on 21 May, with a section at Reggio Calabria, moving to Palermo on 21 May. Both squadriglie moved to Novi Ligure in July, but the Gruppo disbanded on 16 August.

67 GRUPPO OA

Squadriglie 25, 115
Stormo 21

Arrival	Zone	Base	Country	Aircraft	Duties
10 Jun 40	Sqa 1	Bologna Borgo Panigale	Italy	Ro 37bis	AR
10 Jul 40	Sqa 5	Mellaha	Tripolitania	Ro 37bis	AR
Sep 40	Sqa 5	Benina	Cirenaica	Ro 37bis	AR, GA
Oct 40	Sqa 5	Mellaha	Tripolitania	Ro 37bis Ca 310	AR
Feb 41	Sqa 5	Derna	Cirenaica	Ro 37bis	AR
Mar 41	Sqa 5	Mellaha	Tripolitania	Ro 37bis	TG
Dec 41	Sqa 5	Tamet	Tripolitania	Ro 37bis Ro 63	AR
Feb 42	Sqa 5	Sorman	Tripolitania	Ro 37bis	TG
Feb 42	Sqa 1	Novi Ligure	Italy	Ca 314 ?	CE, AS

25 Sq was detached to Jesi for operations against France, under XV Corpo d'Armata, with ten aircraft operational. On 11 June 1940 25 Sq left for 72 Gruppo at Villanova d'Albenga. The following month found 115 Sq in Libya, having been joined by 33 Sq from 61 Gruppo on 1 July.

115 Sq was busy during the advance on Sidi Barrani, returning to Mellaha in October to receive 20 Ca 310s. These were not in operational condition and only a few were used.

In early January 1941 five Ca 310s and some Ro 37s were sent with 33 Sq to Tobruk. Moving to Derna on 6th they lost several aircraft to the strafing RAF. Five days later 33 Sq was at Apollonia with a section at Tobruk T5. There followed a rapid series of moves: Soluch on 28 January, El Agheila on 4 February, Tamet on 5th, Misurata on 7th, evacuation of Cirenaica on 9th. This was typical of the chaotic situation at the time. Wear and tear on the crews and aircraft reduced efficiency to almost nil. 115 Sq used its Ro 37bis during the spring offensive, but on 7 August the crews began returning to Italy. The aircraft were left in Libya for other units to use. On 31 December an Ro 63 was transferred from 30 to 129 Sq at Tamet. The latter had replaced 33 Sq and stayed in Libya when the Gruppo returned to Italy in February 1942. 132 Sq joined in January while based at Ain El Gazala.

The Gruppo disbanded on 10 February and the surviving Ro 37s were collected at Sorman and transferred to the Balkans. Between March and May some of the pilots retrained on CR 42s and formed 158 Gruppo Assalto at Sorman. The observers were passed to the RST units.

The Gruppo reformed by August 1942 with 115 Sq and the Gruppo being part of 19 Stormo. They carried out convoy escorts and anti-submarine duties over the Alto Tirreno.

68 GRUPPO OA

| Squadriglie | 24, 35 |
| Stormo | 21 |

Arrival	Zone	Base	Country	Aircraft	Duties
10 Jun 40	Sqa 1	Verona	Italy	Ro 37	AR
20 Jun 40	Sqa 1	Torino	Italy	Ro 37	AR
Apr 41	AALB	Peqini	Albania	Ro 37	AR
Jan 42	AALB	Scutari	Albania	Ro 37 Ca 111bis	AR
Mar 42	Sqa 1	Venaria Reale	Italy	Ca 311	TG
9 Mar 42	Sqa 5	Zuara	Tripolitania	Ca 311	AR
Jul 42	Sqa 5	Misurata	Tripolitania	Ca 311 Ca312	AR
Nov 42	Sqa 5	Zuara	Tripolitania	Ca 311 Ca312	IT
28 Nov 42	ASIC	Palermo	Sicily	Ca 311 Ca312	AR
Nov 42	Sqa 2	Treviso	Italy	Ca312	TG
Feb 43	Sqa 2	Ronchi	Italy	Ca312	TG
Jul 43	Sqa 2	Jesi	Italy	Ca 314 Ca 313	TG
25 Jul 43	Sqa 1	Lavariano	Italy	Ca 314 Ca 313	TG

Twelve aircraft of this unit were used in the French campaign, under 4 Armata. 35 Sq was detached to Venaria Reale on 20 June under 6 Armata. On 14 April 1941 35 Sq went to Peqini, Albania, with eight Ro 37s for operations against Greece and Yugoslavia in the closing stages of those campaigns. 35 Sq was replaced by 33 Sq at this time.

Re-equipping with 12 Ca 311s 33 Sq left for Libya in March 1942. 24 Sq followed on 23 April. At the end of July 33 Sq was back at Zuara, receiving Ca 312s which never measured up to operational standards. The unit was briefly involved in the Alamein battles, but returned to Italy in November. On 20 September 24 Sq was at Misurata with 5 serviceable Ca 311s, while 33 Sq was at Zuara with 7 serviceable Capronis. The remaining aircraft were passed to 64 Gruppo.

24 Sq left for 73 Gruppo in December. 34 Sq joined from 10 December to 18 June 1943, with a section at Pescara from 21 May. It then moved on to 61 Gruppo. 121 Sq arrived at Pescara in late August. By 7 September there were nine out of fifteen Ca 314s operational, plus two unserviceable Ca 313s.

69 GRUPPO OA

| Squadriglie | 118, 123 |
| Stormo | 19 |

Arrival	Zone	Base	Country	Aircraft	Duties
10 Jun 40	Sqa 1	Levaldigi	Italy	Ro 37bis Ca 311	
				Ca 310	AR
1 Jan 41	Sqa 1	Novi Ligure	Italy	Ca 311 Ca 310	AR
Dec 41	Sqa 5	Zuara	Tripolitania	Ca 311 Ro 63	AR
9 Mar 42	Sqa 5	Benghasi K3	Cirenaica	Ca 311	AR
27 Mar 42	Sqa 5	Barce	Cirenaica	Ca 311	AR
Jul 42	Sqa 3	Capodichino	Italy	Ca 311 Ca 313	
				Ca 314	AS, AR, TG
Sep 43	Sqa 4	Pontecagnano	Italy	Ca 313 Ca 314	AS, AR

On 11 June 1940, 118 Sq was switched from 1 Armata to the control of 11 Corpo d'Armata. 123 Sq had been detached to Novi Ligure to defend the approaches to Levaldigi. During this first month of war the unit exchanged its Ro 37bis for Ca 311s. On 24 June 132 Sq temporarily joined from 76 Gruppo in Sicily. By January 1941 123 Sq was still at Novi Ligure, 118 Sq being at Mondovi. They had received two Ca 310s for training use.

Arriving in Libya by the end of 1941 they received the first Ro 63—the Italian equivalent to the German Fieseler Storch. This aircraft was tried out for liaison and desert rescue duties. The squadriglie were by now based at Zuara (123 Sq) and Misurata (118 Sq). There followed a period of local defence duties. 118 Sq then moved to Barce and 123 Sq to K3. They returned to Italy at the end of July 1942, joining 20 Stormo on 1 October.

In November they became the first OA unit to receive the new Ca 314 light bomber, with 17 on strength by the 13th. The Ca 311s were used for anti-submarine duties until late 1942, with 123 Sq detached to Palese-Macchie. Some Ca 313s and a Ca 164 joined the unit in January 1943. 123 Sq left on the 29th.

103 Sq joined at Bari on 1 March, moved to Gioia del Colle by 14 May, then back to Bari on 30 July. 104 Sq joined in April at Crotone, moving to Manduria on 23 July, Castrovillari on 30 July, Crotone on 6 August, and Sibari on 13 August. 118 Sq was at Pontecagnano until the Armistice, with a section at Capua from 20 to 27 August.

On 7 September they had 11 out of 18 Ca 314s, plus one Ca 313, operational.

70 GRUPPO OA

| Squadriglie | 114 |
| Stormo | Auto |

Arrival	Zone	Base	Country	Aircraft	Duties
Mar 41	Sqa 2	Vicenza	Italy	Ro 37bis	TG
6 Mar 41	AALB	Tirana	Albania	Ro 37bis	AR

Arrival	Zone	Base	Country	Aircraft	Duties
May 41	AALB	Coritza	Albania	Ro 37bis Ca 311	
				Ca 314	AG, AR
May 43	AALB	Valona	Albania	Ca 311 Ca 314	AR

This unit transferred on 6 March 1941, with eight aircraft, to join 25 Sq with nine aircraft at Tirana. They began operations over Yugoslavia and stayed after the surrender to carry out anti-partisan duties from May. Detachments were sent to various bases such as Alture di Pola, Lubiana, Zara, Grobnico, and Mostar.

The Ro 37bis were gradually replaced by Ca 311s and then Ca 314s. 39 Sq joined from September 1942 to March 1943. 25 Sq used a Ca 164 from February 1943 then left next month for 61 Gruppo, having been replaced by 123 Sq from 29 January. 114 Sq had a section at Devoli until 2 July. 123 Sq was at Devoli until 13 August then moved to Valona.

On 7 September 1943, 114 and 123 Sq had eight out of twelve Ca 311s and six out of six Ca 314s operational at Valona.

71 GRUPPO OA

Squadriglie	38, 116
Stormo	22

Arrival	Zone	Base	Country	Aircraft	Duties
10 Jun 40	Sqa 1	Gorizia	Italy	Ro 37bis Ca 111bis	AR
17 Jun 40	Sqa 1	Aosta	Italy	Ro 37bis	AR
Apr 41	Sqa 2	Udine	Italy	Ro 37bis	AR
May 42	CSIR	Stalino	Russia	Ca 311 Ca312	AR
Aug 42	CSIR	Voroscilovgrad	Russia	Ca 311 Ca312	
				BR 20M Fi156C	AR
Feb 43	CSIR	Stalino	Russia	Ca 311 Ca312	
				BR 20M Ca 164	AR
43	CSIR	Saporoshje	Russia	Ca 311 Ca312	
				BR 20M	AR
43	CSIR	Odessa	Russia	Ca 311 Ca312	
				BR 20M	AR, IT
May 43	Sqa 2	Ronchi	Italy	BR 20M	TG
17 Jul 43	Sqa 1	Venaria Reale	Italy	BR 20M	TG
30 Jul 43	Sqa 1	Mirafiori	Italy	BR 20M	AR
3 Sep 43	Sqa 1	Venaria Reale	Italy	BR 20M	TG

This unit began the war under 2 Armata control. The eight Ca 111bis on strength were quickly put into reserve duties. The Gruppo then moved to Aosta and temporarily received 31 Sq, detached to Venaria Reale from 5 Gruppo, for operations against France. This was under I Gruppo Armata Ovest and controlled by Corpo d'Armata Alpino.

By 7 April 1941 the unit was at Udine for operations over Yugoslavia. Earlier, on 1 January they had received three Ca 311s to assist the older Ro 37s.

In the spring of 1942 the unit, Autonomo since 13 May, came under 8 Armata and joined in supporting the advance into Russia. They took over 61 Gruppo's Ca 311s at Stalino. During August and September they received seven BR 20Ms, followed by five more in December. Most of these went to 38 Sq, performing valuable photo-reconnaissance work in the Don area in August. At this time 116 Sq was detached to Kalinovskaja landing ground, with a section of Ca 311s at Kantamirovka. Two Fi 156C liaison aircraft were used from November.

By 18 December the Gruppo was fully reunited at Voroscilovgrad with 17 BR 20Ms and 15 Ca 311s. Both 38 and 116 Sq used a Ca 133S ambulance plane between September 1942 and April 1943. Two Ca 312s also arrived in 1942 for ambulance work, but were soon put on ordinary transport duties. By February 1943 38 Sq had two and 116 Sq had three of these types, along with a Ca 164 each.

Following the retreat across Russia the unit returned to Italy, leaving all its surviving Capronis behind. They re-equipped fully with BR 20Ms and carried on training in northern Italy.

72 GRUPPO OA

Squadriglie	119, 129
Stormo	19

Arrival	Zone	Base	Country	Aircraft	Duties
10 Jun 40	Sqa 1	Villanova d'Albenga	Italy	Ro 37 Ca 311	AR
Oct 40	AALB	Valona	Albania	Ro 37bis	AR
Aug 42	AGRE	Larissa	Greece	Ro 37 Ro 37bis	
				Ca 311 BR 20	
				Ca 164 Ca 313	AS, AR

On the first day of war 129 Sq was detached to Mondovi with Ca 311s under III Corpo d'Armata and was subsequently transferred to 61 Gruppo. 119 Sq stayed at Villanova with Ro 37s under XV Corpo d'Armata. 25 Sq arrived from 67 Gruppo at Jesi and joined 119 Sq. 120Sq joined in October. 119 Sq then transferred to 61 Gruppo in the summer of 1941.

Meanwhile, 42 Sq flew to Valona where the Gruppo now had 27 Ro 37bis. 25 Sq was detached to Coritza and the other new arrival, 120 Sq, was at Argirocastro. In December 120 Sq moved to Valona, and 25 Sq went to Tirana where it joined 70 Gruppo in March 1941. During January 1941 the Gruppo, escorted by CR 42s over the Greek front, became embroiled in several fights with Gladiators.

By April 120 Sq exchanged its Ro 37bis for nine Ca 311s which it took to Durazzo for operations against Yugoslavia. 42 Sq continued to use its nine Ro 37bis from Valona for the same campaign. Both squadriglie then participated in the anti-partisan duties, operating from

Valona. Sections were detached to various bases as required, such as Zara, Lubiana, and Alture di Pola. 120 Sq then left for Villanova for a rest, returning in July 1942 to replace 36 Sq at Mostar. The latter went to Lucca where it carried on using three Ca 164 liaison aircraft on anti-partisan duties. 120 Sq went to 5 Gruppo in February 1943.

72 Gruppo seems to have then reformed as an Autonomo unit in Greece, with 31 Sq at Argos and 35 Sq at Larissa, all on anti-submarine and reconnaissance duties. 31 Sq had six Ro 37s and three Ca 311s, with a section at Araxos. 35 Sq had nine Ro 37bis. Both squadriglie still used a Ca 164 each. They remained in this area until the Armistice. By then, in operation they had eight BR 20s out of eleven, four Ca 311s out of nine, and one Ca 313 out of one.

73 GRUPPO OA

Squadriglie	**127, 137**				
Stormo	**Auto**				

Arrival	Zone	Base	Country	Aircraft	Duties
10 Jun 40	Sqa 5	El Adem	Cirenaica	Ro 37bis Ca 310	AR
Sep 40	Sqa 5	Menastir	Cirenaica	Ro 37bis	AR
26 Sep 40	Sqa 5	Sollum	Egypt	Ro 37bis	AR
Dec 40	Sqa 5	Benghasi	Cirenaica	Ro 37bis	IT
Mar 41	Sqa 5	Castelbenito	Tripolitania	Ro 37bis	AR
Mar 41	Sqa 5	Benghasi K2	Cirenaica	Ro 37bis	AR
Mar 41	Sqa 5	Ain El Gazala	Cirenaica	Ro 37bis	AR
Apr 42	Sqa 1	Novi Ligure	Italy	Ca 311	TG
Apr 42	Sqa 2	Alture di Pola	Italy	Ca 311	AG
22 May 42	Sqa 1	Piemonte	Italy	Ca 311	AR
Jun 42	Sqa 1	Venaria Reale	Italy	Ca 313 Ca 314	TG
May 43	Sqa 1	Novi Ligure	Italy	Ca 313 Ca 314	TG
Jul 43	AALB	Scutari	Albania	Ca 313 Ca 314	AG
Sep 43	AALB	Scjak	Albania	Ca 313 Ca 314	AG, AR

This unit suffered heavily in the first stages of the desert war. Operating under 10th Army, 127 Sq was at Tobruk T2, and 137 Sq was at El Adem with seven Ro 37bis. On 12 June 127 Sq lost three aircraft to RAF attacks, leaving only one operational. Despite replacements from 137 Sq and six Ca 310s received for ground attack duties, the unit was poorly equipped to carry out its work. In September 137 Sq moved to Menastir and both squadriglie went to Sollum on the 26th where three more Ro 37bis were lost to bombing. 136 Sq was temporarily attached for operations against Sidi Barrani in September. In December 137 Sq withdrew to Benghasi, leaving 127 Sq in the frontline where it lost a further seven Ro 37bis abandoned in the retreat. By February 1941 the Gruppo had only eight aircraft left, the Ca 310s having long since been abandoned as useless. It seems that the unit was then withdrawn from action.

In April 1942 137 Sq moved from Novi Ligure to Alture di Pola, and 127 Sq from Venaria Reale to Zara,

both with Ca 311s. Due to bad weather and difficult terrain they returned in May to Piemonte and Liguria. In June 127 Sq received the first Ca 313 at Venaria Reale, followed by a delivery the next month to 137 Sq at Novi Ligure.

In September and December the squadriglie changed. 115 and 24 Sq arriving in those respective months with Ca 313s and Ca 314s. 127 Sq passed to 76 Gruppo in September. 115 Sq received a Ca 164 in February 1943 at Novi Ligure. 24 Sq was still at that base in May, with a section at Venaria Reale until 9 July. Then it moved to Scjak on 13 August. 115 Sq, with a section at Bresso until 11 June, then moved from Novi Ligure to Scutari. On 13 August it moved to Devoli. Meanwhile, 137 Sq had gone to Albenga in February, with nine Ca 313s, and stayed there until the Armistice, under 19 Stormo command.

By 7 September the Gruppo had only two out of ten Ca 313s and four out of eight Ca 314s serviceable.

76 GRUPPO OA

Squadriglie	**132, 30**				
Stormo	**Auto**				

Arrival	Zone	Base	Country	Aircraft	Duties
10 Jun 40	Sqa 2	Boccadifalco	Sicily	Ro 37bis	AR
Jul 42	Sqa 1	Venaria Reale	Italy	Ca 313	AR
Feb 43	APRO	Le Luc	France	Ca 313	AR

This unit started the war in Sicily under the control of XII Corpo d'Armata, with six Ro 37bis. 132 Sq was detached to Catania, then left on 24 June for 69 Gruppo at Levaldigi.

40 Sq joined in 1941, only to become Autonomo again in May 1942. The Gruppo briefly joined 19 Stormo in that month. By July 1942, 30 Sq was at Venaria Reale and 115 Sq at Novi Ligure. The latter exchanged with 127 Sq from 73 Gruppo in September, replacing its Ca 313s with Ca 314s in November. The Gruppo now rejoined 19 Stormo and moved to France when the Italians occupied their portion of that country in 1943. 30 Sq used two Ca 164s for liaison duties.

82 GRUPPO RM

Squadriglie	**139, 184**				
Stormo	**Auto**				

Arrival	Zone	Base	Country	Aircraft	Duties
Aug 42	AGRE	Prevesa	Greece	Z501 Z506B	CE, AR

This unit was formed from the Sezione Costiere under the Greek area command, for the protection of convoys crossing to Cirenaica to supply the Axis forces in front of

El Alamein. They initially had eleven Z501s, boosted by seven Z506Bs by April 1943.

As the squadriglie were uniting a famous incident occurred. On 28 July 1942, a Beaufort of 217 Squadron, RAF, was shot down by a destroyer's anti-aircraft fire while attacking a merchant ship off the southern Greek coast. Lt. E.T. Strever, SAAF, and his crew were picked up and eventually passed to 139 Sq who were to fly them from Greece to Italy and a POW camp. The next morning, during the flight, the prisoners overpowered their captors and forced the pilot, *Tenente* Mastrodicasa, to fly to Malta. Despite Red Cross markings already on the aircraft the defending fighters from Malta attacked, so the Z506B landed on the water. Red Cross aircraft were rumoured by both sides to be used for spotting purposes. The floatplane was subsequently towed to St.Paul's Island then flown in to Kalafrana seaplane base. On 31 July RAF markings were applied, with the intention of using the aircraft for air-sea-rescue duties, but it was felt to be too prone to being accidentally shot down. It disappeared from Malta a few days later.

By early 1943 the Gruppo was patrolling the approaches to the Aegean and the Greek coast, and watching over friendly shipping in the area. On 20 May, 10 Sezione Aerea di Soccorso was formed from 184 Sq at Prevesa. From 3 September 184 Sq was detached to Pola-Puntisella. By the 7th the whole Gruppo had three Z501s and five Z506Bs operational.

83 GRUPPO RM

Squadriglie	184, 186, 189				
Stormo	Auto				

Arrival	Zone	Base	Country	Aircraft	Duties
10 Jun 40	Sqa 2	Augusta	Sicily	Z501 Z506B	
				Z506S RS14B	CE, AR, AS
					ASR

The unit started their operations with 21 Z501s. 189 Sq was detached to Siracusa. 170 Sq joined in the summer of 1940. By 15 March eight Z506Bs had also arrived. On 23 July pilots of 170 Sq were sent to Vigna di Valle to learn to fly the first RS14Bs, which arrived on 11 August 1941. Training was completed by 2 March 1942, and they returned to Augusta with two of the new aircraft. By May they had ten on strength and most crews were trying them out. They also had about nine Z506Bs and several Z501s.

The unit was ready to commit the RS14B to the anti-shipping battles of mid-August. There were about 16 available during that month and September. 184 Sq departed in September, followed by 189 Sq by the end of the year. November saw 170 Sq on convoy and submarine escort duties. Operations continued with reconnaissance, escorts, rescues, and anti-submarine sorties from Augusta.

On 20 May 1943, 7 Sezione Aerea di Soccorso formed from 170 Sq at Siracusa. In July the Gruppo had 20 RS14Bs, four Z506Bs, two Z506Ss, a single Z501 and Breda 25, with 170 and 186 Sq. Twelve of these were operational. Between 12 and 22 July an average six to seven aircraft operated daily from Augusta. On 10 July one RS14B and one Z506B were destroyed by battery fire, but on 22 July the Allies managed to capture intact all the other aircraft in the bay.

The Gruppo administration had moved to Taranto in mid-July, then to Orbetello by the 23rd. It disbanded on 6 August.

84 GRUPPO RM

Squadriglie	147, 185				
Stormo	Auto				

Arrival	Zone	Base	Country	Aircraft	Duties
10 Jun 40	AEGE	Lero	Aegean	Z501 Z506B	AR, CE, AN
Aug 42	AEGE	Suda Bay	Crete, Aegean	Z501 Z506B	CE
Sep 43	Sqa 3	Torre del Lago	Italy	Z501 Z506B	
				RS14B	AR

Formed on 1 October 1937 under Regia Marina control, this unit had 12 Z501s at Lero on 10 June 1940. There was also a Sezione Ricognizione Strategica with two Z506Bs attached to the Gruppo. 147 Sq was originally the 6 Sezione Costiera. The Gruppo joined in the battle of Capo Spada on 19 July and protected shipping between Tripoli and Crete. Two aircraft were lost during an air attack on Lero on 3 October.

In February 1941 the unit was involved in operations against Force H from Gibraltar. The squadriglie continued independent operations through the next year with convoy escorts and maritime reconnaissance between the Aegean and Africa, although the Gruppo was temporarily disbanded until 1 August 1942.

On reforming they moved to Crete to protect convoys crossing to Cirenaica and supplying the Axis forces before Alamein. During 1943 they withdrew to Italy, replacing both squadriglie with 140 and 145 Sq on 11 June. They now covered the Alto Tirreno area.

147 and 185 Sq meanwhile stayed at Lero under the Greek Area Command until the Armistice, at which time they had four Z501s and four Z506Bs operational with a section at Rodi-Mandracchio. On 20 May, 11 Sezione Aerea di Soccorso formed from 185 Sq at Lero. Effectively, 185 Sq disbanded on 10th June when their remaining aircraft and crews were passed to 147 Sq.

On 7 September 1943, 84 Gruppo had three Z501s, two Z506Bs, and five RS14Bs operational.

61 Above: *A well-worn Ju 87R-2 of the 208ᵃ Squadriglia, 101° Gruppo enroute to a target sometime in 1941. By the end of the year the type had been replaced by the assault version of the CR 42. The underwing tanks apppear to be smeared with a temporary black paint, although the rest of the undersurfaces appear to be the original light blue-grey. There is a red number '4' on the wheel spat*

62 Right: *A mechanic lazes under the wing of a 208ᵃ Squadriglia Ju 87. It is unclear whether the underwing fittings are bomb racks or fuel tank shackles. Note the black/white fuselage band*

63 Right: *Close formation flying by Junkers Ju 87Rs of the 208ᵃ Squadriglia. Needless to say, those on the receiving end made no distinction between Italian or German-flown Stukas, consequently the Italian dive-bomber crews have not received their due share of recognition for their work against Allied shipping and over Malta*

64 Left: *Groundcrew re-fuelling a twin-finned Cant Z.1007, possibly of the 210ª Squadriglia, 50° Gruppo. The versatile Alcione was used for both bombing and reconnaissance duties, as shown by the large camera being loaded aboard. Worthy of note is the very smooth finish to the wooden structure, which gave good aerodynamic qualities, but burned easily. The camouflage is the very distinctive so-called polycyclical mottle, unique to CRDA, which used a combination of Giallo Mimetico 3, Verde Mimetico 3 and Marrone Mimetico 53193*

65 Above: *A single-finned Z.1007 of 210ª Squadriglia, probably over Greece in early 1941 as the aircraft does not have the yellow engine cowlings adopted from April that year*

66 Left: *Cant Z.1007bis of the 230ª Squadriglia, 95° Gruppo, during a bombing raid on an unidentified target, possibly in Greece in early 1941. Clearly visible on the fin is the unit emblem, a letter 'M' for Mussolini*

67: *WNr 5688 is a Junkers Ju 87B-2 in service with the 237ᵃ Squadriglia, 96° Gruppo, the first Italian unit to be equipped with the type. It is seen here at Lecce-Galatina in November 1940. Still essentially wearing its original German 70/71/65 finish, the aircraft displays several markings oddities: there are no upperwing markings, the squadron number is on the wheel spats and the rudder cross is very truncated. Visible on the fuselage is the bomb and devil unit emblem*

68: *Front view of a 237ᵃ Squadriglia Junkers Ju 87B-2, probably at Lecce in November 1940*

69 Right: *The diving duck insigne of the 97° Gruppo, painted on the wheel spat of a Ju 87B. The duck wears glasses and carries a large bomb between its legs, with smaller bombs under its wings*

70 Far Right: *Taken at Trapani in Sicily in January 1941, this carefully posed picture shows Italian groundcrew refuelling a Junkers Ju 87R under the watchful eye of a Luftwaffe officer. There is some doubt as to whether the aircraft belongs to StG 2, which had recently arrived in the Mediterranean theatre, or has just been delivered to the RA. The elaborate emblem is suspected of being a propaganda fake*

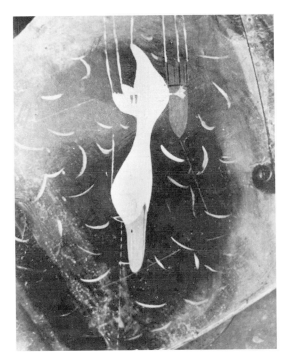

71 Left: *Reggiane Re 2002 fighter-bombers of the 239ª Squadriglia, 102° Gruppo, 5° Stormo Assalto, lined up at Reggio Emilia in May 1943. Thereafter the unit was transferred to Sicily, a few days before the Allied invasion. By September that year the unit had for all practical purposes been annihilated. The indistinct badge on the fin of the nearest machine may be the guitar-playing cockroach emblem of the Gruppo*

72 Left: *Fiat BR 20M of 241ª Squadriglia, 98° Gruppo, probably in late 1940. This unit formed part of the CAI for operations over England in the later stages of the Battle of Britain. The alpine scenery and early style markings seen here suggest that this picture may have been taken during the flight to Germany at the beginning of the campaign*

73 Below: *Another view of 241-5, MM 21532. This aircraft was one of the last of a batch of 44 built between September 1938 and February 1939*

85 GRUPPO RM

Squadriglie	146, 183, 188				
Stormo	Auto				

Arrival	Zone	Base	Country	Aircraft	Duties
10 Jun 40	ASAR	Elmas	Sardinia	Z501	AR, CE
Mar 42	ASIC	Augusta	Sicily	Z501 Z506B	
				RS14B	AR, TG
Jul 42	ASAR	Elmas	Sardinia	Z501 Z506B	
				RS14B	AS, AR
Jul 42	ASIC	Stagnone	Sicily	Z501 Z506B	AR, ASR,
				RS14B Ro43	CE
Apr 43	Sqa 4	Taranto	Italy	Z501 Z506B	
				RS14B	AR

On 16 June 1940 French bombers destroyed seven out of 18 Z501s, with 21 casualties, at Elmas. Six Z506Bs were sent in March 1941 to boost the unit's capability, despite which it disbanded that month.

A year later it reformed with 144 and 197 Sq. On 27 May 1942 it received the first RS14Bs. Numbers of these new aircraft were limited, however, and the unit had to continue with the trusty old Cant floatplanes. In July the unit moved to Sicily and joined the convoy battles of August, They kept an eye on the shipping and picked up naval crews and airmen stranded in the water. An Ro 43 was used for training and liaison at this time. Half a dozen of each combat plane were available, making it a maintenance nightmare. This afflicted most Regia Marina units where policy was to equip them with multiple types because of the unreliability of supply.

By April 1943 the squadriglie were replaced by 142, 196 and 288 Sq, mostly on RS14Bs. 196 Sq had been at Benghasi from 1 November, transferring to Italy on the 15th.

197 Sq became Autonomo and on 20 May formed 8 Sezione Aerea di Soccorso at Stagnone, solely for ASR duties. It then moved to Lago Patria by 23 July, disbanding on 6 August.

85 Gruppo was moved from Stagnone to Taranto as the Allies approached, in order to cover the Ionian and Basso Adriatico areas. A section was detached to Brindisi. At the time of surrender the Gruppo was withdrawing to the north, to completely re-equip with RS14Bs and to cover the Alto Tirreno area.

86 GRUPPO BM

Squadriglie	190, 191				
Stormo	35				

Arrival	Zone	Base	Country	Aircraft	Duties
10 Jun 40	4 ZAT	Brindisi	Italy	Z506B Z1007bis	AN
May 1941	AGRE	Atene Tatoi	Greece	Z1007bis SM82	AR, DB
Dec 41	Sqa 4	Brindisi	Italy	Z1007bis	TG
7 Apr 42	Sqa 5	Castelbenito	Tripolitania	Z1007bis	NB
May 42	Sqa 5	Barce	Cirenaica	Z1007bis	AR, DB, CE
13 Nov 42	Sqa 5	Bir Dufan	Tripolitania	Z1007bis	IT
7 Dec 42	Sqa 4	Gioia del Colle	Italy	Z1007bis	TG
1 Jun 43	Sqa 3	Perugia	Italy	Z1007bis	NB

This unit was formed in 1937, with the Z506B floatplane bomber arriving in November of that year. It supported the occupation of Albania.

In June 1940 the unit briefly flew against Bizerte port and its shipping, then concentrated on sea-warfare. On 9 July it attacked the Royal Navy cruiser HMS *Malaya* in the battle of Punto Stilo. The three days of this battle highlighted the lack of recognition by air and naval units which caused much confusion. This problem remained throughout most of the war.

The Gruppo joined the Greek campaign, and with an average nine out of twelve aircraft operational, continued fighting against the Yugoslavs. From 28 April to 1 May 1941 they assisted in the occupation of Corfu, Zante, and Cefalonia. On 30 April five Z506Bs ferried troops to Cefalonia as part of the occupying force. By 5 May the unit had moved to Greece for a brief stay, while converting to the Z1007bis land-based bomber. Two armed SM 82s were received for long range bombing in May. They were then passed to 145 Gruppo.

On 7 April 1942 the Gruppo was sent to Africa, to replace 13 Stormo. They received aircraft from the disbanding 176 Sq. Night attacks were carried out against Tobruk between April and June. On 22 May 191 Sq was detached to Derna. In May the Gruppo moved to Barce to begin reconnaissance and day bombing duties. 191 Sq was detached to Mersa Matruh on 15 July for reconnaissance missions. During July and August the unit carried out night escorts to convoys and covered the areas where fighters could not reach. The British Special Air Service raided Barce on 14 September and destroyed seven of 35 Stormo's aircraft. On the 20th they still had 8 aircraft at Mersa Matruh. Three were lost on the ground to bombing in October. Ten new aircraft were flown in that month to add to the sixteen 35 Stormo survivors. 191 Sq returned from its forward base on 6 November and the Gruppo then moved to Bir Dufan.

In December they withdrew to Italy, taking only seven aircraft with them, but passing the rest to 95 Gruppo. Armament on the Z1007bis was improved, with the two beam guns becoming 12.7mm in place of the original 7.7mm calibre.

On 1 June 1943 the unit transferred to the Raggruppamento Bombardamento.

87 GRUPPO BT

Squadriglie	192, 193
Stormo	30

Arrival	Zone	Base	Country	Aircraft	Duties
6 Jun 40	Sqa 2	Sciacca	Sicily	SM 79	DB, AR, AN
18 Jul 40	Sqa 2	Castelvetrano	Sicily	SM 79	TG
24 Jul 40	Sqa 2	Sciacca	Sicily	SM 79	NB, AR, DB, AN
27 Aug 41	Sqa 2	Forli	Italy	Z1007bis	TG
29 Jun 42	Sqa 4	Lecce	Italy	Z1007bis	TG
1 Jul 42	AEGE	Gadurra	Aegean	Z1007bis SM82	NB, AR, AN
7 Sep 42	AEGE	Marizza	Aegean	Z1007bis	NB, AR, AN, AS, CE
May 43	AEGE	Gadurra	Aegean	Z1007bis	AR, AS, CE
25 Jun 43	AEGE	Kalamaki	Aegean	Z1007bis	AR, AS, CE

The SM 79 was first received in 1938 and used in Albania the following year. On 12 June 1940 a SM 79 of 193 Sq carried out the unit's first sortie of the war—a ninety minute reconnaissance of Tunisian air bases. Bombing began the next day, in the same areas.

Operations over Malta began on 6 July, two aircraft being lost over La Valetta harbour four days later. The island's shipping routes were also attacked in July. As Sciacca was unsuitable for use at night, training for such duties was done at Castelvetrano. Night procedures subsequently used the latter for night take-off, and Sciacca for day landings and maintenance. The first of these sorties was made on 23 July. From 13 to 23 August the unit was busy training new crews. An escorted day raid over Malta was made the next day. More training then continued until 20 September.

Between January and March 1941 they were the only Italian bomber unit assisting the Germans in operations against Malta. With the night raids, armed reconnaissance, and day raids on shipping, the unit was kept very busy until August when they withdrew to Italy.

Following re-equipment and training with the Z1007bis the unit moved to the Aegean. Thus began a period of night raids on such targets as Port Said, Ismailia, Alexandria, and Cyprus. They also resumed day and night attacks on shipping in the eastern Mediterranean, along with reconnaissance for ships and aircraft missing in that area. In July 1942 five SM 82s of the Sezione Bombardamento Largo Raggio (Long Range Bomber Section) joined the unit for operations against Alexandria. From 15 December the Gruppo also made raids on Beirut, Tripoli, Tobruk, and Haifa.

From January 1943 armed reconnaissance missions were flown along the Syria-Palestine coastline together with convoy escorts and anti-submarine sorties in the Aegean area. These remained the regular duties of the unit until it disbanded on 25 August.

88 GRUPPO BT

Squadriglie	264, 265
Stormo	43

Arrival	Zone	Base	Country	Aircraft	Duties
13 Apr 42	Sqa 1	Bresso	Italy	BR 20M	TG
1 May 42	ASIC	Castelvetrano	Sicily	BR 20M Z1007bis	NB, TG
12 Aug 42	ASIC	Gerbini	Sicily	Z1007bis BR 20M	TG, NB
7 Nov 42	ASAR	Milis	Sardinia	Z1007bis	NB
31 Jan 43	Sqa 3	Viterbo	Italy	Z1007bis	TG
May 43	ASAR	Alghero	Sardinia	Z1007bis	NB
1 Jun 43	Sqa 3	Perugia San Egidio	Italy	Z1007bis	NB

In 1940 this Gruppo may have been at Vigna di Valle with Ro 44 floatplanes. However, it was reformed at Bresso under 43 Stormo and conducted night raids on Malta from May 1942. On 1 August they began receiving the Z1007bis and full conversion to this type was made by November. Initial operations with this new aircraft were over and around Malta. With full conversion the unit moved to Sardinia in time to operate against the Allied invasion forces off the Algerian and Tunisian coastline.

The Gruppo joined 16 Stormo on 31 January 1943. By May they were at Alghero. On 1 June 265 Sq joined the Raggruppamento Bombardamento at Perugia, leaving 264 Sq at Alghero until the Armistice.

89 GRUPPO BT

Squadriglie	228, 229
Stormo	32

Arrival	Zone	Base	Country	Aircraft	Duties
3 Jun 40	ASAR	Decimomannu	Sardinia	SM 79	DB, AN
Sep 41	Sqa 2	Bologna	Italy	SM 84	TG
28 May 42	Sqa 4	Gioia del Colle	Italy	SM 84	TB
1 Jun 42	Sqa 3	Capodichino	Italy	SM 84	TG
Aug 42	ASAR	Villacidro	Sardinia	SM 84	TB
Aug 42	Sqa 4	Gioia del Colle	Italy	SM 84	TG
6 Nov 42	ASAR	Alghero	Sardinia	SM 84	TB
30 Nov 42	Sqa 4	Gioia del Colle	Italy	SM 84	TG
Dec 42	ASAR	Decimomannu	Sardinia	SM 79	TB
May 43	ASAR	Milis	Sardinia	SM 79	TB
1 Jun 43	Sqa 3	Siena Ampugnano	Italy	SM 79	TG
16 Jul 43	Sqa 4	Lecce	Italy	SM 79	TB
30 Jul 43	Sqa 3	Siena	Italy	SM 79	TB

The SM 79 was received in early 1939 and this was the first unit, along with its sister 38 Gruppo, to operate against Tunisia, bombing Bizerte on 12 June 1940. The unit was used in attacks on shipping in July and August, including those against Force H from Gibraltar. The unit was kept busy from January to July 1941 attacking coastal convoys and warships from Gibraltar. Losses were building up so they left Sardinia for Italy in September. On 17 October they received SM 84 bombers in place of the faithful old SM 79. In March 228 Sq transfered to Capodichino under 2 NAS instructors. 229 Sq joined them on 1 May 1942 when they became Aerosilurante, detaching 13 S84s to Capodichino to pick up torpedoes and more crews. Its sister, 38 Gruppo, remained B.T. with the intention of the Stormo using both in combination attacks in order to split the defences.

Returning to Sardinia, on 12 August they attacked the Malta-bound PEDESTAL convoy. Four days later 228 Sq returned to Capodichino. In November Milis was also used as well as Alghero, during anti-invasion sorties against the Allied fleets. Twenty SM 84s were lost in these operations.

On 1 December ten SM 84s attacked Bone harbour, claiming 6 defending fighters but losing only two bombers.

On 14 December they took over the SM 79s of 108 Gruppo and became Autonomo on 10 January 1943. It had been discovered that the SM 84 had insufficient range and performance for torpedo-bombing, consequently the remaining aircraft were passed to 38 Gruppo and the older type reintroduced. Six aircraft were passed to 105 and 130 Gruppi at the end of January. On 28 February the new SM 79s were operating near Capo Bougaroni, often combining operations with other torpedo units such as 131 Gruppo and 205 Sq. By 5 April they had seven serviceable aircraft. On 1 June the squadriglie left for Italy to join the new specialist Raggruppamento Aerosilurante. 89 Gruppo disbanded on 8 August.

90 GRUPPO BT

| Squadriglie | 194, 195 |
| Stormo | 30 |

Arrival	Zone	Base	Country	Aircraft	Duties
6 Jun 40	Sqa 2	Sciacca	Sicily	SM 79	DB, AR, AN
18 Jul 40	Sqa 2	Castelvetrano	Sicily	SM 79	TG
24 Jul 40	Sqa 2	Sciacca	Sicily	SM 79	NB, AR, DB, AN, CE
7 Sep 41	Sqa 2	Forli	Italy	Z1007bis	TG
22 Aug 42	Sqa 4	Lecce	Italy	Z1007bis	TG
23 Aug 42	AEGE	Gadurra	Aegean	Z1007bis	NB, AR, AN
Jan 43	AEGE	Marizza	Aegean	Z1007bis	CE, AR, AN, AS
May 43	AEGE	Gadurra	Aegean	Z1007bis	CE, AR, AS
18 Jun 43	AEGE	Kalamaki	Aegean	Z1007bis	AR, CE
25 Jun 43	AEGE	Marizza	Aegean	Z1007bis	AR

The SM 79 was received in 1938 and used during the occupation of Albania in April 1939. During June 1940 missions were carried out against Tunisian ports, bases, and shipping. A Breda 39 was used for liaison duties and joy-riding.

From 30 June they turned to Malta and its supply

routes. Night training took place from 18 to 23 July, with operations resuming that night. Sciacca was used by day and Castelvetrano by night. Training interrupted operations during August and September, but Malta was still repeatedly attacked in this period. On 16 December a section was detached to Catania. Hampered by bad weather, The Gruppo managed to carry out its allotted shipping reconnaissance and Malta attacks until recalled to Italy for re-equipment.

After several months training they moved to the Aegean to assist 87 Gruppo with reconnaissance and night bombing in the eastern Mediterranean. Apart from ship-hunting, attacks were made on Cyprus, Egypt, Syria, Palestine, and Tripoli. From January 1943 they joined in armed reconnaissance along the Syria-Palestine coastline, as well as convoy escorts and anti-submarine patrols among the Aegean Islands.

On 25 August they became Autonomo when 30 Stormo disbanded. For the last two months before the Armistice they made mainly reconnaissance missions around the Greek islands.

92 GRUPPO BT

| Squadriglie | 200, 201 |
| Stormo | 39 |

Arrival	Zone	Base	Country	Aircraft	Duties
10 Jun 40	AEGE	Marizza	Aegean	SM 81	AN, DB, NB
Nov 40	AEGE	Gadurra	Aegean	SM 81 SM82	AN, NB

This unit was formed on 1 November 1938 at Marizza. During the early months of the war they were very active against shipping in the eastern Mediterranean and targets in Egypt.

On 8 July 1940 they participated in the Battaglia de Punta Stilo, attacking ships leaving Malta for Alexandria. The latter port was regularly attacked from June to October. On 19 July they assisted in damaging the destroyer HMS *Havock*.

Two SM 82s arrived from 41 Gruppo on 5 November for long range bombing sorties. From February to April 1941 the Gruppo made several night attacks on Crete, in support of the imminent German invasion.

Sometime afterwards the unit appears to have ceased operations.

93 GRUPPO BM

| Squadriglie | 196, 197 |
| Stormo | 31 |

Arrival	Zone	Base	Country	Aircraft	Duties
10 Jun 40	ASAR	Elmas	Sardinia	Z506B	AN, DB
41	Sqa		Italy		TG

This unit, having flown the Z506B since November 1937, joined in bombing operations against the French.

By early 1941 they were withdrawn with the intention of re-equipping with the Z1007bis.

196 Sq was at Benghasi from the summer of 1941, moving to Pisida for the first half of 1942, then back to Benghasi from July to September. In the latter months they were only able to use the Z501s. They used Z501s and Z506Bs on ASR and CE duties, before joining 85 Gruppo in Italy.

94 GRUPPO BM

Squadriglie	198
Stormo	31

Arrival	Zone	Base	Country	Aircraft	Duties
10 Jun 40	ASAR	Elmas	Sardinia	Z506B	AN, DB
41	Sqa		Italy		TG

This unit flew bombing sorties against the French, joined by 199 Sq in July for shipping attacks. By early 1941 they were withdrawn with the intention of re-equipping with Z1007bis.

95 GRUPPO BM

Squadriglie	230, 231
Stormo	35

Arrival	Zone	Base	Country	Aircraft	Duties
10 Jun 40	4 ZAT	Brindisi	Italy	Z506B Z1007bis	AN
9 Apr 42	Sqa 5	Benghasi	Cirenaica	Z1007bis SM82	NB
21 Apr 42	Sqa 5	Barce	Cirenaica	Z1007bis	AR, DB, CE
13 Nov 42	Sqa 5	Bir Dufan	Tripolitania	Z1007bis	AR, NB
7 Dec 42	Sqa 5	El Asabaa	Tripolitania	Z1007bis	NB
9 Jan 43	Sqa 5	Misurata	Tripolitania	Z1007bis	IT
9 Jan 43	Sqa 4	Gioia del Colle	Italy	Z1007bis	TG
25 Jun 43	Sqa 2	Bologna	Italy	Z1007bis	NB

This unit was formed in 1937 with the Z506B floatplane bomber and supported the occupation of Albania. In June 1940 they carried out anti-shipping sorties, including involvement in the Battaglia de Punta Stilo on 9 July.

The unit joined the Greek and Yugoslav campaigns. On 16 January 1941 it began converting to the Z1007bis Series II. In May six aircraft of 231 Sq were detached to Marizza for operations over Crete. By 5 May the unit had moved to Greece for a brief stay while conversion to the Z1007bis continued.

In April 1942 they were sent to Africa to replace 13 Stormo. Night attacks were carried out against Tobruk between April and June. Some SM 82s were borrowed from a Trasporto Gruppo for long range bombing. The Gruppo then moved to Barce to begin reconnaissance, night convoy escorts and day bombing duties. 86 Gruppo passed their remaining bombers over at Bir Dufan before returning to Italy. The unit then began night raids on Sirte and Ara Fileni. Then they joined their sister Gruppo in January, with nine surviving aircraft.

At this time the armament of the Z1007bis was improved, all guns now becoming 12.7mm calibre. By September, however, they had only one aircraft operational, at Bologna.

96 GRUPPO BaT

Squadriglie	236, 237
Stormo	Auto

Arrival	Zone	Base	Country	Aircraft	Duties
3 Jun 40	Sqa 2	Pantelleria	Sicily	SM 85	TG
22 Aug 40	Sqa 2	Comiso	Sicily	Ju 87B SM 86W	AN, DB
27 Oct 40	Sqa 4	Lecce Galatina	Italy	Ju 87B SM 86W	DB
8 Jan 41	ASIC	Comiso	Sicily	Ju 87B	IT
Jan 41	Sqa 5	Castelbenito	Tripolitania	Ju 87B Ju 87R	IT
2 Feb 41	Sqa 5	Misurata	Tripolitania	Ju 87B Ju 87R	TG
2 Feb 41	Sqa 5	Benghazi	Cirenaica	Ju 87B Ju 87R	DB
Feb 41	Sqa 5	Bir Dufan		Ju 87B Ju 87R	DB

In June 1940 this was Italy's only dive-bomber unit, having been formed on 20 March with ex-fighter pilots. It was considered they had the qualities required for successful dive-bombing. However, the 14 SM 85s were considered unstable and non-operational, the humid conditions subsequently proving too much for their wooden airframes. This type had been rushed into service in order that the Regia Aeronautica could claim to have a dive-bomber, an aircraft type which was fast becoming *de rigeur* for most air force politicians by then. On 1 July pilots were sent to Graz in Austria to learn to fly the Ju 87. The following month 15 of these were received and the unit took them to Sicily. Because of the urgency from High Command to get units into action, the crews only completed 15 out of the 25 hours of the German training programme.

Operations began on 2 September with attacks on the Royal Navy, west of Malta. Three days later the first sorties over the island of Malta were carried out. September was a very busy initiation month for this unit. In addition to the normal raids, they assisted in trials with an uprated SM 85, the SM 86W which was attached to 236 Sq. This was also a twin-engined dive-bomber and was flown by test-pilot Elio Scarpini on raids over Malta. The Gruppo lost its first aircraft on 17 September, when a Hurricane from 261 Squadron, RAF, shot down a Ju 87B-2 of 237 Sq.

On 27 October the unit was transferred to Italy to join the campaign against Greece until 7 January 1941. The prototype SM 86W was known to have been used over this front, along with the unit's 20 Ju 87Bs. The test pilot was lost in action, flying a Ju 87B during the campaign. It appears the SM 86W was abandoned at Lecce, Galatina. On 11 November eight aircraft were returned to Comiso to form the nucleus of 97 Gruppo.

The unit was now called to action in Africa, arriving there via Sicily on 30 January 1941. 236 Sq, with 5 aircraft, arrived at Castelbenito on 1 February, via Comiso and Pantelleria. 237 Sq flew in with 5 more aircraft to Misurata the next day. Due to the low number of serviceable aircraft, and despite the urgent situation, they were put mainly on training duties, but did operate over Tobruk. The supply situation was critical and so they spent the next three months building up their strength, but ended up disbanding on 15 April. 236 Sq had become Autonomo in February, receiving 237 Squadriglia's aircraft in April.

97 GRUPPO BaT

Squadriglie	238, 239
Stormo	Auto

Arrival	Zone	Base	Country	Aircraft	Duties
Jul 40	Sqa 4	Lecce	Italy	Ju 87B	TG
Aug 40		Graz	Austria	Ju 87B	TG
22 Sep 40	Sqa 1	Lonate Pozzolo	Italy	Ju 87R	TG
Nov 40	Sqa 4	Lecce	Italy	Ju 87R	TG
20 Nov 40	Sqa 2	Comiso	Sicily	Ju 87R	AN
7 Dec 40	Sqa 4	Lecce Galatina	Italy	Ju 87R	DB, AN
15 Mar 43	Sqa 3	Ciampino Sud	Italy	Ro 57bis	TG
19 Jun 43	Sqa 4	Crotone	Italy	Ro 57Bis Ba201	
				Z1018	DF, CE, AS
13 Jul 43	Sqa 3	Tarquinia	Italy	Ro 57bis	DF
Aug 43	Sqa 1	Lonate Pozzolo	Italy	Ro 57bis	TG

This unit formed in November 1940 to supplement 96 Gruppo, who passed them some of their aircraft. They were given the longer ranging version of the Ju 87 (the Ju 87R), and began a successful period of anti-shipping operations around Maltese waters. The CR 42s of 23 Gruppo provided escort when possible.

On 7 December 239 Sq moved to Lecce and 238 Sq to Grottaglie, to support the campaign against Greece. 238 Sq flew to Tirana on 3 March and on 1 April exchanged places with 209 Sq in 101 Gruppo. While 209 Sq stayed at Galatina, 239 Sq, with ten aircraft, was detached to Jesi from 10 to 14 April for operations against Yugoslavia under Squadra 2. When hostilities ceased in the Balkans

the unit briefly patrolled the Mediterranean then disbanded on 7 May. The two squadriglie became Autonomo.

During this period, the commander of 239 Sq, Guiseppe Cenni, developed the tactic of skip-bombing, by pulling out of a dive very low to fly horizontally at the target, thus giving the released bomb added momentum to skim the surface into a ship's hull. The technique demanded very accurate flying.

On 15 March 1943 a new 97 Gruppo, with 226 and 227 Sq, appeared as an Intercettori Gruppo. They received the twin-engined Ro 57bis at Ciampino. This aircraft proved incapable of carrying out its intended function due to poor climb and speed, so a dive-bomber adaptation was made. The pilots began training in ground attack and air-to-air bombing. The unit operated over Sicily in the battles of June 1943. During that month they also received the single-engined Breda 201 second prototype, for comparative trials with the Ro 57bis. This new type was equipped with the Daimler-Benz DB601 engine. Such was the state of Italy's industries by now, that even good designs could not be produced in any numbers. The unit also tried out the night-fighter version of the Z1018 bomber (MM24824), but this had inefficient engines.

226 Sq received eight new pilots in May. They were very young and the difficulty of learning to use the Ro 57bis was aggravated by low serviceability. They needed to train further on G 50s, then progress to the Ro 57bis.

In June the unit made one scramble and carried out one convoy escort, and two anti-submarine missions. On 13 July 1943 ten of the 15 Ro 57bis at Crotone were lost in a B-24 bombing raid. Four surviving serviceable aircraft moved to Tarquinia, and were kept serviceable by spares from Ciampino and Capodichino.

The Gruppo disbanded on 10 August 1943.

98 GRUPPO BT

Squadriglie	240, 241
Stormo	43

Arrival	Zone	Base	Country	Aircraft	Duties
10 Jun 40	Sqa 1	Camera	Italy	BR 20	DB
27 Sep 40	CAI	Frankfurt	Germany	BR 20M	IT
Oct 40	CAI	Chievres	Belgium	BR 20M	DB
Jan 41	Sqa 1	Cameri	Italy	BR 20M	TG
11 Mar 41	Sqa 5	Castelbenito	Tripolitania	BR 20M	IT
11 Mar 41	Sqa 5	Bir Dufan	Tripolitania	BR 20M	NB
5 Apr 41	Sqa 5	Benghasi K2	Cirenaica	BR 20M	NB
7 May 41	Sqa 5	Barce	Cirenaica	BR 20M	NB
20 Jul 41	Sqa 5	Castelbenito	Tripolitania	BR 20M	CE
14 Dec 41	Sqa 2	Reggio Emilia	Italy	BR 20M	TG
42	AALB	Lubiana	Yugoslavia	BR 20M	AG

Arrival	Zone	Base	Country	Aircraft	Duties1
Aug 42	Sqa 2	Ronchi	Italy	BR 20M	TG
Jan 43	Sqa 1	Cameri	Italy	SM 84	TG
May 43	Sqa 1	Bresso	Italy	SM 84	TG
28 May 43	Sqa 1	Cervere	Italy	SM 84	TG
2 Jul 43	Sqa 1	Lonate Pozzolo	Italy	SM 84	TG
21 Jul 43	Sqa 4	Gioia del Colle	Italy	SM 84	AN

This unit was formed in December 1939 and began operations the following June against France.

On 27 September they set off for Belgium, but bad weather scattered them over Germany on the way. Poor navigational training and inadequate instruments resulted in an indifferent performance over Belgium and England. The first raid was on the night of 24 October, against the town of Harwich. Along with 99 Gruppo they carried out two daylight raids: on 29 October against Ramsgate and 11 November against Harwich. The latter was intercepted with the loss of three bombers and three escorting CR 42s. Between 5 November and 2 January 1941 they also made several night raids on Ipswich and Harwich when the weather allowed. After three months they were recalled to Italy. Mussolini had ill-prepared them for a modern campaign.

The next call came to Africa, where the unit's 12 BR 20Ms replaced the SM 81s of 54 Gruppo on night bomber duties in March 1941. The first operation was on the 17th, against Benghasi. On the 31st they made their first day raid. This was against Agedabia, with an escort of Bf 110s of 7./ZG 26. They were intercepted by Hurricanes of 3 Squadron, RAAF, and two bombers and one fighter were downed. The bomber crews were relieved at the relatively light losses, as it was Hurricanes that had severely dealt with them over England.

On 5 April they began night raids on Tobruk, followed by sorties along the Egyptian coast in May. The Gruppo became Autonomo that month. On 25th, eight aircraft made a rare day raid on Agedabia, under escort from Bf 110s of ZG 26 and G 50s of 2 Gruppo. July found them in need of a reduction in pace, so they were transferred to escorting convoys to and from Tripoli.

After recuperating in Italy they were sent to Yugoslavia for a tour of anti-partisan duties. This meant bombing strongholds, protecting motor convoys, and reconnaissance work.

Back in Italy the old BR 20Ms were passed to 63 Gruppo and the unit now came under Squadra 1. Conversion was made to SM 84s, although they were not as popular as the previous aircraft. On 11 July 1943 they used the new aircraft against the invasion forces off Sicily. By 7 September they still had nine aircraft operational.

99 GRUPPO BT

Squadriglie 242, 243
Stormo 43

Arrival	Zone	Base	Country	Aircraft	Duties
10 Jun 40	Sqa 1	Cameri	Italy	BR 20	DB
27 Sep 40	CAI	Frankfurt	Germany	BR 20M	IT
Oct 40	CAI	Chievres	Belgium	BR 20M	DB
Jan 41	Sqa 1	Cameri	Italy	BR 20M	TG
7 Apr 41	Sqa 2	Vicenza	Italy	BR 20M	DB
41	Sqa 2	Forli	Italy	BR 20M	IT
41	Sqa 1	Lonate Pozzolo	Italy	BR 20M	IT
7 May 41	ASIC	Gerbini	Sicily	BR 20M	NB
Jul 42	Sqa 1	Milano Bresso	Italy	SM 84	TG
Jan 43	Sqa 1	Levaldigi	Italy	SM 84	AN
May 43	Sqa 1	Bresso	Italy	SM 84	TG
4 Jun 43	Sqa 1	Lagnasco	Italy	SM 84	TG
11 Jun 43	Sqa 1	Cervere	Italy	SM 84	AN
2 Jul 43	Sqa 1	Lonate Pozzolo	Italy	SM 84	AN
21 Jul 43	Sqa 4	Gioia del Colle	Italy	SM 84	AN
28 Jul 43	Sqa 1	Lonate Pozzolo	Italy	SM 84	AN

Following a similar history to 98 Gruppo, this unit was formed in December 1939 and began operations in June 1940 against France.

On 27 September they transferred to Belgium, along with 98 Gruppo, for what was intended to be a triumphal assault against a weakened foe. Bad weather along the way, however, dispersed the aircraft from both Gruppi all over Germany. In concert with 98 Gruppo, they began operations on 24 October, with a night raid on Harwich. Five days later they made their first daylight raid, escorted by 56 Stormo, with an attack on Ramsgate. They met no opposition but did little damage. After three months they returned to Italy, having discovered that both their training and equipment were inadequate to cope with spirited opposition and the English winter weather.

In April the Gruppo, with 14 aircraft, began operations against Yugoslavia. They subsequently received some ex-Yugoslav Bücker Bü 131 *Jungmann* trainers as spoils of war.

The following month they went to Sicily for night raids on Malta. By this time the Gruppo was Autonomo. Within their limited capabilities they kept up a sporadic nightly effort until the fighter opposition became too strong.

Back to Italy and conversion to the SM 84. Their BR 20Ms went to 63 Gruppo in the Balkans. They were in action again during the Allied invasion of Sicily but after a month had to withdraw to the north to recuperate. On 7 September 1943 they had just seven aircraft on strength.

101 GRUPPO BaT
Squadriglie   208, 209
Stormo   Autonomo

Arrival	Zone	Base	Country	Aircraft	Duties
5 Mar 41	Sqa 1	Lonate Pozzolo	Italy	Ju 87B	TG
20 Mar 41	Sqa 4	Lecce Galatina	Italy	Ju 87B	DB
2 Apr 41	AALB	Tirana	Albania	Ju 87R	AR, DB, AS
28 May 41	Sqa 4	Lecce	Italy	Ju 87R	IT
29 May 41	ASIC	Reggio Calabria	Italy	Ju 87R	IT
29 May 41	ASIC	Trapani Milo	Sicily	Ju 87R	TG, AN, NB
7 Dec 41	Sqa 1	Lonate Pozzolo	Italy	Ju 87R Breda 88	
				CR 42	TG

Arrival	Zone	Base	Country	Aircraft	Duties
4 Jul 42	Sqa 3	Ciampino Sud	Italy	CR 42	IT
5 Jul 42	Sqa 3	Capodichino	Italy	CR 42	IT
6 Jul 42	ASIC	Gerbini Nord	Sicily	CR 42	CE
15 Jul 42	ASIC	Pantelleria	Sicily	CR 42	CE
21 Jul 42	Sqa 5	Castelbenito	Tripolitania	CR 42	IT
24 Jul 42	Sqa 5	Tamet	Tripolitania	CR 42	IT
24 Jul 42	Sqa 5	Benghasi K1	Cirenaica	CR 42	IT
25 Jul 42	Sqa 5	Derna	Cirenaica	CR 42	CE
22 Aug 42	Sqa 5	Abu Nimeir	Egypt	CR 42	GA, NF, AR, NB
31 Oct 42	Sqa 5	Abu Smeit	Egypt	CR 42	CE, AR, NB
5 Nov 42	Sqa 5	Bir el Astas	Egypt	CR 42	IT
6 Nov 42	Sqa 5	Bu Amud	Cirenaica	CR 42	AR
11 Nov 42	Sqa 5	Agedabia	Cirenaica	CR 42	AR
13 Nov 42	Sqa 5	En Nofilia	Tripolitania	CR 42	GA
4 Dec 42	Sqa 5	Buerat	Tripolitania	CR 42	IT
6 Dec 42	Sqa 5	Misurata	Tripolitania	CR 42	IT
8 Dec 42	ASIC	Gerbini	Sicily	CR 42	IT
13 Dec 42	Sqa 1	Lonate Pozzolo	Italy	G 50 Re 2001	
				Re 2002	TG
11 Jul 43	Sqa 4	Crotone	Italy	Re 2002	AN, AR, DF
14 Jul 43	Sqa 4	Manduria	Italy	Re 2002	AN, AR, DF

101 Gruppo Bombardamento at Tuffo formed on 5 March 1941. Two days later 208 Sq arrived, followed by 209 Sq on 15 March. Training on the Ju 87B began with help from the crews of 97 Gruppo at Lecce. SM 81s were attached for liaison and transport work.

On 9 March 208 Sq began operations over Albania, from Lecce, while detached for operational training with 239 Sq. 209 Sq joined them on 18 March. The Gruppo officially moved on 20th March to Lecce for operations against Greece. From 14 March they had received long range fuel tanks, enabling much more action when the weather allowed. To further increase time over the front the unit moved to Albania.

On 1 April 209 Sq exchanged places with 238 Sq in 97 Gruppo. Raids began on 12 April using Scutari and Scjak as forward bases. After several bombing missions, from 22 April they made armed reconnaissance and anti-submarine patrols until the 30th. After one more reconnaissance on 5 May they prepared to transfer to Sicily. During the Balkan campaigns from 12 to 15 aircraft

were kept operational out of 20.

Picking up new Ju 87Rs on the way, the Gruppo arrived in Trapani and began training for operations over and around Malta. Night training started on 5 July. The first mission was on 23rd, against shipping off Malta. Gela was used as a forward base. From 5 August up to six Ju 87Rs were detached to Comiso for night sorties over Malta until September. The aircraft returned to Trapani where the whole unit carried on the same operations until 4 September, with occasional day raids against shipping in September and October. From 18 to 25 November 239 Sq was temporarily attached to this Gruppo. On the 21st the first day raid over Malta was made with MC 200 escorts.

A call for help sent a detachment to Castelbenito. On 29 November the detachment moved on to Benghasi, then to Derna on 8 December. The whole Gruppo returned to Italy in December for a rest and re-equipment. On 20 February 1942 the unit changed title to 101 Gruppo Tuffatori and on 15 May joined 5 Stormo, along with 102 Gruppo. Meanwhile, two Breda 88s were received for trials, followed on 27 April by the assault version of the CR 42.

With Castelvetrano as a forward base, operations began again on 10 July with convoy escorting in the Sicilian Straits. Pantelleria was used by detachments from the 17th.

Another detachment of five CR 42s operated from Castelbenito (26th), Tamet (29th), Benghasi (31st), and Derna (1st August) where they rejoined the Gruppo. From 25th to 31st August four aircraft were detached to Fuka as night fighter protection to 4 Stormo. From 27th ground attack and armed reconnaissance missions began. Night sorties started on 3 September, with an attack on Halam el Halfa. Losses were suffered on the ground at this time from various bombardments. During the El Alamein battles the unit maintained a busy period of night raids. By 20 September they still had 20 aircraft on charge. On 27 October forty-two CR 42s of the Gruppo and 50 Stormo tried a day raid, but met seventy P-40s. 101 Gruppo lost one aircraft with a further eight damaged, so they reverted to night operations. By 30 October they had 18 serviceable CR 42s out of 32, and moved to Abu Smeit (LG15) the next day. On 4 December SM 82s began transferring unit personnel back to Italy. From the 9th the crews were traveling via Naples, Rome, Bologna, Milano, Gallarate, along with the Comando 5 Stormo.

On 2 January Fiat G 50Bs arrived. These were the two-seat trainer versions of the G 50 fighter, and were for training in anticipation of conversion to the Ju 87D. However, Re 2001s, together with one or two D.520s and MC 202s, followed on 6 February for use until June. On 15 April the next operational type flew in—the Re 2002 *Ariete*. The CO of 208 Sq made the first flight on 17 April and expressed his pleasure with Italy's latest fighter-bomber.

With the urgency to repel the Allied invasion of Sicily the unit was sent into action on 12 July with sorties against the invasion fleet and armed reconnaissances. This continued through to the mainland invasion. The unit was also used for bomber interception during this period. Botricello and Crotone were used as forward bases in August. With mixed fortunes and only eleven Re 2002s left, they flew their last operation on 4 September.

102 GRUPPO Tuff

| Squadriglie | 209, 239 |
| Stormo | Autonomo |

Arrival	Zone	Base	Country	Aircraft	Duties
1 May 42	Sqa 1	Lonate Pozzolo	Italy	Ju 87R	TG, AN
23 May 42	Sqa 3	Capodichino	Italy	Ju 87R	IT
24 May 42	ASIC	Gela	Sicily	Ju 87R	NB, AN
13 Jun 42	ASIC	Sciacca	Sicily	Ju 87R	IT
14 Jun 42	ASIC	Chinisia	Sicily	Ju 87R	AN
15 Jun 42	ASIC	Gela	Sicily	Ju 87R	AN, NB
15 Jul 42	ASIC	Castelvetrano	Sicily	Ju 87R	AN
16 Jul 42	ASIC	Gela	Sicily	Ju 87R	NB
11 Aug 42	ASIC	Castelvetrano	Sicily	Ju 87R	IT
12 Aug 42	ASIC	Pantelleria	Sicily	Ju 87R	AN
13 Aug 42	ASIC	Castelvetrano	Sicily	Ju 87R	AN
13 Aug 42	ASIC	Gela	Sicily	Ju 87R	AN
18 Aug 42	ASIC	Chinisia	Sicily	Ju 87R	AN, AS
18 Aug 42	ASIC	Gela	Sicily	Ju 87R Re 2001CN	NB
25 Oct 42	ASIC	Sciacca	Sicily	Ju 87R	NB
7 Nov 42	Sqa 1	Lonate Pozzolo	Italy	CR 42 G 50bis	
				Re 2001 Re 2002	TG
May 43	Sqa 2	Reggio Emilia	Italy	Re 2002	TG
19 Jun 43	Sqa 3	Tarquinia	Italy	Re 2002	TG
10 Jul 43	Sqa 4	Crotone	Italy	Re 2002	AN GA
16 Jul 43	Sqa 4	Manduria	Italy	Re 2002	DF, AN, GA
20 Aug 43	Sqa 4	Crotone	Italy	Re 2002	DF, GA, AN
3 Sep 43	Sqa 4	Manduria	Italy	Re 2002	DF, GA, AN

This unit was formed on 1 May 1942, with 209 Sq from 97 Gruppo and 239 Sq from 101 Gruppo. From 8 May they were on standby for operations against ships in the Alto Tirreno, using Villanova d'Albenga as a staging base until 14 May.

Moving via Capodichino with 18 Ju 87 bombers and an SM 81 transport to Sicily, it began operations over the Sicilian Canal and Malta. The first mission was a night raid on Malta on 28 May. Similar operations continued through to 10 June. Problems arose with the Ju 87's artificial horizon, which made night attacks tricky. As a result the unit switched to daylight missions against Malta and its convoys, often with an escort of MC 202s from 155 Gruppo. On 14 June nine aircraft of 209 Sq and eight of 239 Sq attacked the HARPOON convoy off Cape

Blanc, losing only one Ju 87 which was damaged by flak and ran out of fuel before reaching base. The next day ten aircraft attacked the convoy, losing one aircraft from 239 Sq, but a gunner from 209 Sq claimed a Spitfire from Malta. Despite five days of intensive operations, no ships were hit and the Gruppo was reduced to six serviceable aircraft out of 31. Only two aircraft were lost in direct action. On the 17th Monserrato in Sardinia was used as a forward base.

On 20 June aircraft were detached to Caltagirone to join in the ceremony to award crew members for actions against the recent convoys. More ceremonies followed four days later, with the Cape Governor celebrating the success in what was now known as the 'Battaglia aeronavale di Pantelleria' between 14 and 16 June.

Night operations resumed over Malta from 24 June. Receipt of new radio equipment was hoped to improve success. On 15 July the unit moved with 15 Ju 87s and an SM 81 for operations in the Tunisian Gulf, returning to Gela the next day. In August they were heavily involved in attacks on the PEDESTAL convoy, attacking both incoming and outgoing ships. The vital oil tanker *Ohio* limped into Malta's harbour with one of the Gruppo aircraft embedded in its upper decking. On the 13th sixteen aircraft had attacked and one had crashed into the tanker, brought down by anti-aircraft fire. From 25 August an Re 2001CN nightfighter was attached to the unit, to escort night raids on Malta. The unit lost ten crews over Malta between May and September. From 9 to 19 October German technicians arrived to check the aircraft and discuss the night-flying problems.

Returning to Italy to rest and re-equip with Ju 87D3s, two Ju 87s were detached to Alghero for anti-shipping sorties between 8 and 20 November. On 27 December 239 Sq was detached to Reggio Emilia for training on the G 50bis, then Re 2002 fighter-bombers. 209 Sq stayed at Lonate Pozzolo where it received training on the CR 42, G 50bis, Re 2001, then the Re 2002. The latter arrived on 8 March 1943. By the end of that month the Gruppo had 19 Re 2002s (MM7311-29). On 19 June 239 Sq moved to Tarquinia with ten Re 2002s, and 209 Sq joined them two days later with twelve Re 2002s and a Saiman 202 liaison aircraft.

With the launch of the Sicilian invasion the Gruppo was committed to action on 10 July, flying that day to Crotone with 20 fighter-bombers. 209 Sq stopped at Capua on the way, due to bad weather. On 12 July the whole unit bombed and strafed landing forces in support of German paratroops on the Catania Plain. Due to bomb damage to Crotone in July, the unit gradually withdrew to Manduria via Tortorella, all reuniting by 16 July. Several bomber intercepts were flown at this time, but the confusing information received by the inexperienced intercepting pilots during those chaotic days greatly reduced the chances of actual interception and combat.

By 1 August repaired Re 2002s reinforced the unit and operations were resumed against invasion shipping, ground forces, and enemy bombers.

A detachment was sent to Botricello, 10 km south of Crotone, between 1 and 23 August. This was the last usable airstrip, and not yet spotted by the Allies. 101 Gruppo also used this base, on 2 August. Escorts of MC 202s from 21 Gruppo were used over the Messina area during August.

With the invasion of mainland Italy under way, the unit began opposing shipping off Calabria from 6 August. The unit's 'hack' Ca 133 was still flying men and equipment between Manduria and Sicily on 24 August. On 3 September aircraft were detached to Crotone, and while returning that day to Manduria, three of them, together with nine from 101 Gruppo, flew the unit's last sorties of the war. They strafed and bombed ships near Reggia Calabria, but were then bounced by Spitfires who shot down three for the loss of four. One of those lost was the Gruppo commander, *Maggiore* Giuseppe Cenni, who had survived over 100 operations as one of Italy's top dive-bomber experts. The Gruppo had lost more air crews in the last two months of war, than in the previous twelve.

103 GRUPPO BaT
Squadriglie 207, 237
Stormo Autonomo

Arrival	Zone	Base	Country	Aircraft	Duties
1 Feb 43	Sqa 3	Siena Ampugnano	Italy	Ju 87D-3	TG
18 May 43	ASAR	Decimomannu	Sardinia	Ju 87D-3	NB
24 May 43	ASAR	Chilivani	Sardinia	Ju 87D-3	NB
Jul 43	ASIC	Chinisia	Sicily	Ju 87D-3	AN
14 Jul 43	Sqa 3	Capua	Italy	Ju 87D-3	IT
15 Jul 43	Sqa 3	Siena Ampugnano	Italy	Ju 87D-3	IT
20 Aug 43	Sqa 1	Lonate Pozzolo	Italy	Ba88M	TG

This unit formed on 1 February 1943 to use the new version of the German Ju 87. In mid-April twelve Ju 87D-3s arrived from Graz, in Austria, followed by six more on the 21st. The latter were flown by Italians to Bari-Palese for inspection by the Air Ministry on the 20th, and then to Siena the next day. With German technical help, the unit began intensive training.

In May they moved to Sardinia for anti-shipping and night raiding missions. The night they arrived at Decimomannu, they were bombed and reduced to six operational aircraft. They shortly moved base to escape further bombing. On 10 July four Ju 87Ds of 207 Sq flew to Decimomannu, joining seven escorting fighters from 51 Stormo, and set off to tackle the invasion fleet at Licata Bay. They met 50 enemy fighters, but some ships were hit and all four bombers managed to land at Chinisia. The following day 237 Sq transferred from Gioia del Colle to

Crotone with five aircraft to take on shipping off the Calabria area. The unit then passed its remaining nine aircraft to the newly formed 121 Gruppo.

The next month the unit retired to the north to test the Breda 88M, a rebuilt version of the unsuccessful ground attack aircraft of 1940. They had two of these serviceable on 7 September.

104 GRUPPO BT
Squadriglie 252, 253
Stormo 46

Arrival	Zone	Base	Country	Aircraft	Duties
10 Jun 40	Sqa 3	Pisa San Giusto	Italy	SM 79	DB
4 Nov 40	AALB	Tirana	Albania	SM 79	DB
Nov 40	AALB	Scutari	Albania	SM 79	DB
14 Apr 41	Sqa 4	Foggia	Italy	SM 79	DB
May 42	Sqa 3	Pisa San Giusto	Italy	SM 79	TG
13 Jun 42	ASAR	Decimomannu	Sardinia	SM 79	TB
Jun 42	Sqa 3	Pisa	Italy	SM 79	TB
3 Jul 42	AEGE	Gadurra	Aegean	SM 79	TB, AR
12 Jul 43	Sqa 4	Lecce Galatina	Italy	SM 79	TB
23 Jul 43	Sqa 2	Rimini	Italy	SM 79	IT, AR
25 Jul 43	Sqa 3	Siena Ampugnano	Italy	SM 79	TB
13 Aug 43	Sqa 4	Lecce	Italy	SM 79	TB
27 Aug 43	Sqa 3	Siena	Italy	SM 79	TB

This Gruppo formed on 15 February 1940 with 15 SM 79 bombers. In June they made bombing raids on Corsica, escorted by G 50s of 51 Stormo, and on 21 June nine SM 79s bombed Marseilles naval port.

The unit adopted several camouflage finishes, from banded to mottled in the same squadriglia, as new colour orders filtered through from H.Q. In November they transferred to the Balkans for operations over Greece and Yugoslavia. To save weight the bombers reduced their defensive weapons from four to two, despite several combats with RAF Gladiators. The winter produced heavy snows which reduced the number of operations, but some bombing was still undertaken. Escorting G 50s joined in with ground strafing.

On 1 May 1942 the unit became Aerosilurante and the more experienced crews were sent to Sardinia in June for operations against the HARPOON convoy. On 14 June four aircraft out of twelve were lost, with *Medaglia d'Oro* being posthumously awarded to *Tenente* Ingrellini and *Sergente Maggiore* Compiani. On 3 July the whole Gruppo went to the Aegean to operate against shipping in the eastern Mediterranean. They made armed reconnaissance sorties as far as Haifa, Port Said, and Port Alexander. On 1 September they became Autonomo, often co-operating with Fliegerkorps X on convoy attacks and reconnaissance missions.

By 1 January 1943 they had 8 operational aircraft at Gadurra, on day and night reconnaissance missions along the eastern and central African coastlines. On 15 February two SM 79s were intercepted by P-39s between Tobruk and Mersa Matruh, claiming one fighter shot down. By 20 March six aircraft were still operational out of thirteen.

From January to March crews were transferred between Kalamaki and Gadurra for night training by instructors from 1 and 3 NAS. Despite the setting up at the start of the war of a Blind Flying School (La Scuola di Volo Senza Visibilta) most new pilots had very little experience of instrument or night flying as they were rushed to the front with minimal training.

Pilots briefly trained on the Junkers Ju 88 for dive and torpedo bomber operations, using Luftwaffe aircraft based at Athene. The practical difficulties of acquiring and supporting such a unit precluded further pursuit of this role, despite the initial success with training.

In April 1943 one squadriglia sometimes used Coo and Scarpanto as forward bases. Two aircraft used Timpaklion, Crete, for armed reconnaissance flights between Appollonia and Benghasi. There were very few aircraft operational by mid-May, but morale was high with the recent successful missions which had followed a long wait. On 23 May three SM 79s escorted two unarmed SM 75s from Gadurra to bomb Gura base in Africa at night. 253 Sq was detached to Iraklion on Crete, from 25 June to 16 July. By 9 July the unit had only five out of eleven aircraft serviceable at Gadurra.

In July the Gruppo moved to Italy for re-equipment. They then carried out night attacks against the invasion fleet off Sicily. 253 Sq claimed an enemy night fighter off the Ioinian coast on the night of 18 July. On 7 September eight aircraft were still operational. The two squadriglie commanders took off at 19.30 hours on 8 September to attack ships in the Gulf of Salerno. It was not until they were nearing the target area that the radiomen heard the order for all bomber and fighter units to cancel operations and return to base. They only turned back when a direct order to all torpedo bomber units was received from the H.Q. of Squadra 3, landing at Guidonia and returning to Siena the next day.

Arrival	Zone	Base	Country	Aircraft	Duties
28 Aug 42	Sqa 3	Pisa	Italy	SM 79	TB
Nov 42	ASAR	Decimomannu	Sardinia	SM 79	TB, AR
14 May 43	Sqa 2	Forli	Italy	SM 79	TG

This Gruppo formed on 15 February 1940 with 15 SM 79 bombers. In June they bombed targets in Corsica, escorted by G50s of 51 Stormo. On 21 June they bombed Marseilles naval port.

The unit moved to the Balkans in October for operations over Greece and Yugoslavia. On 1 May 1942 they became Aerosilurante, with 15 torpedo-bombers. From 11 to 28 August they operated from Sardinia against the convoys and coastal vessels in the central and eastern Mediterranean. On 1 September they became Autonomo.

On 16 November two out of three aircraft were lost while on an armed reconnaissance of the Bougie area.

On 1 January 1943 the unit had ten serviceable aircraft. The reduced strengths of all the torpedo units meant they were usually employed on armed reconnaissance, unless an urgent situation appeared. The small numbers meant they became more vulnerable to enemy nightfighters, the RAF Beaufighters being a particularly common and much feared foe. As a result higher command began using the units in combined attacks.

During February and March the Gruppo was active by day and night over the ports of Algiers and Bone. By 28 February the unit had only three serviceable aircraft, due to recent USAAF bombing raids. These continued to operate off Algiers. On 27 March *Capitano* Urbano Mancini led six aircraft of his Gruppo, combined with six from 89 Gruppo, in an attack off the Algerian coast. He did not return and was awarded the *Medaglia d'Oro* for his continuous leadership of the torpedo units. Despite a search through to the next day by an SM 79 of 105 Gruppo and a Z506 of 613 Sq no trace was found of the veteran pilot or his crew. On 5 April the unit had seven serviceable aircraft. In May 1943 they moved to Forli, disbanding on 6 June. The crews and aircraft went to 130 and 132 Gruppi.

105 GRUPPO BT
Squadriglie 254, 255
Stormo 46

Arrival	Zone	Base	Country	Aircraft	Duties
10 Jun 40	Sqa 3	Pisa San Giusto	Italy	SM 79	DB
24 Oct 40	AALB	Tirana	Albania	SM 79	DB
20 Jan 41	Sqa 4	Bari	Italy	SM 79	DB
May 42	Sqa 3	Pisa San Giusto	Italy	SM 79	TG
11 Aug 42	ASAR	Decimomannu	Sardinia	SM 79	TB

106 GRUPPO BT
Squadriglie 260, 261
Stormo 47

Arrival	Zone	Base	Country	Aircraft	Duties
10 Jun 40	Sqa 1	Ghedi	Italy	Z1007bis	TG
Aug 40	Sqa 2	Trapani Milo	Sicily	Z1007bis	IT
Aug 40	Sqa 2	Chinisia	Sicily	Z1007bis	DB
Oct 40	4 ZAT	Grottaglie	Italy	Z1007bis	DB
28 Aug 41	AEGE	Rodi Marizza	Aegean	Z1007bis	DB, AN, AR
31 Aug 42	Sqa 1	Ghedi	Italy	Z1007bis	TG, AN
May 43	ASIC	Sciacca	Sicily	Z1007bis	NB, AN
21 May 43	ASIC	Gela	Sicily	Z1007bis	NB, AN

74: *Lineup of Fiat BR 20Ms of the 242ª Squadriglia, 99° Gruppo of the Corpo Aereo Italiani, seen here on a gloomy autumn day at Chievres, Belgium, in October 1940. The camouflage pattern is a classic C2 style consisting of green blotches over a yellow ochre base*

75: *Often overshadowed by the Savoia Marchetti SM 79, the BR 20 nevertheless saw action in all the different theatres in which the RA was involved. Here a BR 20M of the 243ª Squadriglia, 99° Gruppo, (which together with 242ª Squadriglia formed part of 43° Stormo) is seen in flight. According to the original caption to the picture the machine is over Yugoslavia in 1941, although it does not carry the yellow Balkan theatre markings carried by Axis aircraft from April that year*

76: *Escorted by Fiat CR 42s, SM 79s of the 254ª Squadriglia, 105° Gruppo, 46° Stormo, in attack formation over Malta. The wavy band Type A camouflage patterns and the lack of white fuselage bands on all the aircraft date the picture to summer 1940, when the unit was based at Pisa San Giusto. From 24 October the unit was transferred to Tirana in Albania. Fighter cover was soon discovered to be essential as the SM 79 was vulnerable even to the few Gladiator biplane fighters based on Malta*

77: *SM 79s of 252ᵃ Squadriglia, 104° Gruppo, wear the older type of wavy band camouflage, modified by the addition of the white fuselage band which was introduced from the end of 1940*

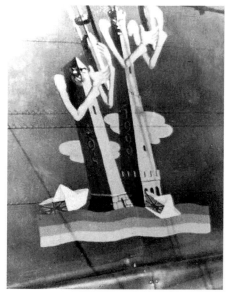

78 Far left: *The emblem of the 36° Stormo, used on SM 79s. It features a caricature of the famous twin towers of Boulogna (where the 108° and 109° Gruppi which made up the Stormo were formed) hurling bombs on two paper boats marked with the Union Jack*

79 Left: *The guitar-playing cockroach badge of the 102° fighter-bomber Gruppo, used on the unit's Reggiane Re 2002s*

80: *Taken on their first operation of the war, these are SM 79s of the 256ᵃ Squadriglia, 108° Gruppo, 36° Stormo, bound for Malta from their base at Castelvetrano in Sicily. 11 June 1940*

81: *This SM 84 (MM 22429?) of the 258ᵃ Squadriglia, 109° Gruppo, 36° Stormo, in flight some where over the Mediterranean from its base at Decimomannu in August 1942, would be unremarkable, except for the fact that it is believed to be finished in the blue-grey E2 camouflage scheme, specially developed for its anti-shipping role*

82: *A pastoral scene on the airfield at Castelvetrano, where an SM 79 of the 257ᵃ, Squadriglia, 108° Gruppo, sits at its dispersal in summer 1940. The air traffic control problems caused by flocks of sheep on the runway can only be wondered at!*

83: *According to the original caption to this picture, this is a CRDA Cant Z.1007bis of the 260ᵃ Squadriglia, 106° Gruppo, 47° Stormo, based at Grottaglie in October 1940. The yellow engine cowlings, however, suggest that the picture was much more likely to have been taken after April 1941, the opening of the campaign against Yugoslavia. Note the early style white backgrounds to the wing markings. As these compromised the camouflage, later machines carried simple black versions*

84: *A very rare picture of one of the few CRDA Cant Z1018 Leone (Lion) bombers to enter service with the 262ᵃ Squadriglia, 101° Gruppo, during early summer 1943 when the unit was based at Vicenza. The first Italian bomber to be fully up to the standards of its opponents, it was yet another example of how an excellent aircraft failed to reach the RA in numbers, in time. Much production effort was wasted by Fiat in updating their out-moded BR 20, which would have been better spent on license building the Leone*

85: *Three Piaggio P.108B bombers of the 274ª Squadriglia B.G.R. just prior to takeoff from Decimomannu on a bombing raid against Gibraltar in October 1942. As this was the only unit to operate the bomber, but with never more than 8 aircraft serviceable, the whole programme was little more than a dissipation of effort. In principle, the idea of the long-range stategic bomber was sound but Italy lacked the resources to produce enough aircraft to support meaningful operations*

86 Left: *Although over 150 Piaggio P.108s were completed only 30 or so saw combat. This is the third P.108B (MM 22003), in which Bruno Mussolini was killed near Pisa on 7 August 1941 during conversion training from the Z.1007*

87 Below: *An SM 79sil of the 278ª Squadriglia, up close to the camera ship shows off its torpedo and unit badge—four black and white cats carrying a torpedo. Date and location unknown*

Arrival	Zone	Base	Country	Aircraft	Duties
1 Jun 43	Sqa 3	Perugia San Egidio	Italy	Z1007bis	NB

This Gruppo was formed just before the war and was sent to Sicily in August for operations over Malta. The first raid was made on 29 August, with ten Cant Z1007bis aircraft against Luqa airbase. They were the first to use this aircraft type in the Mediterranean area.

Two months later the Gruppo was transferred to Italy, to support the campaign against Greece, then Yugoslavia. The aircraft proved less vulnerable than other bomber types and fended off many fighter attacks without loss. Only one or two were shot down and the same number of Gladiators were claimed.

After the Balkan episode the unit moved to the Aegean where, for the next year, they operated against shipping in the eastern Mediterranean and supported the African campaign with raids on Egyptian and Libyan targets. Between September and November they hit several ships around Cyprus.

By 1942 they were sending an average of two or three aircraft on reconnaissance missions, and five to eight on shipping strikes. During the battle against the June convoys, 25 Z1007bis of 47 Stormo were involved, using Derna in Libya as a stop-over base. The intensity of operations meant that by August there were no aircraft left operational, so the Gruppo retired to Italy for a rest and re-equipment.

In the spring of 1943 the unit was in Sicily, attacking the invasion forces off North Africa and Sicily. On 1 June they joined the Raggruppamento Bombardamento.

107 GRUPPO BT

Squadriglie	262, 263
Stormo	47

Arrival	Zone	Base	Country	Aircraft	Duties
10 Jun 40	Sqa 1	Ghedi	Italy	Z1007bis	TG
Aug 40	Sqa 2	Chinisia	Sicily	Z1007bis	DB
Oct 40	4 ZAT	Grottaglie	Italy	Z1007bis	DB
28 Aug 41	AEGE	Rodi Gadurra	Aegean	Z1007bis	DB, AN, AR
31 Aug 42	Sqa 1	Ghedi	Italy	Z1007bis	TG, AN
May 43	Sqa 2	Vicenza	Italy	Z1007bis Z1018	TG

This Gruppo was formed just before the war and was sent to Sicily in August for operations over Malta. They then moved to Italy to support the Balkans campaigns, where the Z1007bis proved less vulnerable than other bomber types to fighter attack and anti-aircraft fire.

For the rest of 1941 they operated from the Aegean, attacking shipping in the eastern Mediterranean, as well as land targets in Egypt and Libya. By 1942 they were

sending an average of six aircraft on shipping strikes. Derna was used as a stop-over base in June, during the convoy battle. By August they only had two operational aircraft left so the Gruppo returned to Italy for rest and re-equipment.

In the spring of 1943 they joined 106 Gruppo in attacking the Allied invasion forces nearing Sicily. In May they moved to Vicenza with eight aircraft, and acted as reserves for 106 Gruppo which were operating as part of Raggruppamento Bombardamento. The unit also received some of the new Z1018 bombers for trials in the last weeks of the war.

108 GRUPPO BT

Squadriglie	256, 257
Stormo	36

Arrival	Zone	Base	Country	Aircraft	Duties
3 Jun 40	Sqa 2	Castelvetrano	Sicily	SM 79	AR, DB, AN
11 Nov 40	Sqa 2	Bologna	Italy	SM 79 SM 84	TG
4 Sep 41	ASAR	Decimomannu	Sardinia	SM 84	TB, CE, TG
13 Sep 42	Sqa 4	Gioia del Colle	Italy	SM 84	IT
15 Sep 42	Sqa 3	Pisa	Italy	SM 84 SM 79	TG
1 Nov 42	ASAR	Decimomannu	Sardinia	SM 79	CE, AR, AN
12 Dec 42	Sqa 3	Pisa	Italy	SM 79	TG
22 May 43	ASAR	Milis	Sardinia	SM 79	AN
Jun 43	Sqa 4	Lecce	Italy	SM 79	AN
30 Jul 43	Sqa 3	Pisa	Italy	SM 79	TG
13 Aug 43	Sqa 4	Brindisi	Italy	SM 79	TG
27 Aug 43	Sqa 3	Pisa	Italy	SM 79	TG

This unit was formed on 4 February 1938 at Bologna Borgo Panigale with crews and aircraft from 8 Stormo. They participated with SM 81s and SM 79s in the occupation of Albania. Their main war began over Bizerte, Tunisia, followed by attacks on Malta. They also joined in the Battaglia de Punta Stilo on 9 July, losing an SM 79 from 257 Sq.

They returned to Italy for retraining and fresh equipment, receiving their first SM 84s on 7 May 1941. With this new aircraft the unit changed role, and on 1 September became a Gruppo Aerosilurante. Three days later, with 14 SM 84s, they went to Sardinia for operations against shipping from Gibraltar.

Operating jointly with 109 Gruppo on the 27th, eleven SM 84s (six from 108, five from 109 Gruppo) took off from Sardinia to attack the convoy off La Galite. Their main targets were the battleship HMS *Nelson* and the carrier HMS *Ark Royal*. At first escorting fighters kept interceptors engaged, then the unit split in two for its attack. The escorts, from 161 and 24 Gruppi, were at the limit of their range and had difficulty following the torpedo bombers all the way in. Indeed, one CR42 was downed by Italian naval anti-aircraft fire in error, and the Royal Navy also shot down two Fulmars amid the massive barrage set up to protect the warships. *Sergente Maggiore* Valotti of 354 Sq flew aerobatics to the amazement and distraction of the naval crews but it was not enough to prevent the torpedo bomber losses, and he was also shot down. Six SM 84s were lost, including the Stormo commander, *Colonello* Riccardo Seidl, and three of his squadriglia commanders. For the first time a whole command section, 36 Stormo, was awarded the *Medaglia d'Oro alle Bandiere* for its dedication and sacrifice to its nation. 38 crew members were lost and 6 wounded out of 70. HMS *Nelson* was put out of action for six months. *Sottotenente* Del Vento of 287 Sq kept watch on the convoy throughout the battle, then landed his Z506B to pick up torpedo crews in the water. Enemy fighters attacked, setting fire to the Cant and he had to land on the water again. When the enemy had left, his observer, *Sottotenente* Majorana, although mortally wounded and unable to speak, guided the crew to land. Both he and Del Vento were awarded the *Medaglia d'Oro*.

On 23 October four SM 84s of 256 and 258 Sq took off from Decimomannu to attack ships west of La Galite. Vichy French anti-aircraft fire from neighbouring ships hit one of the SM 84s. Detachments were sent to Sicily and Pantelleria as needed, but the SM 84 did not prove very capable in the anti-shipping role. On 7 March three aircraft from 257 Sq carried out armed reconnaissance flights, one force landing at Maison Blanche. On the 20th fourteen Stormo aircraft moved to Sciacca in anticipation of approaching convoys for Malta. Two days later nine of them attacked a convoy in the bay of Sollum.

By April 1942, both 108 and its sister Gruppo, 109, were temporarily out of action because their remaining twelve airworthy aircraft were grounded with engine problems. They spent the next few weeks on training sorties and convoy escorts, while the engines were all gradually replaced. On 14 June six out of fourteen Stormo aircraft were lost in a mission south of Sardinia, including two senior crews. This despite an escort of nineteen CR 42s and twenty MC 200s. On 13 September some of the SM 84s were passed to 32 Stormo at Gioia del Colle. Two days later the Gruppo exchanged the remainder for S79s.

Returning to Sardinia they carried out convoy escorts, reconnaissance missions, and anti-shipping strikes. After five weeks they went to Pisa for training in night attacks on shipping. By 28 November the Stormo had sixteen aircraft at Pisa and nine had returned to Decimomannu. They were all returned to action in May 1943. Gerbini was also used about this time. In June the Gruppo moved to Lecce to join the newly formed Raggruppamento Aerosilurante and became Autonomo on 15 July.

109 GRUPPO BT

Squadriglie	258, 259
Stormo	36

Arrival	Zone	Base	Country	Aircraft	Duties
10 Jun 40	Sqa 2	Castelvetrano	Sicily	SM 79	AR, DB, AN
11 Jun 40	Sqa 1	Bologna	Italy	SM 79 SM 84	TG
20 Sep 41	ASAR	Decimomannu	Sardinia	SM 84	AN
13 Sep 42	Sqa 4	Gioia del Colle	Italy	SM 84	IT
15 Sep 42	Sqa 3	Pisa	Italy	SM 84 SM 79	TG
1 Nov 42	ASAR	Decimomannu	Sardinia	SM 79	CE, AR, AN
12 Dec 42	Sqa 3	Pisa	Italy	SM 79	TG
22 May 43	ASAR	Milis	Sardinia	SM 79	AN
May 43	Sqa 3	Pisa	Italy	SM 79	AN

This unit followed the same operational history as 108 Gruppo, its sister unit in 36 Stormo. They carried out their first night missions on 12 August 1940, over Malta.

On 20 September 1941, with 15 SM 84s, they followed 108 Gruppo to Sardinia for operations against shipping from Gibraltar, beginning on the 27th near La Galite. Five aircraft were temporarily transferred to Pantelleria on 29 November, making armed reconnaissances. The next day they land at Castelbenito, one being accidentally shot down by German anti-aircraft fire near Zanzur.

On 18 December three aircraft from 259 Sq attacked ships south of Malta, *Maggiore* Gastaldi receiving a posthumous *Medaglia d'Oro* for his leadership during the attack. Three days later six aircraft from 259 Sq moved to Comiso via Pantelleria, five returning to Decimomannu shortly after.

On 14 June 1942 one aircraft from 256 Sq and one from 259 Sq guided eight CR42 fighter bombers against the HARPOON convoy, claiming a near miss on a cruiser. Two Fiats were downed by Fulmars, as well as the 259 Sq aircraft. The other SM 84 claimed two of the intercepting fighters.

On 13 August three aircraft were detached to Chinisia via Castelvetrano, joining two from 3NAS and ten from 130 Gruppo for attacks on the PEDESTAL convoy. After intensive operations they reorganised in Italy, returning to Sardinia with 15 SM 79s in November, together with ten from 1, 2, and 3 NAS.

Joint operations continued with their sister unit until July 1943. By 9 July they had no serviceable aircraft. 36 Stormo was disbanded on the 15th, followed by the Gruppo on 9 August.

114 GRUPPO BT

Squadriglie	Unknown
Stormo	Autonomo

Arrival	Zone	Base	Country	Aircraft	Duties
Oct 40	Sqa 5	Ain el Gazala	Cirenaica	SM 82 SM 79	DB, NB

This unit originally formed as the Gruppo Speciale Bombardamento, under Squadra 5 command, for long range attacks around the Mediterranean. On 9 October 1940 three SM 82s were received, commencing operations against airfields in the Alexandria and Port Said areas on the 17th.

By 2 December they had five SM 82s and two SM 79s. The latter were used for close support duties south of Sidi Barrani, flying on low level bombing missions.

From 1 January 1941 the aircraft returned to Italy and the unit disbanded at the end of the month.

116 GRUPPO BT

Squadriglie	276, 277
Stormo	37

Arrival	Zone	Base	Country	Aircraft	Duties
Oct 40	4 ZAT	Lecce Galatina	Italy	BR 20	DB, CE, AR
5 Oct 41	ASIC	Fontanarossa	Sicily	BR 20M	NB
Nov 41	Sqa 4	Lecce	Italy	BR 20M	TG
2 Jun 42	ASIC	Castelvetrano	Sicily	BR 20M	NB
29 Jul 42	Sqa 4	Lecce	Italy	Z1007bis	TG, CE
24 Sep42	ASIC	Reggio Emilia	Sicily	Z1007bis	NB
28May43	Sqa	Littoria	Italy	Z1007bis	TG
May 43	Sqa 1	Cameri	Italy	BR 20M Z1007bis	TG

This unit formed in October 1940 for operations over Yugoslavia and Greece. They initially used both BR 20s and BR 20Ms. Bad weather and difficult terrain made finding targets a hard task. After the land campaign ended, the unit flew escort and reconnaissance missions over the adjacent seas.

In October 1941 they moved to Sicily for the night bombing of Malta. 276Sq was detached to Trapani. After training they resumed operations in June 42, 220 Sq having replaced 277 Sq on the 5th. Within six months they were reduced from twelve to two operational aircraft, at least five having lost to Maltese defences.

Once more in Italy, they began re-equipping with later production models of the Z1007bis. 276 Sq stayed in Lecce, while 220 Sq went with the Gruppo to Reggio Emilia. The Gruppo disbanded on 15 June 1943 at Cameri while still under training.

121 GRUPPO BaT

Squadriglie	206, 216
Stormo	Autonomo

Arrival	Zone	Base	Country	Aircraft	Duties
2 Jul 43	Sqa 1	Lonate Pozzolo	Italy	Ju 87R5	TG
10 Jul 43	Sqa 3	Capua	Italy	Ju 87R5	IT
10 Jul 43	Sqa 4	Gioia del Colle	Italy	Ju 87R5 Ju 87D-3	IT
11 Jul 43	Sqa 4	Crotone	Italy	Ju 87R5 Ju 87D-3	AN
Jul 43	Sqa 4	Manduria	Italy	Ju 87D-3	TG
26 Jul 43	Sqa 4	Lecce Galatina	Italy	Ju 87D-3	AN, NB
8 Aug 43	Sqa 4	Brindisi	Italy	Ju 87D-3	AN, NB
22 Aug 43	Sqa 4	Lecce Galatina	Italy	Ju 87D-3	TG
27 Aug 43	ASAR	Chilivani	Sardinia	Ju 87D-3	AN, NB

This unit was formed from aircraft and crews of the Nucleo Addestramento Tuffatori (Dive-bomber training unit), with eight Ju 87Rs. They received some Ju 87Ds at Gioia del Colle, moving to Crotone to attack shipping around Sicily. Their first operation was on 12 July 1943, when seven Ju 87Ds attacked Allied naval vessels off Augusta, losing two aircraft to Spitfires and P-38s, with two more force-landing at Fontanarossa. Despite the obvious vulnerability of their aircraft the crews are ordered to attack again on the next day. Eight Ju 87Bs set out, without escort, and seven were shot down by enemy fighters.

After this the unit retired to Manduria, receiving nine Ju 87Ds from 103 Gruppo, together with their crews. Time did not allow much training and the unit was soon thrown into night attacks on shipping with an average four to five aircraft per mission. For better strike ability, and because the base had not yet been discovered, the unit moved to Chilivani. It remained there until the surrender, when it still had seven Ju 87Ds operational.

130 GRUPPO AS

Squadriglie	280, 283
Stormo	Autonomo

Arrival	Zone	Base	Country	Aircraft	Duties
1 Sep 41	ASAR	Elmas	Sardinia	SM 79	TB
20 Mar 42	ASIC	Catania	Sicily	SM 79	TB
Apr 42	ASIC	Pantelleria	Sicily	SM 79	TB
May 42	ASAR	Elmas	Sardinia	SM 79	TB
6 Nov 42	ASIC	Catania	Sicily	SM 79	TB
1 Mar 43	Sqa 3	Littoria	Italy	SM 79	TG

This unit formed from the previously Autonomo 280 and 283 Sq, with five additional crews and aircraft. Their first operation was made on 27 September 1941 with 14 torpedo-bombers, operating against ships off La Galite. Despite escorting CR 42s of 24 Gruppo, three were lost to intercepting Fulmars, in the same action that cost 36 Stormo six SM 84s. Five aircraft tried to repeat the attack the next day.

On 14 November two aircraft were detached to Sicily, from where they sank *Empire Pelican* east of La Galite. The next day eight crews (two from 280 Sq, six from 283

Sq) transferred temporarily to Catania for armed reconnaissance around Malta. Ten days later three of these moved to Misurata, one moving on to Castelbenito for more armed reconnaissance flights. On 28 December all eight returned to Elmas.

The unit was kept busy with shipping attacks for the next 18 months, including battles with the Malta convoys, most notably HARPOON in June. On 22 March twelve aircraft from 280 and 278 Sq took off from Catania to attack a convoy in the bay of Sollum. Bad weather prevented level bombers from operating against this convoy (Force B) from Alexandria, so the operation fell upon the torpedo bombers alone. A combined attack from nine aircraft from 36 Stormo at Sciacca, four from 279 Sq at Benghasi, plus four more from Eraklion, resulted in four merchant ships being lost. Four 130 Gruppo aircraft were downed by anti-aircraft fire.

By 1 January 1943 the unit had nine serviceable aircraft, and withdrew to Forli later that month to reform and retrain, their commanders going to 1 and 2 NAS to instruct new recruits. On 1 March they transferred to Littoria to reform yet again. By 9 July they had only two out of nine aircraft serviceable. However, such was the supply state that the crews were posted to the Raggruppamento Aerosilurante on 8 August, the 130 Gruppo formally disbanding on the 10th.

131 GRUPPO AS

Squadriglie	279, 284
Stormo	Autonomo

Arrival	Zone	Base	Country	Aircraft	Duties
25 Mar 42	Sqa 5	Benghasi K2	Cirenaica	SM 79	TB
3 Jul 42	Sqa 5	El Ftehja	Cirenaica	SM 79	TB
15 Jul 42	Sqa 5	Derna	Cirenaica	SM 79	TB
8 Nov 42	Sqa 5	Misurata	Tripolitania	SM 79	TB
22 Nov 42	Sqa 3	Napoli	Italy	SM 79	IT
23 Nov 42	Sqa 3	Pisa	Italy	SM 79	TG
Nov 42	ASIC	Castelvetrano	Sicily	SM 79	TB
May 43	Sqa 3	Pisa	Italy	SM 79	TG
23 Jul 43	Sqa 4	Lecce	Italy	SM 79	TB
6 Aug 43	Sqa 3	Pisa	Italy	SM 79	TB
13 Aug 43	Sqa 4	Grottaglie	Italy	SM 79	TB
27 Aug 43	Sqa 3	Siena	Italy	SM 79	TB

This unit formed from the previously Autonomo 279 and 284 Sq, to create the southern arm of a two-pronged attack on Allied convoys. During the attack on the HARPOON convoy in June 1942 the unit took off in the morning with 28 MC 202s escorting. Unfortunately, because the German reconnaissance location was in error, they failed to make contact. Ten aircraft tried again in the late afternoon, but were prevented from pressing home their attack by covering Beaufighters.

In July they moved to Derna, with a section detached to Marsa Matruh. There were twelve aircraft on strength at this time. In September they assisted in attacking convoys near Tobruk. With the Allied invasion of North West Africa in November the unit returned to Italy, simultaneously picking up eleven new SM 79s and absorbing crews and aircraft from the disbanding 133 Gruppo. Detachments were transferred to Castelvetrano, Sicily for torpedo operations. Through January and February the Gruppo underwent intensive night training at Littoria. On 28 March 279 Sq joined 41 Gruppo on combined operations from Furbara while 284 Sq continued to work up to operational efficiency.

279 Sq went to Gerbini on 1 April 1943 to replace 132 Gruppo, beginning night operations on 20 May off Biserta and Bone. 284 Sq remained at Pisa, detaching crews to Milis through May and June for operations off Algeria. They had joined Raggruppamento Aerosilurante on 1 June. On 10 July they began combining with three other Gruppi for joint torpedo operations. On the 11th a section was hurried to Sicily on standby. 279 Sq disbanded at Gerbini on 14 July, with no serviceable aircraft left, having had only one out of four available on the 9th.

On 23 August 131 Gruppo moved with 108 Gruppo to Pisa, leaving a detachment at Grottaglie. More new aircraft and crews arrived.

On 8 September 131 Gruppo sent eight aircraft to attack shipping in Salerno bay but were recalled as they approached the target area.

132 GRUPPO AS

Squadriglie	278, 281
Stormo	Autonomo

Arrival	Zone	Base	Country	Aircraft	Duties
1 Apr 42	Sqa 3	Littoria	Italy	SM 79	TB
Apr 42	ASIC	Castelvetrano	Sicily	SM 79	TB
14 Jun 42	ASIC	Gerbini	Sicily	SM 79	TB
11 Aug 42	ASIC	Pantelleria	Sicily	SM 79	TB
16 Nov 42	ASIC	Castelvetrano	Sicily	SM 79	TB
27 Nov 42	ASAR	Decimomannu	Sardinia	SM 79	TB
10 Dec 42	ASIC	Chinisia	Sicily	SM 79	TB
9 Jan 43	ASAR	Decimomannu	Sardinia	SM 79	TB
3 Mar 43	ASIC	Gerbini	Sicily	SM 79	TB
5 Apr 43	Sqa 2	Gorizia	Italy	SM 79	TB, TG
12 Aug 43	Sqa 3	Littoria	Italy	SM 79	TB, TG

This unit was formed with 21 pilots, 45 specialists, and 16 SM 79s and was almost immediately sent to Sicily. The newly reformed 281 Sq went to Catania and 278 Sq went to Castelvetrano, with the command nucleo under *Maggiore* Carlo Buscaglia going to Gerbini. Two months later they reunited at Gerbini with fifteen aircraft, in time for the attacks on the HARPOON convoy on its way to Malta, usually escorted by Re 2001s or MC 202s of 51 Stormo.

The unit was very busy in the next few months, operating around the central Mediterranean against Allied shipping. In November they carried out some daring raids against the invasion fleet in Bougie Bay. On the 11th the CO, *Maggiore* Buscaglia, led four SM 79s over the bay. Seven Spitfires gave chase, but the only bomber lost was brought down by anti-aircraft fire. The next day he led six torpedo-bombers into the same area. This time the Spitfires shot down his aircraft, and damaged the others. He, along with his crewmember *1st Aviere* Francesco Maiore who was mortally hit, was given the *Medaglia d'Oro* (Gold Medal), his country's highest award. The Gruppo was named in his honour and turned to night attacks. Despite the dangers involved and lessons being learned, Bomber H.Q. ordered another day raid on 30 November, resulting in the loss of four out of five SM 79s to thirteen intercepting Spitfires. Operations were severely limited by the few serviceable aircraft and low availability of fuel, which restricted training especially for the replacement crews.

In February 1943 the crews found that while the power of the aircraft engines could be raised, higher vibrations caused more engine malfunctions. Despite the gallant efforts of the defending 24 Gruppo who made several claims, aircraft were lost on the ground during February as RAF and USAAF bombing raids concentrated on Sardinian bases. On the 7th four enemy bombers were claimed, but two SM 79s and four Z506Bs were destroyed at Decimomannu and Elmas respectively. By the 28th, 132 Gruppo only had four serviceable aircraft left. On 3rd March the Gruppo transferred to Sicily to reorganise and train new crews.

Between 27 March and 10 April the torpedo units on Sardinia had lost ten crews out of 25 used from the 63 on strength. Lack of operational aircraft and poor fuel supplies kept the others from flying. As a result of this situation, fighter-bombers became more frequently used. On 8 June, for example, three SM 79s from Sardinia with 15 MC 200 and MC 205V fighter-bombers, escorted by a further 23 MC 205Vs from Pantelleria, operated against a convoy, with the fighter-bombers managing to attack several warships.

Operations were carried out against Gibraltar from Istres, France, in June. On the 27th three aircraft moved to Gerbini for night operations on Malta, returning to Littoria shortly after to join the long range squadriglia. By then the unit was reduced to only five aircraft. All of these were unserviceable by 9 July.

A report concluded that the low strengths of the torpedo units were due to :
a)   heavy losses in combat
b)   intense use of units, especially in night and bad weather operations,

c)   no rest for crews, continuous operations over 18 months reducing efficiency,
d)   poor supplies in essentials such as food, fuel, and weapons.

The Gruppo moved to Littoria in August to rest and re-equip. While there, on the 12th, three aircraft operated against a convoy off Sicily, losing all three. The leader, *Tenente Colonello* Canniavello, was posthumously awarded the *Medaglia D'Oro*. Three days later five aircraft transferred to Milis, sinking the *Empire Kestrel* the following day. Two aircraft were lost. Two replacements arrived on the 19th, but only two were left by the time the detachment returned to Littoria on the 26th. On 1 September nine SM 79s attacked ships off Calabria. They still had six aircraft available on the day of surrender.

133 GRUPPO AS

| Squadriglie | **174, 175** |
| Stormo | **Autonomo** |

Arrival	Zone	Base	Country	Aircraft	Duties
5 Apr 42	Sqa 5	Benghasi K2	Cirenaica	SM 79	TB
Jun 42	Sqa 5	EL Ftehja	Cirenaica	SM 79	TB
Jul 42	Sqa 5	Benghasi K3	Cirenaica	SM 79	TB, CE, AR
14 Nov 42	Sqa 5	Misurata	Tripolitania	SM 79	TB, AR
1 Dec 42	Sqa 3	Roma	Italy	SM 79	TG
Dec 42	Sqa 3	Pisa	Italy	SM 79	TG

This unit formed from two previously reconnaissance squadriglie, 174 Sq being at Benghasi and 175 Sq at Castelbenito. Instructors from 2 NAS arrived to set up training on torpedo bombing operations. With ten aircraft they joined in the battles against the HARPOON convoy. Following that the national markings were darkened to help them approach the enemy at low level more easily.

By 15 July 175 Sq was detached to Castelbenito. The unit still carried on with reconnaissance duties as well as convoy escorts and torpedo attacks. Both squadriglie were at K3 in time for the August convoy to Malta. There were eight aircraft available for action. During September 174 Sq joined 35 Stormo BT and 87 Sq OA in continuous armed reconnaissance missions. They used Agedabia as a temporary base at this time. On 20 September 175 Sq had six serviceable SM 79s at Castelbenito, and 174 Sq had two at K3.

In November some bombers and crews went to 21 Sq at Misurata, and other crews went to 132 Gruppo. 174 Sq moved from K3 to Misurata on the 14th. Most of the surviving aircraft went to the newly formed 102 Sq at Castelbenito on 1 December, although six had already gone to Pisa on the 24 November. The unit then withdrew to Italy. At the end of the month the unit disbanded and the crews were sent to 131 Gruppo.

144 GRUPPO T

Squadriglie	617, 618
Stormo	48

Arrival	Zone	Base	Country	Aircraft	Duties
Mar 42	ASIC	Castelvetrano	Sicily	SM 82	TR
Mar 42	Sqa 4	Lecce	Italy	SM 82	TR
25 Mar 42	Sqa 3	Roma Centocelle	Italy	SM 82	TR
Oct 42	AGRE	Atene Tatoi	Greece	SM 82	TR
7 Nov 42	ASIC	Castelvetrano	Sicily	SM 82	TR
Jul 43	Sqa 3	Roma Marcigliana	Italy	SM 82	TR
Sep 43	Sqa 2	Fano	Italy	SM 82	TR

This unit formed in Sicily in 1942 and then went to southern Italy to replace 44 Stormo at Lecce. On 25 March they joined 148 Gruppo to complete 48 Stormo.

On 1 October five SM 82s were sent to Castelvetrano to ferry supplies to Tripoli. Meanwhile six more ferried fuel from Tatoi to Tobruk for the next two months. The Axis forces in Africa were being pushed westwards so the unit was sent to Sicily. They continued transport runs between Castelvetrano and Tripoli with an average fourteen serviceable aircraft. As the Allies advanced the ferry route switched to Tunisia, each aircraft making two trips a day.

In April 1943 three SM 82s of 618 Sq were detached to Elmas, from where they delivered saboteurs to Algeria and Tunisia behind Allied lines. By July the unit was in Rome, with 25 aircraft. Some were at Centocelle. They had moved further north by September.

145 GRUPPO T

Squadriglie	604, 610
Stormo	Autonomo

Arrival	Zone	Base	Country	Aircraft	Duties
Jun 40	ALIB	Benghasi	Cirenaica	SM 75	TR
Feb 41	Sqa 5	Castelbenito	Tripolitania	SM 75 S74 SM 81	TR
9 Apr 41	Sqa 5	Agedabia	Cirenaica	SM 75 S74 SM 81	TR
Apr 41	Sqa 5	Castelbenito	Tripolitania	SM 75 S74 SM 81	
				SM 73 SM 83 SM 82	TR
Dec 41	Sqa 5	Benghasi	Cirenaica	SM 75 S74 SM 81	
				SM 82	TR
20 Dec 41	Sqa 5	Misurata	Tripolitania	SM 75 S74 SM 81	
				SM 82	TR
Jun 42	AGRE	Atene Tatoi	Greece	SM 75 S74 SM 81	
				SM 82	TR
Jul 42	Sqa 5	Castelbenito	Tripolitania	SM 75 S74 SM 81	
				SM 82 Ca312	TR, DB
20 Jan 43	Sqa 3	Roma Urbe	Italy	S74 SM 82	TR
May 43	ASIC	Pantelleria	Sicily	S74 SM 82	TR
Jul 43	Sqa 3	Roma Urbe	Italy	SM 82	TR

604 Sq formed at Roma-Urbe on 9 June 1940 with six ex-civilian SM 75s. Two days later they moved to Benghasi.

610 Sq was formed at Benghasi with eight SM 75s received from the Italian airline, Ala Littoria. The two squadriglie united as the Gruppo SAS under Libyan command. At the time this was the only transport unit with desert experienced crews. They were mostly ex-civilian aircrew and went on to help 146 and 149 Gruppi when they joined the desert arena.

604 Sq began a shuttle between Tripoli and Tobruk, reinforcing troops at the Bir el Gobi fort on 22 June, from Tobruk T2. Other aircraft were on the Benghasi-Rodi run. On 9 July three more SM 75s were transferred from 602 Sq at Benghasi. Three four-engined SM 74s arrived on 7 July, and in August they helped supply the oasis garrisons at Giarabub and Cufra until January. The SM 74s could carry twice the payload of the SM 75s. In September the unit began evacuating civilians from Benghasi to Catania, sometimes using Tamet.

As the SM 81 bomber units were being shot up in the retreat across Libya, they were disbanded and their surviving aircraft passed to 145 Gruppo. This became the most active transport unit in Libya, evacuating personnel and civilians from Cirenaica to Tripolitania and Sicily respectively. Up to 31 January 1941, they had flown 3,200 hours, transported 11,600 men and 1,140 tons of equipment over Cirenaica and to and from Sicily. Five SM 81S ambulances ferried 587 wounded from Sidi Barrani, Bardia, and Tobruk. On 5 February the last unit aircraft withdrew from Benghasi to Castelbenito. 604 Sq was then detached to Fontanarossa and Gerbini.

On 25 February they reinforced Giarabub again, via Tamet. In April they supported the counter-offensive, supplying the 'Ariete' Division from the 9th. 610 Sq was temporarily detached to Benina. On 30 July an unarmed SM 74 of 604 Sq fought off a Blenheim north of Pantelleria, while en route to Gerbini. It force-landed at Pantelleria. Due to the increasing losses of the unarmed transports, the unit received its first SM 82s in July, two bomber-transport versions arriving from 35 Stormo. By 15 September eight of these aircraft had arrived from 146 and 149 Gruppi. The unit then began a supply run from Sicily to Libya, reinforcing the Axis advanced positions. An SM 74 was destroyed by enemy strafing at Castelbenito on 2 November. Another was disabled by collision with a Z1007bis of 59 Sq at Castelvetrano.

Serviceability was running low, even with other transport units assisting. Aircraft were sent to Roma-Urbe for repairs, and the Ala Littoria offices at Tripoli provided a very efficient maintenance network. However, the number of aircraft from all units requiring their services was often overwhelming. Only three SM 75s were left by now, and just four out of ten SM 82s were operational.

On 28 March 1942 an SM 73 was received from the Gruppo Complementare (Reserve unit for the Gruppo). 610 Sq used this aircraft between Castelbenito and

Benghasi, and in May between Agedabia and Gialo.

On 13 April two SM 82s of 610 Sq, with an escort of six Messerschmitt Bf 110s of 7./ZG 26 and three Bf 109s, flew from Derna to an enemy landing ground 270 km south east of Derna and 120 km north west of Giarabub. While the escort flew top cover the 25 soldiers disembarked and destroyed three Blenheim aircraft and the oil and fuel dumps on the base. The aircraft then all returned to Derna. (Publisher's note: Not confirmed, but possible candidates for this misfortune were from 14 Squadron, RAF, or 15 Squadron, SAAF, both of which were equipped with Blenheims and had detachments in the general area at the time).

In May 610 Sq received an SM 83 which was equipped with cameras. Using Gatrun and Hon, this aircraft flew from the Atlantic coast to Egypt, obtaining information on the Allied reinforcement routes. It returned to Italy on 18 November.

June saw an intensive period of activity during the buildup to the battles at El Alamein. Aircraft flew Gerbini-Benghasi-Derna and Atene-Fuka. The latter run was used to fly in the 'Folgore' Division, which took five transport Gruppi. During this period armed SM 82s flew night-bombing raids in the Capuzzo and Akroma areas.

By August there were only two SM 75s remaining and SM 82s were now the main equipment. By 20 September the Gruppo had only seven serviceable aircraft. Between 19 and 21 October three SM 82s carried out ten day-bombing raids at low level in the Agheila-Gialo area. In November the Gruppo moved personnel from Castelbenito to K3, to help reinforce the fighting units. The increasing Allied air offensive caused more and more losses. By January the unit was withdrawn to Italy, taking nine SM 82s, two SM 81s, and five Ca133Ss. Between the 6th and 9th the SM 82s were used for bombing the Sirte area. On 1 February the Gruppo joined 48 Stormo.

During the spring it ferried troops to Tunisia and Tripoli, losing its last SM 74 to bombing at Urbe on 19 July. In May and June the unit made successful night runs to Pantelleria, despite nightfighters, aerial bombing, and naval shelling. Good use was made of the island's caves as underground hangars.

146 GRUPPO T

| Squadriglie | 603, 609 |
| Stormo | Autonomo |

Arrival	Zone	Base	Country	Aircraft	Duties
1 Mar 41	Sqa 3	Roma Urbe	Italy	SM 82 SM 79	
				Ca 164	TR
Sep 41	ASIC	Castelvetrano	Sicily	SM 82	TR
23 Jan 42	Sqa 3	Roma Urbe	Italy	SM 82	TR

Arrival	Zone	Base	Country	Aircraft	Duties
Mar 42	ASIC	Castelvetrano	Sicily	SM 82	TR
May 42	Sqa 3	Roma Urbe	Italy	SM 82	TG
Jul 42	AGRE	Atene Tatoi	Greece	SM 82	TR
1 Sep 42	Sqa 5	Tobruk	Cirenaica	SM 82	TR
7 Sep 42	AGRE	Atene Tatoi	Greece	SM 82	TR
30 Sep 42	ASIC	Castelvetrano	Sicily	SM 82	TR
Oct 42	AGRE	Atene Tatoi	Greece	SM 82	TR
Nov 42	Sqa 4	Lecce	Italy	SM 82	TR
Dec 42	ASIC	Gerbini	Sicily	SM 82	TR
Jul 43	Sqa 3	Roma Marcigliana	Italy	SM 82	TR
Sep 43	Sqa 2	Ferrara	Italy	SM 82	TR

This unit formed in Rome, receiving 603 Sq from 147 Gruppo and 609 Sq from 149 Gruppo. Initially there were seventeen SM 82s, one SM 79, and one Ca 164 on strength. The first operation was to Tamet on 12 March. The next four months saw intense use during the reconquest of Cirenaica. On 3 August a recently acquired armed SM 75 was lost to a Beaufighter near Nettuno Bay. By September the unit had 21 SM 82s on the Roma-Castelvetrano-Tripoli run.

The new year found them joining 149 Gruppo as 44 Stormo on 23 January. On 3 February they reinforced ground forces in Croatia, via the Squadra 2 area. The following month they resumed supply runs to Libya. In May they prepared for the invasion of Malta, but as this was deemed unnecessary by the Axis leaders, they helped airlift the 'Folgore' Division to Fuka just before the battles at El Alamein. They then ran supplies from Greece to Tobruk, in support of the frontline. From 1 September they temporarily moved to Tobruk, operating as local transports to the Germans, although still under Squadra 5 Command.

After a brief return to Greece, they switched to Sicily then back to Greece. By this time they had only eleven SM 82s left serviceable. Three were lost to bombing at Benina on 17 November. That month saw them on the Lecce-Ara Fileni run, followed by the Gerbini-Misurata route in December. On 5 May 1943, six SM 82s of 609 Sq flew from Sicily on one of the last troop reinforcement runs to Tunisia.

July 1943 found them in Rome with about twenty SM 82s, having supported the retiring Axis forces across Tunisia and Sicily. On 18 July an SM 75bis, operating from Urbe, fought an enemy aircraft east of Corsica, losing one engine. By September the Gruppo had moved north.

147 GRUPPO T

| Squadriglie | 601, 602, 603 |
| Stormo | Autonomo |

Arrival	Zone	Base	Country	Aircraft	Duties
10 Jun 40	Sqa 3	Littoria	Italy	SM 75	TG

Arrival	Zone	Base	Country	Aircraft	Duties
14 Jun 40	Sqa 3	Capodichino	Italy	SM 75	TR
Nov 40	Sqa 4	Brindisi	Italy	SM 75	TR
2 Nov 40	Sqa 3	Ciampino	Italy	SM 75 SM 82 G 12	TR
Mar 42	Sqa 4	Lecce	Italy	SM 82	TR
Oct 42	ASIC	Castelvetrano	Sicily	SM 82	TR
Jul 43	Sqa 2	Rimini	Italy	SM 82	TR

This unit formed with 13 SM 75s received from the Italian airlines. Operations began on 14 June 1940 on the Capodichino-Catania-Benghasi-Tobruk run, ferrying mostly ammunition. Three aircraft were transferred from 602 Sq to 610 Sq on 9 July. In October the Gruppo ferried troops and equipment from Brindisi to Tirana and other Albanian bases, in support of the Greek campaign.

On 2 November the unit reorganised, receiving their first two armed SM 82s four days later. These were used on the Aegean run. The unit was called on to transport VIPs around the Aegean and Balkans until mid-1941. Between 6 and 17 May an SM 75 of 601 Sq was used by King Vittorio Emanuele III for a tour around Albania.

On 1 March 603 Sq passed to 146 Gruppo. On 10 June 601 Sq received a Fiat G 12 at Ciampino, followed by three more in October. They were used on the Ciampino-Brindisi-Rodi-Benghasi run. The unit also had four SM 75s left, although these were wearing out fast. On 18 October and 30 December one and three G 12s respectively were passed to 606 Sq in 148 Gruppo. By 29 September the unit had 17 SM 82s on the Ciampino-Castelvetrano-Tripoli run.

On 23 January 1942 they joined 148 Gruppo at Ciampino, to form 45 Stormo. From March they flew the Lecce-Benghasi run. In May they prepared for the invasion of Malta with paratroop training drops. With the cancellation of that operation, they helped airlift the 'Folgore' Division to Fuka, only eleven days before the battle of El Alamein. On 3 July two armed SM 82s were detached to Rodi, for bombing operations in the eastern Mediterranean. Both had been lost by 25 August. Twelve SM 82s were used in July on the Lecce-Derna run. In October this route was used to evacuate prisoners-of-war.

The unit then switched to the Castelvetrano-Tripoli run. As the Axis forces retreated, so the unit's base moved northwards, ending at Rimini on the northeast coast of Italy with about twenty SM 82s still on strength.

148 GRUPPO T

Squadriglie	605, 606
Stormo	Autonomo

Arrival	Zone	Base	Country	Aircraft	Duties
Jun 40	Sqa 3	Littoria	Italy	SM 73	TR
4 Jul 40	Sqa 2	Fontanarossa	Sicily	SM 73	TR

Arrival	Zone	Base	Country	Aircraft	Duties
1 Nov 40	Sqa 3	Ciampino	Italy	SM 73 SM 83	
				SM 82 G 12	TR
5 Dec 41	CSIR	Bucharest	Romania	SM 73 SM 82 G 12	TR
Jan 42	ASIC	Castelvetrano	Sicily	SM 82 G 12	TR
23 Jan 42	Sqa 3	Ciampino	Italy	SM 82 G 12	TR
Mar 42	Sqa 4	Lecce	Italy	SM 82 G 12	TR
25 Mar 42	Sqa 3	Roma Centocelle	Italy	SM 82 G 12	TR
Jul 42	ASIC	Castelvetrano	Sicily	SM 82 G 12	TR
Apr 43	ASIC	Sciacca	Sicily	G 12	TR
Jul 43	Sqa 3	Roma Centocelle	Italy	G 12	TR
Sep 43	Sqa 2	Fano	Italy	G 12	TR

In June 1940 eight SM 73s from Ala Littoria formed 605 Sq and five SM 73s from Avia Linee Italiane formed 606 Sq. Some aircraft arrived from Reggio Calabria. The unit was used to carry the French Armistice Party from Roma-Urbe to France, and back via Rabat, in Algiers. From 4 July seven aircraft were on the Catania-Benghasi-Tobruk run, delivering ammunition. There followed a very busy period, keeping Libyan forces supplied during the advance on Sidi Barrani. In September and October they flew VIPs around Libya. Four ex-Sabena (Belgian Air Line) SM 73s arrived from Algiers for 605 Sq, increasing the Gruppo strength to sixteen.

On 1 November the unit was transferred to Italy, to support the campaign in Greece. They flew the Ciampino-Brindisi-Valona-Tirana run. Sorties were still being made to North Africa, delivering personnel and equipment, and evacuating wounded and civilians. Two SM 83s from Sabena arrived in November for 605 Sq. These were kept busy flying between Italy and French West Africa in 1941. However, the age of the SM 73s was showing, along with crew fatigue, as several were lost in take-off and landing accidents during the course of the year.

From time to time the unit was asked to help transfer the personnel of combat air units. On 1 April an SM 73 of 606 Sq ferried 8 Stormo men and material from Alghero to Libya. For most of 1941 the unit liaised between Italy and Vichy France. By September it was switched to ferrying troops on the Ciampino-Trapani-Tripoli run. A detachment of three aircraft was sent to Trapani to ease the transfer.

From 17 October night flights were undertaken as well as day missions. The following day a G 12 was received by 606 Sq, from 147 Gruppo. The SM 73s were slow and vulnerable, so the unit was to be re-equipped with more modern aircraft. In December three more G 12s arrived along with some SM 82s. 605 Sq used the latter type, while 606 Sq used the G 12s.

Meanwhile, on 1 November six of 605 Sq's remaining SM 73s went to Milano-Linate then Venezia-Lido to support the Russian bound units. On the 6th they moved to Belgrade, flew on to Bucharest on the 7th, then arrived at Saporoshje on the 9th. One aircraft crashed on take-

88: *A Savoia Marchetti SM 84bis of the 282ª Squadriglia Sil on the airfield at Gerbini, Sicily, sometime between August to mid-November 1941. This unit was short-lived, only being formed in June 1941 and disbanding in January 1942. Note the extended leading edge wing slots and the ubiquitous fuel drums*

89: *A close study of an SM 84 of the 282ª Squadriglia at Gerbini in September 1941 which reveals evidence of overspray on the arms of the rudder cross. This is probably the result of dissatisfaction with the standard camouflage schemes which were felt to be unsuited to the low-level torpedo bombing role. An unofficial light blue-grey scheme was consequently evolved and applied in the field. This is believed to have been further modified by the addition of a dark blue mottle and has been referred to as the E2 scheme. See photo 81*

90: *A Savoia Marchetti SM 79 of the 284ª Squadriglia Sil, operating out of Benghazi K2 during February 1942 on low-level anti-shipping torpedo strikes. This unit obviously also felt unhappy with the camouflage of their aircraft as the white fuselage band has been obscured with a dark mottle*

91: *Seen at Cagliari-Elmas sometime between July 1940 and April 1943, this CRDA Cant Z.506B of the 287ª Squadriglia R.M. waits to be lifted out of the water by a giant crane. The ventral window for the bomb-aimer is clearly visible. What appears to be a mottle finish under the wing is probably no more than reflections off the water*

92: *In-flight study of another Cant Z.506B of the 287ª Squadriglia R.M. The location is somewhere over the sea around Sardinia where the unit was based throughout the war on ASR and reconnaissance duties*

93: *Another dark grey Cant Z.506B of the 287ª Squadriglia R.M. some where over the Tyrrhenian Sea. The scenery is typical for the vast majority of missions carried out by this unit*

94: *This is one of the earliest Fiat G 50s in service with the 351ª Squadriglia, (20° Gruppo, 51° Stormo,) probably at Ciampino Sud, shortly before Italy joined the war. Finished in a mottle scheme first tried out in Spain, the aircraft still retains the red/white/green rudder stripes and the original sliding glazed canopy. This was deleted in later batches on account of pilot complaints about poor visibility, although this picture indicates that the pilot's view was better than in a great many later aircraft. Never as popular as the Macchi MC 200, the G 50 was simply a workhorse*

95: *Seen over the Alps on the way to the CAI bases in Belgium in September 1940, this is a Fiat G 50 of the 352ª Squadriglia, 20° Gruppo, 56° Stormo CT. There is no record of any of the 45 G 50s of the CAI being shot down during the Italian operations against England, or even being engaged in combat*

96: *An XI series Macchi MC 202 of the 353ª Squadriglia, 20° Gruppo. This particular machine, MM 9691, was built by Breda sometime between November 1942 and April 1943. Notable features are the armoured windscreen and single tailwheel fairing. Location could be Sardinia, Sicily or Italy*

97 Above: *Pilots of the 354ª Squadriglia, 24° Gruppo, scramble for the camera, probably in late 1940, soon after they had arrived in Albania. Camouflage appears to be the D1A variant of the 'colonial' scheme*

98 Left: *Fiat G 50, MM 5362, of the 355ª Squadriglia, (21° Gruppo, 51° Stormo). The markings style and the presence of numerous Fiat CR 42s in the background suggest that the location could be Capodichino in summer 1940 when the unit first began converting to the G 50 from the CR 32*

99 Left: *Reggiane Re 2001CN night fighters of the 358ª Squadriglia, 2° Gruppo CT, probably sometime in May 1943 after the unit had reformed and been given the task of night defence of the La Spezia area. The aircraft in the background still carries the markings of 150ª Squadriglia, which had been disbanded in September 1942. Presumably, the machine was passed on to the 358ª, who had not had time to repaint it*

off at Bucharest. The other five formed a chain link, spread to cover Bucharest-Linate. The aircraft returned to Italy on 17 November.

On 5 December all the SM 73s returned to Bucharest. 606 Sq stayed in Rome, receiving eight G 12s by February 1942. On 23 January the Gruppo joined 147 Gruppo to form 45 Stormo at Ciampino. For the next six months 606 Sq flew the Roma-Castelvetrano-Tripoli run.

On 25 March the Gruppo transferred to 48 Stormo, with 144 Gruppo, at Centocelle. 605 Sq had seven SM 73s detached to Roma-Urbe. Four more were operating the Russian supply line, Linate-Saporoshje until 4 April. In May they became 247 Sq. Three more G 12s had arrived from 147 Gruppo by March, giving 606 Sq a total of eight. These were used on the Lecce-Benghasi route.

On 29 June two G 12s transported *Il Duce* and his officials from Rome to Tripoli. The following month 605 Sq returned to the Gruppo, receiving brand new G 12s and joining 606 Sq at Castelvetrano. Some SM 82s were used for trips to Tripoli, but 606 Sq was sent with ten G 12s on the Roma-Tatoi-Marsa Matruh-Tobruk run until November. By now both squadriglie were fully equipped with G 12s. Thirteen were operational on 14 November.

Between November 1942 and May 1943 the unit suffered several losses on the Castelvetrano-Tunis-Tripoli runs. During this time, the Transport Arm, SAS, delivered 72,000 men and over 5,000 tons of equipment for the loss of 82 aircraft and 220 men. On 5 April four G 12s were destroyed by enemy aircraft while landing at Tunisi. The unit was now flying the Sciacca-Tunisi and Roma-Decimomannu routes, reinforcing Sardinian ground forces as well as Tunisian.

By 1 August they had 28 operational G 12s in Rome. The unit moved north the following month. One SM 75 may have been used at Fano.

149 GRUPPO T

| Squadriglie | 607, 608, 609 |
| Stormo | Autonomo |

Arrival	Zone	Base	Country	Aircraft	Duties
Jun 40	Sqa 3	Capodichino	Italy	SM 82	TR
Jun 40	Sqa 2	Catania	Sicily	SM 82	TR
19 Jul 40	Sqa 3	Roma Urbe	Italy	SM 82 SM 75 SM 83	TR
Apr 41	Sqa 5	Tripoli	Tripolitania	SM 82 SM 75	TR
Dec 41	ASIC	Castelvetrano	Sicily	SM 82 SM 75	TR
23 Jan 42	Sqa 3	Roma Urbe	Italy	SM 82 SM 75	TR
Mar 42	ASIC	Castelvetrano	Sicily	SM 82	TR
Jul 42	AGRE	Atene Tatoi	Greece	SM 82	TR
1 Sep 42	Sqa 5	Tobruk	Cirenaica	SM 82	TR
7 Sep 42	AGRE	Atene Tatoi	Greece	SM 82	TR
30 Sep 42	ASIC	Castelvetrano	Sicily	SM 82	TR
Nov 42	Sqa 4	Lecce	Italy	SM 82	TR
Dec 42	ASIC	Gerbini	Sicily	SM 82	TR
Jul 43	Sqa 3	Roma Urbe	Italy	SM 82 SM 75	TG
Sep 43	Sqa 2	Ferrara	Italy	SM 82	TR

This unit formed at Capodichino with twelve SM 82s. On 17 June 1940, five aircraft from 607 Sq were sent to Tobruk via Comiso-Benghasi. 608 Sq followed with four aircraft, via Catania-Benghasi on 20 June. Four days later the Gruppo had eleven SM 82s at Tobruk. Two were detached to Giarabub oasis the next day. The Gruppo ferried supplies from Sicily to Tobruk until 19 July, when the unit reunited in Rome.

This unit had the only aircraft with the range and capacity to supply Italian East Africa, so they began to fly the Roma-Benghasi-Asmara run. When the British overran Benghasi they switched to a Roma-Rodi Marizza-Addis Abeba run. 609 Sq received an ex-Sabena SM 83 at Guidonia in August, two more arriving in September. These three aircraft flew several trips between Rome and Libya. On 2 November one SM 83 was passed to 605 Sq.

From October 1940 to March 1941 the unit staged through Squadra 4 bases and Tirana in support of the Balkan campaigns. They proved most useful, and contributed greatly to the movement of the 17,000 men and 2,400 tons of equipment carried by SAS units in this period. Despite difficult terrain, poor facilities and bad weather, the transport units kept at least 50 out of 80 aircraft serviceable for these operations.

Only three SM 75s were serviceable by December. On 1 March 1941 609 Sq transferred to 146 Gruppo. By the end of that month 149 Gruppo had carried 51 Fiat CR 42 fighters to East Africa in the capacious fuselages of their SM 82s. It was the only type capable of carrying the dismantled fighter in this way, and that far.

In April two of these outstanding aircraft were transferred to the Germans—who were so pleased with them that they ordered 300 more in October. From April to December the Gruppo backed up the reconquest of Cirenaica, using the Benghasi-Tripoli run.

Three SM 82s were diverted in May to ferry weapons and ammunition to Iraq, evacuating civilians from Syria on the return journey.

On 29 September fifteen SM 82s were operating the Roma-Castelvetrano-Tripoli run. Two SM 75s were still on strength. Three SM 82s were lost to bombing on 4th January. On the 23rd the unit joined 146 Gruppo to form 44 Stormo at Urbe. The first operation as a Stormo was carried out on 3rd February, reinforcing ground units in Croatia via the Squadra 2 area. That same day an SM 82 of 607 Sq, evacuating civilians from Tripoli to Sicily, became a victim of one of the war's minor tragedies when it came under attack by four Beaufighters. It force-landed at Pantelleria with seven dead (including four women and a baby) and nine wounded.

The unit returned to the Castelvetrano-Tripoli run in March, then prepared for the invasion of Malta. When this was cancelled, they assisted in airlifting 6,000 men of the 'Folgore' Division to Fuka in May. Two months later they were busy supplying the African front, via Tatoi-Tobruk. On 3 July two armed SM 82s were detached to Rodi for bombing targets in Egypt.

From 1 to 7 September the unit operated from Tobruk as local transport to the Germans, under Squadra 5 command. They returned to the Castelvetrano-Tripoli run in October. The following month they flew Lecce-Derna, losing two aircraft to bombing at Benina on the 17th while delivering fuel. December saw them on the Gerbini-Misurata run.

By early 1943 the unit had some SM 82s equipped with a 12.7 mm machine gun in a dorsal turret. The Gruppo began supplying units in Tunisia from February. By July the unit was back in Rome, re-equipping with twenty SM 82s. One SM 75 was still found to be flyable. They had moved north by September.

150 GRUPPO CT

Squadriglie 363, 364, 365
Stormo 53

Arrival	Zone	Base	Country	Aircraft	Duties
10 Jun 40	Sqa 1	Torino Caselle	Italy	CR 42	DF, AE
23 Oct 40	AALB	Valona	Albania	CR 42 MC 200	DF, AE
41	AGRE	Araxos	Greece	MC 200	CE
Dec 41	AGRE	Atene Tatoi	Greece	MC 200	CE
14 Dec 41	Sqa 5	Castelbenito	Tripolitania	MC 200	DF
Dec 41	Sqa 5	En Nofilia	Tripolitania	MC 200	DF
Jan 42	Sqa 5	El Merduma	Tripolitania	MC 200	DF
Jan 42	Sqa 5	Ara Fileni	Tripolitania	MC 200	DF
26 Jan 42	Sqa 5	Agedabia	Cirenaica	MC 200	AE, AR, GA
2 Feb 42	Sqa 5	Benghasi K3	Cirenaica	MC 200	AE, AR, GA
13 Feb 42	Sqa 5	Martuba	Cirenaica	MC 200	AE, AR, GA
15 May 42	Sqa 5	Benghasi K3	Cirenaica	MC 200 MC 202	DF, CE, GA
9 Nov 42	Sqa 4	Lecce	Italy	MC 200 MC 202	
				Bf 109F-4 Bf 109G-4	
				Bf 109G-6	TG, DF
Apr 43	Sqa 3	Ciampino	Italy	Bf 109G-6	TG
13 Apr 43	ASIC	Caltagirone	Sicily	Bf 109F-4 Bf 109G-4	
				Bf 109G-6	TG
15 Apr 43	ASIC	Sciacca	Sicily	Bf 109F-4 Bf 109G-4	
				Bf 109G-6	DF
16 Jul 43	ASIC	Palermo	Sicily	Bf 109G-6	IT
17 Jul 43	Sqa 3	Ciampino Sud	Italy	Bf 109G-6	DF
28 Jul 43	Sqa 1	Torino Caselle	Italy	Bf 109G-6	DF, TG

This unit first received the CR 42 in May 1939,

replacing its CR 32s which it had flown since 1936. Operations began over metropolitan France. A CR 42 from 364 Sq intercepted RAF bombers, based in France, over Torino on 14 June. On 23 October the Gruppo became Autonomo and moved to Albania.

From 28 October 1940 the unit was very active over Greece. They were split, with twelve fighters each, between Tirana (363 Sq), Valona (364 Sq), and Argirocastro (365 Sq). During initial operations they began converting to MC 200s. Scutari was sometimes used by 365 Sq. During this period there were many clashes with RAF Gladiators. At the start of the Yugoslav campaign they had twenty Macchis operational, mainly at Valona.

After the Balkan success one squadriglia was detached to Greece for convoy escort duties. The other two followed from Tirana, after a brief period of anti-partisan patrols.

At the end of the year they left for Africa. There followed an intensive period of escort duties, low level strafing, and fighter sweeps through the spring of 1942. A section of MC 202s was used in July from Benghasi. Besides protecting the port they also escorted convoys between Tripoli and Tobruk. On 20 September the unit had 25 MC 200s on charge. On November they left their surviving aircraft to 8 Gruppo and, four days later, flew by SAS from Derna to Lecce.

1943 found the unit re-equipping with Messerschmitt Bf 109 fighters, transferred from the Luftwaffe's JG 53. After the initial reaction to its comparative lack of manouevrability, the pilots began to appreciate its potent weaponry and speed. Conversion did not take long, much to the surprise of the Germans. While working up on these, a section of three MC 202s was detached to Furbara. By April the Gruppo was involved in defensive operations over Sicily. They received 49 Bf 109F-4s, G-4s, and G-6s. Many of these aircraft were, however, lost to bombing raids before they could be effective. It is thought only one or two Bf 109Fs were used operationally.

In May only three contacts were made with enemy aircraft. A local investigation reported that cover was insufficient because of a slow take-off procedure, poor interception rate, and the late return of airborne aircraft preventing follow-up scrambles (a condition aggravated by German operations in the same area). The unit suggested better warning systems (similar to the Germans), and combining all cannon-armed fighters under one command for anti-bomber operations, leaving other aircraft free to take on the escorts. Time was against setting this up, with the appropriate training required.

Training was delayed because of continuous scrambles and bombings, and the scarcity of spares and supplies. Altitude performance training was especially limited. The pilots were very enthusiastic but were wearing out due to constant readiness, and many of their aircraft were war-weary.

Most of the pilots were experienced and managed to control the skies over Pantelleria in June. On the 10th problems with tyres grounded all the unit's aircraft. Oil and petrol supplies were supplemented by the Germans. While the latter could scramble twice, the Italians frequently had to sit and wait for fuel and oil, often under bombing. Even though the Axis units were at opposite ends of the base, there were problems when the Germans scrambled in all directions, while the Italians lined up for take-off.

About 25 Bf 109Gs were available for use against the invasion forces in July. On the 3rd of that month, fourteen fighters scrambled to intercept a formation of South African Baltimore light bombers. The escort, from the 324 FS, USAAF, who were on their first operational mission, chased off two squadriglie but the third dived in on the unprotected formation and shot down two bombers and damaged several others while braving the South Africans' return fire and heavy German flak. Two more bombers were downed by the German anti-aircraft fire, along with one of the Bf 109Gs. Seven P-40s were claimed in the covering dogfight.

The Gruppo was withdrawn to help defend Rome, then sent north to protect the industrial areas. By 7 September they were still at Torino, having left a detachment at Ciampino with four aircraft, and a Nucleo at Littoria. On the 8th the detachment scrambled before noon against a formation of USAAF bombers nearing Rome. A B-17F from the 97 BG was shot down, becoming what appears to be the last Regia Aeronautica aerial victory of the war.

151 GRUPPO CT

Squadriglie	366, 367, 368
Stormo	53

Arrival	Zone	Base	Country	Aircraft	Duties
10 Jun 40	Sqa 1	Casabianca	Italy	CR 42	DF AE
8 Sep 40	Sqa 5	El Adem	Cirenaica	CR 42	DF
Dec 41	Sqa 5	Agedabia	Cirenaica	CR 42	DF
22 Dec 41	Sqa 5	Ara Fileni	Tripolitania	CR 42	DF
Dec 41	Sqa 5	Sorman	Tripolitania	CR 42	IT
1 Jan 42	Sqa 1	Torino Caselle	Italy	G 50bis	TG
31 Jul 42	AGRE	Araxos	Greece	G 50bis	CE, DF
6 Nov 42	ASIC	Chinisia	Sicily	G 50bis	CE, DF
May 43	ASIC	Pantelleria	Sicily	MC 202	DF
May 43	ASIC	Chinisia	Sicily	MC 202	DF
21 May 43	ASIC	Palermo	Sicily	MC 202	DF
2 Jul 43	Sqa 1	Torino Caselle	Italy	MC 202 G55	TG

This unit was the first to receive the CR 42, in March

1939. Escorts and sweeps were carried out in the French campaign in June 1940. Three Ca 133s were used as the unit transports.

After the French surrender the unit was sent to Libya, to support the offensive on Sidi Barrani. Sections were detached to both Derna and Gazala. The Gruppo had a total of thirty CR 42s in September, and became Autonomo on 23 October. Three days later they began the return to Italy.

On 1 January 1942 they rejoined 53 Stormo, having left their aircraft for 160 Gruppo, back in Libya. Having re-equipped with G 50s, they were sent to Greece to patrol the shipping lanes and act against any aerial intrusions the enemy might make.

A year later, in January 1943, 368 Sq was detached to Sfax, in Tunisia, for ground attack duties. They were often used in combined German-Italian air attacks, but the poor communications between the commands blunted the effects, with scattered timing or poor target information. The Squadriglie relied mainly on MC 202 escorts from 13 Gruppo to cover them. They retired on 2 March to Pantelleria with seven surviving G 50bis, eventually rejoining the Gruppo in Sicily to attack the Allied invasion forces. The main unit had meanwhile arrived there, equipped with Macchis. In July the Gruppo was back in Italy. One of the new Fiat G55 fighters was received for training purposes, but such was the supply situation by then that by 7 September they still had just the single example.

152 GRUPPO CT

Squadriglie	369, 370. 371
Stormo	54

Arrival	Zone	Base	Country	Aircraft	Duties
10 Jun 40	Sqa 1	Airasca	Italy	MC 200	TG
Dec 40	Sqa 1	Treviso	Italy	MC 200	TG

On account of technical problems with their new fighters this unit was not operational at the start of the war. Most pilots were veterans from the Spanish Civil War and were looking forward to trying out their modern aircraft in action.

The Gruppo disbanded, however, on 18 December 1940 before they could fight as a unit. 369 Sq went to 22 Gruppo, and 370 Sq had transferred to Foggia on 7 December for operations over Greece. The latter used eight Macchis, operating from Grottaglie by April.

On 6 March 1941 371 Sq, by now Autonomo, moved from Ciampino to Valona with ten aircraft for operations over Yugoslavia. It eventually joined 22 Gruppo later that year.

153 GRUPPO CT

Squadriglie 372, 373, 374
Stormo 54

Arrival	Zone	Base	Country	Aircraft	Duties
10 Jun 40	Sqa 1	Vergiate	Italy	MC 200	TG
Nov 40	Sqa 1	Treviso	Italy	MC 200	TG
26 Nov 40	Sqa 4	Bari	Italy	MC 200	DF
Nov 40	Sqa 4	Brindisi	Italy	MC 200 CR 42	DF
2 Jul 41	Sqa 5	Castelbenito	Tripolitania	MC 200	DF, GA, AE
Sep 41	Sqa 5	Derna	Cirenaica	MC 200	DF, AE
18 Dec 41	Sqa 5	Sidi Magrum	Cirenaica	MC 200	DF, GA
20 Dec 41	Sqa 5	En Nofilia	Tripolitania	MC 200	GA, DF
21 Dec 41	Sqa 5	Agedabia	Cirenaica	MC 200	DF
22 Dec 41	Sqa 5	Misurata	Tripolitania	MC 200	DF
Dec 41	Sqa 1	Torino Caselle	Italy	MC 200 MC 202 CR 42	TG
1 Sep 42	ASIC	Caltagirone	Sicily	MC 200	DF
Oct 42	ASIC	Chinisia	Sicily	MC 200	AE, DF
Nov 42	ASIC	Palermo	Sicily	MC 202	IT
6 Nov 42	ASAR	Decimomannu	Sardinia	MC 202	DF
May 43	ASIC	Sciacca	Sicily	MC 202	IT
21 May 43	ASIC	Chinisia	Sicily	MC 202	DF
Jul 43	Sqa 1	Torino Caselle	Italy	MC 202	TG

This unit contained several Spanish Civil War veterans but their aircraft were technically not ready for action. The Gruppo left 54 Stormo in November for operations over the Balkans. They patrolled over the lower Adriatic Sea, protecting the supply lines and escorting raids where needed. 373 Sq was at Bari and 374 Sq was at Grottaglie. 372 Sq operated from Brindisi at the start of the Greek campaign, joining the Gruppo in November. 370 Sq also operated with them from November to April, although remaining Autonomo. This squadriglia used Grottaglie, then Tirana, before exchanging their MC 200s for G 50s and moving to Italy to join 24 Gruppo.

The entire Gruppo used 38 MC 200s and 9 CR 42s during the Yugoslav campaign. As early as December some aircraft were at Guidonia, adding sand filters in preparation for a tour in Libya.

On 19 April 374 Sq moved to Castelbenito with eleven Macchis, followed later by the rest of the Gruppo. They carried out mainly intercepts and ground strafing, sometimes joining 2 Gruppo as dive-bomber escorts. 372 Sq replaced its MC 200s with CR 42s during this phase, to assist in the ground attacks. In late December the Gruppo returned to Italy, leaving their aircraft to 8 Gruppo.

By 1942 they were replacing their MC 200s with MC 202s. In September they moved to Sicily, ready for operations over Malta. During the Allied invasion of North West Africa they were ordered to Sardinia, with 24 aircraft available. Operations began against Bone and Bougie ports, and the invasion fleet on the day of arrival. A section was detached to Palermo from 9 to 16 July 1943.

By 7 September they were in northern Italy with no serviceable aircraft left.

154 GRUPPO CT

Squadriglie 361, 395
Stormo Autonomo

Arrival	Zone	Base	Country	Aircraft	Duties
25 Oct 40	AALB	Berat	Albania	G 50	AE, GA, DF
16 Jan 41	AALB	Devoli	Albania	G 50	DF, AE
14 May 41	Sqa 4	Brindisi	Italy	G 50	TG
19 Jul 41	Sqa 4	Grottaglie	Italy	G 50 CR 42	DF, NF
10 Oct 41	Sqa 4	Crotone	Italy	G 50 CR 42	DF, NF, CE
May 42	AEGE	Rodi Gadurra	Aegean	G 50 CR 42 MC 200 MC 202	DF, NF, CE, AS, AR

This unit was formed on 25 October 1940 for operations in the Balkans, under the direct control of AALB command. The next day 361 Sq arrived from 24 Gruppo, and on 5 November 395 Sq arrived from 160 Gruppo. On 27 November a section was detached to Valona, reuniting with the Gruppo at Devoli on 4 April 1941. The unit had moved there because Berat had proved inadequate.

Despite the bad weather and primitive bases this unit became the most successful in the Greek campaign. With up to 27 G 50s operational, they claimed 52 aircraft plus 29 probables for the loss of only five pilots and one technician between November and April. They escorted bombers, army co-operation and reconnaissance planes, undertook ground attacks, and joined in local defence scrambles. For their achievement the Gruppo was awarded the *Medaglia d'Argento al Valor Militare*.

Immediately the Gruppo moved to Italy 361 Sq was detached to Lecce. On 25 May both squadriglie transferred to 24 Gruppo and 154 Gruppo disbanded.

Reforming on 19 July they reunited with 361 Sq, already at Grottaglie, and 395 Sq flew in from Brindisi. Both squadriglie had returned from 24 Gruppo. G 50s were used for day missions and CR 42s were received for night work. On 10 October pilots and aircraft from both squadriglie formed a third, 396 Sq, at Crotone.

With sections spread between Grottaglie, Lecce, Manduria, and Crotone, the unit defended the ports and areas of Taranto and Brindisi. Much time was taken up with convoy escorts for Libya-bound shipping. 395 Sq had been at Grottaglie since December 1941, but temporarily used Valona between 7 and 23 February 1942. In March another compementary squadriglia was formed within the Gruppo (number not known). The new sub-unit comprised spare Gruppo pilots together with some ex-bomber pilots.

In May 395 and 396 Sq moved to the Aegean while 361 Sq, equipped with MC 200s, left for 21 Gruppo. On the 29th 396 Sq was detached to Gadurra, with a section at Coo. The latter base was only suitable for short stops and emergencies. By August the pilots were finding that static on radio reception often prevented orders from being heard properly.

On 13 September aircrew and ground personnel from the Gruppo defeated a group of enemy saboteurs at Gadurra and Marizza.

In January 1943 the G 50s practiced dropping 50 kg bombs over the Passimada area. Some MC 200s arrived on 26 February in time for an intensive period of activity, as Allied convoys crossed the eastern Mediterranean. The unit undertook day and night defence, anti-submarine and reconnaissance patrols, and shipping escort. Although limited by bad weather in March, they still made three convoy escorts, six standing patrols, five submarine hunts, seven armed reconnaissances, three scrambles, and one torpedo-bomber escort. A total of 72 sorties in just over 105 hours. Problems recurred with the B5 radio crystals, preventing efficient communications.

April saw 106 sorties in 67 missions, including thirty-nine scrambles, five convoy escorts, three patrols, two submarine hunts, and seven armed reconnaissances. By mid-May the squadriglie were split between Marizza and Gadurra. The Gruppo was still in this area on 7 September, having by then also received some MC 202s. 396 Sq had been detached to Antimachia landing ground, on the island of Kos.

155 GRUPPO CT

Squadriglie	360, 378
Stormo	51

Arrival	Zone	Base	Country	Aircraft	Duties
Sep 40	Sqa 3	Ciampino	Italy	G 50	TG
29 Jan 41	Sqa 5	Agheila	Cirenaica	G 50	DF, AE
Apr 41	Sqa 5	Benina	Cirenaica	G 50	DF, AE
9 Apr 41	Sqa 5	Derna	Cirenaica	G 50bis	DF, AE
Nov 41	Sqa 5	Gambut	Cirenaica	G 50bis	DF, AE
24 Mar 42	Sqa 3	Ciampino	Italy	MC 202	TG
30 May 42	ASIC	Gela	Sicily	MC 202	AE, AR
14 Jun 42	ASIC	Chinisia	Sicily	MC 202	AE
Jun 42	ASIC	Gela	Sicily	MC 202	AE, AR
11 Nov 42	ATUN	El Aouina	Tunisia	MC 202	DF, GA
11 Dec 42	ASIC	Gela	Sicily	MC 202	DF
Dec 42	Sqa 3	Ciampino	Italy	MC 202	TG
Mar 43	Sqa 3	Lazio	Italy	MC 202 MC205V	TG
Apr 43	Sqa 3	Capua	Italy	MC 202 MC205V	DF
May 43	Sqa 3	Ciampino	Italy	MC 202 MC205V	DF
16 May 43	ASAR	Monserrato	Sardinia	MC 202 MC205V	DF
11 Jul 43	ASIC	Chinisia	Sicily	MC205V	DF
Aug 43	ASAR	Monserrato	Sardinia	MC205V	DF
21 Aug 43	ASAR	Casa Zeppera	Sardinia	MC 202 MC205V	
				P-38G	DF

This unit was originally formed in 1939, and by September 1940 was receiving sand filters for its G 50s in readiness for desert operations. 360 Sq left for 22 Gruppo by October, but rejoined this Gruppo in March 1941. 351 Sq transferred from 20 Gruppo in April, and the unit left for Libya in the new year.

The poor supply system and difficult terrain caused many damaged G 50s to be abandoned during the retreat in 1941. Even with sand filters, the unit was worn down by the fine dust. Soon after arriving they were escorting Italian and German Ju 87s in the first joint Axis attacks. By April they were busy joining Bf 110s and Bf 109s escorting Ju 87s over Tobruk, maintaining these escorts through the year. Other known units involved in the Tobruk attacks were 96 Gruppo, 18 Gruppo, III./ZG 26, II./StG 2, and III./StG 1. On the night of 21 November the Gruppo lost several aircraft to a bombing raid. Serviceability was now very low so they returned to Italy in the new year.

At this time they rejoined 51 Stormo, which had been disbanded from September 1940 to 1 January 1942. Receiving the MC 202 in March, the unit was then ordered to Sicily for operations over Malta. They claimed a Spitfire on 2 June in their first operation over the island. On 14 June they moved to Chinisia to escort torpedo-bombers during the attacks on the Malta-bound Harpoon convoy. They returned to Gela when the convoy had gone. Following the Allied invasion of North West Africa, the unit took 21 fighters to Tunisia to help defend the Axis forces.

By December 1942 they were back in Italy, receiving more MC 202s. During March 1943 their 28 MC 202s made eight scrambles in the defence of Rome. Training continued, meanwhile, from Ciampino, Capua, and Capodichino, for the next few weeks. The new fighters, including the more modern MC 205Vs, needed modification. (See 20 Gruppo comments).

By May the unit was in Sardinia, with twelve MC 205Vs and over twenty MC 202s, escorting and intercepting around the Tunisian coastline as well as local defence. 351 and 360 Sq were rushed to Sicily to help fight the invasion, but were back in Sardinia after three weeks of heavy action.

On 11 August 360 Sq used a captured P-38G (in Italian markings), sent from Guidonia, and downed a B-24. The Italian fuel corroded the tanks, so it quickly became unserviceable. On the 12th fresh aircraft were passed over by 20 Gruppo to replace the recent losses in Sicily. Some success was had against USAAF fighters in August, mainly P-40s. 378 Sq was detached to Milis from 21 August.

The unit had four MC 202s and eight MC 205Vs still operational on 7 September, at Casa Zeppera.

156 GRUPPO CT

| Squadriglie | 379, 380 |
| Stormo | Autonomo |

Arrival	Zone	Base	Country	Aircraft	Duties
20 Jan 41	ASIC	Comiso	Sicily	CR 42	AE

This unit was briefly formed with nine aircraft taken from 23 Gruppo, which was on its way to Africa. The unit carried out escort missions over Malta until 1 April 1941, when the pilots and thirty-one aircraft were passed back to 23 Gruppo on its return. The Gruppo then disbanded on 8 April. A Re 2000 was tested in late March, possibly the same one as tried out by 6 Gruppo a few days later.

157 GRUPPO CT

| Squadriglie | 384, 385, 386 |
| Stormo | 1 |

Arrival	Zone	Base	Country	Aircraft	Duties
10 Jun 40	Sqa 2	Trapani Milo	Sicily	CR 42	AE
Dec 40	Sqa 1	Torino Caselle	Italy	MC 200	TG
25 Feb 41	Sqa 3	Ciampino Sud	Italy	MC 200	DF
Jul 41	Sqa 5	Derna	Cirenaica	MC 200	DF, GA
13 Dec 41	Sqa 5	Benghasi K2	Cirenaica	MC 200	DF
14 Dec 41	Sqa 5	Tamet	Tripolitania	MC 200	IT
Dec 41	Sqa 1	Torino Caselle	Italy	MC 200	TG
3 Jan 42	AEGE	Kalamata	Aegean	MC 200	CE, DF
Jul 43	ASIC	Reggio Calabria	Italy	MC 200 Re2005	DF
10 Jul 43	AGRE	Paramithia	Greece	MC 200	CE
14 Jul 43	Sqa 4	Grottaglie	Italy	MC 200	DF, CE

This unit was temporarily attached to 1 Stormo in June 1940, for operations against France. It escorted bombing raids on Tunisian targets. At the end of July it became Autonomo, and on 9 December re-equipped with 36 MC 200s.

On 25 February 1941 they joined 52 Stormo for the defence of Rome. 385 Sq became Autonomo, and 386 Sq joined 21 Gruppo. They were replaced by 357 and 371 Sq, both from 22 Gruppo. A few days later 371 Sq became Autonomo under Squadra 4. Once more the Gruppo became Autonomo, in September.

While operating in Libya they received a newly formed 383 Sq on 15 September, and 385 Sq rejoined in October. In late December they passed their aircraft to 150 Gruppo and returned to Italy. Moving to the Aegean with fifteen Macchis, they began a series of convoy escorts.

371 Sq, with modified and improved radio communications, then replaced 385 Sq in December. For a while this squadriglia used a Caproni Vizzola F6M received from 167 Gruppo. 383 Sq disbanded, reforming a year later on 17 January 1943 at Zara, as a Squadriglia Autonomo Assalto.. The whole Gruppo received better communications equipment, for use over land and sea. It was fully operational by February.

384 Sq left to train on MC 200 fighter-bombers, flying out via Sciacca and using these aircraft from El Aouina in Tunisia in January. A Beaufighter was claimed during a convoy escort off Greece that month. They withdrew to Castelvetrano on 3 March with only four MC 200s left. By July the Gruppo was back in Italy, with 50% serviceability. 371 Sq received two Re2005s on 14 July at Reggio Calabria, but these were soon lost to a bombing raid before much use was made of them. 163 Sq joined the Gruppo from 11 June to 30 July, before returning to 161 Gruppo.

On 7 September only seven out of twelve MC 200s were operational.

158 GRUPPO Assalto

| Squadriglie | 236, 387, 388 |
| Stormo | Autonomo |

Arrival	Zone	Base	Country	Aircraft	Duties
Dec 41	Sqa 5	Sorman	Tripolitania	CR 42	TG
10 May 42	Sqa 2	Aviano	Italy	CR 42	TG
13 May 42	Sqa 5	Benghasi K3	Cirenaica	CR 42	GA
26 May 42	Sqa 5	El Ftehja	Cirenaica	CR 42	GA
Jun 42	Sqa 5	Derna	Cirenaica	CR 42	GA
26 Jun 42	Sqa 5	Sidi Barrani	Egypt	CR 42	GA
30 Jun 42	Sqa 5	Abu Nimeir	Egypt	CR 42	GA
29 Oct 42	Sqa 5	Martuba 4	Cirenaica	CR 42	CE
11 Nov 42	Sqa 5	Benghasi K1	Cirenaica	CR 42	IT
12 Nov 42	Sqa 5	Ara Fileni	Tripolitania	CR 42	DF
15 Nov 42	Sqa 5	Buerat	Tripolitania	CR 42	GA, CE
7 Dec 42	Sqa 2	Aviano	Italy	CR 42 G 50bis	TG
May 43	Sqa 2	Osoppo	Italy	CR 42 G 50bis	GA
10 Jul 43	ASIC	Reggio Calabria	Italy	G 50bis	GA
16 Jul 43	Sqa 4	Crotone	Italy	G 50bis	GA
23 Jul 43	Sqa 3	Pistoia	Italy	G 50bis	IT
25 Jul 43	Sqa 1	Lonate Pozzolo	Italy	G 50bis	TG

In December 1941 this unit began forming on CR 42s at Sorman. The pilots came mainly from the withdrawing OA units, their observers going to the RST units. 236 Sq arrived at K2 by 9 February and joined the Gruppo. The whole Gruppo then returned to Italy for a course on ground attack duties, joining 50 Stormo Assalto. Then they moved back to Africa ready to support the push into Egypt. Operations resumed on 24 May.

The next month they entered Egypt with eleven aircraft, and continued to operate through the Alamein battles until attrition took its toll. They fought several combats against Beaufighters in July. By 20 September they still had over 20 fighter-bombers on charge. In October they passed their surviving CR 42s to 101 Gruppo at Abu Nimeir, and moved to Martuba to pick up replacement aircraft. During November, as well as ground attacks, they helped protect the Regia Marina warships along the Misurata-Sirte coastline. On 7 December they passed their aircraft to 159 Gruppo, and left for Italy.

Once home they began re-equipping with G 50bis fighter-bombers. 236 Sq handed over its last CR 42s in June 1943. On 9 July, with 24 fighters operational out of 37, they carried out attacks on the invasion forces off Sicily. As the Allies gained the upper hand the unit retired to the north, with only seven serviceable aircraft out of thirteen left by 7 September. They were awaiting re-equipment with Re 2002s.

159 GRUPPO Assalto

Squadriglie	389, 390, 391
Stormo	50

Arrival	Zone	Base	Country	Aircraft	Duties
4 May 42	Sqa 2	Aviano	Italy	CR 42	TG
25 May 42	Sqa 5	Castelbenito	Tripolitania	CR 42	GA
28 May 42	Sqa 5	El Ftehja	Cirenaica	CR 42	GA
Jun 42	Sqa 5	Derna	Cirenaica	CR 42	GA
24 Jun 42	Sqa 5	El Adem	Cirenaica	CR 42	GA
26 Jun 42	Sqa 5	Sidi Barrani	Egypt	CR 42	GA
30 Jun 42	Sqa 5	Abu Nimeir	Egypt	CR 42	GA, AE, AR
15 Sep 42	Sqa 5	Benghazi K3	Cirenaica	CR 42	TG AR
Sep 42	Sqa 5	Abu Nimeir	Egypt	CR 42	GA
29 Oct 42	Sqa 5	Martuba 4	Cirenaica	CR 42	CE
11 Nov 42	Sqa 5	Benghasi K1	Cirenaica	CR 42	IT
12 Nov 42	Sqa 5	Ara Fileni	Tripolitania	CR 42	DF
15 Nov 42	Sqa 5	Buerat	Tripolitania	CR 42	GA, CE
10 Dec 42	Sqa 5	Misurata	Tripolitania	CR 42	DF, GA
18 Dec 42	Sqa 5	Gars Garabulli	Tripolitania	CR 42	GA
Jan 43	Sqa 5	Zuara	Tripolitania	CR 42	GA
15 Jan 43	Sqa 2	Aviano	Italy	CR 42 G 50bis	TG
May 43	Sqa 2	Osoppo	Italy	G 50bis	TG
4 Jun 43	Sqa 3	Pistoia	Italy	G 50bis	GA
11 Jun 43	ASIC	Gela	Sicily	G 50bis	GA
18 Jun 43	Sqa 3	Pistoia	Italy	G 50bis	GA
10 Jul 43	ASIC	Reggio Calabria	Italy	G 50bis	GA
16 Jul 43	Sqa 4	Crotone	Italy	G 50bis	GA
23 Jul 43	Sqa 3	Pistoia	Italy	G 50bis	IT
30 Jul 43	Sqa 1	Lonate Pozzolo	Italy	G 50bis Re 2002	GA

After a ground attack course, this unit transferred with 30 CR 42AS to Libya ready to support the push into Egypt. Operations began jointly with 158 Gruppo, on 25 May 1942.

They entered Egypt in June, but by 1 July 391 Sq had only one CR 42 operational out of the ten they set out with. After a brief rest they received fresh aircraft, eventually operating nine aircraft among ten pilots. Losses increased during the run up to the battles around El Alamein. The Gruppo was recalled to K3 on 15 September with 23 CR 42AS. In October the Gruppo transferred their remaining aircraft to 101 Gruppo, and picked up replacements at Martuba. They then carried out shipping protection duties alongside 158 Gruppo. In December one squadriglia supported the defence of Hon, using Buerat then Misurata. The Gruppo may have used Bir Dufan in November.

On 8 December four SM 82s flew some of the personnel from Misurata to Gerbini, followed by the rest of the Gruppo which withdrew to Italy and re-equipped with G 50bis. Some personnel were passed to 101 Gruppo. 391 Sq received its first new fighter-bomber on 16 March 1943, and detached four aircraft to Gela on 10 June. The rest of the Gruppo followed the next day, but were decimated during July in the defence of Sicily. On the 13th 28 aircraft were destroyed in a raid by 200 B-24s, leaving only 7 serviceable. In September efforts were made to equip them with the more modern Re 2002, but they were still training on these aircraft when Italy surrendered. Only one G 50bis and four Re 2002s were available by then.

160 GRUPPO CT

Squadriglie	393, 394
Stormo	Autonomo

Arrival	Zone	Base	Country	Aircraft	Duties
10 Jun 40	AALB	Tirana	Albania	CR32 CR 42 Ro41	DF, AE
28 Oct 40	AALB	Drenova	Albania	CR 42 CR32 Ro41	DF, AE
29 Oct 40	AALB	Devoli	Albania	CR 42 CR32 Ro41	
				G 50	DF, AE
41	Sqa 2	Osoppo	Italy	CR 42	TG

Arrival	Zone	Base	Country	Aircraft	Duties
Nov 41	Sqa 5	Gialo	Cirenaica	CR 42	GA
Dec 41	Sqa 5	Benghasi	Cirenaica	CR 42	DF
20 Dec 41	Sqa 5	Agedabia	Cirenaica	CR 42	GA
22 Dec 41	Sqa 5	Ara Fileni	Tripolitania	CR 42	GA
Dec 41	Sqa 5	Sorman	Tripolitania	CR 42 G 50bis	GA
Mar 42	Sqa 5	Castelbenito	Tripolitania	CR 42 G 50bis	GA
Jul 42	Sqa 5	Sorman	Tripolitania	CR 42 G 50bis	GA
Dec 42	Sqa 2	Osoppo	Italy	Re 2001	TG
Mar 43	ASAR	Decimomannu	Sardinia	Re 2001	DF, AE, GA
Apr 43	ASAR	Olbia Venafiorita	Sardinia	Re 2001 CR 42	
				G 50bis	DF, AE, GA, CE

This unit began the war with eight CR 32s and eight CR 42s, having been formed at Tirana during the occupation of Albania. 395 Sq became Autonomo the day war broke out and went to join 154 Gruppo on 5

November. Six Ro 41s were attached to each squadriglia for training purposes, although they were briefly used in action in the initial days of the Greek campaign. On 21 October two Ca 133s were received, the unit initiating use of this type as an air ambulance.

394 Sq was detached to Berat on 29 October but this base proved too limited so they rejoined 393 Sq at Devoli on 16 January 1941. 375 Sq, formerly Autonomo, joined the Gruppo from Tirana, possibly as early as February. The Gruppo now fielded 30 CR 42s for operations against Yugoslavia. They also received some G 50s towards the end of the campaign.

After a brief period of anti-partisan duties, they retired to Italy for rest. By the end of the year they were in Africa on ground attack duties. The first operation was on 26 November, with nine Fiats attacking Allied columns near Agheila. The summer of 42 found them with eight CR 42s and twenty G 50bis, preparing for the offensive on Egypt. By 20 September they had 23 G 50bisAS still serviceable. After many exhaustive ground support missions, where they suffered from heavy groundfire and enemy fighters, they withdrew to Italy.

Re-equipping with Re 2001s they moved to Sardinia in March 1943. Sections were detached in April to Ajaccio (Re 2001s), and Sarzana (CR 42s, G 50bis). They fought numerous battles around Sardinian waters in the next few months. The unit suffered many problems with their radios, trying to liaise with shipping when on protective patrols. In June a short-wave length radio was considered for both ships and aircraft, but the urgent situation prevented this being implemented. By 7 September the unit had twelve serviceable Re 2001s at Venafiorita, and two CR 42s and one G 50bis serviceable at Ajaccio.

161 GRUPPO CT

Squadriglie	162, 163, 164				
Stormo	Autonomo				

Arrival	Zone	Base	Country	Aircraft	Duties
11 Jun 41	AEGE	Rodi Marizza	Aegean	CR 42 G 50bis	
				G 50B	DF, CE
May 42	Sqa 4	Grottaglie	Italy	G 50bis MC 200	TG, CE, DF
Mar 43	ASIC	Palermo	Sicily	MC 200 CR 42CN	DF
18 Mar 43	ASIC	Chinisia	Sicily	MC 200	CE
24 Mar 43	Sqa 4	Grottaglie	Italy	MC 200	CE, DF
Mar 43	ASIC	Castelvetrano	Sicily	MC 200	DF
Apr 43	Sqa 5	El Aouina	Tunisia	MC 200	DF
15 May 43	ASIC	Reggio Calabria	Italy	MC 200 MC 202	
				D.520	DF
22 Jul 43	Sqa 3	Cerveteri	Italy	MC 202	DF
26 Jul 43	Sqa 3	Castiglione del Lago	Italy	MC 202 SAI207	D

This unit formed in June 1941 to help protect the Aegean Islands and its supply ships. 162 Sq had formed

in 1941, and between 20 and 31 May had supported operations against Crete using Scarpanto. They made several bombing and strafing attacks in their CR 42s. 164 Sq formed on 4 June from CR 42s returning from supporting the Iraqi revolt, where they had claimed one for the loss of four against the RAF.

These two squadriglie joined 163 Sq to form the Gruppo. Each of them also formed a night-fighter section. Some G 50bis were received during the year, together with two G 50B two-seat trainers for converting pilots from biplanes to monoplanes.

In May 1942 they moved to Italy, using Grottaglie and Lecce. 164 Sq was detached to Reggio Calabria on 2 December, with eight MC 200s, for the protection of Taranto and convoy escort duties. From the 13th they escorted German air convoys to Tunisia, staying in that country between 14 and 17 December, to help cover the incoming formations.

During the following spring 162 Sq was at Crotone, 163 Sq at Grottaglie, and 164 Sq at Reggio Calabria. They now used the Radio 1000 system, which greatly improved communications. The increase in Allied air attacks led to the unit being moved to Sicily in March. They still maintained a night-fighter section, with two CR 42CNs. For the next two months they helped protect the supply routes to and from Tunisia.

Returning to southern Italy, they received MC 202s along with seven D.520s delivered direct from France. They operated against the invasion forces off Sicily and patrolled the Messina Straits and north-west Sicily. In April 164 Sq claimed nine B-24s over Calabria in four combats. 371 Sq joined them at Reggio Calabria on 15 May until late July. 163 Sq briefly joined 157 Gruppo, from 11 June to 30 July, then returned to the Gruppo. Many aircraft were lost to bombing and eventually the unit had to move further north.

During the early part of August it was intended to re-equip with the new lightweight fighter, the SAI 207. There were not enough available, however, and by 7 September no MC 202s or SAI 207s were serviceable.

162 GRUPPO Assalto

Squadriglie	109, 110				
Stormo	Autonomo				

Arrival	Zone	Base	Country	Aircraft	Duties
12 Mar 43	ASIC	Palermo	Sicily	MC 200	GA
10 Apr 43	ATUN	Uadi Ghindel	Tunisia	MC 200	GA
6 May 43	ASIC	Castelvetrano	Sicily	MC 200	GA

This Gruppo was formed in Sicily as a fighter-bomber unit using aircraft from 13 Gruppo. The pilots were mostly

100 Right: *This Macchi MC 202, liberally marked with red lines and arrows is an 'Arlecchino' (Harlequin-joker), an aircraft built up from spares and parts cannibalised from other machines. These were usually issued to second line units. The Fiat CR 42 in the background sports a night black finish, shrouded exhausts and underwing bomb racks. The number 1 in a circle on the fuselage gives no clue to its identity*

101 Above: *Personnel of the 360ª Squadriglia, 155° Gruppo, 51° Stormo, inspect one of their new Macchi MC 205s, MM 9291. Location is probably Trapani-Chinisia, Sicily, June 1943*

102 Right: *A Macchi MC 200 of the 362ª Squadriglia, 22° Gruppo, CSIR, at Krivoi Rog, Russia. The Caproni Ca 133 in the background suggests that the date is 26 September 1941, the day three of these machines joined the Gruppo—this may be a welcoming ceremony for them. Soon afterwards they moved to Stalino*

103: *A Macchi MC 200 of the 363ᵃ Squadriglia, 150° Gruppo, 2° Stormo in flight over the wastes of Cirenaica in spring 1942.Camouflage appears to be a field-modified C1C type consisting of large green and brown patches on a yellow ochre background. The engine cowling also appears to have once been yellow and then been thinly re-camouflaged. Fuel overspill has run down over the unit emblem*

104: *A Messerschmitt Bf 109G-6/R6 Trop of 363ᵃ Squadriglia, 3° Gruppo at its dispersal on a Sicilian airfield in June 1943. The number '7' identifies the aircraft as that of Tenente Ugo Drago, who used it as his lucky number on all his aircraft. Camouflage is the original German 74/75/76 scheme with the national insignia roughly over-painted by approximate shades of Italian paint. There is no unit emblem to be seen*

105: *A Messerschmitt Bf 109G-6 of 364ᵃ Squadriglia, 3° Gruppo, on a crowded Sicilian dispersal in June 1943. As the machine carries the famous 'Gigi Tre Osei' unit badge on its fuselage and the number '1' this may indicate it is the CO's air-craft. What appears to be an all-black Fiat CR 42 can be seen in the background*

106: *Fiat G.50bis fighters of the 366ᵃ Squadriglia, 151° Gruppo, probably at Araxos in Greece in summer 1942. All wear the Fiat-applied D1A 'lizard' style camouflage. The 'Ace of Sabres' emblem of the Gruppo can be made out on the fuselage band. White numbers were fairly uncommon on Italian fighters*

107: *An early production Macchi MC 200 of 369ᵃ Squadriglia, 152° Gruppo, 54° Stormo. Manned by Spanish Civil War veterans, the squadron had many technical problems with their new aircraft. They thus saw no action until December 1940 when they were transferred to 22° Gruppo at Ciampino. As seen here the location is Treviso in spring 1940. The aircraft appears to have minor damage below the open gun access panel and wears the 'Cucaracha' emblem of the Gruppo. It retains the pre-war tail stripes on its C8 type camouflage*

108: *A Macchi MC 202, Serie VII, of the 369ᵃ Squadriglia, 22° Gruppo, 53° Stormo displays its classic lines. Based at Capdichino in June 1943, The aircraft wears Macchi's standard D3 'smoke rings' camouflage consisting of Verde Oliva Scuro 2 rings on a Nocciola Chiaro 4 base. This pattern was also applied to most MC 205 models. The scarecrow badge is that of the Stormo.*

109: *During a raid on Malta on 27 July 1942 by nine Luftwaffe Junkers Ju 88s, this Macchi MC 202, MM7842, of the 378ª Squadriglia, 155° Gruppo, which formed part of the fighter escort, became the first of four victories that day by Sergeant George 'Screwball' Beurling of 249 Squadron, RAF. The Italian pilot, Sergent Maggiore Falerio Gelli managed to crashland on the island of Gozo and escaped with bruises. Gelli had previously claimed three Spitfires shot down over Malta. The aircraft wears a D1 type camouflage, the official 'colonial' pattern*

110: *Fiat CR 42 of the 379ª Squadriglia, 156° Gruppo, somewhere over Sicily. This unit had only the briefest of existence, being formed with nine aircraft from 23° Gruppo on 20 January 1941 and was based at Comiso. After a few escort missions over Malta, the pilots were all transferred to 23° Gruppo on 1 April, the squadron officially disbanding on the 8th*

111: *Another view of the same Fiat CR 42 of the 369ª Squadriglia seen in photo 110. The elaborate mottle camouflage on the upper wing appears to be a thickly applied C1 type, and is noticeably darker than that on the fuselage. possibly the wing was a replacement. Note how the white backgrounds to the national insignia stand out—these were often obscured in the field, and were eventually dropped altogether, the new markings being just the black ring and fasces*

fresh trainees. The desperate situation in Tunisia meant committing them to action before training was complete. 110 Sq used Crotone before moving to Tunisia.

109 Sq moved to base K41 on 25 March 1943, continuing training there and then at Achichina. 110 Sq joined them at Uadi Ghindel on 10 April, giving them a total of fifteen MC 200s. The first operation was carried out on 15 April, with a bombing attack on armour near Djebibina escorted by MC 200s of 54 Stormo. From then on the unit was constantly busy with ground attacks, usually covered by 7 Gruppo. On 2 May, escorted by 24 MC 202s (9 from 16 Gruppo, 15 from 7 Gruppo), they attacked Enfidaville, joining combat with P-40s after bombing. Three days later eight aircraft of 110 Sq attacked the enemy south of Djebibina. This was the last offensive mission by the Regia Aeronautica based in Tunisia. One aircraft was hit by anti-aircraft fire. The next day the unit retired to Sicily, where the survivors seem to have been distributed to other units. The Gruppo was disbanded on 31 May.

167 GRUPPO Int.

Squadriglie	300, 303
Stormo	Autonomo

Arrival	Zone	Base	Country	Aircraft	Duties
10 May 42	Sqa 3	Ciampino	Italy	CR 42CN CVF5	
				MC 200 CVF4 G 50	
				CVF6 Ca 164	
				Ca 313	NF, DF
43	Sqa 4	Grottaglie	Italy	CR 42CN CVF5	
				CVF4 Re 2001CN	
				FC20bis D.520	NF
May 43	Sqa 3	Ciampino Sud	Italy	CR 42CN CVF5	
				Re 2001CN	NF
20 Jul 43	Sqa 3	Littoria	Italy	Re 2001CN	NF

This unit formed in May 1942 with the previously Autonomo 300 and 303 Sq, as the night fighter defence of Rome and Naples. The initial aircraft intake was a Quartermasters nightmare. They had 10 CR 42s, 13 CV F5s, and 1 CV F 6—all fighters—and 4 Ca 164 and 1 Ca 313 trainers.

300 Sq used the Caproni Vizzola fighters, along with some MC 200s and G 50s. The latter types were used to boost the day defences of Rome. A single CV F4 was received by 303 Sq for trials at Capua and Capodichino.

In November the aircraft received modified B5/B30 radios, which reduced communication problems. On 6 December 303 Sq passed its sole CV F6M to 157 Gruppo. In January they made 23 night scrambles over Naples and Rome, with no claims. In February 26 scrambles were made, claiming one victim south of Capris. The next month, although there were 33 scrambles, the unit was

short of trained pilots—there were only twelve in the Gruppo. By April the CR 42 was proving

By April the CR42 was proving almost useless in catching four-engined bombers, and only seven pilots were fully night trained. 303 Sq moved from Capua to Ciampino Sud in May. To add to their problems the Gruppo was now experiencing problems with severe oil loss in flight.

During the summer of 1943 a French D.520 was tried out for night operations. It proved more practical in some ways than the CR 42, especially with its cannon armament. By June all the pilots had learned to fly the D.520. However, the usual supply problems occurred, so both squadriglie settled for the Re 2001CN as the standard nightfighter. By 9 June six of these were operational in the night defence of Rome, from Ciampino Sud. The Gruppo joined 42 Stormo between 10 May and 24 June.

In April the prototype twin-engined FC 20bis was flown from Guidonia to Capua by *Maggiore* Ricci. It made only one intercept and was found to be too slow to catch the B-24s it was sent after. After that it moved to Furbara.

On 21 June four MC 200s moved from Grottaglie to Paramithia for convoy escort duties, returning on 11 July. These aircraft were recorded as part of this Gruppo. On the day of surrender this unit had seven serviceable Re 2001CNs.

171 GRUPPO Int.

Squadriglie	301, 302
Stormo	Autonomo

Arrival	Zone	Base	Country	Aircraft	Duties
1 Oct 41	ASIC	Gela	Sicily	CR 42CN	NF

This was the first nightfighter unit to form. The defences of Sicily required a counter to the RAF night bomber raids, so 301 and 302 Sq were reformed with CR 42CNs. The lack of modern equipment and facilities limited the usefulness of the unit. The Germans took over their base in November and they then disbanded. The pilots and aircraft split up to form three individual nightfighter sections.

Battaglione Aviazione Sahariana

Squadriglie	26, 99				
Arrival	Zone	Base	Country	Aircraft	Duties
Jul 42	Sqa 5	Hon	Tripolitania	CR 42 Ca309	
				SM 79 SM 81	AR, DF
Jan 43	Sqa 5	Zuara	Tripolitania	Ca309 SM 79	AR

This unit was formed for the protection of the oases

in the south of Libya. 99 Sq had been at Hon since the outbreak of war, and 26 Sq was at Cufra. Both units had six Ca 309s and were part of the Aviazione Sahariana. They covered the western and eastern oasis respectively. 26 Sq moved to Hon on 1 March 1941 after successfully defending Cufra from an armoured car attack.

In June 1942 several SM 81s arrived from 103 Sq, along with some CR 42s for local defence and armed reconnaissances. On 20 September the unit had the following serviceable aircraft 7 Ca 309s, 2 SM 79s, 5 CR 42s, and 2 SM 81s all at Hon. Between 25 December and 1 January 1943 the unit was very active against enemy ground units. A section of 26 Sq was detached to Sebha until 4 January when it moved to El Asabaa. Three days later the unit left Hon. On 20 January the Aviazione Sahariana returned to Italy, via Zuara, with four SM 79s and six Ca 309s.

Gruppo Gasbarrini BT

Squadriglie	41, SMSN
Stormo	Autonomo

Arrival	Zone	Base	Country	Aircraft	Duties
10 Jun 40	AOI	Agordat	Eritrea	Ca133	AR

Named after its commander, this unit of twelve Ca 133s comprised 41 Sq and the Squadriglia Stato Maggiore Settore Nord. Their duties included patrolling the northern borders of Eritrea and the southern Red Sea. No mention is made in records after the initial outbreak of war, so it may have been dispersed to other units to boost their offensive capabilities. This may also have happened to the squadriglie SMSC at Dembidollo, SMSO at Addis Abeba, and SMSS at Mogadiscio. These units were all equipped with six Ca133s for border and sea patrols. The SMSO Squadriglia was given nine aircraft and held in reserve for operations against British Somaliland. SMSS Squadriglia was dispersed on 20 June to Villaggio Duca di Abruzzi.

Raggruppamento Bombardamento

Arrival	Zone	Base	Country	Aircraft	Duties
1 Jun 43	Sqa 3	Perugia San Egidio	Italy	Z1007bis Z1007ter	NB

This unit was created to make maximum use of the remaining experienced bomber crews by placing them under one command. 28 Gruppo (10, 19 Sq), 86 Gruppo (190, 191 Sq), 88 Gruppo (264, 265 Sq) and 106 Gruppo (260, 261 Sq) formed this unit. They used the remaining airworthy bombers and also received about fifty of the new Z1007ter, which retained the good characteristics of the 'bis' but was more powerful and better equipped. An average twenty out of thirty were operational daily.

It was intended that the unit would re-equip with the excellent Z1018, which was equal to the American B-25 Mitchell in performance and capability. Due to industrial problems in converting production to a totally new design at this late stage, it meant only a trickle of examples became available. These went to 262 Sq.

Between July and August the unit made over 100 raids on the invasion forces around Sicily. By mid-August they were reduced from 31 fully operational aircraft to 13 out of 19. The entire bomber capability of the Regia Aeronautica was now reduced to the size of one Gruppo. On 21 July they hit *Ocean Virtue* in a night strike off Sicily. By 7 September they had only nine operational aircraft left, plus four SM 82 transports.

Raggruppamento Aerosilurante

Arrival	Zone	Base	Country	Aircraft	Duties
3 Jun 43	Sqa3	Siena Ampugnano	Italy	S79	TB
17 Jul 43	Sqa4	Lecce	Italy	S79	TB
23Aug43	Sqa3	Pisa	Italy	S79	TB

This unit was created to make the most effective use of the surviving experienced torpedo-bomber crews, by bringing them directly under Squadra 3 control. 89 Gruppo (228, 229 Sq) and 41 Gruppo (204 Sq) used the home base, while 108 Gruppo (256, 257 Sq) and 131 Gruppo (284 Sq) used Pisa San Giusto. They had a total of 44 SM 79s available.

In July they moved to Lecce under Squadra 4, for operations against the Sicilian invasion fleets. 41 Gruppo dispersed to Gioia del Colle, and 131 Gruppo to Pisa. 104 Gruppo, arriving at Lecce from Gadurra, joined the unit. 132 Gruppo at Littoria also joined. It may have been one of these units that disabled the aircraft carrier HMS *Indomitable* in a night attack on 16 July, causing her to retire to Gibraltar, although credit was claimed by 130 Gruppo. On 8 August the crews and aircraft of 89, 109, and 130 Gruppi were absorbed by this unit, which by now comprised elements of 41, 108, 131, 132, 104 Gruppi. One aircraft was lost off Sicily when 24 from 131/108/41 Gruppi took off from Lecce on 15 August to attack shipping.

On 23 August new crews arrived from 1 NAS at Gorizia and 3 NAS at Salon. The unit moved to Pisa, 131 Gruppo arriving from Grottaglie, 108 Gruppo from Lecce, and 132 Gruppo staying at Littoria. To reduce the risk of major loss in a bombing raid, 104 Gruppo from Lecce and 41 Gruppo from Gioia del Colle both moved to Siena. On the 24th four aircraft went to Pisa, to attack ships off Philippeville.

On 1 September 39 aircraft operated against shipping off Calabria. Seven days later twelve took off from Pisa, Siena, and Littoria in the late afternoon for an attack on ships at Salerno. Eight returned on hearing the Armistice orders, but four made the attack, unaware of the signal. This was the last operation carried out by the Regia Aeronautica against the Allies. By that day, 131 Gruppo had moved to Siena, joined by 279 Sq. 41 Gruppo had also received 205 Sq there. A total of 22 SM 79s was then available.

Out of 39 SM 79s, based at both Pisa and Siena, six were serviceable. 104 Gruppo had 8 out of 12 at Siena, while 132 Gruppo had 6 out of 9 serviceable at Littoria. A Sezione Autonomo was being formed at Capodichino with a single SM 79.

Centrale Sperimentale di Guidonia

The RAF had Boscombe Down, the Luftwaffe had Rechlin, the USAAF had Wright Field, and the Regia Aeronautica had Guidonia. A test unit operated there throughout the war, testing ideas and developing aircraft. Through this base passed most of the bomber and fighter prototypes, some soon to see production and others remaining experimental. As well as these, several captured enemy aircraft were also put through their paces.

Among the more important issues covered were the development and study of level and dive bombing procedures, and test flying of new potential frontline aircraft.

Indeed, by 1943, some prototypes were being used to intercept incoming Allied bombing raids over Italy due to the desperate shortage of aircraft.

Some examples of the aircraft types seen at this base (often for many months) are shown in the tables below.

112 Below: Among the aircraft tested at Guidonia was an IMAM Ro 57bis, intended as a single-seat fighter-bomber. This is MM75335, believed to be at Guidonia in summer 1942. It is carrying a 500kg bomb under the fuselage, and one of 160kg under each wing

Aircraft tested at Guidonia June 1940-September 1943					
Date	Aircraft	Type	Reason	Pilot	Comments
1940					
Jun	SM 83	3E transport	Under test		range/load combinations
Jun	SM 82	3E transport	under test		range/load combinations
Jun	Z 1018	2E bomber	under test	Stoppani	MM467
Jun	SAI 7	SE trainer	under test		
Jun	AUT 18	SE fighter	under test	Tondi, Vignoli	
				Mantelli	Abandoned after 50 flights—intended to replace Ba65—beat CR42, G50, MC200, and Bf 109E in mock combat but deemed systems and fuel tanks too vulnerable.
Jul	Ca 602	SE trainer	under test	Gasperi	
Jul	SM 82	3E transp/bom	operational trials		Three used in experimental ops against Gibraltar between 9th and 17th
Jul	Ro 63	SE liason	under test	Mantelli	
Aug	MC 201	SE fighter	under test		
1940	Re 2000GA	SE fighter	under test	Mantelli	Endurance tests for increased tankage
Aug	Re 2001	SE fighter	under test		
Aug	MC202	SE fighter	under test		
Aug	SM 86	2E dive bom	under test	Scarpini	Used later over Malta and Greece
Sep	G 50bis	SE fighter	under test		

Date	Aircraft	Type	Reason	Pilot	Comments
1940					
Sep	Blenheim 4	2E bomber	affiliation		Landed at Pantelleria en route to Malta 13th, used in fighter affiliation with CR42 and MC200s
Sep	LN411	SE dive bom	affiliation		Ex-Aeronavale, force landed on south coast of Sardinia in June
Sep	Fi 156C-2	SE liaison	under test		
Oct	Cansa FC12	SE fig bom trainer	under test		Two-seater
Oct	P108B	4E bomber	under test	Lana	
Oct	Ro 57	2E fighter	under test	Mantelli	Long test period
Oct	Caproni V F4	SE fighter	under test		Testing DB601 engine
Nov	SM 84	3E bomber	under test		
Nov	Ca 603	SE trainer	under test	Mantelli	Tested until May 1942
1941					
Feb	Swordfish	SE torp bomb	affiliation		Ex-FAA '4F', P4127, (820 NAS) captured 2 August at Bacu Abis
Mar	Ca 164	SE trainer	under test	Rosetti	
Mar	Re 2002	SE fighter	under test		Testing manoeuvrability, and potential use as fighter bomber
Apr	Fiat G12T	3E transport	under test		
May	Caproni C4	SE trainer	under test	Korompai Mantelli	Built for colonial and desert use
May	Fury II	SE fighter	affiliation		Ex-Yugoslav Hawker biplane
May	Gladiator	SE fighter	affiliation		Captured in Yugoslavia
1941	Ca 331A	2E night fighter	under test		
1941	CR 42DB	SE fighter	under test	Cus	MM469 tested with DB601 engine
Jun	D.520	SE fighter	under test		Checked out by pilots of 2 Stormo—impressed by French HS404 cannon
Jun	Ca 313	2E bomber	under test		Tested for torpedo carrying
Jun	MS 406	SE fighter	under test		Joined D.520 on cannon trials, and potential equipping of RA units
Jul	Ba 201	SE dive bom	under test	Acerbi	Badly damaged in March 1942 after 94 flights
Jul	Bü 131	SE trainer	under test		
Jul	Bestetti BN1	2E aircraft	under test		Twin boomed
Jul	SAI 107	SE fighter	under test		First of lightweight fighters
Sep	CV F6M	SE fighter	under test		Tested different German engines including DB605
Sep	Hurricane 1	SE fighter	affiliation		Two ex-Yugoslav captured at Mostar, still present in full RA camouflage and markings in early 1942. After suffering light damage during a heavy handed landing one was used only for ground instruction.
1942					
Jan	Beaufighter 1	2E fighter	affiliation		Landed in error at Siracuse, while on a flight between Gibraltar and Malta. Destroyed in a landing accident on 29 January 1943.
Jan	SM 85	2E dive bom	under test	Busnengo	
Jan	FN 315	SE trainer	under test		
1942	Re 2001	SE fighter	under test		Testing for carrier trials
1942	Ro 58	2E fighter	under test	Mantelli Moci	Tested in mock combat with Me 410
May	Cansa C6	SE trainer	under test		
May	Ba 201	SE dive bom	under test		Second prototype. On 14 June flew to Chinisia via Reggio Calabria for op against Malta convoy. Returned to Guidonia the next day.

Date	Aircraft	Type	Reason	Pilot	Comments
1942					
1942	G 55	SE fighter	under test	Cus	Mock combats with Bf109G and Fw 190A and Ro 58—voted the best even by the German pilots who took turns to fly each type
May	MC 205V	SE fighter	under test	Carestiato	Placed in production as it used most MC202 components, later MC205N was the real equivalent to G55 and Re 2005 fighter generation.
Jun	Ro 57bis	2E fighter	under test		Being converted for dive bombing trials
Jun	SAI 207	SE fighter	under test		Six examples passed to 83 Sq for ops on 1 July 1943
Jul	Re 2005	SE fighter	under test	De Prato	
Sep	BR 20bis	2E bomber	under test	Rolandi	Tested until November
Sep	Z1018	2E bomber	under test	Stoppani	MM24290 several examples on trials, eventually going to 262 Sq by July 1943
Sep	Spitfire V	SE fighter	affiliation		Force landed at Scoglitti by 51 Stormo. Checked out by them at Gela before transferring to Guidonia
Oct	SM 89	2E attack aircraft	under test	Moggi	Assigned with FC20 to op trials with 173 Sq in April 1943
Oct	Re 2003	SE recce	under test	Caracciolo	Two seat version of Re 2002
Oct	AL12	Glider	under test		Aeronautica Lombarda 14 seat troop carrier
Oct	Go 242A1	Glider	under test		
Oct	DFS 230	Glider	under test		
Oct	G 50B	SE fighter trainer	under test		Two seat version of G 50bis on trials for both carrier use (G 50bis AN) and for training schools (G 50B)
Nov	Re 2001CN	SE nightfighter	under test		Day fighter converted to night fighting
Nov	MC 205N-1	SE fighter	under test		
Dec	P108T	4E transport	under test		Present until at least April 1943
Dec	P108C	4E transport	under test		Present until at least April 1943
Dec	Re 2001 Delta	SE fighter	under test		Tested with Isotta Fraschini engine. Pilot baled out 27 January 1943, aircraft lost
1943					
Jan	SAI 403	SE fighter	under test		Produced at a fraction of cost and time compared to MC 202
Feb	B-24D-1-CO	4E bomber	affiliation	Raina	*Blonde Bomber II*, 41-123659, brought in from Pachino, via Catania, Sicily where it force landed after being hit in the engines over Naples. Flew to Rechlin in June 1943.
Mar	FC20bis	2E fighter	under test		Used unsuccessfully to intercept Liberators— insufficient speed at height
Mar	SM 91	2E fighter	under test	Moggi	Twin boom fighter with DB605 engines
Mar	LeO 451	2E bomber	under test		
Mar	SM 75GA	3E transport	under test		Two with Nucleo C LATI for long range ops
Apr	SAIMAN 208	SE trainer	under test		
Apr	SAI 403	SE fighter	under test		Second series of tests
May	MC 205N-2	SE fighter	under test		joined first prototype in intercepts in August—no recorded successes known
Jun	AR	SE bomb	under test		Disposable radio guided flying bomb built by Aeronautica Lombarda—too late for use
Jun	P-38G	2E fighter	affiliation		See over for full story*
1943	Beaufighter	2E fighter	affiliation		Study of IFF system
Aug	SM 95	4E transport	under test		Intended for flights to New York

*On 12 June 1943 a USAAF Lockheed P-38G Lightning fighter was on a sortie between Gibraltar and Malta. The inexperienced pilot found himself low on fuel. Due to a 30° compass error he thought he was over friendly territory, but had flown over Sicily and then southern Sardinia. He landed at Cagliari-Capoterra and was captured. The next day an Italian test pilot, *Colonello* Angelo Tondi, arrived to supervise the control of this enemy fighter. The local pilots of 51 Stormo were intrigued, and Tondi instructed the aircraft to be repainted in Italian markings for the flight to the Test and Research Centre at Guidonia. During the initial transfer to Italy the aircraft was attacked over central Sardinia by Luftwaffe Bf 109s who broke off when they saw the Italian insignia.

During the next few days Tondi flew several test flights, and the mechanics studied the aircraft systems and weapons. He eventually received permission to use the P-38G to intercept Allied bombers who were attacking Rome. He felt that he could avoid the escorts who would assume he was friendly, and shoot down a bomber and escape before they could react.

On 11 August he took off from Guidonia to intercept Twelfth Air Force bombers—Italian sources say B-24s, German sources say B-17s. Even with an escort of MC 202s, he was still attacked by a MC 205V but evaded this. He then approached fifteen bombers, attacking the last in the formation. The bomber was shot down over Torvajanica, six parachutes being seen to emerge. The crew were retrieved from the sea by PBYs the next day.

A report was issued to all Allied bomber formations to be alert for a lone P-38. If in doubt, they were to shoot the loner down.

Several further attempts were made to use the captured fighter but were not successful. The lower octane Italian fuel eventually damaged the engines and corrosion was found in the fuel tanks. Consequently, the aircraft was grounded.

Other bases used for testing and training (refer to the section on torpedo units for their test units) were:

Test Units
Furbara	weapons testing (Centrale Sperimentale)
Gorizia	external equipment testing (Centrale Sperimentale)
Ditta	internal equipment testing (Centrale Sperimentale)

Bomber Training
Aviano	Scuolo di Bombardamento
Ghedi	Scuolo di Bombardamento
Jesi	Scuolo di Bombardamento
Grosseto	Scuolo di Bombardamento

Dive Bomber Training
Guidonia	Scuolo Volo a Tuffo—later moved
Lonate Pozzolo	Nucleo Addestramento Tuffatori

Reconnaissance Training
Cerveteri	observer training (Scuolo Osservazione Aerea)

Night Fighter Training
Treviso	Nucleo Addestramento Intercettori

Glider Training
Cameri	Nucleo Addestramento Volo formed 15 June 1942

Ground Attack Training
Ghedi	Scuolo Assalto
Ravenna	Scuolo Assalto

Fighter Training
Gorizia	Scuolo Caccia
Rimini	Scuolo Caccia
Foligno	Scuolo Caccia
Castiglione del Lago	Scuolo Caccia
Campoformido	Scuolo Caccia
Levaldigi	Scuolo Caccia added later
Osoppo	Scuolo Caccia added later
Mostar	Croatians trained at Scuolo Volo

113 Right: *Engine running on a Fiat CR 42 nightfighter of the 377ᵃ Squadriglia Autonomo. This unit had originally been formed to fly the Reggiane Re 2000 on convoy escort duties. Problems with the Re 2000s led to an anti-submarine and nightfighter section, equipped with CR 42CNs, being created in September 1942 and based at Pantelleria. These remained in use until the beginning of 1943. The aircraft seen here still retains its daytime camouflage*

114 Right: *Pilots pose by their 377ᵃ Squadriglia Fiat CR 42CN. This one is finished overall blue-black with black and red codes. Pantelleria, autumn 1942. Note the long flame damper just under the trailing edge of the lower wing*

115 Below: *A Fiat CR 42, MM5024, of the 385ᵃ Squadriglia, 157° Gruppo. Built between December 1939 and March 1940, the aircraft is having its pneumatic system replenished. The lightning flash is the personal insignia of the Gruppo commanding officer, Maggiore Guido Nobile. Trapani-Milo in June 1940*

116 Left: *An early-model Savoia-Marchetti SM 75 of the little-known 610ª Squadriglia, 145° Gruppo. This unit had eight SM 75s on charge at the end of 1941 taken over from Ala Littoria. Civil registrations were I-TACO,-TIMO, -TESO, -TOSA, -TILO, -TAIO, -TOGO and -TEMI Probably seen somewhere in Libya in use as an aerial ambulance, it is not known which of them is shown here*

117 Left: *The first of only three built in 1935, this is a Savoia-Marchetti SM 74, c/n 21001, of the 604ª Squadriglia. Originally registered I-URBE while in service with Ala Littoria, the aircraft was used extensively in Libya until it was destroyed on the ground by enemy action at Castel Benito in Libya on 2 November 1941*

118 Below: *An anonymous Savoia-Marchetti SM 82 seen on a Tunisian airfield has been hastily camouflaged while ground crew struggle to repair the damage caused by enemy action*

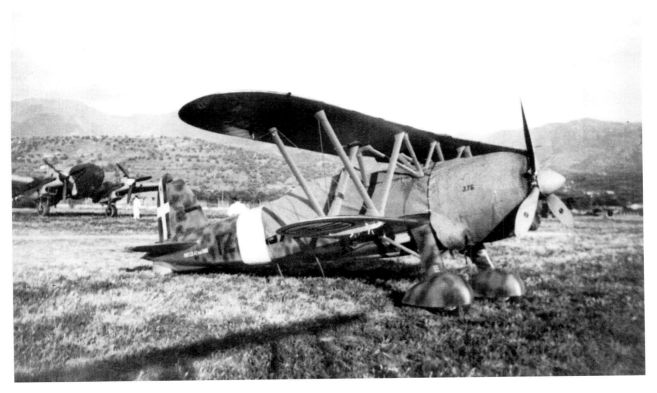

COMBAT UNITS
The Independent Squadriglie

110 Squadriglia R.T.

Arrival	Zone	Base	Country	Aircraft	Duties
10 Jun 40	AOI	Dire Daua	Ethiopia	Ro 37bis	AR DF
Sep 40	AOI	Mogadiscio	Ethiopia	Ro 37bis	AR DF
Jan 41	AOI	Dire Daua	Ethiopia	Ro 37bis CR 42	AR DF
24 Mar 41	AOI	Gimma	Ethiopia	Ro 37bis CR 42	AR DF

Originally 108, 109 and 110 Sq were on policing duties in the Italian colony of Ethiopia. On account of lack of supplies only 110 Sq was left operational by June 1940. On the day war broke out sections of three aircraft each were detached to Auarech and Giggiga, leaving three others at the home base. These aircraft all carried out armed reconnaissance of British and French Somaliland, also acting as reserve fighters in case of British counter-attack.

On 27 June three aircraft went to Assab, from where the following day one of them fought three Blenheims of 39 Squadron RAF. There were no losses, but the Ro 37 was badly damaged. The section returned to Dire Daua on 6 July.

119 Above: A well protected Fiat CR 42 Assalto of the 376ª Squadriglia. The aircraft appears to be brand new, which suggests that the location is Ciampino in Italy soon after the unit formed in April 1941. Visible in the background is a Luftwaffe Heinkel He 111 used by General Rommel as a transport

On 23 August three aircraft moved to Mogadiscio to protect the southern sector. The rest of the unit followed during September, and several battles were fought with SAAF Battle bombers. On 18 December two Ro 37s went to Bardera for operations against the British offensive.

On 17 January 1941 the unit received four CR 42s to boost its low numbers. Their first operation was on that day, and the pilots became quite aggressive with their new aircraft over the next two months. Ironically, the Ro 37 scored its only known victory on 22 January, downing a Hartbeeste of 41 Squadron SAAF over Gerille.

Operating jointly with 413 Sq on 13 March, the unit lost its CO, *Capitano* Palmera, who had claimed at least one Battle and one Hurricane since 22 February. Dire Daua was evacuated by 2 March for Gimma. Also being threatened by the advancing enemy, this base was evacuated by 5 June, all aircraft now being unserviceable.

120 Squadriglia O.A.

Arrival	Zone	Base	Country	Aircraft	Duties
10 Jun 40	AALB	Tirana	Albania	Ro 37bis	AR
Dec 40	AALB	Valona	Albania	Ro 37bis	AR
41	Sqa 1	Villanova d'Albenga	Italy	Ca 311	TG
Jul 42	AALB	Mostar	Yugoslavia	Ca 311	AG

This unit supported 26 Corpo d'Armata with ten aircraft in June 1940. From October 1940 to July 1942 it joined 72 Gruppo, receiving 9 Ca 311s at Durazzo at the end of 1940. These were used against Yugoslav partisans.

In the summer of 1941 they were at Albenga from where they moved to Mostar. From 5 August they transferred from 19 Stormo to 21 Stormo, and joined 5 Gruppo the following February.

124 Squadriglia O.A.

Arrival	Zone	Base	Country	Aircraft	Duties
10 Jun 40	ASAR	Elmas	Sardinia	Ro 37	AR
Feb 43	ASAR	Bastia	Corsica	Ro 37	AR

This unit supported 13 Corpo d'Armata with four aircraft. It made 36 operational flights in 66.25 hours between 10 and 30 June 1940.

A Ca 111 was received at Elmas in April 1941 for liaison duties. The unit joined 65 Gruppo from July 1942 to February 1943. Then it became Autonomo, directly under 20 Stormo from 1 February. They were based at Bastia until the Armistice, with a section detached to Ajaccio until 23 July.

129 Squadriglia O.A.

Arrival	Zone	Base	Country	Aircraft	Duties
Mar 41	Sqa 5	Castelbenito	Tripolitania	Ro 37bis	AR
Mar 41	Sqa 5	Benghasi K2	Cirenaica	Ro 37bis	AR
Mar 41	Sqa 5	Ain el Gazala	Cirenaica	Ro 37bis	AR

This unit is believed to have been Autonomo between January and November 1941, and February to May 1942. While at Gazala all the aircraft were destroyed on the ground which left the unit without aircraft for the remainder of 1941. The crews may have gone to 158 Gruppo in May 1942.

The squadriglia was attached at various times to 72 Gruppo (June 1940), 61 Gruppo (July to December 1940), 64 Gruppo (December 1940 to about March 1941), and 67 Gruppo (possibly Aug 1941 to January 1942).

131 Squadriglia O.A.

Arrival	Zone	Base	Country	Aircraft	Duties
Sep 42	Sqa 5	?	Egypt	Ca 311	AR

During the el Alamein battles this little known unit kept up reports on the Allied vehicle convoys. Possibly this was a temporary allocation.

138 Squadriglia R.M.

Arrival	Zone	Base	Country	Aircraft	Duties
1 Aug 42	ASAR	Olbia	Sardinia	Ro43 Z501	AR
25 Jun 43	ASAR	Portovecchio	Corsica	Z501	AR

This unit formed from the Sezione Costiera at Olbia, with one Ro 43 and seven Z501s operational. By the following June it was in Corsica with sections at Olbia and La Maddelena.

140 Squadriglia R.M.

Arrival	Zone	Base	Country	Aircraft	Duties
1 Aug 42	Sqa 3	Torre del Lago	Italy	Z501 Z506B RS14B	AR

This unit formed from the Sezione Costiera with four operational Z501s, covering the Alto Tirreno from near Pisa. In April 1943 they were still there, with two RS14Bs and two Z506Bs. By 11 June they had joined 84 Gruppo.

141 Squadriglia R.M.

Arrival	Zone	Base	Country	Aircraft	Duties
10 Jun 40	Sqa 1	La Spezia Cadimare	Italy	Z501	AR, CE
12 Jul 40	4 ZAT	Brindisi	Italy	Z501	AR, ASR

This unit formed part of 79 Gruppo which disbanded on 11 June 1940. It patrolled the Alto Tirreno, escorting shipping and watching for enemy vessels.

In July 1940 they moved to the base which was to remain theirs until the Armistice. On 2 November 1940 one of the Z501s fought off a Blenheim, receiving 67 hits but surviving after a temporary sea landing.

With duties extended to patrolling the Jonio e Bassio Adriatico, the unit received some Z506Bs in 1943. On 20 May that year 9 Sezione Aerea di Soccorso (Air Sea Rescue section) formed from this squadriglia at Brindisi.

142 Squadriglia R.M.

Arrival	Zone	Base	Country	Aircraft	Duties
10 Jun 40	4 ZAT	Taranto	Italy	Z501 Z506B	AR, CE, AS, ASR

The unit stayed at this base throughout the war. Initially, six Z501s covered the Jonio e Basso Adriatico. In September 1940, the unit was very busy with anti-submarine operations, covering the transfer of supplies to Albania.

120: *Ground attack Fiat CR 42s of 376ª Squadriglia, believed to be at Ciampino in early summer 1941. From August they were stationed in Cirenaica, beginning operations from Ain el Gazala in October. In November they returned to Italy for conversion training onto the Macchi MC 200*

121: *Another view of a 376ª Squadriglia Fiat CR 42AS. This is the same machine shown covered by tarpaulins in photo 118. The underwing bomb racks are clearly visible. Although rather dark in tone, it is believed that the engine cowling has been given a solid coat of yellow paint*

122: *Looking rather like the offspring of a marriage between a Fieseler Storch and a Percival Proctor, this is an IMAM Ro 63, MM 11592. This was the second of only six built between summer 1940 and May 1941. Four aircraft were intended to be delivered from 28 September for initial training of maintenance personnel of the 132ª Squadriglia, 76° Gruppo OA. In the event this aircraft did not arrive until 23 October, only to be written off on 11 November as a result of bomb splinter damage. It had completed 24 hours and 20 minutes of flying time*

123 *Left: A CRDA CANT Z.501 in typical pre-war all-aluminium finish upper surfaces and undersides in anti-fouling black. The meaning of the unit marking is not known. Date and location unknown*

124 *Below: An IMAM Ro 43 from the 'Condottieri' Class cruiser* Armando Diaz *in flight over an unidentifed anchorage. The aircraft still wears the pre-war silver-grey finish. Whether the aircraft was aboard when the parent vessel was sunk by the Royal Navy submarine HMS* Upright *on 25 February 1941 is not known*

125 Right: *Engine maintenance on a CRDA Cant Z.506B at Tripoli in 1942. The aircraft is finished in the typical light and dark greys used for most maritime aircraft later in the war*

126 Below: *Another Cant Z.506B of an unidentified unit, probably sometime in 1942. The exact meaning of the fuselage code is not known, but the Roman 'II' could represent the Regia Marina operational area, the letter the home base (Lido di **R**oma?) and the number, the individual aircraft*

127 Right: *One of the scores of aircraft prototypes developed by the Italian aircraft industry destined not to see service was the CRDA Cant Z.515. Intended as a reconnaissance bomber, it first flew in 1939. Not developed, something of its elegant nose profile surfaced in the later Cant Z.1018*

128: *Among the great variety of aircraft seized by the Germans at the time of the Armistice was this Caproni Ca 309, MM52134, completed round about June 1943. Seen taxying out for takeoff from an unidentified location, the wheel spats to the fixed undercarriage have been removed. This fact and the bare trees suggest that the picture was taken in Northern Italy sometime in winter 1943-1944*

129: *This experimental Caproni Ca 111, powered by a Fiat A.80 RC.41 1,000 hp radial engine was tested in October 1942. Like many other odd machines it was pressed into service as a general purpose transport. Finish is overall dark green*

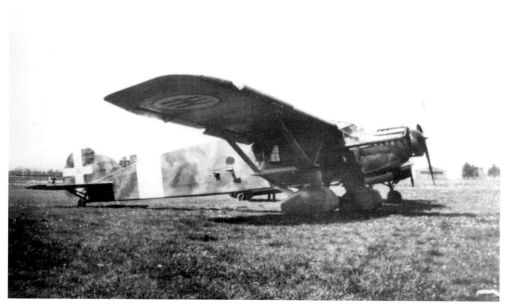

130: *Many elderly Caproni Ca 111s continued to give service well into the war years. There are no clues to which unit this one belonged to, but it could have been used as a hack by almost any operational Gruppo. The camouflage scheme is probably field-applied and the white backgrounds to the underwing markings suggest that the date is early in the war*

By April 1943 they had seven Z506Bs at Taranto. They joined 85 Gruppo before the Armistice.

143 Squadriglia R.M.

Arrival	Zone	Base	Country	Aircraft	Duties
10 Jun 40	ASIC AS	Menelao	Cirenaica	Z501	AR, ASR
Aug 42	AALB	Divulje	Yugoslavia	Z501 Ro43	AR, AS
Apr 43	Sqa 2	Venezia	Italy	Z501 Z506B	AR, AS

Although based in Libya, the six aircraft of this unit were still under Sicilian command. They were occupied with anti-submarine duties in November 1940.

Records next show them at Divulje with one Ro 43 (probably for training) and five Z501s, covering the Alto Adriatico. In mid 1942 they were watching the Dalmatian coast, following the Yugoslav partisan rebellion. They attacked submarines which were trying to reinforce and supply the partisans.

By April 1943 they had moved to Venezia, where they stayed until the Armistice.

144 Squadriglia R.M.

Arrival	Zone	Base	Country	Aircraft	Duties
10 Jun 40	ASIC	Stagnone	Sicily	Z501 Z506B RS14B	AR, ASR CE, AS
May 43	Sqa 3	Orbetello	Italy	Z501 Z506B	AR, ASR, AS

Six aircraft covered the waters around Sicily, and in September and November 1940 were kept busy on anti-submarine duties.

The following year they received some Z506Bs after losing several Z501s at their base to strafing fighters from Malta in July. The surviving Z501s were on convoy escort duties at the end of the year.

In March 1942 they joined 85 Gruppo for a year. RS14Bs were received and carried out anti-submarine sorties from October to December. In the latter month there were frequent encounters with marauding Allied fighters, one Spitfire being successfully fought off by a Z506B on the 24th.

In February 1943 the RS14Bs carried out rescues and escorts in the Cap Bon area. Three months later the unit appeared at Orbetello. 3 Sezione Aerea di Soccorso formed from the squadriglia on 20 May. The Sezione stayed at this base until the Armistice, covering the Basso Tirreno with Z501s and Z506Bs.

145 Squadriglia R.M.

Arrival	Zone	Base	Country	Aircraft	Duties
10 Jun 40	4 ZAT	Brindisi	Italy	Z501	AR, ASR
Jul 40	Sqa 5	Benghasi	Cirenaica	Z501	AR, CE, ASR
Apr 41	Sqa 5	Tripoli Caramanlis	Tripolitania	Z501	AR, ASR
Jul 42	Sqa 5	Menelao	Cirenaica	Z501 Z506B	AR, ASR
Aug 42	Sqa 5	Pisida	Tripolitania	Z501 Z506B	AR, ASR
Sep 42	Sqa 5	Tripoli	Tripolitania	Z501 Z506B	AR, ASR
Nov 42	Sqa 5	Pisida	Tripolitania	Z501 Z506B	AR, ASR
19 Jan 43	Sqa 1	La Spezia Cadimare	Italy	Z501 RS14B	AR, ASR
Jun 43	Sqa 3	Torre del Lago	Italy	Z501 RS14B	AR, ASR

This unit began the war with six aircraft covering the Jonio e Basso Adriatico. The next month they were ordered to Libya, to cover the incoming convoys supplying the advance on Sidi Barrani. They remained in this theatre until the Allied advance through Libya. The move to Menelao may have occurred earlier in 1942. On 20 September they had 8 serviceable aircraft at Tripoli.

Re-equipping in Italy they joined 84 Gruppo by 11 June 1943 at Torre del Lago.

146 Squadriglia R.M.

Arrival	Zone	Base	Country	Aircraft	Duties
Jun 40	ASAR	Elmas	Sardinia	Z501 Z506B RS14B	AR, ASR, AN
Apr 43	ASAR	Oristano	Sardinia	Z506B RS14B	AR, ASR
21 May 43	ASAR	Ajaccio	Corsica	Z506B RS14B	AR, ASR

This unit was part of 85 Gruppo in June 1940 and covered Sardinian waters throughout the war. During the battles of mid-1942 they co-operated with patrols of CR 42 fighter-bombers against isolated ships. In August that year they had ten operational Z506Bs out of twelve. Five RS14Bs joined in December.

On 10 January 1943 a Z506B on air sea rescue fought off an aggressive Hudson. On 14 May five RS14Bs were destroyed by strafing P-38s at Oristano, leaving only one serviceable together with six of the older Z506Bs. The unit moved to Corsica. 6 Sezione Aerea di Soccorso formed at Ajaccio on 20 May, using aircraft and crews from this squadriglia.

The Armistice found them still at Ajaccio, with a section at Porto Vecchio from 9th July.

148 Squadriglia R.M.

Arrival	Zone	Base	Country	Aircraft	Duties
10 Jun 40	Sqa 3	Vigna di Valle	Italy	Z501 Z506B	
				RS14B	AR, ASR
Jul 42	Sqa 5	Menelao	Cirenaica	Z501	AR
11 Nov 42	Sqa 5	Pisida	Tripolitania	Z501	AR
15 Nov 42	Sqa 3	Vigna di Valle	Italy	Z501 Z506B	
				RS14B	AR

The unit began with seven Z501s covering the Basso Tirreno from 11 June 1940. Z506Bs were received by January 1942, although a RS14B Series III was on trials from 30 May 1941 to 17 July 1942. This was the first to be used by any unit.

In July 1942 the unit replaced 145 Sq at Menelao, returning to Italy in November for reforming. They had lost seven Z501s at Menelao to strafing Beaufighters on 6 and 7 October. On 14 September a Z501 of this unit spotted and helped prevent a surprise British naval landing near Tobruk.

During 1943 they covered the Basso Tirreno, but with few serviceable aircraft. On 10 February, 1 Sezione Costiera was disbanded at Vigna di Valle and their aircraft and crews joined 148 Squadriglia.

149 Squadriglia R.M.

Arrival	Zone	Base	Country	Aircraft	Duties
1 Aug 42	Sqa 2	Pola Puntisella	Italy	Ro43 Z501 Z506B	AR, ASR
Jul 43	Sqa 2	Castelnuovo	Italy	Ro43 Z501 Z506B	AR, ASR
Sep 43	AALB	Kumbor	Yugoslavia	Z501 Z506B	AR, ASR

This unit formed from a Sezione Costiera, with four Ro 43s, three Z501s, and Z506Bs. They covered the Alto Adriatico until at least April 1943.

The Armistice found them still covering the same area, with five out of eight Z501s operational.

161 Squadriglia C.M.

Arrival	Zone	Base	Country	Aircraft	Duties
10 Jun 40	AEGE	Lero	Aegean	Ro 44 Ro 43	DF, GA
Jun 41	AEGE	Rodi	Aegean	CR 42	DF, CE

This was the only fighter-floatplane unit left operational by June 1940. The Ro 43 was used for training. The eight Ro 44s flew continuous patrols around the Aegean Islands, and joined in all the actions in the area for the next twelve months. In April 1941 they bombed and strafed the naval bay of Milos, prior to the German attacks on Crete. In June 1941 they transformed from

Caccia Marrittima to Caccia Terrestre, receiving CR 42s at Rodi.

It may have been this squadriglia that transferred from Grottaglie to Sicily on 6 November 1942 with 16 MC 200s and 5 G 50s, to help protect the supply routes to Tunisia.

163 Squadriglia C.T.

Arrival	Zone	Base	Country	Aircraft	Duties
10 Jun 40	AEGE	Marizza	Aegean	CR 32 CR 42	DF
Apr 41	AEGE	Gadurra	Aegean	CR 32 CR 42	DF, GA, AE

This unit formed in June 1935, transferring from Ciampino to the Aegean in December of that year. They began the war with 11 CR 32s. In July 1940, 9 CR 42s, specially modified for fighter-bomber duties, were received for training in this new role. On 4 September the CR 32s intercepted an attack by the Royal Navy aircraft carrier HMS *Eagle,* claiming five out of the twelve Swordfish from 813 and 824 Squadrons FAA. Three others force landed.

During the late spring of 1941 the unit moved to Gadurra. In April they used 8 CR 32s in the operations against Crete. A section of these aircraft were detached to Cattavia landing ground in May. Between 20 and 31 May the unit also used the fighter-bomber CR 42s against Crete and Castelrosso, bombing and strafing in support of the German paratroops. After the conquest of Crete, the CR 32s were relegated to training duties. On 11 June 1941 the squadriglia joined 161 Gruppo.

170 Squadriglia R.M.

Arrival	Zone	Base	Country	Aircraft	Duties
10 Jun 40	ASIC	Augusta	Sicily	Z506B	AR, ASR

This unit, with seven aircraft, came under the orders of the Sicilian Maritime Command. During the summer of 1940 they joined 83 Gruppo until it disbanded in July 1943.

171 Squadriglia R.M.

Arrival	Zone	Base	Country	Aircraft	Duties
10 Jun 40	4 ZAT	Brindisi	Italy	Z506B	AR, ASR
Jun 40	4 ZAT	Taranto	Italy	Z506B	AR, ASR, CE
1 Feb 43	APRO	Tolone	France	Z506B Z501	AR, ASR

This unit, with six aircraft, helped cover the Jonio e Basso Adriatico. They soon moved to Taranto, with a section at Menelao, covering the convoy routes to Libya and the approaches to the Taranto naval base.

After two years the number of serviceable aircraft had dropped to two out of eleven on strength. In 1943, as the Allies pressed forward the unit transferred to Tolone, receiving six Z501s to help the Z506Bs cover the Alto Tirreno. On 20 May, 1 Sezione Aerea di Soccorso formed from the squadriglia. This unit was still at Tolone when the Armistice was declared.

172 Squadriglia B.T.

Arrival	Zone	Base	Country	Aircraft	Duties
13 Jun 40	Sqa 1	Bresso	Italy	BR 20M Z1007bis	DB
19 Oct 40	CAI	Chievres	Belgium	Z1007bis	DB, TR
Jan 41	CAI	Frankfurt	Germany	Z1007bis	IT
Jan 41	Sqa	Viterbo?	Italy	Z1007bis	TG
Mar 41	AEGE	Marizza	Aegean	Z1007bis	AR, NB
Jun 43	Sqa 3	Viterbo	Italy	Ju88D	TG

This unit formed on 13 June 1940 with six BR 20Ms. Two days later they operated over Camet des Maures, near patrolling CR 42s of 3 Stormo. French D.520s of GCIII/6 intercepted, losing two but claiming four CR 42s and one BR 20M.

On 24 August five of the more modern Z1007bis were received for reconnaissance missions. These were taken to Belgium, under the orders of 56 Stormo. Because the German reconnaissance system was deemed very efficient, the aircraft were not required for their primary role. Consequently they carried out diversionary raids with fighter escort, and made liaison trips among the other CAI units. On 11 November they made a feint attack towards Great Yarmouth.

Returning to Italy for a rest, they detached three aircraft to the Aegean to watch the North African coast. This was prior to supporting bombing raids by 50 Gruppo against Tobruk from April 1941. During the next five months they made 18 reconnaissance missions to Alexandria, losing three aircraft. They also made eight night-bombing raids against the same target. On 14 September 1941 the unit disbanded.

In June 1943 they reformed, training on the Ju 88D. They were not, however, ready for operations before the Armistice intervened.

173 Squadriglia R.S.T.

Arrival	Zone	Base	Country	Aircraft	Duties
Jul 41	Sqa 1	Torino Caselle	Italy	CR25	TG
14 Jul 41	Sqa 3	Ciampino Nord	Italy	CR25	IT
20 Jul 41	ASIC	Boccadifalco	Sicily	CR25 Ca314	AR, CE
25 Jan 43	Sqa 3	Reggio Emilia	Italy	CR25	TG
21 Feb 43	Sqa 3	Cameri	Italy	CR25	TG
5 Apr 43	Sqa 3	Cerveteri	Italy	Ca314 FC20bis	CE, TG

This unit was the only one to use the twin-engined Fiat CR 25 escort-fighter. Only ten were supplied, and they were used until January 1943. They were easy to maintain, but because Italy's resources were spread over too many aircraft types, production of this competent aircraft was not built up. Their first operation was on 24 July 1941, searching for a submarine off Palermo.

On 5 August six aircraft were detached to Sciacca as anti-submarine escort to a convoy returning from Libya. The following day they flew to Trapani to escort merchant shipping over the next few weeks, sometimes using Pantelleria as a staging base.

On 6 September they made a reconnaissance sortie over Malta, running into Hurricanes near Capo Passero. From 11 to 13 September, two sections of CR25s were detached to Pantelleria and Castelbenito, for anti-torpedo-bomber operations. Four aircraft were detached to Catania on 17 October. The following month ten aircraft were at Catania, carrying out shipping reconnaissances, protection of the 3rd Naval Divison against torpedo-bombers, and at least two reconnaissance missions over Malta. On 13 December six aircraft were detached to Reggio Calabria for convoy escorts, returning to Palermo on the 20th. By now the unit had only five serviceable aircraft.

Three aircraft were detached to Sciacca to assist 10 Stormo on 2 January 1943. On 2 February they came under the direct command of 10 Stormo B.T. at Boccadifalco. A Blenheim was claimed as a 'probable' on the 6th while on convoy escort. The unit also escorted the SM 79s of 10 Stormo while they carried out anti-submarine missions. During this period they were visited by a Japanese party, who were very interested in the twin-engined fighter.

On 23 April six aircraft were detached to Pantelleria to escort a convoy between Brindisi and Benghasi, the aircraft returning to Palermo the same day. This pattern of operations continued, with most bases in the area being used by sections during their escort and anti-submarine duties over the central Mediterranean. They met both Beaufighters and Beauforts in June 1942, notably claiming two on the 21st.

From October 1942 some Ca 314s were received to boost operational numbers as the CR 25s were now getting worn out. The unit patrolled the seas north of Sicily, escorting convoys and watching for enemy shipping. During January 1943 CR25s and Ca 314s clashed several times with P-38s between Palermo and Philippeville.

By this time there were four CR 25s serviceable, although fourteen Ca 314s were also on strength. On 25 January the squadriglia became Autonomo, transferring to Cerveteri by 5 April with no aircraft left. The intention was to re-equip with the FC20bis, but only three were received by the time the squadriglia disbanded on 1 August 1943.

174 Squadriglia R.S.T.

Arrival	Zone	Base	Country	Aircraft	Duties
Dec 41	Sqa 5	Benghasi	Cirenaica	SM 79	AR
20 Dec 41	Sqa 5	Agedabia	Cirenaica	SM 79	AR
25 Dec 41	Sqa 5	Tamet	Tripolitania	SM 79	AR
Jan 42	Sqa 5	Sirte	Tripolitania	SM 79	AR
13 Jan 42	Sqa 5	En Nofilia	Tripolitania	SM 79	AR
Jan 42	Sqa 5	Ara Fileni	Tripolitania	SM 79	AR
29 Jan 42	Sqa 5	Agedabia	Cirenaica	SM 79	AR
9 Feb 42	Sqa 5	Benghasi K2	Cirenaica	SM 79	AR

This unit appears in December 1941 as one of the frontline reconnaissance units, occasionally used in the bombing role. They covered both land and sea areas, and were very active in the ebb and flow of this period. On 5 April 1942 they joined 175 Sq at K2 to form 133 Gruppo, in the anti-shipping role.

175 Squadriglia R.S.T.

Arrival	Zone	Base	Country	Aircraft	Duties
Sep 40	Sqa 5	Gambut	Cirenaica	SM 79	AR
9 Mar 41	Sqa 5	Derna	Cirenaica	SM 79	AR
Jun 41	Sqa 5	Benghasi K2	Cirenaica	SM 79	AR, CE
Dec 41	Sqa 5	Castelbenito	Tripolitania	SM 79	AR

This unit received some experienced crews from 172 Sq and formed in September 1940 in Libya, for reconnaissance duties with the advancing Axis forces. During the advance on Sidi Barrani one section was at T5, another at Gambut. Two aircraft were destroyed by a British Special Air Service raid on Derna in March. The unit had an average of three operational aircraft for land and sea reconnaissance duties in 1941. During March they patrolled the area surrounding Tripoli port. On 28 June one aircraft was sent from Benghasi to Gialo to reconnaissance Cufra Oasis and the enemy units in that area. They may have used some Z1007bis in 1941.

In April 1942 they joined 174 Sq to form 133 Gruppo at Benghasi.

176 Squadriglia R.S.T.

Arrival	Zone	Base	Country	Aircraft	Duties
Dec 41	Sqa 5	Derna	Cirenaica	Z1007bis	AR
12 Dec 41	Sqa 5	Barce	Cirenaica	Z1007bis	AR
Dec 41	Sqa 5	Misurata	Tripolitania	Z1007bis	AR
Jan 42	Sqa 5	Sirte	Tripolitania	Z1007bis	AR
Jan 42	Sqa 5	Tamet	Tripolitania	Z1007bis	AR
Mar 42	Sqa 5	Castelbenito	Tripolitania	Z1007bis	AR
26 Mar 42	Sqa 5	Barce	Cirenaica	Z1007bis	AR

This unit formed in December 1941 to take over from 175 Sq, carrying out reconnaissance duties over the Libyan land and sea fronts. On 9 April 1942 they disbanded, passing their twelve aircraft to 35 Stormo.

182 Squadriglia R.M.

Arrival	Zone	Base	Country	Aircraft	Duties
10 Jun 40	Sqa 3	Napoli Pisida	Italy	Z501 Z506B	
				RS14B	AR, ASR

This unit stayed at the same base throughout the war, covering the Basso Tirreno area. They started with four Z501s, receiving Z506Bs and RS14Bs in 1942 to supplement the worn out Z501s. In August that year a section was detached to Vigna di Valle, replacing 148 Sq which had moved to Libya. By 23 October the RS14B was no longer used by this unit.

On 20 May 1943, 4 Sezione Aerea di Soccorso was formed from this unit, using the remaining Z506Bs. The Armistice found them at Pisida with two out of four Z506Bs serviceable.

183 Squadriglia R.M.

Arrival	Zone	Base	Country	Aircraft	Duties
10 Jun 40	ASAR	Elmas	Sardinia	Z501	AR, ASR
Jul 42	Sqa 3	Orbetello	Italy	Z501	AR, AS, ASR
Aug 42	AALB	Divulje	Yugoslavia	Z501 Z506B	AR, AS, ASR

This unit was part of 85 Gruppo from June 1940 to March 1941, covering Sardinian waters. By 1942 they were in Italy, patrolling the Alto Adriatico with seven Z501s. 4 Sezione Costiera joined the squadriglia, and they moved to Yugoslavia. Patrols were made along the Balkan coast, watching for submarines and vessels attempting to supply the partisans.

By April 1943 the unit was also using a Z506B for rescue duties. A section was at Kumbor until 6 August. Another section was detached to Paludi, near Divulje, in

July. Two months later the unit still had five Z501s operational when the order arrived to surrender.

187 Squadriglia R.M.

Arrival	Zone	Base	Country	Aircraft	Duties
10 Jun 40	Sqa 1	La Spezia Cadimare	Italy	Z501 Z506B	
				RS14B	AR, ASR

This unit stayed at Cadimare throughout the war, protecting the naval base at La Spezia. They were initially part of 79 Gruppo, but this disbanded on 11 June 1940. In February 1941 the unit monitored the progress of Force H from Gibraltar.

By July 1942 they had received six Z506Bs to help cover the Alto Tirreno. An RS14B arrived in 1943. On 20 May that year 2 Sezione Aerea di Soccorso was formed from the unit, using mainly Z506Bs.

By the Armistice they were only able to operate one RS14B, one Z506B, and two, out of eleven, Z501s.

188 Squadriglia R.M.

Arrival	Zone	Base	Country	Aircraft	Duties
10 Jun 40	ASAR	Elmas	Sardinia	Z501 Z506B	AR, ASR
Apr 43	ASAR	Arbatax	Sardinia	Z501 Z506B	AR, ASR
Jul 43	ASAR	Elmas	Sardinia	Z501 Z506B	AR, ASR
Sep 43	ASAR	Porto Vecchio	Corsica	Z506B RS14B	AR, AS

This unit was part of 85 Gruppo from June 1940 to March 1941. It continued to operate Z501s in Sardinian waters until at least May 1943. Six Z506Bs were used from around January 1943, one fighting two Blenheims off Sardinia on the 5th, and claiming both. The Z506Bs were moved to Arbatax in April, returning to Elmas in early July. On 20 May, 5 Sezione Aerea di Soccorso formed from the squadriglia for rescue duties. The Sezione was officially disbanded at Elmas on 5 August.

On the day of the Armistice the unit was in Corsica with only one RS14b serviceable, and no Z506Bs available. A detached section was at La Maddelena.

209 Squadriglia B.a.T.

Arrival	Zone	Base	Country	Aircraft	Duties
7 May 41	Sqa 4	Lecce	Italy	Ju 87R	DB
5 Jul 41	ASIC	Trapani Milo	Sicily	Ju 87R	IT
8 Jul 41	Sqa 5	Castelbenito	Tripolitania	Ju 87R	IT
11 Jul 41	Sqa 5	Tamet	Tripolitania	Ju 87R	IT
11 Jul 41	Sqa 5	Benghasi K2	Cirenaica	Ju 87R	TG
18 Jul 41	Sqa 5	Derna	Cirenaica	Ju 87R	AR, AN

Arrival	Zone	Base	Country	Aircraft	Duties
29 Jul 41	Sqa 5	Gambut	Cirenaica	Ju 87R	AN
30 Jul 41	Sqa 5	Derna	Cirenaica	Ju 87R	TG
2 Aug 41	Sqa 5	Gambut	Cirenaica	Ju 87R	AN
3 Aug 41	Sqa 5	Derna	Cirenaica	Ju 87R	DB, AN
13 Sep 41	Sqa 5	Gars el Arid	Cirenaica	Ju 87R	DB
18 Sep 41	Sqa 5	Derna	Cirenaica	Ju 87R	TG
31 Oct 41	Sqa 5	Benghasi K2	Cirenaica	Ju 87R	TG
5 Dec 41	Sqa 5	Derna	Cirenaica	Ju 87R	IT
8 Dec 41	Sqa 5	Martuba	Cirenaica	Ju 87R	DB
14 Dec 41	Sqa 5	Derna	Cirenaica	Ju 87R	DB
18 Dec 41	Sqa 5	Maraua	Cirenaica	Ju 87R	DB
20 Dec 41	Sqa 5	Sidi el Magrum	Cirenaica	Ju 87R	IT
21 Dec 41	Sqa 5	En Nofilia	Tripolitania	Ju 87R	IT
28 Dec 41	Sqa 5	Ara Fileni	Tripolitania	Ju 87R	DB
30 Dec 41	Sqa 5	El Merduma	Tripolitania	Ju 87R	DB
11 Jan 42	Sqa 5	El Agheila	Cirenaica	Ju 87R	DB
29 Jan 42	Sqa 5	Agedabia	Cirenaica	Ju 87R	AR
12 Feb 42	Sqa 5	Martuba 3	Cirenaica	Ju 87R	DB, AN
23 Feb 42	Sqa 5	Benghasi K2	Cirenaica	Ju 87R	IT
24 Mar 42	Sqa 5	Castelbenito	Tripolitania	Ju 87R	IT
25 Mar 42	Sqa 1	Lonate Pozzolo	Italy	Ju 87R	TG

This unit left 97 Gruppo on 7 May 1941, after several operations over the Greek front. In May they were on anti-naval standby during the occupation of the Ionian Islands. There followed a quiet period of training then they were ordered to Africa.

Two SM 82s of the SAS assisted in moving the unit, and by 15 July the whole squadriglia with eight aircraft was established at Benghasi. Their first operation was on 21 July with an armed reconnaissance over Tobruk. They were escorted by 153 Gruppo who had also performed the same role for them in Greece. The unit remained active over the Tobruk area, joining German Ju 87s in several raids up to mid-September.

On the 14 September ten aircraft lost their way near Sidi Barrani and force-landed out of fuel all over the desert. One theory has it that in view of the general shortage of fuel among the Axis forces, the aircraft were deliberately under-fuelled by German ground crew. The RAF captured at least one intact and flew it on fighter affiliation duties. At least three others were found, one with the crew stabbed to death. For the next eight days 155 Gruppo, 20 Gruppo, 19 Sq, 129 Sq, and 209 Sq, as well as German Bf 110s searched for the missing crews. A few members were found on the 17th. Eighteen had been reported captured by the Allies, but at least two were dead and three returned so this figure is suspect unless the number of aircraft lost was greater than accepted. Despite receiving four replacement aircraft on 2 September bringing strength to 13 aircraft, but by the 18th the squadriglia only had two aircraft left and were declared non-operational.

Between 28 November and 8 December, 101 Gruppo passed nine of their aircraft over when they returned to

Italy. This enabled the unit to resume operations , with eleven aircraft, alongside German units. They launched attacks in the Gazala area then they were back over Tobruk in January. Some attacks were carried out on shipping near the Tobruk harbour.

Reduced by losses again, the unit withdrew to Italy and disbanded on 26 March 1942. They reformed in May joining 102 Gruppo.

236 Squadriglia C.B.

Arrival	Zone	Base	Country	Aircraft	Duties
Jan 41	Sqa 5	Misurata	Tripolitania	Ju 87R CR 42AS	DB, GA
Nov 41	Sqa 5	Agedabia	Cirenaica	CR 42AS	GA
Dec 41	Sqa 5	Sorman	Tripolitania	CR 42AS	GA
25 Dec 41	Sqa 5	Ara Fileni	Tripolitania	CR 42AS	GA
15 Jan 42	Sqa 5	El Merduma	Tripolitania	CR 42AS	GA
Jan 42	Sqa 5	Agheila	Cirenaica	CR 42AS	GA
29 Jan 42	Sqa 5	Agedabia	Cirenaica	CR 42AS	GA
9 Feb 42	Sqa 5	Benghasi K2	Cirenaica	CR 42AS	GA

This squadriglia arrived from Lecce on 30 January 1941, with Ju 87Rs. In February they were joined by 237 Sq of 96 Gruppo for operations over Tobruk. They received the latter unit's aircraft in April to bolster their strength. On 14 May the pilots picked up replacement aircraft at Tripoli. On 3 November they re-equipped with nine CR 42 fighter-bombers and new pilots, moving to Agedabia that month. They sometimes operated in conjunction with 209 Sq during January. After a tour of close support missions, they joined the newly formed 158 Gruppo on 9 February 1942.

239 Squadriglia B.a.T.

Arrival	Zone	Base	Country	Aircraft	Duties
7 May 41	ASIC	Comiso	Sicily	Ju 87R	IT
11 May 41	Sqa 5	Castelbenito	Tripolitania	Ju 87R	IT
20 May 41	Sqa 5	Benghasi	Cirenaica	Ju 87R	IT
21 May 41	Sqa 5	Derna	Cirenaica	Ju 87R	AN, DB
29 Jun 41	Sqa 5	Gambut	Cirenaica	Ju 87R	DB
30 Jun 41	Sqa 5	Derna	Cirenaica	Ju 87R	DB, AN
18 Jul 41	Sqa 5	Benghasi	Cirenaica	Ju 87R	TG, AR, AS CE
1 Nov 41	Sqa 5	Derna	Cirenaica	Ju 87R	TG
15 Nov 41	Sqa 5	Castelbenito	Tripolitania	Ju 87R	TG
18 Nov 41	ASIC	Trapani Milo	Sicily	Ju 87R	IT, DB
26 Nov 41	Sqa 5	Castelbenito	Tripolitania	Ju 87R	IT
27 Nov 41	Sqa 5	Derna	Cirenaica	Ju 87R	DB
18 Dec 41	Sqa 5	Maraua	Cirenaica	Ju 87R	IT
20 Dec 41	Sqa 5	Benghasi	Cirenaica	Ju 87R	IT
21 Dec 41	Sqa 5	Castelbenito	Tripolitania	Ju 87R	IT
23 Dec 41	ASIC	Boccadifalco	Sicily	Ju 87R	IT
26 Dec 41	Sqa 3	Ciampino	Italy	Ju 87R	IT

Arrival	Zone	Base	Country	Aircraft	Duties
28 Dec 41	Sqa 1	Lonate Pozzolo	Italy	Ju 87R	TG

This unit was part of 97 Gruppo operating in the Greek and Yugoslav campaigns against enemy shipping in the Adriatic Sea. On 7 May 1941 it took ten Ju 87s and an SM 81 to the Libyan front.

The first operation was on 25 May with an anti-shipping patrol off Tobruk, which resulted in the sinking of a tanker. They were escorted by G 50s of 2 Gruppo. For the next two months they carried out dive-bombing missions in the Tobruk area, sometimes with 153 Gruppo escorting. By 18 July the five surviving aircraft were resting at Benghasi. Sections were used for escorting coastal shipping, submarine spotting, and local reconnaissances. In November three aircraft operated over Malta. During that month the unit was temporarily attached to 101 Gruppo.

From 27 November they rejoined the main action, operating in the Gazala and Bir el Gobi areas, alongside German units. A mixture of Bf 109s and G 50s provided escorts. The following month the serviceable aircraft were passed to 209 Sq, and the unit withdrew to Italy, taking nine damaged aircraft homewards. In May 1942 the squadriglia joined 102 Gruppo.

244 Squadriglia B.T.

Arrival	Zone	Base	Country	Aircraft	Duties
18 Mar 41	Sqa 3		Italy	SM 81	CE
7 May 41	Sqa 5		Libya	SM 81	CE

This unit formed in 1941 with six SM 81s for convoy escort duties, moving to Libya in May. By December their aircraft were passed to 103 Sq for transport duties.

245 Squadriglia T.

Arrival	Zone	Base	Country	Aircraft	Duties
Sep 41	CSIR	Krivoi Rog	Russia	SM 81	TR
May 42	CSIR	Voroscilovgrad	Russia	SM 81	TR
Jan 43	CSIR	Stalino	Russia	SM 81	TR
Feb 43	CSIR	Odessa	Russia	SM 81	TR
Mar 43	Sqa		Italy	SM 81	TR

This unit formed (in Russia?) in September 1941 with SM 81s from Italy and two from 22 Gruppo. During the summer of 1942 they reinforced the units at Voroscilovgrad. They supplied isolated troops and evacuated wounded during the following winter. Support was given to both the ground and air units until they were recalled to Italy in March 1943.

246 Squadriglia T.

Arrival	Zone	Base	Country	Aircraft	Duties
25 Nov 41	CSIR	Stalino	Russia	SM 81	TR
May 42	CSIR	Voroscilovgrad	Russia	SM 81	TR
May 43	CSIR	Odessa	Russia	SM 81	TR
May 43	Sqa		Italy	SM 81	TR

This unit arrived in Russia with six SM 81s from Italy. They supported the ground units until recalled to Italy at the end of May 1943.

247 Squadriglia T.

Arrival	Zone	Base	Country	Aircraft	Duties
May 42	CSIR	Otopeni	Romania	SM 73	TR
Jun 42	CSIR	Saporoshje	Russia	SM 73 SM 81	TR
42	CSIR	Stalino	Russia	SM 73 SM 81	TR
Mar 43	CSIR	Bucharest	Romania	SM 73 SM 81	TR
May 43	Sqa	Linate?	Italy	SM 73 SM 81	TR

Four SM 73s were detached from 148 Gruppo to assist the supply lines to the Russian front. Initially they acted as a link between Italy and the Russian front, flying Stalino-Saporoshje-Bucharest-Venezia. Six SM 81s were added for the Bucharest-Stalino run. Eventually, eight SM 81s were used. This unit was kept continually busy until withdrawn to Italy at the end of May 1943.

248 Squadriglia T.

Arrival	Zone	Base	Country	Aircraft	Duties
15 Apr 43	Sqa 3	Viterbo	Italy	P108T	TR
11 Jun 43	Sqa 3	Orvieto	Italy	P108T	TR
25 Aug 43	Sqa 3	Foligno	Italy	P108T	TR

This unit was intended to equip with the transport version of the P108B bomber. However, although several P108T and P108C models were supplied by Piaggio before the Armistice, only one (possibly three) reached the unit. It was used in Italy from August.

274 Squadriglia B.G.R.

Arrival	Zone	Base	Country	Aircraft	Duties
1 Jun 41	Sqa 3	Pisa	Italy	P108B	TG
13 Feb 42	Sqa 3	Guidonia	Italy	P108B	AN
26 Jun 42	Sqa 3	Decimomannu	Sardinia	P108B	NB, AN
1 Feb 43	Sqa 3	Siena Ampugnano	Italy	P108B	TG
11 May 43	Sqa 3	Guidonia	Italy	P108B	AN, NB
24 Jul 43	Sqa 3	Pontedera	Italy	P108B	NB
8 Sep 43	Sqa 3	Foligno	Italy	P108B	IT

This was the only strategic bomber unit in the Regia Aeronautica, formed for long range shipping and land target attacks. Another unit, 275 Sq, was created in 1942 but disbanded after a few days because of a lack of future aircraft supplies. The bomber was extremely expensive to produce from Italy's meagre resources. Thus, only one unit existed which kept up a balance of loss and supply until the Armistice.

The crews trained in the anti-shipping role, although the aircraft was rarely used in this way. The trainee crews were sent to Guidonia for flying lessons, Littoria for instrument flying, Furbara for bombing lessons, and Gorizia for torpedo drops. On 7 August 1941 Bruno Mussolini, son of *Il Duce*, died when his aircraft crashed during a landing approach. He was CO of the unit, and a popular commander. This accident coloured Mussolini Senior's attitude towards the bomber, and practically ensured a lack of support that could have given the Italian bomber arm a much-needed heavy weapon. In fact the costs of building such aircraft were probably too prohibitive anyway.

The unit never had more than eight aircraft, averaging four serviceable at any one time. Operations began on 9 June 1942, with unsuccessful attacks on the Royal Navy in the western Mediterranean. On 26 June they moved to Sardinia, carrying out their first night raid on Gibraltar three days later. On account of the inexperience of the crews, three of the five participants landed in Spain, low on fuel. Two were damaged and retained but the third was returned to Italy.

From July to September the unit continued training, receiving Series II models with a modified nose for night flying. Operations resumed from 24 September with spasmodic raids being made on Gibraltar until November. Bad weather and low numbers limited success. On 28 October one aircraft force-landed in Algiers due to bad weather. The unit turned its attention to the invasion ports of North Africa, once again with poor results.

Early in December all bombers were sent to the Piaggio works for new engines. On 6 January 1943 operations were resumed against the same ports. Seven days later two bombers were shot down over Algiers by Beaufighters of 153 Squadron, RAF. Victory claims by the RAF for 22 January, 1 March, and 23 March are something of a mystery and remain unsubstantiated, as the Piaggios were not operating on those nights.

From February to July the unit continued training, with attacks on invasion shipping off Sicily commencing on 11th July. They retired further north at the end of July, and still had five aircraft on the day of the Armistice.

278 Squadriglia Sil

Arrival	Zone	Base	Country	Aircraft	Duties
3 Sep 40	Sqa 5	El Adem T3	Cirenaica	SM 79	TB
Dec 40	Sqa 5	Benghasi	Cirenaica	SM 79	TB
1 Jan 41	Sqa 5	Ain el Gazala	Cirenaica	SM 79	TB
15 Feb 41	ASIC	Pantelleria	Sicily	SM 79	TB
Mar 42	ASIC	Castelvetrano	Sicily	SM 79	TB

This unit formed from the Reparto Sperimentale Aerosilurante with five SM 79 torpedo bombers. On 4 September 1940 aircraft began operating in ones and twos on armed reconnaissance missions. Sorties began at 4,000 metres for better spotting. From 30 September to 7 October two aircraft were detached to Gadurra. They became very busy when the war extended around Greece and Crete. Initial successes were hits on the cruisers HMS *Kent* on 17 September, HMS *Liverpool* on 14 October, and various coastal vessels. The HMS *Glasgow* was sunk on 3 December.

On 7 November, for their services in developing and operating the torpedo bombers, ten pilots received the *Medaglia d'Argento*, and ten specialists received the *Medaglia di Bronzo*. The Fleet Air Arm attack on Taranto naval base served to reinforce the determination and potential of this unit. The squadriglia searched for the attackers but bad weather prevented their location. In November four aircraft were detached to Gadurra to pass on the lessons learned to 34 Gruppo BT.

Newly trained torpedo bomber sections joined the squadriglia on 16 December. During December they moved several times during the retreat from Cirenaica, but continued training and attacks on the ports of both Sollum and Alexandria. On the 10th four aircraft were damaged by British artillery and they were sent to Benina for repairs by the Servizia Riparazioni Aeromobili e Motori and returned after eight days. On 21st detachments used Berka, then Ain el Gazala, as staging bases for night raids on the Gulf of Sollum.

By the end of the year the six aircraft on strength had carried out 34 armed reconnaissance missions, 25 attacks on ships at sea, 6 attacks on ships in port, and numerous training exercises. Having proved the worth and promise of this method of attack they helped set up 1 NAS and instruct 279 Sq, the next unit to form.

Meanwhile, on 1 January 1941, nine RAF bombers destroyed three SM 79s at Gazala. On the 28th a section was detached to Castelbenito, with two aircraft moving to Pantelleria on 15 February. The squadriglia covered the eastern Mediterranean while 279 Sq covered the central area, both combining armed reconnaissance with planned convoy attacks. It is worth comparing the size of this area with that which the RAF's Beaufort torpedo squadrons had to cover—the North Sea and English Channel—to appreciate the task confronting the unit. The squadriglia

moved to Pantelleria in February where they had more chance of positive results, but the inaction of the Royal Navy at that time meant time was used more on training than operations. On 21 April a section was at Berka. On 14 May a section of two aircraft moved to Gerbini while the rest stayed on Pantelleria. On 25 July they operated against a convoy near Benghasi.

In March 1942 the unit was in Sicily, joining 132 Gruppo on 1 April.

279 Squadriglia Sil

Arrival	Zone	Base	Country	Aircraft	Duties
Dec 40	Sqa 2	Gorizia	Italy	SM 79	TG
28 Dec 40	ASIC	Catania	Sicily	SM 79	TB
10 Jan 41	ASIC	Fontanarossa	Sicily	SM 79	TB
14 Apr 41	AEGE	Gadurra	Aegean	SM 79	TB
7 May 41	Sqa 5	Benghasi K2	Cirenaica	SM 79	TB
27 May 41	Sqa 5	El Ftehja	Cirenaica	SM 79	TB
15 Dec 41	Sqa 5	Benghasi K3	Cirenaica	SM 79	TB
21 Dec 41	Sqa 5	Misurata	Tripolitania	SM 79	TB
Feb 42	Sqa 5	Benghasi K2	Cirenaica	SM 79	TB

This was the first unit to be created from the first torpedo-training school, with six SM 79s leaving for Sicily at the end of 1940. On 9 January two aircraft joined with 32 Stormo in attacks on Force H from Gibraltar.

In April 1941 they went to the Aegean to operate against Allied convoys from Alexandria. On 20 April they joined 34 Gruppo which subsequently disbanded the following month. On 7 May three aircraft went to Benghasi K2 and three to Benina, all aircraft uniting on the 27th at El Ftehja (Derna), for operations around Crete and convoy escorts.

On 24 June two aircraft took off from Derna to search for two light cruisers north east of Tobruk. They were intercepted by Hurricanes while attacking a 3,000 ton tanker. *Capitano* Bernadini was hit by anti-aircraft fire and the enemy fighters. The radio operator, Riccardo Balagna was badly wounded as well as the commander and observer. The gunner, *Maresciallo* Vito Sinisi, fought back and managed to hit the fighters. Unfortunately, the SM 79 was too badly damaged to continue flying so it was ditched in the sea. The two worst wounded stayed in the aircraft dinghy while the others took turns in treading water (two in and two out). Sinisi, weakened by exposure, kept his friends spirits up then tried to throw himself into the water in order to increase their chances. The wounded Balagna, on sighting a Royal Navy destroyer, said he would rather die than be rescued by the enemy. The dinghy eventually floated to the African coast. For their courage and fortitude both Balagna and Sinisi were awarded posthumous *Medaglia d'Oro*.

131: *The pilot of a Macchi MC 202 of the 164ª Squadriglia, 161° Gruppo Autonomo CT, dismounts from his fighter which is finished in the sparsely blotched C2B desert camouflage pattern, sometimes called 'serir'. The number '1' on the fuselage and '164' on the fin probably indicates that he is the Squadriglia leader. Note how the sand and dust has worn away the paint from the propeller blades. Reggio Calabria, May 1943*

132: *A Fiat CR 42CN of the 300ª Squadriglia based at Ciampino and tasked with the night defence of Rome, seen at the beginning of 1942. This particular machine, 300-7, flown by Capitano Corrado Ricci, is fitted with a searchlight under the port wing, but still retains its daytime camouflage. The small propeller above the uppper wing is probably a wind-driven generator for the searchlight*

133: *"I can't even sleep at night" says the legend on this unidentified Fiat CR 42CN. It wears matt black night camouflage and was photographed at Boccadifalco but nothing else is known*

134 Above: *Magnificent shot of the Caproni-Vizzola F.4, MM5932, in July 1940. In 1942 it was used as a night fighter by the 303ª Squadriglia*

135 Left: *One of 13 Caproni-Vizzola F.5s in service with the 300ª Squadriglia, 167° Gruppo, as nightfighters defending Rome in 1942-1943*

136 Left: *The prototype Savoia-Marchetti SM 95 under test at Guidonia in August 1943. Intended for use as a four-engined transatlantic airliner, only three were built before the end of the war. Production continued after the war and the type saw service with the Italian Air Ministry and Alitalia. Could it have been the Italian Condor?*

137 Right: A Savoia-Marchetti SM 81A/R of the 202ᵃ Squadriglia, 40° Gruppo, 38° Stormo, in use as a transport over Albania in spring 1941. Note the unusual glazing to the turret

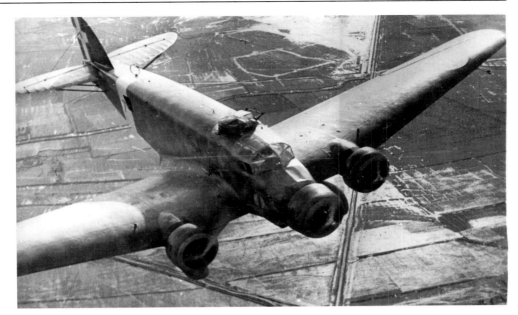

138 Below: Savoia-Marchetti SM 75 in service with the 604ᵃ Squadriglia. Once owned by Ala Littoria as I-LOLA, the aircraft survived until the end of 1941, when it was apparently damaged by enemy air attack. If correct, this is the result at Benghasi. The camouflage is a field-applied mix of blotches and bands

139 Right: The Italian aircraft industry failed to produce a credible dive bomber during the war. One of the great disappointments was the Savoia-Marchetti SM 85. Thirty-two were issued to the 96° Gruppo, but the lack of power and erratic flight behaviour doomed it. In June 1940, fourteen were sent to Pantelleria where the wooden airframes quickly deteriorated. In July the pilots went to Germany to train on the Ju 87

140: *Seen early in 1939, this is MM21599, the third production Savoia-Marchetti SM 85 dive bomber under test at Guidonia. The machine wears a C1 type camouflage scheme. Points of note are the external strengthening longerons and the large mass balances*

141: *The Breda 65 had many faults—lack of firepower was not one of them. This picture of one of the type (16-12) during the Spanish Civil War shows that it could carry a 12.7mm and 7.7mm machine gun in each wing, as well as a 100kg bomb under each wing. Unfortunately for the RA, the aircraft proved to be under-powered, tiring to fly and extremely vulnerable to enemy fire. The engine was also found to be easily damaged by sand or dust*

142: *Piloted by Tullio De Prato this Reggiane Re 2001, MM90760, is testing 20mm Mauser cannon in underwing gondolas. Known as the CN (Caccia Notturno) this variant was intended for use as a night fighter. Trials were successful and eventually 124 in several batches were built, although few pictures of them seem to have survived. The bright finish on this aircraft is noteworthy. This could be overall yellow with a dark green rudder*

Operations continued along the African coast, with for example three aircraft searching for ships north east of Marsa Matruh on 24 October. On 28 May 1942 they joined 131 Gruppo.

280 Squadriglia Sil

Arrival	Zone	Base	Country	Aircraft	Duties
8 Feb 41	Sqa 2	Gorizia	Italy	SM 79	TG
10 Feb 41	ASAR	Elmas	Sardinia	SM 79	TB

Formed with five aircraft, this unit operated in Sardinian waters. On 3 May 1941 they combined attacks with 32 Stormo north of Capo de Fer. On the 8th five aircraft, escorted by 15 CR 42s of 3 Stormo operated against Force H. Intercepted by enemy fighters, *Sottotenente* Marini was hit and crashed near La Galite. A French flying boat took the crew to Tunisia. *Sottotenente* Cappa, hit by cannonfire, launched a torpedo against a large ship from close range, then disappeared into the water with the loss of all the crew. He was awarded a posthumous *Medaglia d'Oro*. Both 278 and 281Sq were also involved in this attack.

On 23 July three aircraft attempted to attack the carrier HMS *Ark Royal* while she was avoiding level bombing from 32 Stormo and 51 Gruppo. At least one 32 Stormo SM 79 was shot down by interceptors, and one Hurricane was claimed by 280 Sq gunners. On 1 September 1941 they joined 130 Gruppo.

281 Squadriglia Sil

Arrival	Zone	Base	Country	Aircraft	Duties
15 Mar 41	Sqa 4	Grottaglie	Italy	SM 79	TG
20 Mar 41	AEGE	Gadurra	Aegean	SM 79	TB
May 41	Sqa 5	Castelbenito?	Tripolitania	SM 79	TB

This unit formed from the second torpedo-training school, 2 NAS, with four aircraft under the command of Capitano Buscaglia, formerly with 278 Sq. They went to the Aegean for attacks on the east Mediterranean convoys, joining 34 Gruppo in April 1941. On 21st they joined 279 Sq under 34 Gruppo. Between 5 March and 20 May the unit claimed 5 definite and 19 probable torpedo hits during the battle of Crete.

By 1 July they were Autonomo again and moved to Africa. Five pilots of this squadriglia were to receive their country's highest award, the *Medaglia d'Oro*, three of them posthumously.

On the 4th four aircraft attacked ships in Famagusta Bay, Cyprus. During the attack engineer *Sergente Maggiore* Nicola Gaesta was badly wounded by anti-aircraft fire from a destroyer. After his crewmates applied dressings to his wounds, he continued to control the engines on the long flight back, for which he was awarded the *Medaglia d'Argento*.

On 21 August, after operating against shipping west of Alexandria, the unit was temporarily reorganised, with new crews boosting strength, and resuming operations soon after.

On 13 October, a very clear day, three aircraft attacked the battleships *Queen Elizabeth* and *Barham*, but the defences were too strong, even though photographer *1ª Aviere* Tommaso di Paolo managed to photograph the former from only feet away as they completed their attack run. During this he took several good close photographs of the action.

On 23 November two aircraft were searching around Marsa Matruh when they were intercepted by three P-40s. The gunners claimed one 'probable'.

On 14 December six aircraft were split into two sections, one at Ain el Gazala and the other at Gadurra. Three days later, four aircraft attacked Alexandria harbour to prevent Royal Navy interference with a convoy crossing the Aegean to Libya. Attacking from both south and north of the ships, they flew into a solid wall of water thrown up by salvoes of heavy guns, together with a barrage of lesser calibre weapons. The highly experienced Buscaglia, Faggioni, and Cimicchi attempted several approaches but were all hit, although not fatally. On his first mission, *Sottotenente* Forzinetti pressed home his attack on a tanker, was caught in a hail of fire, burst into flames but continued to fly at his target until he eventually hit the water. For his dedication he was awarded a posthumous *Medaglia d'Oro*, and his four crew members were also given posthumous awards. No ships were hit.

On the 28th four aircraft attacked and sank the merchantship *Volo*, despite intercepts by P-40s, losing one aircraft to these and one to anti-aircraft fire. *Tenente* Rovello's aircraft caught fire but he continued his attack, launching his torpedo seconds before his aircraft disintegrated in flames over the sea. He was awarded the *Medaglia d'Oro*. By this time the crews had reverted to using two pilots in the front seats, instead of one pilot and one observer, on account of the severe punishment being received from flak. During the previous four weeks the unit had lost twenty per cent of its crews.

On 15 January 1942 they disbanded, passing their crews and aircraft to 41 Gruppo. On 1 April they reformed and joined 132 Gruppo.

282 Squadriglia Sil

Arrival	Zone	Base	Country	Aircraft	Duties
28 Jun 41	Sqa 3	Littoria	Italy	SM 84	TG
1 Jul 41	AEGE	Rodi Gadurra	Aegean	SM 84	TB
30 Jul 41	ASIC	Gerbini	Sicily	SM 84	TB
15 Nov 41	ASIC	Fontanarossa	Sicily	SM 84	TB
9 Dec 41	ASIC	Castelvetrano	Sicily	SM 84	TB

Formed with four SM 84s, they moved to Rodi and joined 41 Gruppo, alongside 204 and 205 Sq. Leaving the Gruppo on 30 July 1941 they moved to Sicily for operations in the Sicilian Canal. On 24 October two aircraft were intercepted by two Gladiators west of Malta with no losses to either side. On 9 November two aircraft, operating around the Maltese waters, hit a light cruiser of the *Leander* type. Enemy fighters prevented further attacks. Two aircraft from 278 Sq followed up the attack. Experiments were carried out during the month, with night attacks against La Valetta Harbour, Malta, using special anti-warship 1,000 kg bombs at night. These were used on the 12, 15, 19 and 20 November, but were no more successful than normal bombs.

On 15 January 1942 they disbanded, with the crews and aircraft passing to 41 Gruppo.

283 Squadriglia Sil

Arrival	Zone	Base	Country	Aircraft	Duties
4 Jul 41	Sqa 3	Ciampino Nord	Italy	SM 79	TG
15 Jul 41	ASAR	Elmas	Sardinia	SM 79	TB

Formed with seven aircraft, they operated around Sardinia, joining 280 Sq. Between 22 and 25 July 1941 they operated with 278 Sq against the Royal Navy's 'Force H'. On the 23rd four aircraft set out, escorted by 20 G 50s of 24 Gruppo from Monserrato. Due to their inexperience the escorts soon lost their charges. Six enemy fighters attacked, downing two and damaging the other two, but also losing two of their own. Five crew members were wounded. The squadriglia ceased operations for a few days to repair aircraft and receive replacement crews. On 1 August 1941 they joined 130 Gruppo.

284 Squadriglia Sil

Arrival	Zone	Base	Country	Aircraft	Duties
7 Nov 41	Sqa 3	Ciampino	Italy	SM 79	TG
23 Nov 41	ASIC	Fontanarossa	Sicily	SM 79	TB
27 Nov 41	Sqa 5	Derna	Cirenaica	SM 79	TB
12 Dec 41	Sqa 5	Benghasi K3	Cirenaica	SM 79	TB
21 Dec 41	Sqa 5	Misurata	Tripolitania	SM 79	TB
13 Feb 42	Sqa 5	Benghasi K2	Cirenaica	SM 79	TB

Formed with seven aircraft, they operated in the central Mediterranean. Four aircraft were transferred to K3 on 15 December 1941, joining the other three at K2 the next day. They joined 131 Gruppo on 25 March 1942.

287 Squadrilgia R.M.

Arrival	Zone	Base	Country	Aircraft	Duties
Jul 40	ASAR	Elmas	Sardinia	Z506B RS14B	AR, ASR
Apr 43	ASAR	Porto Conte Alghero	Sardinia	Z506B RS14B	AR, ASR

On 10 June 1940, 199 Sq was based at Oristano San Giusta, in Sardinia, with seven Z506Bs. That month it switched from bombing to reconnaissance duties, and renumbered as 287 Sq when a new 199 Sq formed in 94 Gruppo.

The unit remained in Sardinian waters throughout the war, assisting stranded airmen and seamen, and watching for enemy shipping. In 1941 they had several battles with enemy aircraft. On 27 September for example, a Z506B was out looking for an SM 84 crew who were down in the sea. During the rescue six enemy fighters attacked, losing two to the gunners, but setting the flying boat on fire. It landed in the sea, and the occupants waited with the bomber crew for seventeen hours before rescue came. They were among the lucky ones.

In the summer of 1942 they co-operated with CR 42 fighter-bombers, looking for stray ships during the Malta convoy runs. Shortly after they received RS14Bs, six being on strength by September.

As the Allies continued to advance the unit took its five Z506BS and five RS14Bs to northern Sardinia, continuing their duties until the Armistice. A section was detached to La Maddelena from 25 June to 9 July 1943.

288 Squadrilgia R.M.

Arrival	Zone	Base	Country	Aircraft	Duties
Mar 41	Sqa 4	Taranto	Italy	Z506B RS14B Z501	AR, ASR, CE

This unit may have been at Taranto since 1940. On 15 March 1941 they had seven Z506Bs there, of which only two were serviceable. The unit patrolled the Jonio e Basso Adriatico, with a section of three aircraft detached in August 1942 to Suda Bay, Crete, for the protection of convoys sailing to Cirenaica.

By April 1943 the whole unit had joined 85 Gruppo at the main base, covering the approaches to southern Italy and co-operating with German aircraft in anti-submarine operations.

300 Squadriglia C.T.

Arrival	Zone	Base	Country	Aircraft	Duties
41	Sqa 3	Ciampino	Italy	CR 42	NF

This unit formed from the Sezione Caccia Noturne at Guidonia, for the night defence of Rome. From January to May 1942 they came under the control of 51 Stormo, then joined 167 Gruppo.

310 Squadriglia C.T.

Arrival	Zone	Base	Country	Aircraft	Duties
24 Jul 43	Sqa 3	Guidonia	Italy	MC205V	AR

This unit was formed as a special fast reconnaissance unit, covering the Allied advance in the west and central Mediterranean. In 1943 they were effectively the only unit with a good chance of surviving such missions in daylight. They were possibly operating in June, although not appearing on the daily returns until July.

The only other similar unit had been 73 Sq of 4 Stormo, with modified MC 202s in 1942.

375 Squadriglia C.T.

Arrival	Zone	Base	Country	Aircraft	Duties
1 Feb 41	AALB	Tirana	Albania	CR 42	DF, AE
Dec 41	Sqa 5	Agedabia	Cirenaica	CR 42	DF, GA
Jan 42	Sqa 5	En Nofilia	Tripolitania	CR 42	DF, GA

Ten aircraft and their pilots left 152 Gruppo and formed this squadriglia at Tirana for operations against Yugoslavia. During 1941 they joined 160 Gruppo, although this may have not been until the Gruppo reunited at Sorman in January 1942.

376 Squadriglia Assalto

Arrival	Zone	Base	Country	Aircraft	Duties
20 Apr 41	Sqa 1	Torino Caselle	Italy	CR 42AS	TG
Apr 41	Sqa 3	Ciampino	Italy	CR 42AS	TG
21 May 41	Sqa 5	Castelbenito	Tripolitania	CR 42AS	GA, TG
8 Aug 41	Sqa 5	Ain el Gazala	Cirenaica	CR 42AS	GA
15 Nov 41	Sqa 5	Bir Hacheim	Cirenaica	CR 42AS	GA
25 Nov 41	Sqa 5	Ain el Gazala	Cirenaica	CR 42AS	GA
Nov 41	Sqa 3	Capodichino	Italy	MC 200	DF
29 Sep 42	Sqa 4	Gioia del Colle	Italy	MC 200	DF
May 43	AALB	Durazzo	Albania	MC 200 G 50bis	
				FN305	CE
Sep 43	AALB	Tirana	Albania	MC 200 G 50bis	DF, GA

This unit formed with twelve fighter-bombers and took them to Libya. They had been training at Ciampino on ground attack duties, but this was rushed due to the urgent need for more aircraft on the frontlines. After a further period of training the unit began operations on 24 October, with seven aircraft also using Gambut. They often co-operated with 239 Sq in ground attacks.

From Gazala they operated over Bir Hacheim, then Bir el Gobi, operating jointly with 160 Gruppo. In November they returned to Italy where they defended Naples.

During May 1943 they escorted six convoys in the Adriatic, and practiced radio communications with naval units. June saw five more convoy escorts, with twelve G 50s and two FN 305s operational. The following July they were training at Tirana, with a section detached to Devoli. They had six fighter-bombers operational on 7 September.

377 Squadriglia C.T.

Arrival	Zone	Base	Country	Aircraft	Duties
1 Aug 41	ASIC	Comiso	Sicily	Re 2000	DF, CE
9 Aug 41	ASIC	Trapani Milo	Sicily	Re 2000	DF
Aug 41	ASIC	Chinisia	Sicily	Re 2000	DF, CE, GA
Sep 41	ASAR	Monserrato	Sardinia	Re 2000	DF, AR
Dec 41	ASIC	Reggio Calabria	Italy	Re 2000	CE
19 Dec 41	ASIC	Trapani Milo	Sicily	Re 2000	DF, AR, CE
22 Mar 42	Sqa 2	Reggio Emilia	Italy	Re 2000	TG
23 May 42	ASIC	Boccadifalco	Sicily	Re 2000	DF, AR, CE
Aug 42	ASIC	Pantelleria	Sicily	Re 2000	DF, AR
12 Aug 42	ASIC	Boccadifalco	Sicily	Re 2000	CE, DF
Sep 42	ASIC	Sciacca	Sicily	Re 2000 CR 42	
				MC 200	DF. CE. GA
Feb 43	ASIC	Boccadifalco	Sicily	MC 202	DF, CE

A Sezione Sperimentale was attached to 74 Sq of 23 Gruppo at Comiso in 1941. This unit was equipped with six Re 2000 Series I, which had been a contender for major production orders along with the MC 200 and G 50. Although considered the better aircraft, it lost the major contract due to more vulnerable fuel tanks. The Regia Marina needed a modern catapult fighter for its warships, and so a limited number were produced. The need for fighters was such, however, that most equipped this land based unit. They were very useful for convoy escort work because of a greater fuel capacity than the other single-seaters. In August they moved to Trapani then Chinisia, having become 377 Sq and receiving twelve Series III long-range versions with bomb-carrying capacity. These were used against Malta.

The unit used various bases in Sicily, including Pantelleria, in 1941. During the convoy battles in September they moved to Sardinia. Using Comiso as a forward base some Re 2000s operated over Malta in November. When 23 Gruppo went to Libya the squadriglia became Autonomo on 12 December. A short stay in southern Italy followed, escorting ships off Calabria. Then the unit returned to Sicily, defending the island and escorting its shipping. A few CR 42CN night fighters may have been used while the fighters continued operational training.

In March 1942 ten more Series III machines were received in Italy to replace losses, and the unit moved to Palermo-Boccadifalco for interceptor duties. In June they escorted the 7th Naval Division during operations against the *Harpoon* convoy. That month they received the B30 radio transmitter system, but this did not improve communications between the navy and air force. August found them at Pantelleria, participating in the battles around Malta. On 12 August a section was detached to Chinisia for local defence.

The pilots had been complaining that the Re 2000 was harder to fly than the CR 42, and the lack of spares was reducing the operational numbers. Consequently, an anti-submarine and night-fighter section of CR 42CNs was attached in September. The Re 2000s were replaced by twelve MC 200s, and the CR 42s were detached to Pantelleria.

In January 1943 they received a modified version of the B30 radio, which improved air-to-air and air-to-ground communications. Despite this, high static density was still suffered when flying over metropolitan Italy. Some CR 42s were still used for anti-submarine patrols, but the downward view was too limited to be efficient for this role. These CR 42s were eventually passed to 379 Sq. Co-operating with German searchlights, the remaining CR 42 nightfighters still found electrical interference on their radios. On the other hand, sufficient artificial horizons were now arriving to cure yet another of the night flying problems.

By February 1943 the unit was re-equipped with six MC 202s at Bocccadifalco. After several scrambles against American bombers they were grounded for five days in March for inspection of weapons and radios. The next month they were severely bombed, which hindered operations and training. Three four-engined bombers were claimed at this time. The unit temporarily moved to Catania, due to several unexploded bombs on their home base. They disbanded on 26 May, passing aircraft and crews to 53 Stormo.

384 Squadriglia Assalto

Arrival	Zone	Base	Country	Aircraft	Duties
Dec 42	Sqa		Italy	MC 200	TG
2 Jan 43	ATUN	El Aouina	Tunisia	MC 200	GA
12 Feb 43	ATUN	Tunis	Tunisia	MC 200	GA
3 Mar 43	ASIC	Castelvetrano	Sicily	MC 200	GA, AN

Arrival	Zone	Base	Country	Aircraft	Duties
Jul 43	ASIC	Reggio Calabria	Italy	MC 200	DF

This unit left 157 Gruppo to train on fighter-bombers in late 1942. They were then hurried into battle in northern Tunisia, retiring to Sicily with only four surviving aircraft after two months of intensive action.

They were heavily bombed while defending Sicily before the Allied invasion. The pilots then reunited with 157 Gruppo to defend the island and southern Italy.

392 Squadriglia C.T.

Arrival	Zone	Base	Country	Aircraft	Duties
1 Mar 43	AALB	Tirana	Albania	CR 42 G 50bis	DF, GA, CE
24 Jun 43	AALB	Airport 917?	Albania	CR 42 G 50bis	
				MC 200 Ro41	CE, DF

This unit formed from the Sezione Caccia Terrestre based at Tirana in 1943. Convoy escorts were made from Durazzo in May and June, over the Adriatic. On 24 June the unit had four CR 42s, six G 50s, five Ro 41s, two MC 200s, and one CR 30D on strength. Initially training on the CR 42 through to July, by 7 September they had nine out of eleven CR 42s and two G 50bis serviceable.

410 Squadriglia C.T.

Arrival	Zone	Base	Country	Aircraft	Duties
10 Jun 40	AOI	Dire Daua	Ethiopia	CR32	DF, AE
Jul 40	AOI	Giggiga	Ethiopia	CR32	DF, AE
Mar 41	AOI	Addis Abeba	Ethiopia	CR32	DF, AE
5 Apr 41	AOI	Gimma	Ethiopia	CR32	DF
5 Jun 41	AOI	Gondar	Ethiopia	CR32	DF

This unit arrived in Ethiopia by sea in 1938 as 155 Sq, being renumbered in August 1939. There were nine fighters on strength at the start of the war, and these moved to Giggiga in July in preparation for the offensive against British Somaliland.

On 7 August 1940 two CR32s were sent to Hargeisa in British Somaliland for fighter patrols in that area. They were given bomb-racks for two 50 kg bombs and began assault duties during the offensive, operating with 411 and 413 Sq as a Gruppo. Two more aircraft joined them on 10 August. The detachment moved to Aauax in September and two CR 32s returned to home base on 27 September when British Somaliland was occupied.

On 16 December two CR 32s downed a Free French Martin 167F from Aden, over their own base. In February 1941 two fighters were detached to Makale, returning in mid-March. On 9 March three fighters forced down one out of six Blenheims over their base. The fighters were only now given radios. On 28 March two CR32s were sent to Gauani for operations against Giggiga.

By April some aircraft had been lost at Addis Abeba, so the unit left for Gimma. On 9 April two were destroyed on the ground and two were shot down, leaving only two operational at that base. By 5 June they had evacuated to Gondar but it is unlikely they had any aircraft left by then.

411 Squadriglia C.T.

Arrival	Zone	Base	Country	Aircraft	Duties
10 Jun 40	AOI	Addis Abeba	Ethiopia	CR32	DF, AE
20 Jun 40	AOI	Javello	Ethiopia	CR32	DF
18 Jul 40	AOI	Addis Abeba	Ethiopia	CR32	DF
30 Jul 40	AOI	Dire Daua	Ethiopia	CR32	DF
Aug 40	AOI	Addis Abeba	Ethiopia	CR32	DF
Mar 41	AOI	Asmara	Ethiopia	CR32	DF
Mar 41	AOI	Dessie	Ethiopia	CR32	DF
Apr 41	AOI	Addis Abeba	Ethiopia	CR32	DF
Apr 41	AOI	Gimma	Ethiopia	CR32	DF
May 41	AOI	Gondar	Ethiopia	CR32	DF

This unit had nine fighters on strength at the start of hostilities. Three were sent to Javello on 19 June, fighting that same day against three Ju 86s and two Hurricanes of the SAAF. One fighter from each side was lost. The next day more Fiats were flown in. On 30 June two were detached from Javello to Neghelli followed by two more on 1 July. The five survivors all returned to Addis Abeba on 18 July.

On the 30th, nine CR32s moved to Dire Daua where three were passed to 410 Sq, and together with 413 Sq, the three squadriglie formed a fighter gruppo for operations during the offensive against British Somaliland. Giggiga was used as a staging base.

Returning to Addis Abeba in August, the unit sent three fighters back to Dire Daua on the 16th in case of a British counter-offensive. They returned on the 22nd as the threat receded.

On 27 September two CR 32s flew from Dessie to Sciasciamanna via Addis Abeba. The unit used both Dessie and Asmara during operations over the Cheren area. By March or April the unit had moved to Gimma then on to Gondar where they probably ran out of aircraft.

412 Squadriglia C.T.

Arrival	Zone	Base	Country	Aircraft	Duties
10 Jun 40	AOI	Massaua	Eritrea	CR 42	DF, AE
Aug 40	AOI	Agordat	Eritrea	CR 42	DF
Sep 40	AOI	Asmara	Eritrea	CR 42	DF
30 Sep 40	AOI	Gura	Eritrea	CR 42	DF
Oct 40	AOI	Barentu	Eritrea	CR 42	DF
Jan 41	AOI	Gura	Eritrea	CR 42	AE, GA
16 Mar 41	AOI	Dessie	Ethiopia	CR 42	DF, AE
22 Mar 41	AOI	Asmara	Eritrea	CR 42	DF
31 Mar 41	AOI	Dessie	Ethiopia	CR 42	DF
7 Apr 41	AOI	Alomata	Ethiopia	CR 42	DF, GA, AR
Apr 41	AOI	Gimma	Ethiopia	CR 42	DF, AE
Jun 41	AOI	Gondar	Ethiopia	CR 42	DF

There were nine fighters on strength at the start of the war, with five detached to Gura. Some pilots were received from 409 Sq which had disbanded in early 1940. This was a very experienced unit, with two years of flying in this theatre, but because of the primitive conditions and poor supplies they could not make the best use of all the bases available. Several Wellesley bombers were shot down over the Massaua area. Three new CR 42s arrived on the 28 June.

In August or September the unit moved to Agordat in preparation for the British counter-offensive. By 30 September nine fighters were at Gura, fighting Blenheims, Gladiators and Wellesleys in protection of the area. On 16 October they all joined escort with one SM 79 on a raid against Gedaref where eight Wellesleys of 47 Squadron and two Vincents of 430 Flight were destroyed.

Three CR 42s were lost to strafing Gladiators at Barentu. Many combats were fought with these SAAF fighters over the Metemma area. During the British offensive on Eritrea and northern Ethiopia the unit was heavily involved. Six claims for no loss in the three days of operations gained air superiority for the Italians. The British supply situation was as bad as the Italian and thus the attack was called off. In early December radios were fitted to some CR 42s, enabling detachments to be sent more effectively to Burie, Gura, and Addis Abeba for operations in the north.

By 29 January 1941 the unit was carrying out bomber escort and ground attack duties from Gura. A raid on Agordat on 9 February destroyed two Wellesleys, two Hartebeestes, two Lysanders, and damaged four others. Two days later the unit lost *Capitano* Mario Visintini when he fatally crashed into Mount Nefasit while looking for a fellow pilot. He had over 15 victories at this time, and was the most successful fighter pilot in the campaign.

On 16th March the unit took twelve CR 42s to Dessie for operations in the Cheren area. A detachment was sent to Combolcia landing ground on 6 April, evacuating on the 22nd to Gimma. By early April the aircraft were on intercept, close support, and reconnaissance duties. Another detachment went to Cer Cer then on to Gondar.

By 14 April the unit was reunited at Gimma but soon had to transfer to Gondar as the Allies sought out all known bases.

On 5 June the fighters had no ammunition, until an SM 75 delivered fresh supplies on the 10th. A detachment was then sent to Azozo. By the 11th only two CR 42s were operational at Gondar. The last dogfight was over Ambazzo when one was shot down by the SAAF. The remaining fighter carried out a strafing raid in the Kulkaber area on the 22 November as its last sortie. Four days later it was burnt to prevent capture.

413 Squadriglia C.T.

Arrival	Zone	Base	Country	Aircraft	Duties
10 Jun 40	AOI	Assab	Ethiopia	CR 42	TG, DF
Jul 40	AOI	Dire Daua	Ethiopia	CR 42	DF
Aug 40	AOI	Gondar	Ethiopia	CR 42	DF
Sep 40	AOI	Adi Ugri L.G.	Ethiopia	CR 42	DF
Sep 40	AOI	Dessie	Ethiopia	CR 42	DF
Sep 40	AOI	Addis Abeba	Ethiopia	CR 42	DF
28 Mar 41	AOI	Gauani	Ethiopia	CR 42	DF, AE
Apr 41	AOI	Addis Abeba	Ethiopia	CR 42	DF
5 Apr 41	AOI	Dessie	Ethiopia	CR 42	DF, GA
7 Apr 41	AOI	Sciasciamanna	Ethiopia	CR 42	DF, GA
Apr 41	AOI	Gimma	Ethiopia	CR 42	DF, AE

By the outbreak of war this unit had mostly novice pilots but with an experienced leader. On 15 June three fighters were detached to Addis Abeba. Two months later the unit joined 410 and 411 Sq as a Gruppo for operations against British Somaliland, using Giggiga as a forward base. They then moved to Gondar, in anticipation of a counter-attack.

Two fighters were detached to Assab on 6 July, with three others to Bahar Dar on 27 September. By December some aircraft had radios, and on 18th three flew to Bardera for operations against the Allied attacks. On 16 December three CR 42s flew from Burie to Addis Abeba then on to Lugh Ferrandi. The fighters were called on for ground attack duties, and as escorts to the Ca 133s and SM 79s operating against the northern attacks.

On 13 March they joined with 110 Sq for fighter sweeps. Nine days later two flew from Addis Abeba to Dire Daua for operations against SAAF units at Giggiga, returning on 24th March. The unit's five remaining fighters flew to Gauani to continue sorties against Giggiga from 28 March. They returned on 4 April, flying out the next day to Dessie for close support and intercept duties. The last known action was on 9 July when a Wellesley was claimed over Gimma.

414 Squadriglia C.T.

Arrival	Zone	Base	Country	Aircraft	Duties
10 Jun 40	AOI	Gura	Eritrea	CR 42	DF, AE
28 Jun 40	AOI	Assab	Ethiopia	CR 42	DF, AE

In early 1940 this unit received pilots from the disbanded 409 Sq. However, the aircraft were limited to the main bases because runways were usually too short for the CR 42. Six of these fighters were available at the start of hostilities.

On 15 June three were detached to Assab to replace the 413 Sq detachment. The rest of the unit joined them on 28 June. By 10 July the last of the six fighters was lost at Assab. It is assumed that on account of a lack of reserves the unit then ceased to exist and its personnel were dispersed to the other fighter squadriglie.

600 Squadriglia T.

Arrival	Zone	Base	Country	Aircraft	Duties
Sep 41	Sqa 5	Castelbenito	Tripolitania	Ca 133S SM 81S	
				Ca 309	TR
Aug 42	Sqa 5	Fuka Nord	Egypt	Ca 133S	TR
Nov 42	Sqa 5	Marsa Matruh	Egypt	Ca 133S	TR
Jan 43	Sqa 5	Zuara	Tripolitania	Ca 133S	TR
Jan 43	ASIC	Sciacca	Sicily	Ca 133S	TR

This unit was formed for ambulance duties around Libya. It initially had three Ca 133Ss, two SM 81Ss, and one Ca 309, sharing the same facilities as 145 Gruppo. During 1942 the aircraft operated singly all over Libya and occupied Egypt. They evacuated Marsa Matruh in November, taking seven Ca 133Ss with them and leaving one unserviceable aircraft behind.

The unit evacuated civilians and wounded by night, from Tripoli to Sicily in January 1943. In February they came directly under 18 Stormo command.

611 Squadriglia T.

Arrival	Zone	Base	Country	Aircraft	Duties
Jun 40	AALB	Tirana	Albania	Ba 44	TR

This unit formed with five ex-civil Breda 44s. They supported operations against Greece from October, also using Valona and Argirocastro bases. In November they ferried troops between Durazzo, Tirana, and Coritza.

From April 1941 they supported anti-partisan units in Yugoslavia. It is believed that two of these aircraft survived until September 1943, after eight years of constant flying.

612 Squadriglia Soccorso

Arrival	Zone	Base	Country	Aircraft	Duties
8 Jun 40	Sqa 3	Roma Lido	Italy	Z506C	ASR

Arrival	Zone	Base	Country	Aircraft	Duties
Jun 40	Sqa 2	Stagnone Marsala	Sicily	Z506C Z506S	ASR
23 Dec 40	ASIC	Stagnone	Sicily	Z506C Z506S	ASR

This unit was formed on 8 June 1940 for air sea rescue duties in Sicily, with five aircraft. A section of two was detached to Torre del Lago under Squadra 3 until 27 August. During that month three aircraft were at Siracusa and three more were at Stagnone. The squadriglia initially had ex-civilian Z506Cs, but in May 1941 received the purpose-built Z506S. They were kept busy rescuing airmen shot down into the sea during the battles around Malta.

On 12 June 1941 a Z506C and a Z506S were downed by enemy fighters. By 1942 they had evolved four Autonomo sections, operating from various bases around the Sicilian islands, because of the vast area to be covered by the unit.

613 Squadriglia Soccorso

Arrival	Zone	Base	Country	Aircraft	Duties
8 Jun 40	Sqa 3	Roma Lido	Italy	SM 66C	ASR
12 Jun 40	ASAR	Cagliari Elmas	Sardinia	SM 66C	ASR

This unit was formed for air sea rescue duties around Sardinia, with five ex-civilian SM 66C flying boats. A section of two aircraft was detached to Olbia, becoming Autonomo on 15 July when the squadriglia disbanded. The section temporarily moved to Brindisi.

The squadriglia then reformed on 6 August 1940 with the same five S66Cs, at Elmas. On 10 September some of the aircraft received stretchers and medical equipment. Z506S ambulance aircraft joined them in 1941, the unit operating them together until well into 1942.

The unit evolved into four Autonomo sections with other ex-civilian aircraft. Two SM 66Cs were converted into properly equipped ambulance aircraft, redesignated SM 66Ss. On 31 August 1942 the unit had three Z506Ss, two SM 66Cs, and one SM 66S. In the summer of 1943, after ten years flying, three of the sedate SM 66Cs were still pulling Axis and Allied airmen out of the Sardinian waters.

614 Squadriglia Soccorso

Arrival	Zone	Base	Country	Aircraft	Duties
12 Jun 40	Sqa 3	Roma Lido	Italy	Z506C	ASR

Arrival	Zone	Base	Country	Aircraft	Duties
13 Jun 40	ALIB	Tripoli Caramanlis	Tripolitania	Z506C Z506S	
				Z509	ASR

This unit formed with six aircraft, for rescue duties off the Tripolitanian coast. To help cover the large area, the six Z506Cs were split into sections, one each in Menelao, Benghasi, and Tripoli. A section of two aircraft was initially detached to Lero from 14 June, moving to Rodi-Mandracchio on 8 July when it became Autonomo. Both this section and the main unit received some Z506Ss from November 1940.

Initially the squadriglia was also on transport duties between Benghasi, Tripoli, and Siracusa. On 15 August 1940 they passed from the SAS to Squadra 5 command, and permanently detached a section to Menelao.

In January 1941 the unit helped evacuate civilians from Benghasi to Tripoli. Between 5 April and 23 October they used a Z509, borrowed from 104 Sq. Between 18 April and 9 July they rescued 31 men from the sea.

In September 1942 the squadriglia evolved into four Autonomo sections, including the detachments in the Aegean and in Benghasi. On 20 September the unit had two serviceable aircraft at Tripoli. The main unit was still at Caramanlis on 31 December, being one of the last units left in Libya.

615 Squadriglia T.

Arrival	Zone	Base	Country	Aircraft	Duties
Jun 40	Sqa 3	Guidonia	Italy	SM 83	TR

This unit formed with eight SM 83s for liaison duties between Libya and Italian East Africa. The first trip was made on 15 June using Guidonia-Benghasi-Asmara. In February 1941 this route ceased to operate when the British occupied Benghasi. The unit switched to Guidonia-Catania-Tripoli until they could no longer reach Italian bases in Ethiopia.

616 Squadriglia T.

Arrival	Zone	Base	Country	Aircraft	Duties
10 Jun 40	Sqa 3	Roma Littorio	Italy	SM 74	TR

This unit formed with three SM 74s. These were passed on to 604 Sq on 7 July before much use had been made of them.

Squadriglia Baylon CT

Arrival	Zone	Base	Country	Aircraft	Duties
23 April 41	Sqa 5	Derna	Cirenaica	G 50	AE

On 23 April 1941 *Maggiore* Baylon was promoted to *Tenente Colonele* and ordered to create a unit purely for escorting the dive-bombers and ground forces attacking Tobruk. He received some G 50s from 2 Gruppo but supplies did not allow a Gruppo sized operation as originally intended. Between 23 April and 6 July they flew 51 missions. On 22 July the unit was disbanded and the personnel left for Italy.

1 Nucleo Addestramento Silurante

Arrival	Zone	Base	Country	Aircraft	Duties
28 Oct 40	Sqa 2	Gorizia	Italy	SM 79	TG

This training unit was formed with ten aircraft and the help of 278 Sq members to study the weapon installations and bomb-aimers position in the SM 79. Methods of torpedo attack, manoeuvres, training of new crews, and operations under different conditions of light (day and night) were all tried out. Ship recognition and low level flying were also covered.

The unit went to Capodichino to study torpedoes, returning to Gorizia to deal with the practical problems of hitting moving ships at sea. This had been studied since the 1930s when the Italian commission in China in 1937 investigated the RAF use of Vickers Vildebeeste torpedo-bombers in Singapore. Eventually a 'Manuale del Siluriste Aeronautico' was developed for all torpedo units.

The initial four aircraft were called on to join in operations, where necessary, against the more important Allied convoys. During 1941 six aircraft and crews were released for combat while continuing training. In mid-1941 experienced crews from 279, 280 and 281 Sq were brought to Gorizia to help form new squadriglie. By 9 July 1943, the unit still had six out of twelve aircraft serviceable at Gorizia. After the armistice the aircraft and crews went on to form the ANR's only torpedo unit.

The 2nd NAS formed at Capodichino in November 1940 and was disbanded by September 1943 due to lack of aircraft. In June 1942, six of their aircraft and more advanced trainees had joined five from 3 NAS in Sardinia for operations against the Malta convoys. On the 15th three of these aircraft attacked the HARPOON convoy; the leader, *Tenente* Silva, receiving a posthumous *Medaglia d'Oro* after being shot down by fighters during an attack on the cruiser, HMS *Liverpool*.

The 3rd NAS formed at Pisa in January 1942. The following month they began training 46 Stormo in day and night flying and torpedo attack methods. They moved to Salon in France on 1 July 1943 in order to make room for Luftwaffe units. Instructors and the more advanced trainee crews were often called into action. By 9 July 3 NAS had eight out of ten aircraft serviceable. All aircraft and crews were captured by the Germans in September.

Reparto Speciale Aerosilurante

Arrival	Zone	Base	Country	Aircraft	Duties
11 Jun 43	APRO	Istres	France	SM 79bis	TB, AR
27 Jun 43	Sqa 3	Littoria	Italy	SM 79bis	TB

Sometimes noted as 'La Squadriglia Grande Autonomia', this unit was specially formed with ten of the new uprated S79bis, for long range night torpedo operations against Gibraltar and the western Mediterranean. The idea for this type of unit was planned from February 1943, and several experiments were tried out. On 13 June three SM 82s took off from Salon, France, to deliver parachutists to sabotage bases in Oran and Algiers. Earlier, eleven SM 82s had delivered 140 parachutists from Crete to Africa. Damage was done to Benghasi base—*1st Aviere* Procida and Cargnel receiving the *Medaglia d'Argento* each.

The SM 79bis were stripped down to increase fuel capacity, and ten veteran crews from 130 Gruppo, 132 Gruppo, 1 NAS, and 3 NAS were acquired. Training was hindered by the Mistral winds but eventually the unit was declared operational.

On the morning of 20 June nine crews took off at 00.18 am for a night raid on the shipping around Gibraltar. The flight route took them over Spain, arriving over Gibraltar from landward and returning over the water. Engine problems causing variable fuel consumptions forced the return of at least one, and bad weather en route split the formation causing extra navigational problems and the return of five others. Only two managed to reach the target area between 05.10 and 05.20 am and launch their torpedoes (*Capitano* Faggioni and *Capitano* Cimicchi), but the results were not seen. Both aircraft landed at Barcelona on the way back. The Spanish authorities allowed the crews to leave but kept the aircraft. There was no fighter opposition, although searchlights were very effective. The potential effect upon the course of the war had the other aircraft found targets in that packed bay can only be wondered at. The raid was not repeated due

xxx Above: An IMAM Ro 43, coded '32', which may indicate that it belongs to 3 Squadriglia Forze Navali of the Regia Marina air arm. It is seen here perched on the bow catapult of the heavy cruiser Trento. *This vessel was torpedoed early on 15 June 1942 by a Beaufort of 217 Squadron RAF, based on Malta and flown by F/Lt Arthur Aldridge. The ship was subsequently sunk by the Royal Navy submarine HMS* Umbra, *whose commander had watched the air attack through his periscope*

to the difficulties of finding torpedo aircraft with sufficient range for a successful attack.

On 19 and 24 June the unit operated over the bay of Bone and off the Tunisian coast. Orders were received on the 24th to make armed reconnaissance missions to the ports of Oran and Algiers. The Germans insisted on taking over the Istres base by 27 June, and thereby ended further Italian torpedo attacks on Gibraltar.

Reparto Sperimentale Aerosilurante

Arrival	Zone	Base	Country	Aircraft	Duties
25 Jul 40	Sqa 2	Gorizia	Italy	SM 79	TG
10 Aug 40	Sqa 3	Ciampino	Italy	SM 79	IT
Aug 40	ASIC	Catania	Sicily	SM 79	IT
12 Aug 40	Sqa 5	Benghasi	Cirenaica	SM 79	TB
15 Aug 40	Sqa 5	El Adem	Cirenaica	SM 79	TB

Poor results from high level bombing of moving ships led to the formation of this unit. This was the first torpedo-bomber unit to form, with six aircraft adapted for torpedo drops. The crews were introduced to a low level altimeter and rearranged crew duties. An observer (*Osservatore*), usually a shipping specialist and/or naval observer, replaced the second pilot and was put in command of the aircraft. He judged the angle of attack and time of release. The pilot (*pilote*) was supported by an engineer (*motoriste*) who maintained engine performance during the attack. A dorsal gunner (*cacciatore*) watched for enemy fighters and the results of the torpedo launch, and the radio operator (*marconista*) manned the waist guns as well as kept contact with base. Navigation was primarily the responsibility of the observer but could be shared with the pilot with the support of the radio operator.

Operations began on 15 August, with a low level attack on Alexandria port in conjunction with conventional level bombing by 10 Stormo. One aircraft was lost by running out of fuel and landing in the desert. A similar attack was made on 23 August with only one SM 79, this time at night, but once again heavy anti-aircraft fire and bad weather prevented success. Adjustments were made to the instruments and torpedo holding brackets as a result of experience gained.

The unit now turned to attacks on shipping at sea. Due to inexperience the crews often reported columns of water and explosions as hits when they were mostly defensive fire. Torpedo launches were initially too far from the target but the crews were learning all the time.

Meanwhile, the unit had become 278 Sq on 3 September 1940 operating directly under Squadra 5 command.

143 Below: Derived from the SM 84 bomber, the Savoia Marchetti SM 89 was a heavily armed attack aircraft carrying 2 x 37mm and 3 x 12.7mm guns in the nose and a 12.7mm gun each in dorsal and ventral turrets. Under test at the Armistice, it would probably have been overshadowed by the competing CANSA FC20

144: *Easily the most potent Italian bomber of the war, the CRDA Cant Z.1018 had something of both the Mitsubishi Ki 67 and the Tupolev Tu 2 about it. Reflecting Italy's chronic shortage of raw materials, this is MM24290, the first of a pre-series of ten built from wood. Production aircraft were intended to be built from metal. Finish here is the typical late-war simple dark green uppersurfaces*

145: *The elegant nose of a CRDA Cant Z.1018. Note the soft demarcation line between upper and lower surface colours and that the port propeller is not fitted with a spinner here*

146: *Fiat devoted considerable efforts to developing their own designs, even when it would have been more beneficial to the overall war effort if they had just license-built other company's designs. An example is the BR 20 bis, which offered only marginal improvement of the earlier versions. By 1943 the original design was seven years old. Rightly, the RA was much more interested in the Cant Z.1018 which had far more potential. Nevertheless, Fiat still managed to find enough resources to build fifteen examples of the BR 20 bis between March and July 1943*

147: *Another dead-end experimental aircraft was the Caproni Ca 313G (G-Germania) trainer. Three were built at the behest of the Germans in 1943. Oddly, although the aircraft is finished in typical Italian overall dark green with Italian markings, the data on the rear fuselage is in German.*

148: *There is nothing special about this picture of a Caproni Ca 313, taken from the manufacturer's brochure, except for the fact that it is from the original material supplied to the RAF for assessment by the Royal Aircraft Establishment prior to a British order for the type. In November 1939 an order for 400 Ca 311 and Ca 313 trainers was duly placed, only to be cancelled on 23 April 1940. What if the RAF had received them? What if the 300 Reggiane Re 2000s also ordered for the RAF in 1940 had been delivered? Would the Italians have joined the Germans? What if...*

149: *The final development of the Savoia-Marchetti SM 85 dive bomber was the improved SM 86. Fitted with Isotta-Fraschini inline engines and a greatly refined airframe, one was delivered in late 1940. Finished in combat markings as seen here at Lonate Pozzolo, it took part in a raid on Hal Far, Malta, with twelve Ju 87s of the 96° Gruppo on 15 September. On 4 November it attacked a Greek target. After that it remained in the hangar until an order for it to be broken up was issued on 17 August 1941*

150 Left: *Much effort was expended in trying to improve the striking power of the Caproni Ca 314. Here an experimental Ca 314C (MM12053) has been fitted with a 37mm cannon in an underfuselage gondola, three 12.7mm machine guns in and under the wings plus racks for a variety of light bombs in an attempt to make it into a more effective light attack aircraft. Note the soft demarcation between the upper and lower surface colours*

152 Right: *An IMAM Ro 43 on the bow catapult of the heavy cruiser* Trento, *which was torpedoed and sunk by the submarine HMS* Umbra *on 15 June 1942. The aircraft colour scheme appears to be the standard Grigio Azzurro Scuro 3 upper-surfaces and Grigio Azzurro Chiaro 1 below. The deck seems remarkably cluttered; note the conveniently pro-vided benches for sailors to take their ease*

151 Left: *Capua, August 1943. Two surviving Junkers Ju 87Ds from the 216ᵃ Squadriglia, 121° Gruppo. 49 were supplied between April and June 1943 and used to form two new Gruppi: the 103° and 121°. Thrown into the jaws of the Allied invasion force over Sicily in July, the remnants of 121° returned to Sardinia in August. The other Gruppo did not—it had been wiped out*

SQUADRIGLIE ALLOCATIONS
1940-1941

The number in each line is, where known, the Gruppo controlling the squadriglia. Where a question mark (?) is shown it is not clear that the unit was then constituted. The 'b' notation relates to the bomber units operating in East Africa whose numbers were duplicates of those in other theatres. An 'a' indicates a member of Gruppo APC (colonial patrols). Letter 'o' indicates the unit was part of a Gruppo OA. Capital 'A' means the squadriglia is Automono—independent. A blank means it probably did not operate, while a dash (-) indicates that the unit was nominally on the records but not active. It must be stressed that these are not official designations, but are used solely for clarity.

Squadriglia	Gruppo in 1940							Gruppo in 1941											
	Jun	Jul	Aug	Sep	Oct	Nov	Dec	Jan	Feb	Mar	Apr	May	Jun	Jul	Aug	Sep	Oct	Nov	Dec
1	11	11	11	11	11	11	11	11	11	11	11	11	11	11	11	11	11	11	11
2	45	45	45	45	45	45	45	45											
3	43	43	43	43	43	43	43	43	43	43	43	43	43	43	43	43	43	43	43
4	11	11	11	11	11	11	11	11	11	11	11	11	11	11	11	11	11	11	11
5	43	43	43	43	43	43	43	43	43	43	43	43	43	43	43	43	43	43	43
6	44	44	44	44	?														
6b	44b	44b	44b	44b	44b	44b	44b	44b	44b	44b	44b								
7	44	44	44	44	?														
7b	44b	44b	44b	44b	44b	44b	44b	44b	44b	44b	44b								
8	25	25	25	25	25	25	25	25	25	25	25	25	25	25	25	25	25	25	
8b	25b	25b	25b	25b	25b	25b	25b	25b	25b	25b	25b	25b	25b	25b					
9	25	25	25	25	25	25	25	25	25	25	25	25	25	25	25	25	25	25	
9b	25b	25b	25b	25b	25b	25b	25b	25b	25b	25b	25b	25b	25b	25b					
10	28	28	28	28	28	28	28	28	28	28	28	28	28	28	28	28	28	28	
10b	28b	28b	28b	28b	28b	28b	28b	28b	28b	28b	28b								
11	26	26	26	26	26	26	26	26											

Squadriglia	Jun	Jul	Aug	Sep	Oct	Nov	Dec	Jan	Feb	Mar	Apr	May	Jun	Jul	Aug	Sep	Oct	Nov	Dec	
	Gruppo in 1940							**Gruppo in 1941**												
11b	26b	26b																		
12	1a	1a	1a	1a	1a	1a	1a	1a	1a	1a	1a	1a	1a	1a	1a	1a	1a	1a	1a	
13	26	26	26	26	26	26	26	26												
13b	26b	26b																		
14	4	4	4	4	4	4	4	4	4	4	4	4	4	4	4	4	4	4		
14b	4b	4b	4b	4b	4b	4b	4b	4b	4b	4b										
15	4	4	4	4	4	4	4	4	4	4	4	4	4	4	4	4	4	4		
15b	4b	4b	4b	4b	4b	4b	4b	4b	4b	4b										
16	2a	2a	2a	2a	2a	2a	2a	2a	2a	2a	2a	2a	2a	2a	2a	2a	2a	2a		
17																				
18	27	27	27	27	27	27	27	27	27	27	27	27	27	27	27	27	27	27	27	
18b	27b	27b	27b	27b	27b	27b	27b	27b	27b	27b	27b									
19	28	28	28	28	28	28	28	28	28	28	28	28	28	28	28	28	28	28	28	
19b	28b	28b	28b	28b	28b	28b	28b	28b	28b	28b	28b									
20	46	46	46	46	46	46	46	46	46	46	46	46	46	46	46	46	46	46		
21	46	46	46	46	46	46	46	46	46	46	46	46	46	46	46	46	46	46		
22	45	45	45	45	45	45	45	45												
23	2a	2a	2a	2a	2a	2a	2a	2a	2a	2a	2a	2a	2a	2a	2a	2a	2a	2a		
24	68	68	68	68	68	68	68	68	68	68	68	68	68	68	68	68	68	68		
25	67/72	72	72	72	72	72	72	72	72	72/70	70	70	70	70	70	70	70	70		
26																				
27	1o	1o	1o	1o	1o	1o	1o	1o	1o	1o	1o	1o	1o	1o	1o	1o	1o	1o	*1o = 1 Gruppo OA*	
28	62	62	62	62	62	62	62	62	62?											
29	62	62	62	62	62	62	62	62	62	62	62	62	62	62	62	62	62	62		
30	76	76	76	76	76	76	76	76	76	76	76	76	76	76	76	76	76	76		
31	5/71	5	5	5	5	5	5	5	5	5	5	5	5	5	5	5	5	5		
32	15	15	15	15	15	15	15	15	15	15	15	15	15	15	15	15	15	15		
33	61	67	67	67	67	67	67	67	67	67	68	68	68	68	68	68	68	68		
34	61/65	65/61	61	61	61	61	61	61	61	61	61	61	61	61	61	61	61	61		
35	68	68	68	68	68	68	68	68	68	68	68									
36	65	65	65	65	65	65	65	65	65	65	65	65	65	65	65	65	65?	72?	72?	
37																				
38	71	71	71	71	71	71	71	71	71	71	71	71	71	71	71	71	71	71		
39	5	5	5	5	5	5	5	5	5	5	5	5	5	5	5	5	5	5		
40	5	5	5	5	5	5	5										76?	76		
41	GG/63	63	63	63	63	63	63	63	63	63	63	63	63	63	63	63	63	63	*GG=Gruppo Gasbarrini*	
42	66	66	66	66	66	66	72?	72	72	72	72	72	72	72	72	72?	62?	62	62	
43	35	35	35	35	35															
44	35	35	35	35	35															
45	36	36	36	36	36															
46	36	36	36	36	36															
47	37	37	37	37	37	37	37	37	37	37	37	-	-	37	37	37	37	37	37	
48	37	37	37	37	37	37	37	37	37	37	37	-	-	37	37	37	37	37	37	
49	38	38	38	38	38	38	38	38	38	38	38	38	38	38	38	38	38	38		
50	38	38	38	38	38	38	38	38	38	38	38	38	38	38	38	38	38	38		
51	39	39	39	39	39	39	39	39	39	39	39	39	39	39	39	39	39	39		
52	27	27	27	27	27	27	27	27	27	27	27	27	27	27	27	27	27	27		
52b	27b	27b	27b	27b	27b	27b	27b	27b	27b	27b	27b									
53	47	47	47	47	47	47	47	47	47	47	47	47	47	47	47	47	47	47		
54	47	47	47	47	47	47	47	47	47	47	47	47	47	47	47	47	47	47		
55	30	30	30	30	30	30	30	30	30	30	30	30	30	30	30	30	30	30		
56	30	30	30	30	30	30	30	30	30	30	30	30	30	30	30	30	30	30		
57	32	32	32	32	32	32	32	32	32	32	32	32	32	32	32	32	32	32		

Squadriglia	Gruppo in 1940							Gruppo in 1941											
	Jun	Jul	Aug	Sep	Oct	Nov	Dec	Jan	Feb	Mar	Apr	May	Jun	Jul	Aug	Sep	Oct	Nov	Dec
58	32	32	32	32	32	32	32	32	32	32	32	32	32	32	32	32	32	32	32
59	33	33	33	33	33	33	33	33	33	33	33	33	33	33	33	33	33	33	33
60	33	33	33	33	33	33	33	33	33	33	33	33	33	33	33	33	33	33	33
61																			
61b	49b	49b	49b	49b	49b	49b	49b	49b	49b	49b	49b	49b	49b	49b	49b	49b			
62	29	29	29	29	29	29	29	29	-	-	-	29	29	29	29	29	29	29	29
62b	29b	29b	29b	29b	29b	29b	29b	29b	29b	29b									
63	29	29	29	29	29	29	29	29	-	-	-	29	29	29	29	29	29	29	29
63b	29b	29b	29b	29b	29b	29b	29b	29b	29b	29b									
64																			
64b	49b	49b	49b	49b	49b	49b	49b	49b	49b	49b	49b	49b	49b	49b	49b	49b			
65	31	31	31	31	31	31	31	31	31	31	31	31	31	31	31	31	31	31	31
65b	31b	31b	31b	31b	31b/29b	29b	29b/49b	49b	49b	49b	49b	49b	49b	49b	49b	49b			
66	31	31	31	31	31	31	31	31	31	31	31	31	31	31	31	31	31	31	31
66b	31b	31b	31b	31b	31b														
67	34	34	34	34	34	34	34	34	34	34	34								
68	34	34	34	34	34	34	34	34	34	34	34								
69	39	39	39	39	39	39	39	39	39	39	39	39	39	39	39	39	39	39	39
70	23	23	23	23	23	23	23	23	23	23	23	23	23	23	23	23	23	23	23
71	17	17	17	17	17	17	17	17	17	17	17	17	17	17	17	17	17	17	17
72	17	17	17	17	17	17	17	17	17	17	17	17	17	17	17	17	17	17	17
73	9	9	9	9	9	9	9	9	9	9	9	9	9	9	9	9	9	9	9
74	23	23	23	23	23	23	23	23	23	23	23	23	23	23	23	23	23	23	23
75	23	23	23	23	23	23	23	23	23	23	23	23	23	23	23	23	23	23	23
76	7	7	7	7	7	7	7	7	7	7	7	7	7	7	7	7	7	7	7
77	13	13	13	13	13	13	13	13	13	13	13	13	13	13	13	13	13	13	13
78	13	13	13	13	13	13	13	13	13	13	13	13	13	13	13	13	13	13	13
79	6	6	6	6	6	6	6	6	6	6	6	6	6	6	6	6	6	6	6
80	17	17	17	17	17	17	17	17	17	17	17	17	17	17	17	17	17	17	17
81	6	6	6	6	6	6	6	6	6	6	6	6	6	6	6	6	6	6	6
82	13	13	13	13	13	13	13	13	13	13	13	13	13	13	13	13	13	13	13
83	18	18	18	18	18	18	18	18	18	18	18	18	18	18	18	18	18	18	18
84	10	10	10	10	10	10	10	10	10	10	10	10	10	10	10	10	10	10	10
85	18	18	18	18	18	18	18	18	18	18	18	18	18	18	18	18	18	18	18
86	7	7	7	7	7	7	7	7	7	7	7	7	7	7	7	7	7	7	7
87	65	65	65	65	65	65	65	65	65	65	65	65	65	65	65	65	65/66	66	66
88	6	6	6	6	6	6	6	6	6	6	6	6	6	6	6	6	6	6	6
89	1a	1a	1a	1a	1a	1a	1a	1a											
90	10	10	10	10	10	10	10	10	10	10	10	10	10	10	10	10	10	10	10
91	10	10	10	10	10	10	10	10	10	10	10	10	10	10	10	10	10	10	10
92	8	8	8	8	8	8	8	8	8	8	8	8	8	8	8	8	8	8	8
93	8	8	8	8	8	8	8	8	8	8	8	8	8	8	8	8	8	8	8
94	8	8	8	8	8	8	8	8	8	8	8	8	8	8	8	8	8	8	8
95	18	18	18	18	18	18	18	18	18	18	18	18	18	18	18	18	18	18	18
96	9	9	9	9	9	9	9	9	9	9	9	9	9	9	9	9	9	9	9
97	9	9	9	9	9	9	9	9	9	9	9	9	9	9	9	9	9	9	9
98	7	7	7	7	7	7	7	7	7	7	7	7	7	7	7	7	7	7	7
99																			
100	19	19	19	19	19	19	19	-											
101	19	19	19	19	19	19	19	-											
102	19	19	19	19	19	19	19	-											
103																		AS	
104	1a	1a	1a	1a	1a	1a	1a	1a	1a	1a	1a	1a	1a	1a	1a	1a	1a	1a	1a

Squadriglia	Jun	Jul	Aug	Sep	Oct	Nov	Dec	Jan	Feb	Mar	Apr	May	Jun	Jul	Aug	Sep	Oct	Nov	Dec	
	Gruppo in 1940							**Gruppo in 1941**												
105																				
106																				
107																				
108																				
109																				
110	A	A	A	A	A	A	A	A	A	A	A	A	A							
111																				
112																				
113	63	63	63	63	63	63	63	63	63	63	63	63	63	63	63	63	63	63	63	
114	15									70	70	70	70	70	70	70	70	70	70	
115	67	67	67	67	67	67	67	67	67	67	67	67	67	67	67	67	67	67	67	
116	71	71	71	71	71	71	71	71	71	71	71	71	71	71	71	71	71	71	71	
117																				
118	69	69	69	69	69	69	69	69	69	69	69	69	69	69	69	69	69	69	69	
118b	27b	27b																		
119	72/61	61	61	61	61	61	61	61	61	61	61	61	61	61	61	61	61	61	61	
120	A	A	A	A	A/72	72	72	72	72	72	72	72	72	72	72	72	72	72	72	
121	1o	1o	1o	1o	1o	1o	1o	1o	1o	1o	1o	1o	1o	1o	1o	1o	1o	1o	1o	*1o = 1 Gruppo OA*
122	64	64	64	64	64	64	64	64	64	64	64	64	64	64	64	64	64	64	64	
123	69	69	69	69	69	69	69	69	69	69	69	69	69	69	69	69	69	69	69	
124	A	A	A	A	A	A	A	A	A	A	A	A	A	A	A	A	A	A	A	
125	15	15	15	15	15	15	15	15	15	15	15	15	15	15	15	15	15	15	15	
126																				
127	73	73	73	73	73	73	73	73	73	73	73	73	73	73	73	73	73	73	73	
128	61	61	61	61	61	61	61	61	61	61	61	61	61	61	61	61	61	61	61	
129	72/61	61	61	61	61	61	61/64	64	64	64?	-	-	-	-	67?	67	67	67	67	
130																				
131	66	66	66	66	66	A	A	A	A	A	A	A	A	A	A	A	A	A	A	
132	76/69																			
133																				
134																				
135																				
136	64	64	64	64	64	64	64	64	64	64	64	64	64	64	64	64	64	64	64	
137	73	73	73	73	73	73	73	73	73	73	73	73	73	73	73	73	73	73	73	
138																				
139																				
140																				
141	79/A	A	A	A	A	A	A	A	A	A	A	A	A	A	A	A	A	A	A	
142	A	A	A	A	A	A	A	A	A	A	A	A	A	A	A	A	A	A	A	
143	A	A	A	A	A	A	A	A	A	A	A	A	A	A	A	A	A	A	A	
144	A	A	A	A	A	A	A	A	A	A	A	A	A	A	A	A	A	A	A	
145	A	A	A	A	A	A	A	A	A	A	A	A	A	A	A	A	A	A	A	
146	85	85	85	85	85	85	85	85	85	85/A	A	A	A	A	A	A	A	A	A	
147	84	84	84	84	84	84	84	84	84	84	84	84	84	84	84	84	84	84		
148	A	A	A	A	A	A	A	A	A	A	A	A	A	A	A	A	A	A	A	
149	A	A	A	A	A	A	A	A	A	A	A	A	A	A	A	A	A	A	A	
150	2	2	2	2	2	2	2	2	2	2	2	2	2	2	2	2	2	2		
151	2	2	2	2	2	2	2	2	2	2	2	2	2	20	20	20	20	20		
152	2	2	2	2	2	2	2	2	2	2	2	2	2	2	2	2	2	2		
153	3	3	3	3	3	3	3	3	3	3	3	3	3	3	3	3	3	3		
154	3	3	3	3	3	3	3	3	3	3	3	3	3	3	3	3	3	3		
155	3	3	3	3	3	3	3	3	3	3	3	3	3	3	3	3	3	3		
156																				

Squadriglia	Gruppo in 1940							Gruppo in 1941											
	Jun	Jul	Aug	Sep	Oct	Nov	Dec	Jan	Feb	Mar	Apr	May	Jun	Jul	Aug	Sep	Oct	Nov	Dec
157																			
158																			
159	12	12	12	12	12	12	12	12	12	12	12	12	12	12	12	12	12	12	12
160	12	12	12	12	12	12	12	12	12	12	12	12	12	12	12	12	12	12	
161	A	A	A	A	A	A	A	A	A	A	A	A	A	A	A	A	A	A	A
162												A	161	161	161	161	161	161	161
163	A	A	A	A	A	A	A	A	A	A	A	A	161	161	161	161	161	161	161
164												-	161	161	161	161	161	161	161
165																			
166																			
167	16	16	16	16	16	16	16	16	16	16	16	16	16	16	16	16	16	16	16
168	16	16	16	16	16	16	16	16	16	16	16	16	16	16	16	16	16	16	
169								16	16	16	16	16	16	16	16	16	16		
170	A	A/83	83	83	83	83	83	83	83	83	83	83	83	83	83	83	83	83	83
171	A	A	A	A	A	A	A	A	A	A	A	A	A	A	A	A	A	A	A
172	A	A	A	A	A	A	A	A	A	A	A	A	A	A	A/-	-	-	-	
173														A	A	A	A	A	A
174																			A
175			-	A	A	A	A	A	A	A	A	A	A	A	A	A	A	A	A
176																		-	A
177																			
178																			
179																			
180																			
181																			
182	A	A	A	A	A	A	A	A	A	A	A	A	A	A	A	A	A	A	A
183	85	85	85	85	85	85	85	85	85	85/-	A	A	A	A	A	A	A	A	A
184	83	83	83	83	83	83	83	83	83	83	83	83	83	83	83	83	83	83	83
185	84	84	84	84	84	84	84	84	84	84	84	84	84	84	84	84	84	84	84
186	83	83	83	83	83	83	83	83	83	83	83	83	83	83	83	83	83	83	83
187	s	A	A	A	A	A	A	A	A	A	A	A	A	A	A	A	A	A	A
188	85	85	85	85	85	85	85	85	85	85/-	A	A	A	A	A	A	A	A	A
189	83	83	83	83	83	83	83	83	83	83	83	83	83	83	83	83	83	83	83
190	86	86	86	86	86	86	86	86	86	86	86	86	86	86	86	86	86	86	86
191	86	86	86	86	86	86	86	86	86	86	86	86	86	86	86	86	86	86	86
192	87	87	87	87	87	87	87	87	87	87	87	87	87	87	87	87	87	87	87
193	87	87	87	87	87	87	87	87	87	87	87	87	87	87	87	87	87	87	87
194	90	90	90	90	90	90	90	90	90	90	90	90	90	90	90	90	90	90	90
195	90	90	90	90	90	90	90	90	90	90	90	90	90	90	90	90	90	90	90
196	93	93	93	93	93	93	93	93	93	93?			A?	A	A	A	A		A
197	93	93	93	93	93	93	93	93	93	93?									
198	94	94	94	94	94	94	94	94	94	94?									
199	A/94	94	94	94	94	94	94	94	94	94?									
200	92	92	92	92	92	92	92	92	92	92	92								
201	92	92	92	92	92	92	92	92	92	92	92								
202	40	40	40	40	40	40	40	40	40	40	40	40	40	40	40	40	40	40	
203	40	40	40	40	40	40	40	40	40	40	40	40	40	40	40	40	40	40	
204	41	41	41	41	41	41	41	41	41	41	41	41	41	41	41	41	41	41	
205	41	41	41	41	41	41	41	41	41	41	41	41	41	41	41	41	41	41	
206	42	42	42	42	42	42													
207	42	42	42	42	42	42													
208										101	101	101	101	101	101	101	101	101	101
209										101	101/97	97/A	A	A	A	A	A	A	A

Squadriglia	Gruppo in 1940							Gruppo in 1941											
	Jun	Jul	Aug	Sep	Oct	Nov	Dec	Jan	Feb	Mar	Apr	May	Jun	Jul	Aug	Sep	Oct	Nov	Dec
208										101	101	101	101	101	101	101	101	101	101
209									101	101/97	97/A	A	A	A	A	A	A	A	A
210	50	50	50	50	50	50	50	50	50	50	50	50	50	50	50	50	50	50	50
211	50	50	50	50	50	50	50	50	50	50	50	50	50	50	50	50	50	50	50
212	51	51	51	51	51	51	51	51	51	51	51	51	51	51	51	51	51	51	51
213	51	51	51	51	51	51	51	51	51	51	51	51	51	51	51	51	51	51	51
214	52	52	52	52	52	52	52	52	52?										
215	52	52	52	52	52	52	52	52	52?										
216	53	53	53	53	53	53	53	53	53?										
217	53	53	53	53	53	53	53	53	53?										
218	54	54	54	54	54	54	54	54	54	54									
219	54	54	54	54	54	54	54	54	54	54									
220	55	55	55	55	55	55	55	55	55	55	55	55	55	55	55	55	55	55	55
221	55	55	55	55	55	55	55	55	55	55	55	55	55	55	55	55	55	55	55
222	56	56	56	56	56	56	56	56	56	56	56	56	56	56	56	56	56	56	56
223	56	56	56	56	56	56	56	56	56	56	56	56	56	56	56	56	56	56	56
224																	57	57	57
225																	57	57	57
226																			
227																			
228	89	89	89	89	89	89	89	89	89	89	89	89	89	89	89	89	89	89	89
229	89	89	89	89	89	89	89	89	89	89	89	89	89	89	89	89	89	89	89
230	95	95	95	95	95	95	95	95	95	95	95	95	95	95	95	95	95	95	95
231	95	95	95	95	95	95	95	95	95	95	95	95	95	95	95	95	95	95	95
232	59	59	59	59	59	59	59	59	59	59	59	59	59	59	59	59	59	59	59
233	59	59	59	59	59	59	59	59	59	59	59	59	59	59	59	59	59	59	59
234	60	60	60	60	60	60	60	60	60	60	60	60	60	60	60	60	60	60	60
235	60	60	60	60	60	60	60	60	60	60	60	60	60	60	60	60	60	60	60
236	96	96	96	96	96	96	96	96	96/A	A	A	A	A	A	A	A	A	A	158
237	96	96	96	96	96	96	96	96	96	96	96	-							
238						97	97	97	97	97	101	101	101	101	101	101	101	101	101
239						97	97	97	97	97	97	97/A	A	A	A	A	A	101	A
240	98	98	98	98	98	98	98	98	98	98	98	98	98	98	98	98	98	98	98
241	98	98	98	98	98	98	98	98	98	98	98	98	98	98	98	98	98	98	98
242	99	99	99	99	99	99	99	99	99	99	99	99	99	99	99	99	99	99	99
243	99	99	99	99	99	99	99	99	99	99	99	99	99	99	99	99	99	99	99
244								-	A	A	A	A	A	A	A	A	A	A	A
245																A	A	A	A
246																		A	A
247																			
248																			
249																			
250																			
251																			
252	104	104	104	104	104	104	104	104	104	104	104	104	104	104	104	104	104	104	104
253	104	104	104	104	104	104	104	104	104	104	104	104	104	104	104	104	104	104	104
254	105	105	105	105	105	105	105	105	105	105	105	105	105	105	105	105	105	105	105
255	105	105	105	105	105	105	105	105	105	105	105	105	105	105	105	105	105	105	105
256	108	108	108	108	108	108	108	108	108	108	108	108	108	108	108	108	108	108	108
257	108	108	108	108	108	108	108	108	108	108	108	108	108	108	108	108	108	108	108
258	109	109	109	109	109	109	109	109	109	109	109	109	109	109	109	109	109	109	109
259	109	109	109	109	109	109	109	109	109	109	109	109	109	109	109	109	109	109	109
260	106	106	106	106	106	106	106	106	106	106	106	106	106	106	106	106	106	106	106

Squadriglia	Gruppo in 1940							Gruppo in 1941											
	Jun	Jul	Aug	Sep	Oct	Nov	Dec	Jan	Feb	Mar	Apr	May	Jun	Jul	Aug	Sep	Oct	Nov	Dec
261	106	106	106	106	106	106	106	106	106	106	106	106	106	106	106	106	106	106	106
262	107	107	107	107	107	107	107	107	107	107	107	107	107	107	107	107	107	107	107
263	107	107	107	107	107	107	107	107	107	107	107	107	107	107	107	107	107	107	107
264																			
265																			
266																			
267																			
268																			
269																			
270																			
271																			
272																			
273																			
274													A	A	A	A	A	A	A
275																			
276					116	116	116	116	116	116	116	116	116	116	116	116	116	116	116
277					116	116	116	116	116	116	116	116	116	116	116	116	116	116	116
278			A	A	A	A		A	A	A	A	A	A	A	A	A	A	A	A
279							A	A	A	A	A/34	34/A	A	A	A	A	A	A	A
280								-	A	A	A	A	A	A	A	130	130	130	130
281									-	A	A/34	34/A	A	A	A	A	A	A	A
282												-	A	41	A	A	A	A	A
283														-	A	A/130	130	130	130
284																	-	A	A
285																			
286																			
287	A	A	A	A	A	A	A	A	A	A	A	A	A	A	A	A	A	A	A
288	A	A	A	A	A	A	A	A	A	A	A	A	A	A	A	A	A	A	A
289																			
290																			
300																		A?	A
301																-	171	171	-
302																-	171	171	-
303																			
310																			
351	20	20	20	20	20	20	20	20	20	20	20	20	20	20	155	155	155	155	155
352	20	20	20	20	20	20	20	20	20	20	20	20	20	20	20	20	20	20	20
353	20	20	20	20	20	20	20	20	20	20	20	20	20	20	20	20	20	20	20
354	21	21	21	21	21/A	24	24	24	24	24	24	24	24	24	24	24	24	24	24
355	21	21	21	21	21/A	A	A	A	A	24	24	24	24	24	24	24	24	24	24
356	A	A	21	21	21	21	21	21	21	21	21	21	21	21	21	21	21	21	21
357	22	22	22	22	22	22	22	22	157	157	157	157	157	157	157	157	157	157	157
358	22	22	22	22	22	22	22/2	2	2	2	2	2	2	2	2	2	2	2	2
359	22	22	22	22	22	22	22	22	22	22	22	22	22	22	22	22	22	22	22
360	155	155	155	155	22	22	22	22	22	22?	155?	155	155	155	155	155	155	155	155
361	24	24	24	24	24/154	154	154	154	154	154	154	154/24	24	24/154	154	154	154	154	154
362	24	24	24	24	24	24	24/22	22	22	22	22	22	22	22	22	22	22	22	22
363	150	150	150	150	150	150	150	150	150	150	150	150	150	150	150	150	150	150	150
364	150	150	150	150	150	150	150	150	150	150	150	150	150	150	150	150	150	150	150
365	150	150	150	150	150	150	150	150	150	150	150	150	150	150	150	150	150	150	150
366	151	151	151	151	151	151	151	151	151	151	151	151	151	151	151	151	151	151	151
367	151	151	151	151	151	151	151	151	151	151	151	151	151	151	151	151	151	151	151
368	151	151	151	151	151	151	151	151	151	151	151	151	151	151	151	151	151	151	151

Squadriglia	| Jun	Jul	Aug	Sep	Oct	Nov	Dec	| Jan	Feb	Mar	Apr	May	Jun	Jul	Aug	Sep	Oct	Nov	Dec
	Gruppo in 1940							**Gruppo in 1941**											
369	152	152	152	152	152	152	152/22	22	22	22	22	22	22	22	22	22	22	22	22
370	152	152	152	152	152	152	152/A	A	A	A	24	24	24	24	24	24	24	24	24
371	152	152	152	152	152	152	152/A	A	157	A	A	A	A	A	22	22	22	22	22
372	153	153	153	153	153	153	153	153	153	153	153	153	153	153	153	153	153	153	153
373	153	153	153	153	153	153	153	153	153	153	153	153	153	153	153	153	153	153	153
374	153	153	153	153	153	153	153	153	153	153	153	153	153	153	153	153	153	153	153
375								-	A/160	160	160	160	160	160	160	160	160	160	160
376									-	A	A	A	A	A	A	A	A	A	
377															23	23	23	23	23/A
378	155	155	155	155	155	155	155	155	155	155	155	155	155	155	155	155	155	155	155
379								156	156	156	156	-							
380								156	156	156	156	-							
381																			
382										21	21	21	21	21	21	21	21	21	21
383															-	157	157	157	157
384	157	157	157	157	157	157	157	157	157	157	157	157	157	157	157	157	157	157	157
385	157	157	157	157	157	157	157	157	157	A	A	A	A	A	A	A	157	157	157
386	157	157	157	157	157	157	157	157	157	21	21	21	21	21	21	21	21	21	21
387																			158
388																			158
389																			
390																			
391																			
392																			
393	160	160	160	160	160	160	160	160	160	160	160	160	160	160	160	160	160	160	160
394	160	160	160	160	160	160	160	160	160	160	160	160	160	160	160	160	160	160	160
395	160/A	A	A	A	A/154	154	154	154	154	154	154	154/24	24	24/154	154	154	154	154	154
396																-	154	154	154
397																			
398																			
399																			
410	A	A	A	A	A	A	A	A	A	A	A	A	A						
411	A	A	A	A	A	A	A	A	A	A	A								
412	A	A	A	A	A	A	A	A	A	A	A	A	A	A	A	A	A	A	
413	A	A	A	A	A	A	A	A	A	A	A	A	A	A					
414	A	A																	
600																A	A	A	A
601	147	147	147	147	147	147	147	147	147	147	147	147	147	147	147	147	147	147	147
602	147	147	147	147	147	147	147	147	147	147	147	147	147	147	147	147	147	147	147
603	147	147	147	147	147	147	147	147	147	147/146	146	146	146	146	146	146	146	146	146
604	145	145	145	145	145	145	145	145	145	145	145	145	145	145	145	145	145	145	145
605	148	148	148	148	148	148	148	148	148	148	148	148	148	148	148	148	148	148	148
606	148	148	148	148	148	148	148	148	148	148	148	148	148	148	148	148	148	148	148
607	149	149	149	149	149	149	149	149	149	149	149	149	149	149	149	149	149	149	149
608	149	149	149	149	149	149	149	149	149	149	149	149	149	149	149	149	149	149	149
609	149	149	149	149	149	149	149	149	149	149/146	146	146	146	146	146	146	146	146	146
610	145	145	145	145	145	145	145	145	145	145	145	145	145	145	145	145	145	145	145
611	A	A	A	A	A	A	A	A	A	A	A	A	A	A	A	A	A	A	A
612	A	A	A	A	A	A	A	A	A	A	A	A	A	A	A	A	A	A	A
613	A	A/-	-/A	A	A	A	A	A	A	A	A	A	A	A	A	A	A	A	A
614	A	A	A	A	A	A	A	A	A	A	A	A	A	A	A	A	A	A	A
615	A	A	A	A	A	A	A	A	A	A	A	A	A	A	A	A	A	A	A
616	A	A																	

Squadriglia	Gruppo in 1940							Gruppo in 1941											
	Jun	Jul	Aug	Sep	Oct	Nov	Dec	Jan	Feb	Mar	Apr	May	Jun	Jul	Aug	Sep	Oct	Nov	Dec
617																			
618																			
1 NAS					A	A	A	A	A	A	A	A	A	A	A	A	A	A	
2 NAS						A	A	A	A	A	A	A	A	A	A				
3 NAS																			
RscA																			
RsrA		A	A	A															

153: *The pilot's mascot poses on the engine cowling of his Macchi MC 202 of the 4° Stormo, whose later emblem is written large. This commemorates Francisco Baracca, the Italian World War I fighter ace. Date and location unknown. Note how the propeller tips follow RAF practice and are painted yellow for safety*

154: *Led by an aircraft from the 73ª Squadriglia, the Fiat CR 42s of the 96ª Squadriglia, both from the 9° Gruppo, 4° Stormo, ride the desert sky somewhere over Cirenaica in summer 1940. All the aircraft carry the early 'Cavallino Rampante' stallion badge of the Stormo, but only those from the 96ª carry their squadron badge ('Gamba di Ferro'—iron leg) on the fin. Note the freshly-applied white wing tips and the lack of any white fuselage bands. Camouflage scheme appears to be the three-tone C1 type*

155: *Visiting Luftwaffe personnel watch with interest as the pilot of a Fiat CR 42 of the CAI climbs into his machine on a cold day in late 1940. Location is probably Ursel in Belgium, although it could be Vlissingen, where two of the fighters were detached for reconnaisance and night intercept duties. The three Squadriglie (83ᵃ, 85ᵃ, 95ᵃ) which made up the 18° Gruppo, all equipped with the biplanes, were all based at Ursel in October. The field must have been very crowded as they shared it with the Fiat G 50-equipped 20° Gruppo. By 10 January 1941 the 18° Gruppo was on its way home*

156: *A Savoia-Marchetti SM 75 on its way to Belgium is seen outside a hangar at Novi Ligure in September 1940. It was used as the personal aircraft of Gen-s of erale Rino Corso Fougier, commander of the CAI in Belgium. The large pennant on the nose is the Savoia-Marchetti trademark. Clearly war is war, but business is business*

157 Left: *This is the Fiat CR 42, 95-13, of Sergent Pietro Salvadori of the 95ᵃ Squadriglia who was shot down on 11 November 1940 at Orfordness. Both he and his aircraft were virtually undamaged and it is seen here under test with the RAF as BT474. It now resides in the RAF Museum at Hendon*

158 Above right: *An SM 79Sil of the 278ᵃ Squadriglia, 132° Gruppo, with torpedo, on its way to a strike somewhere in the Mediterranean. Of note is the 'air tail' on the torpedo which broke off on impact with the water, but served to stabilise the weapon as it was dropped*

SQUADRIGLIE ALLOCATIONS
1942-1943

The number in each line is, where known, the Gruppo controlling the squadriglia. Where a question mark (?) is shown it is not clear that the unit was then constituted. The East African bomber units earlier identified wih a 'b' notation had all been overrun by mid-1941 after the campaign was lost and so are not shown below. The 'a' indicates a member of Gruppo APC (colonial patrols). Capital 'A' means the squadriglia is Automono—independent. A blank means it probably did not operate, while a dash (-) indicates that the unit was nominally on the records but not active. It must be stressed that these are not official designations, but are used solely for clarity.

Squadriglia	Gruppo in 1942												Gruppo in 1943											
	Jan	Feb	Mar	Apr	May	Jun	Jul	Aug	Sep	Oct	Nov	Dec	Jan	Feb	Mar	Apr	May	Jun	Jul	Aug	Sep	Oct	Nov	Dec
1	11	11	11	11	11	11	11	11	11	11	11	11	11	11	11	11	11	11	11	11	-			
2																								
3	43	43	43	43	43	43	43	43	43	43	43	43	43	43	43	43	43	43	43	43	43			
4	11	11	11	11	11	11	11	11	11	11	11	11	11	11	11	11	11	11	11	11	-			
5	43	43	43	43	43	43	43	43	43	43	43	43	43	43	43	43	43	43	43	43	43			
6																								
7																								
8	25	25	25	25	25	25	25	25	25	25	25	25	25	25	25	25	25	25	-	-	-			
9	25	25	25	25	25	25	25	25	25	25	25	25	25	25	25	25	25	25	-	-	-			
10																		28	28	28	28			
11																								
12	1a	1a	1a	1a	1a	1a	1a	1a	1a	1a	1a	1a	-	-	-	-	-	-	-	-	-			
13																								
14	4	4	4	4	4	4	4	4	4	4	4	4	4	4	4	4	4	4						
15	4	4	4	4	4	4	4	4	4	4	4	4	4	4	4	4	4	4						
16	2a	2a	2a	2a	2a	2a	2a	2a	-															
17																								
18	27	27	27	27	27	27	27	27	27	27	27	27	27	27	27	27	27	27	27	27	27			
19																			28	28	28	28		
20	46	46	46	46	46	46	46	46	46	46	46	46	46	46	46	46	46	46	46	46	46			
21	46	46	46	46	46	46	46	46	46	46	46	46	46	46	46	46	46	46	46	46	46			
22																								
23	2a	2a	2a	2a	2a	2a	2a	2a	-															
24	68	68	68	68	68	68	68	68	68	68	68	68/73	73	73	73	73	73	73	73	73	73			
25	70	70	70	70	70	70	70	70	70	70	70	70	70	70	70/61	61	61	61	61	61	61			
26						BS?	BS	BS	BS	BS	BS	BS	BS	BS	BS	BS	BS	BS	BS	BS	BS			

Squadriglia	Gruppo in 1942												Gruppo in 1943											
	Jan	Feb	Mar	Apr	May	Jun	Jul	Aug	Sep	Oct	Nov	Dec	Jan	Feb	Mar	Apr	May	Jun	Jul	Aug	Sep	Oct	Nov	Dec
27	1o	1o																						
28							65	65	65	65	65	65	65	65?										*1o = 1 Gruppo O A*
29	62	62	62																					
30	76	76	76	76	76	76	76	76	76	76	76	76	76	76	76	76	76	76	76	76	76			
31	5	5	5	5?																				
32	15	15	-	-	-	-	-	-	-	-	-	-	-	-	-	-	-	-	-	-	-			
33	68	68	68	68	68	68	68	68	68	68	68	68	68	68	68	68	68	5	5	5	5			
34	61	61	61	61	61	61	61	61	61	61	61	61/68	68	68	68	68	68	68/61	61	61	61			
35															72?	72	72	72	72	72	72			
36	72	72	72	72	72	72	72/5	5																
37															1o	1o	1o	1o	1o	1o	1o			*1o = 1 Gruppo O A*
38	71	71	71	71	71	71	71	71	71	71	71	71	71	71	71	71	71	71	71	71	71			
39	5	5	5	5	5	5	5	5	5/70	70	70	70	70	70	70/61	61	61	61	61	61	61			
40	76	76	76	76	76							66	66	66	66	66	66	66	66	66				
41	63	63	63	63	63	63	63	63	63	63	63	63	63	63	63	63	63	63	63	63	63			
42	62	62	62																					
43																								
44																								
45																								
46																								
47	37	37	37	37	37	37	37	37	37	37	37	37	37	37	37	37	-	-	-	-	-			
48	37	37	37	37	37	37	37	37	37	37	37	37	37	37	37	37	-	-	-	-	-			
49	38	38	38	38	38	38	38	38	38	38	38	38	38	38	38	38	38	38	-	-	-			
50	38	38	38	38	38	38	38	38	38	38	38	38	38	38	38	38	38	38	-	-	-			
51	39	39	39	39	39	39	39	39	39	39	39	39	39	39	39	39	39	39						
52	27	27	27	27	27	27	27	27	27	27	27	27	27	27	27	27	27	27	27	27	27			
53	47	47	47	47	47	47	47	47	47	47	47	47	47	47	47	47	47	47	47	47	47			
54	47	47	47	47	47	47	47	47	47	47	47	47	47	47	47	47	47	47	47	47	47			
55	30	30	30	30	30	30	30	30	30	30	30	30	30	30	30	30	30	30	30	30	30			
56	30	30	30	30	30	30	30	30	30	30	30	30	30	30	30	30	30	30	30	30	30			
57	32	32	32	32	32	32	32	32	32	32	32	32	32	32	32?									
58	32	32	32	32	32	32	32	32	32	32	32	32	32	32	32?									
59	33	33	33	33	33	33	33	33	33	33	33	33	33	33	33	33	33	33	33	33	33			
60	33	33	33	33	33	33	33	33	33	33	33	33	33	33	33	33	33	33	33	33	33			
61																								
62	29	29	29	29	29	29	29	29	29	29	29	29	29	29	29	29	29	29	29	29	29			
63	29	29	29	29	29	29	29	29	29	29	29	29	29	29	29	29	29	29	29	29	29			
64																								
65	31																							
66	31																							
67																								
68																								
69	39	39	39	39	39	39	39	39	39	39	39	39	39	39	39	39	39	39						
70	23	23	23	23	23	23	23	23	23	23	23	23	23	23	23	23	23	23	23	23	23			
71	17	17	17	17	17	17	17	17	17	17	17	17	17	17	17	17	17	17	17	17	17			
72	17	17	17	17	17	17	17	17	17	17	17	17	17	17	17	17	17	17	17	17	17			
73	9	9	9	9	9	9	9	9	9	9	9	9	9	9	9	9	9	9	9	9	9			
74	23	23	23	23	23	23	23	23	23	23	23	23	23	23	23	23	23	23	23	23	23			
75	23	23	23	23	23	23	23	23	23	23	23	23	23	23	23	23	23	23	23	23	23			
76	7	7	7	7	7	7	7	7	7	7	7	7	7	7	7	7	7	-	-	-	-			
77	13	13	13	13	13	13	13	13	13	13	13	13	13	13	13	13	13	13	13	13	13			
78	13	13	13	13	13	13	13	13	13	13	13	13	13	13	13	13	13	13	13	13	13			
79	6	6	6	6	6	6	6	6	6	6	6	6	6	6	6	6	6	6	6	6	6			

Squadriglia	Gruppo in 1942												Gruppo in 1943											
	Jan	Feb	Mar	Apr	May	Jun	Jul	Aug	Sep	Oct	Nov	Dec	Jan	Feb	Mar	Apr	May	Jun	Jul	Aug	Sep	Oct	Nov	Dec
80	17	17	17	17	17	17	17	17	17	17	17	17	17	17	17	17	17	17	17	17	17			
81	6	6	6	6	6	6	6	6	6	6	6	6	6	6	6	6	6	6	6	6	6			
82	13	13	13	13	13	13	13	13	13	13	13	13	13	13	13	13	13	13	13	13	13			
83	18	18	18	18	18	18	18	18	18	18	18	18	18	18	18	18	18	18	18	18	18			
84	10	10	10	10	10	10	10	10	10	10	10	10	10	10	10	10	10	10	10	10	10			
85	18	18	18	18	18	18	18	18	18	18	18	18	18	18	18	18	18	18	18	18	18			
86	7	7	7	7	7	7	7	7	7	7	7	7	7	7	7	7	7	-	-	-	-			
87	66	66	66	66	66	66	66	66	66	66	66	66	66	66	66	66	66	66	66	66	-			
88	6	6	6	6	6	6	6	6	6	6	6	6	6	6	6	6	6	6	6	6	6			
89																								
90	10	10	10	10	10	10	10	10	10	10	10	10	10	10	10	10	10	10	10	10	10			
91	10	10	10	10	10	10	10	10	10	10	10	10	10	10	10	10	10	10	10	10	10			
92	8	8	8	8	8	8	8	8	8	8	8	8	8	8	8	8	8	8	8	8	8			
93	8	8	8	8	8	8	8	8	8	8	8	8	8	8	8	8	8	8	8	8	8			
94	8	8	8	8	8	8	8	8	8	8	8	8	8	8	8	8	8	8	8	8	8			
95	18	18	18	18	18	18	18	18	18	18	18	18	18	18	18	18	18	18	18	18	18			
96	9	9	9	9	9	9	9	9	9	9	9	9	9	9	9	9	9	9	9	9	9			
97	9	9	9	9	9	9	9	9	9	9	9	9	9	9	9	9	9	9	9	9	9			
98	7	7	7	7	7	7	7	7	7	7	7	7	7	7	7	7	7							
99						BS*?	BS	BS	BS	BS	BS	BS	BS	BS	BS	BS	BS	BS	BS	BS	BS			
100																								
101																								
102											-	1a	1a	1a	1a	-	-	-	-	-	-			
103	AS‡	AS	AS	AS	AS	1a	1a	1a	1a	1a	1a	1a	1a	1a	69	69	69	69	69	69	69			
104	1a	1a	1a	1a	1a	1a	1a	1a	1a	1a	1a	ia	1a	1a	1a	1a/69	69	69	69	69	69			
105																								
106																								
107																								
108																								
109															162	162	162	-	-	-	-			
110															162	162	162	-	-	-	-			
111																								
112																								
113	63	63	63	63	63	63	63	63	63	63	63	63	63	63	63	63	63	63	63	63	63			
114	70	70	70	70	70	70	70	70	70	70	70	70	70	70	70	70	70	70	70	70	70			
115	67	67		76	76	76	76	76/73	73	73	73	73	73	73	73	73	73	73	73	73	73			
116	71	71	71	71	71	71	71	71	71	71	71	71	71	71	71	71	71	71	71	71	71			
117																								
118	69	69	69	69	69	69	69	69	69	69	69	69	69	69	69	69	69	69	69	69	69			
119	61	61	61	61	61	61	61	61	61	61	61	61	61	61	61/63	63	63	63	63	63	63			
120	72	72	72	72	72	72	72	72	5	5	5	5	5	5	5	5	5	5	5	5				
121	1o	1o	1o/A	A	A?				5	5	5	5	5	5	5	5	5	5	5	5/68	68			
122	64	64	64	64	64	64	64	64	64	64	64	64	64	64	64	64	64	64	64	64	64			
123	69	69	69	69	69	69	69	69	69	69	69	69	69/70	70	70	70	70	70	70	70	70			
124	A	A	A	A	A	A	65	65	65	65	65	65	65	A	A	A	A	A	A	A	A			
125	15	15	-																					
126																								
127	73	73	73	73	73	73	73	73	73/76	76	76	76	76	76	76	76	76	76	76	76	76			
128	61	61	61	61	61	61	61	61	61	61	61	61	61	61	5	5	5	5	5	5	5			
129	67	67/A	A	A	A																			
130																								
131								66	66	66	66	66	65	65	65	65	65	65	65	65	65			

*Battaglione Sahariana

‡Aviazione Sahariana- (Automono)

Squadriglia	Gruppo in 1942												Gruppo in 1943											
	Jan	Feb	Mar	Apr	May	Jun	Jul	Aug	Sep	Oct	Nov	Dec	Jan	Feb	Mar	Apr	May	Jun	Jul	Aug	Sep	Oct	Nov	Dec
132	67	67	-					67?	67?															
133																								
134																								
135																								
136	64	64	64	64	64	64	64	64	64	64	64	64	64	64	64	64	64	64	64	64	64			
137	73	73	73	73	73	73	73	73	73	73	73	73	73	73	A	A	A	A	A	A	A			
138							-	A	A	A	A	A	A	A	A	A	A	A	A	A	A			
139								82	82	82	82	82	82	82	82	82	82	82	82	82	82			
140								A	A	A	A	A	A	A	A	A	A	A/84	84	84	84			
141	A	A	A	A	A	A	A	A	A	A	A	A	A	A	A	A	A							
142	A	A	A	A	A	A	A	A	A	A	A	A	A	A	A	85	85	85	85	85	85			
143	A	A	A	A	A	A	A	A	A	A	A	A	A	A	A	A	A	A	A	A	A			
144	A	A	85	85	85	85	85	85	85	85	85	85	85	85	85	85	A							
145	A	A	A	A	A	A	A	A	A	A	A	A	A	A	A	A	A	A/84	84	84	84			
146	A	A	A	A	A	A	A	A	A	A	A	A	A	A	A	A	A							
147	84	84	84?					84	84	84	84	84	84	84	84	84	84	84	A	A	A			
148	A	A	A	A	A	A	A	A	A	A	A	A	A	A	A	A	A	A	A	A	A			
149	A	A	A	A	A	A	A	A	A	A	A	A	A	A	A	A	A	A	A	A	A			
150	2	2	2	2	2	2	2	2	2								22	22	22	22	22			
151	20	20	20	20	20	20	20	20	20	20	20	20	20	20	20	20	20	20	20	20	20			
152	2	2	2	2	2	2	2	2	2	2	2	2	2	2	2	2	2	2	2	2	2			
153	3	3	3	3	3	3	3	3	3	3	3	3	3	3	3	3	3	3	3	3	3			
154	3	3	3	3	3	3	3	3	3	3	3	3	3	3	3	3	3	3	3	3	3			
155	3	3	3	3	3	3	3	3	3	3	3	3	3	3	3	3	3	3	3	3	3			
156														-	A	A	2	-	-					
157																								
158																								
159	12	12	12	12	12	12	12	12	12	12	12	12	12	12	12	12	12	12						
160	12	12	12	12	12	12	12	12	12	12	12	12	12	12	12	12	12	12						
161	A	A	A	A	A	A	A	A	A	A	A	A	A	A	A	A	A	A	A	A	A			
162	161	161	161	161	161	161	161	161	161	161	161	161	161	161	161	161	161	161	161	161	161			
163	161	161	161	161	161	161	161	161	161	161	161	161	161	161	161	161	161	157	157	161	161			
164	161	161	161	161	161	161	161	161	161	161	161	161	161	161	161	161	161	161	161	161	161			
165							12?	12	12	12	12	12	12	12	12	12	12	12	-	-	-			
166																								
167	16	16	16	16	16	16	16	16	16	16	16	16	16	16	16	16	16	-	-	-	-			
168	16	16	16	16	16	16	16	16	16	16	16	16	16	16	16	16	16							
169	16	16	16	16	16	16	16	16	16	16	16	16	16	16	16	16	16							
170	83	83	83	83	83	83	83	83	83	83	83	83	83	83	83	83	83	83	83	83				
171	A	A	A	A	A	A	A	A	A	A	A	A	A	A	A	A	A							
172	-	-	-	-	-	-	-	-	-	-	-	-	-	-	-	-	-	A	A	A	A			
173	A	A	A	A	A	A	A	A	A	A	A	A	A	A	A	A	A	A	A	A	-			
174	A	A	A	133	133	133	133	133	133	133	133	133												
175	A	A	A	133	133	133	133	133	133	133	133	133												
176	A	A	A	A/																				
177																								
178																								
179																								
180																								
181																								
182	A	A	A	A	A	A	A	A	A	A	A	A	A	A	A	A	A							
183	A	A	A	A	A	A	A	A	A	A	A	A	A	A	A	A	A	A	A	A				
184	83	83	83	83	83	83	83	83/82	82	82	82	82	82	82	82	82	82	82	82	82	82			

Squadriglia	Gruppo in 1942												Gruppo in 1943											
	Jan	Feb	Mar	Apr	May	Jun	Jul	Aug	Sep	Oct	Nov	Dec	Jan	Feb	Mar	Apr	May	Jun	Jul	Aug	Sep	Oct	Nov	Dec
185	84	84					/84	84	84	84	84	84	84	84	84	84	84	84/A	A	A	A			
186	83	83	83	83	83	83	83	83	83	83	83	83	83	83	83	83	83	83	83	83	-			
187	A	A	A	A	A	A	A	A	A	A	A	A	A	A	A	A	A							
188	A	A	A	A	A	A	A	A	A	A	A	A	A	A	A	A	A							
189	83	83	83	83	83	83	83	83	83	83	83	83												
190	86	86	86	86	86	86	86	86	86	86	86	86	86	86	86	86	86	86	86	86	86			
191	86	86	86	86	86	86	86	86	86	86	86	86	86	86	86	86	86	86	86	86	86			
192	87	87	87	87	87	87	87	87	87	87	87	87	87	87	87	87	87	87	87	87	-			
193	87	87	87	87	87	87	87	87	87	87	87	87	87	87	87	87	87	87	87	87	-			
194	90	90	90	90	90	90	90	90	90	90	90	90	90	90	90	90	90	90	90	90	90			
195	90	90	90	90	90	90	90	90	90	90	90	90	90	90	90	90	90	90	90	90	90			
196	A	A	A	A	A	A	A	A	A	85?	85	85	85	85	85	85	85	85	85	85	85			
197		85	85	85	85	85	85	85	85	85	85	85	85	85	85	85	A	A	A	A	-			
198																								
199																								
200														42	42	42	42	42	42	42	42			
201																								
202	40	40	40	40	40	40	40	40	40	40	40	40	40	40	40	40	40	40	40	40	40			
203	40	40	40	40	40	40	40	40	40	40	40	40	40	40	40	40	40	40	40	40	40			
204	41	41	41	41	41	41	41	41	41	41	41	41	41	41	41	41	41	41	41	41	41			
205	41	41	41	41	41	41	41	41	41	41	41	41	41	41	41	41	41	41	41	41	41			
206																			121	121	121			
207														103	103	103	103	103	103	103	103			
208	101	101	101	101	101	101	101	101	101	101	101	101	101	101	101	101	101	101	101	101	101			
209	A	A	A/	102	102	102	102	102	102	102	102	102	102	102	102	102	102	102	102	102	102			
210	50	50	50	50	50	50	50	50	50	50	50	50	50	50	50	50	50	50	50	50	50			
211	50	50	50	50	50	50	50	50	50	50	50	50	50	50	50	50	50	50	50	50	50			
212	51	51	51	51	51	51	51	51	51	51	51	51	51	51	51	51	51	51	51	51	51			
213	51	51	51	51	51	51	51	51	51	51	51	51	51	51	51	51	51	51	51	51	51			
214																								
215																								
216																			121	121	121			
217																								
218																								
219																								
220	55	55	55	55	55	55											116	116	-	-	-			
221	55	55	55	55	55	55	55	55	55	55	55	55	55	55	55	55	55	-	-	-	-			
222	56	56	56	56	56	56	56	56	56	56	56	56	56	56	56	56	56	56	56	56	56			
223	56	56	56	56	56	56	56	56	56	56	56	56	56	56	56	56	56	56	56	56	56			
224	57	57	57	57	57	57	57	57	57	57	57	57	57	57	57	57	57	57	57	57	57			
225	57	57	57	57	57	57	57	57	57	57	57	57	57	57	57	57	57	57	57	57	57			
226															97	97	97	97	97	97	97			
227															97	97	97	97	97	97	97			
228	89	89	89	89	89	89	89	89	89	89	89	89	89	89	89	89	89	89	89	89	89			
229	89	89	89	89	89	89	89	89	89	89	89	89	89	89	89	89	89	89	89	89	89			
230	95	95	95	95	95	95	95	95	95	95	95	95	95	95	95	95	95	95	95	95	95			
231	95	95	95	95	95	95	95	95	95	95	95	95	95	95	95	95	95	95	95	95	95			
232	59	59	59	59	59	59	59	59	59	59	59	59	59	59	59	59	59	59	59	59	59			
233	59	59	59	59	59	59	59	59	59	59	59	59	59	59	59	59	59/60	60	60/59	59	59			
234	60	60	60	60	60	60	60	60	60	60	60	60	60	60	60	60	60/59	59	59/60	60	60			
235	60	60	60	60	60	60	60	60	60	60	60	60	60	60	60	60	60	60	60	60	60			
236	158	158	158	158	158	158	158	158	158	158	158	158	158	158	158	158	158	158	158	158	158			
237														103	103	103	103	103	103	103	103			

Squadriglia	Gruppo in 1942												Gruppo in 1943											
	Jan	Feb	Mar	Apr	May	Jun	Jul	Aug	Sep	Oct	Nov	Dec	Jan	Feb	Mar	Apr	May	Jun	Jul	Aug	Sep	Oct	Nov	Dec
238	101	101	101	101	101	101	101	101	101	101	101	101	101	101	101	101	101	101	101	101	101			
239	A	A	A	A	102	102	102	102	102	102	102	102	102	102	102	102	102	102	102	102	102			
240	98	98	98	98	98	98	98	98	98	98	98	98	98	98	98	98	98	98	98	98	98			
241	98	98	98	98	98	98	98	98	98	98	98	98	98	98	98	98	98	98	98	98	98			
242																								
243																								
244																								
245	A	A	A	A	A	A	A	A	A	A	A	A	A	A	A									
246	A	A	A	A	A	A	A	A	A	A	A	A	A	A	A	A	A							
247					148	148	148	148	148	148	148	148	148	148	148	148	148							
248																A	A	A	A	A	A			
249																								
250																								
251																								
252	104	104	104	104	104	104	104	104	104	104	104	104	104	104	104	104	104	104	104	104	104			
253	104	104	104	104	104	104	104	104	104	104	104	104	104	104	104	104	104	104	104	104	104			
254	105	105	105	105	105	105	105	105	105	105	105	105	105	105	105	105	105	105						
255	105	105	105	105	105	105	105	105	105	105	105	105	105	105	105	105	105	105						
256	108	108	108	108	108	108	108	108	108	108	108	108	108	108	108	108	108	108	108	108	108			
257	108	108	108	108	108	108	108	108	108	108	108	108	108	108	108	108	108	108	108	108	108			
258	109	109	109	109	109	109	109	109	109	109	109	109	109	109	109	109	109	109	109	109				
259	109	109	109	109	109	109	109	109	109	109	109	109	109	109	109	109	109	109	109	109				
260	106	106	106	106	106	106	106	106	106	106	106	106	106	106	106	106	106	106	106	106	106			
261	106	106	106	106	106	106	106	106	106	106	106	106	106	106	106	106	106	106	106	106	106			
262	107	107	107	107	107	107	107	107	107	107	107	107	107	107	107	107	107	107	107	107	107			
263	107	107	107	107	107	107	107	107	107	107	107	107	107	107	107	107	107	107	107	107	107			
264				88	88	88	88	88	88	88	88	88	88	88	88	88	88	88	88	88	88			
265					88	88	88	88	88	88	88	88	88	88	88	88	88	88	88	88	88			
266																								
267																								
268																								
269																								
270																								
271																								
272																								
273																								
274	A	A	A	A	A	A	A	A	A	A	A	A	A	A	A	A	A	A	A	A	A			
275																								
276	116	116	116	116	116	116	116	116	116	116	116	116	116	116	116	116	116	116						
277	116	116	116	116	116	55	55	55	55	55	55	55	55	55	55	55	55	-	-		-		-	
278	A	A	A	A/132	132	132	132	132	132	132	132	132	132	132	132	132	132	132	132	132	132			
279	A	A	A	A	A/131	131	131	131	131	131	131	131	131	131	131	131	131	131	131	131	131			
280	130	130	130	130	130	130	130	130	130	130	130	130	130	130	130	130	130	130	130	130				
281	A/-	-	-	132	132	132	132	132	132	132	132	132	132	132	132	132	132	132	132	132	132			
282	A/-	-																						
283	130	130	130	130	130	130	130	130	130	130	130	130	130	130	130	130	130	130	130	130				
284	A	A	A/131	131	131	131	131	131	131	131	131	131	131	131	131	131	131	131	131	131	131			
285																								
286																								
287	A	A	A	A	A	A	A	A	A	A	A	A	A	A	A	A	A	A	A	A	A			
288	A	A	A	A	A	A	A	A	A	A	A	A	A	A	A	85	85	85	85	85	85			
289																								
290																								

Squadriglia	1942 Jan	Feb	Mar	Apr	May	Jun	Jul	Aug	Sep	Oct	Nov	Dec	1943 Jan	Feb	Mar	Apr	May	Jun	Jul	Aug	Sep	Oct	Nov	Dec
300	A	A	A	A	167	167	167	167	167	167	167	167	167	167	167	167	167	167	167	167	167			
301																								
302																								
303				A	167	167	167	167	167	167	167	167	167	167	167	167	167	167	167	167	167			
304																								
305																								
306																								
307																								
308																								
309																								
310																	A?	A	A	A				
351	155	155	155	155	155	155	155	155	155	155	155	155	155	155	155	155	155	155	155	155	155			
352	20	20	20	20	20	20	20	20	20	20	20	20	20	20	20	20	20	20	20	20	20			
353	20	20	20	20	20	20	20	20	20	20	20	20	20	20	20	20	20	20	20	20	20			
354	24	24	24	24	24	24	24	24	24	24	24	24	24	24	24	24	24	24	24	24	24			
355	24	24	24	24	24	24	24	24	24	24	24	24	24	24	24	24	24	24	24	24	24			
356	21	21	21	21	21	21	21	21	21	21	21	21	21	21	21	21	21	21	21	21	21			
357	157	157	157	157	157	157	157	157	157	157	157	157	157	157	157	157	157	157	157	157	157			
358	2	2	2	2	2	2	2	2	2	2	2				2?	2	2	2	2					
359	22	22	22	22	22	22	22	22	22	22	22	22	22	22	22	22	22	22	22	22	22			
360	155	155	155	155	155	155	155	155	155	155	155	155	155	155	155	155	155	155	155	155	155			
361	154	154	154	154	154	21	21	21	21	21	21	21	21	21	21	21	21	21	21	21	21			
362	22	22	22	22	22	22	22	22	22/2	2								22	22	22	22			
363	150	150	150	150	150	150	150	150	150	150	150	150	150	150	150	150	150	150	150	150	150			
364	150	150	150	150	150	150	150	150	150	150	150	150	150	150	150	150	150	150	150	150	150			
365	150	150	150	150	150	150	150	150	150	150	150	150	150	150	150	150	150	150	150	150	150			
366	151	151	151	151	151	151	151	151	151	151	151	151	151	151	151	151	151	151	151	151	151			
367	151	151	151	151	151	151	151	151	151	151	151	151	151	151	151	151	151	151	151	151	151			
368	151	151	151	151	151	151	151	151	151	151	151	151	151	151	151	151	151	151	151	151	151			
369	22	22	22	22	22	22	22	22	22	22	22	22	22	22	22	22	22	22	22	22	22			
370	24	24	24	24	24	24	24	24	24	24	24	24	24	24	24	24	24	24	24	24	24			
371	22	22	22	22	22								22/157	157	157	157	157/161	161	161	157	157			
372	153	153	153	153	153	153	153	153	153	153	153	153	153	153	153	153	153	153	153	153	153			
373	153	153	153	153	153	153	153	153	153	153	153	153	153	153	153	153	153	153	153	153	153			
374	153	153	153	153	153	153	153	153	153	153	153	153	153	153	153	153	153	153	153	153	153			
375	160	160	160	160	160	160	160	160	160	160	160	160	160	160	160	160	160	160	160	160	160			
376	A	A	A	A	A	A	A	A	A	A	A	A	A	A	A	A	A	A	A	A	A			
377	A	A	A	A	A	A	A	A	A	A	A	A	A	A	A	A	A							
378	155	155	155	155	155	155	155	155	155	155	155	155	155	155	155	155	155	155	155	155	155			
379																								
380																								
381																								
382	21	21	21	21	21	21	21	21	21	21	21	21	21	21	21	21								
383	157												A	A	A	A	A	A	A	A	A			
384	157	157	157	157	157	157	157	157	157	157	157	157/A	A	A	A	A	A	A	A/157	157	157			
385	157	157	157	157	157	157	157	157	157	157	157	157												
386	21	21	21	21	21	21	21	21	21	21	21	21	21	21	21	21	21	21	21	21	21			
387	158	158	158	158	158	158	158	158	158	158	158	158	158	158	158	158	158	158	158	158	158			
388	158	158	158	158	158	158	158	158	158	158	158	158	158	158	158	158	158	158	158	158	158			
389					159	159	159	159	159	159	159	159	159	159	159	159	159	159	159	159	159			
390					159	159	159	159	159	159	159	159	159	159	159	159	159	159	159	159	159			
391					159	159	159	159	159	159	159	159	159	159	159	159	159	159	159	159	159			
392													-	A	A	A	A	A	A	A				

Squadriglia	Gruppo in 1942												Gruppo in 1943											
	Jan	Feb	Mar	Apr	May	Jun	Jul	Aug	Sep	Oct	Nov	Dec	Jan	Feb	Mar	Apr	May	Jun	Jul	Aug	Sep	Oct	Nov	Dec
393	160	160	160	160	160	160	160	160	160	160	160	160	160	160	160	160	160	160	160	160	160			
394	160	160	160	160	160	160	160	160	160	160	160	160	160	160	160	160	160	160	160	160	160			
395	154	154	154	154	154	154	154	154	154	154	154	154	154	154	154	154	154	154	154	154	154			
396	154	154	154	154	154	154	154	154	154	154	154	154	154	154	154	154	154	154	154	154	154			
397																								
398																								
600	A	A	A	A	A	A	A	A	A	A	A	A	A	A	A	A	A	A	A	A	A?			
601	147	147	147	147	147	147	147	147	147	147	147	147	147	147	147	147	147	147	147	147	147			
602	147	147	147	147	147	147	147	147	147	147	147	147	147	147	147	147	147	147	147	147	147			
603	146	146	146	146	146	146	146	146	146	146	146	146	146	146	146	146	146	146	146	146	146			
604	145	145	145	145	145	145	145	145	145	145	145	145	145	145	145	145	145	145	145	145	145			
605	148	148	148	148	148	148	148	148	148	148	148	148	148	148	148	148	148	148	148	148	148			
606	148	148	148	148	148	148	148	148	148	148	148	148	148	148	148	148	148	148	148	148	148			
607	149	149	149	149	149	149	149	149	149	149	149	149	149	149	149	149	149	149	149	149	149			
608	149	149	149	149	149	149	149	149	149	149	149	149	149	149	149	149	149	149	149	149	149			
609	146	146	146	146	146	146	146	146	146	146	146	146	146	146	146	146	146	146	146	146	146			
610	145	145	145	145	145	145	145	145	145	145	145	145	145	145	145	145	145	145	145	145	145			
611	A	A	A	A	A	A	A	A	A	A	A	A	A	A	A	A	A	A	A	A	A			
612	A	A	A	A	A	A	A?																	
613	A	A	A	A	A	A	A?																	
614	A	A	A	A	A	A	A	A	A	A	A?													
615	A	A	A	A	A	A	A	A	A	A	A	A	A	A	A	A	A	A	A	A	A?			
616																								
617			144	144	144	144	144	144	144	144	144	144	144	144	144	144	144	144	144	144	144			
618			144	144	144	144	144	144	144	144	144	144	144	144	144	144	144	144	144	144	144			
1 NAS	A	A	A	A	A	A	A	A	A	A	A	A	A	A	A	A	A	A	A	A	A			
2 NAS	A	A	A	A	A	A	A	A	A	A	A	A	A	A	A	A	A	A	A	A?				
3 NAS	A	A	A	A	A	A	A	A	A	A	A	A	A	A	A	A	A	A	A	A	A			
RscA																		A	A	A	A			
RsrA																								

159 Left: *An unidentifed pilot and his Macchi MC 200, probably in northern Italy. He wears some very fancy gloves!*

160 Above right: *Fiat CR 42s of the 85ª Squadriglia, 18° Gruppo of the CAI. The barely visible serial indicates that 85-7 was only four months old. Camouflage is probably the C1 mottle pattern, with a yellow engine cowling and spinner. The Gruppo insignia is an interesting interpretation of the Fascist symbols of axe and arrows. It originated in Spain with the Fiat CR 32 'Frecce' (Arrow) squadrons of the Aviazione Legionaria*

ORDERS OF BATTLE
June 1940-September 1943

The tables show all the available combat units on strength on the specific dates stated. These were subject to frequent change—within days, weeks, or months other units became involved—but these lists apply only to the day noted. For example, 7 Gruppo is often listed as being available for operations on 10 June 1940, but did not actually enter the front line until 19th June when it transferred to Squadra 1.

Unit strength listings and loss returns often disappeared in the heat of battle, or were later lost, so some units do not have accurate figures or base details.

See glossary for explanation of abbreviations.

1. Units available for operations against the British and French*
10 June 1940

*This is NOT a complete line up of the Regia Aeronautica, but relates only to those units directly opposing the British and French forces

Squadra 1

Gruppo	Squadriglie	Aircraft type	Number on strength	Duties	Base
1	27, 121	Ro 37	10	AR	Arezzo
4	14, 15	BR 20	16	DB	Lonate Pozzolo
5	31, 39, 40	Ro 37	27	TG, AR	Venaria Reale
11	1, 4	BR 20	17	DB, TG	Piacenza
18	83, 85, 95	CR 42	17	GA, AE, AR	Novi Ligure
23	70, 74, 75	CR 42	25	GA, AE, DF	Cervere

Gruppo	Squadriglie	Aircraft type	Number on strength	Duties	Base
25	8, 9	BR 20	16	DB	Ghemme
31	65, 66	BR 20	16?	DB	Aviano
43	3, 5	BR 20	16	DB	Cascina Vega
61	34, 128	Ro 37/Ca 311	4/7	AR	Parma
67	25 only	Ro 37	10	AR	Jesi
68	24, 35	Ro 37	12	AR	Verona
69	118	Ro 37	7	AR	Levaldigi
69	123	Ro 37	7	AR	Novi Ligure
72	119	Ro 37	9	AR	Albenga
72	129	Ca 311	9	AR	Mondovi
98	240, 241	BR 20	16	DB	Cameri
99	242, 243	BR 20	16	DB	Cameri
150	363, 364, 365	CR 42	20	DF, AE	Torino Caselle
151	366, 367, 368	CR 42	19	DF, AE	Casabianca
Autonomo	114	Ro 37	4	AR	Torino Mirafiori

Squadra 2

Gruppo	Squadriglie	Aircraft type	Number on strength	Duties	Base
17	71, 72, 73	CR 32	26	DF	Boccadifalco
33	59, 60	SM 79	17	AN	Comiso
34	67, 68	SM 79	16	AN	Comiso
52	214, 215	SM 79	14	AN	Fontanarossa
53	216, 217	SM 79	13	AN	Fontanarossa
59	232, 233	SM 79	9	DB	Gela
60	234, 235	SM 79	9	DB, AN	Gela
76	30, 132	Ro 37	9	AR	Boccadifalco
87	192, 193	SM 79	14	DB, AR, AN	Sciacca
90	194, 195	SM 79	13	DB, AR, AN	Sciacca
96	236, 237	S85	14	TG/DB	Pantelleria
108	256, 257	SM 79	16	AR, DB, AN	Castelvetrano
109	258, 259	SM 79	16	AR, DB, AN	Castelvetrano
157	384, 385, 386	CR 42	17	AE	Trapani Milo

Squadra 3

Gruppo	Squadriglie	Aircraft type	Number on strength	Duties	Base
20	351, 352, 353	G 50/CR 32nf	25/5	DF, NF	Ciampino Sud
21	354, 355	G 50	19	NF, DF	Ciampino Sud
22	357, 358, 359	G 50	28	AE	Pontedera
24	361, 362	CR 32	10	DF	Sarzana
26	11, 13	SM 79	14	DB	Viterbo
29	62, 63	SM 79	13	DB	Viterbo
41	204, 205	SM 79	16	DB	Ciampino Nord
42	206, 207	SM 79	16	DB, AN	Orvieto
62	28, 29	Ro 37	14	AR	Lucca
104	252, 253	SM 79	15	DB	Pisa San Giusto
105	254, 255	SM 79	15	DB	Pisa San Giusto
Autonomo	356	G 50	9	DF	Capodichino

Aeronautica della Sardegna

Gruppo	Squadriglie	Aircraft type	Number on strength	Duties	Base
3	153, 154, 155	CR 32	27	DF, AE	Monserrato
19	100, 101, 102	Ba88	13	GA	Alghero
27	18, 52	SM 79	16	DB, AN	Villacidro
28	10, 19	SM 79	16	DB, AN	Villacidro
38	49, 50	SM 79	15	DB, AN	Decimomannu
89	228, 229	SM 79	15	DB, AN	Decimomannu
93	196, 197	Z 506	12	AN, DB	Elmas
94	198 only	Z 506	6	AN, DB	Elmas
Autonomo	124	Ro 37	4	AR	Elmas

Aeronautica della Libia

Gruppo	Squadriglie	Aircraft type	Number on strength	Duties	Base
1 APC	12, 89, 104	Ca 309	12	AR	Mellaha
2 APC	16 , 23	Ca 309	7	AR	El Adem
8	92, 93, 94	CR 32	25	DF, CE, AE	Tobruk T2
10	84, 90, 91	CR 42	27	DF	Tobruk T2
12	159, 160	Ca 310/Ba 65	10/11	GA	Sorman
16	167, 168	Ca 310	14		Sorman
30	55, 56	SM 79	15	AN	Benina
32	57, 58	SM 79	15	AR, DB	Benina
35	43, 44	SM 79	16	AR, DB, GA	Bir el Behra
36	45, 46	SM 79	15	AR, DB, AN	Bir el Behra
44	6, 7	SM 79	11	AN	El Adem
45	2, 22	SM 81	19	AN	El Adem
46	20, 21	SM 79	18	DB	Tarhuna T18
47	53, 54	SM 79/SM 81	9/8	DB	Tarhuna T18
64	122, 136	Ro 37	7	AR	Mellaha
73	137	Ro 37	4	AR	El Adem
73	127	Ro 37	3	AR	Tobruk T2
145	604	SM 75	8	TR	T2
Autonomo	99 Av Sah	Ca 309	6	AR	Hon
Autonomo	143	Z506	6	AR, ASR, AS	Menelao

Aeronautica dell'Egeo

Gruppo	Squadriglie	Aircraft type	Number on strength	Duties	Base
56	222, 223	SM 81	10	AN, DB, NB	Gadurra
92	200, 201	SM 81	10	AN, DB	Marizza
Autonomo	163	CR 32	11	DF	Marizza

Comando Superiore Aviazione per La Regia Marina

Gruppo	Squadriglie	Aircraft type	Number on strength	Duties	Base
79	187, 141	Z501	7	AR ASR	Cadimare
83	184, 186	Z501	14	CE, AR, AS, ASR	Augusta
83	189	Z501	7	CE, AR, AS, ASR	Siracusa
85	146, 183, 188	Z501	18	AR CE	Elmas
86	190, 191	Z506	12	AN DB	Brindisi
Autonomo	144	Z506	6	AR, ASR, CE, AS	Stagnone
Autonomo	148	Z506	7	AR ASR	Vigna di Valle
Autonomo	170	Z506	7	AR ASR	Augusta
Autonomo	199	Z506	7	AN AR	Santa Giusta
Autonomo	613	SM 66C soc.	5	ASR	Roma Lido

SAS

Gruppo	Squadriglie	Aircraft type	Number on strength	Duties	Base
148	605, 606	S73	13	TR	Littoria
149	607, 608, 609	SM 82	12	TR	Capodichino
Autonomo	615	S83	8	TR	Guidonia
Autonomo	616	S74	3	TR	Littorio

Africa Orientale Italiana

Gruppo	Squadriglie	Aircraft type	Number on strength	Duties	Base
4	14, 15	SM 81	12	DB	Scenele
25	8	Ca133	6	DB	Gabuen
25	9	Ca 133	6	DB	Lugh Ferrandi
26	11 only	Ca133	6	AR	Gondar
27	18, 52, 118	Ca133	18	DB	Assab
28	10, 19	SM 81	12	AR, NB	Zula
29	62, 63	SM 81	12	DB, NB	Assab
31	65, 66	Ca133	12	AR	Neghelli
44	6, 7	SM 79	12	DB	Ghiniele
49	61, 64	Ca133	12	AR	Jimma

Gruppo	Squadriglie	Aircraft type	Number on strength	Duties	Base
Gruppo Gasbarrini	41, SSM del S Nord	Ca133	12	AR	Agordat
Autonomo	65	Ca133	6	AR	Neghelli
Autonomo	66	Ca133	3	AR	Yavello
Autonomo	110	Ro 37	9	AR, DF	Dire Daua
Autonomo	410	CR 32	9	DF, AE	Dire Daua
Autonomo	411	CR 32	9	DF, AE	Addis Abeba
Autonomo	412	CR 42	9	DF, AE	Massawa/Gura
Autonomo	413	CR 42	9	TG, DF	Assab
Autonomo	414	CR 42	6	DF, AE	Gura
Autonomo	SSM del S Centrale	Ca133	6	AR	Dembidollo
Autonomo	SSM del S Ovest	Ca133	9	AR	Addis Abeba
Autonomo	SSM del S Sud	Ca133	7	AR	Mogadishu

2. The advance on Sidi Barrani: first Italian offensive in the desert
1 September 1940

Squadra 5

Gruppo	Squadriglie	Aircraft type	Number on strength	Duties	Base
1 APC	12, 89, 104	Ca 309	21	AR	Mellaha
7	6, 86, 98	Ba 88	32	GA	Derna
8	92, 93, 94	CR 42	11	DF, AE	Derna
10	84, 90, 91	CR 42	22	DF, AE	Bir el Gobi
12	159, 160	Ba 65/CR 32	7/10	GA	Tobruk T2
13	77, 78, 82	CR 42	28	DF	Berka
16	167, 168	CR 32/Ba 65	10/5	GA	Tobruk T2
32	57, 58	SM 79	5	AR, AN	Derna
33	59, 60	SM 79	?	AN	Benina
35	43, 44	SM 79	?	DB	Bir el Bhera
36	45, 46	SM 79	?	DB	Bir el Bhera
44	6, 7	SM 79	11	DB	El Adem
46	20, 21	SM 79	?	DB	Benina
47	53, 54	SM 81/SM 79	?	DB	Benina
54	218, 219	SM 81	13	NB	Ain el Gazala
63	41, 113	Ro 37	16	AR	(Cirenaica)
64	136 only	Ro 37	?	AR	Gambut
145	604, 610	SM 74/SM 75	3/14	TR	Benghasi
147	601, 602, 603	SM 75	13	TR	Benghasi/Tobruk
148	605, 606	SM 73	7	TR	Benghasi
151	366, 367, 368	CR 42	30	DF	Derna/Ain el Gazala
Bat Av Sah	99 only	Ca 309	7	AR	Hon
67	115 only	Ro 37	10	AR	(Libya)
73	136, 137	Ro 37/Ca 310	7/6	AR	Menastir
Autonomo	145	Z501	6	AR, CE, ASR	Benghasi
Autonomo	175	SM 79	5	AR	Gambut/T5

3. Corpo Aereo Italiano: the fight over the English Channel
22 October 1940

CAI

Gruppo	Squadriglie	Aircraft type	Number on strength	Duties	Base
11	1, 4	BR 20	19	DB	Melsbroech
18	83, 85, 95	CR 42	50	AE	Maldegem
20	351, 352, 353	G 50	45	DF	Ursel
43	3, 5	BR 20	19	DB	Melsbroech
98	240, 241	BR 20	19	DB	Chievres

Gruppo	Squadriglie	Aircraft type	Number on strength	Duties	Base
99	242, 243	BR 20	18	DB	Chievres
Autonomo	172	Z1007	5	AR	Chievres

4. Campaign against Greece
28 October 1940

Comando Aeronautica Albania

Gruppo	Squadriglie	Aircraft type	Number on strength	Duties	Base
24	354, 361, 362	G 50	24	AE	Berat
39	51, 69	SM 81	12	TR/DB	Valona
40	202, 203	SM 81	12	TR/DB	Valona
72	42, 120 only	Ro 37	18	AR	Valona/ Argirocastro
105	254, 255	SM 79	15	DB	Tirana
150	363, 364, 365	CR 42	36	DF	Tirana/ Valona/ Argirocastro
160	393, 394, 395	CR 32/CR 42/Ro 41	14/8/18	DF, AE	Drenova
Autonomo	354	G 50		DF	(Albania)
Autonomo	355	G 50		DF	(Albania)
Autonomo	611	Ba 44	5	TR	Tirana

Comando 4 ZAT

Gruppo	Squadriglie	Aircraft type	Number on strength	Duties	Base
50	210, 211	Z1007	20	DB	Brindisi
55	220, 221	SM 81	18	DB	Lecce Galatina
86	190, 191	Z506	12	AN	Brindisi
95	230, 231	Z506	11	AN	Brindisi
96	236, 237	Ju87B/S86W	20/1	DB	Lecce Galatina
106	260, 261	Z1007	12	DB	Grottaglie
107	262, 263	Z1007	12	DB	Grottaglie
116	276, 277	BR 20	18	DB, CE, AR	Lecce Galatina
147	601, 602, 603	SM 75	10	TR	Brindisi
149	607, 608, 609	SM 82/SM 75/SM 83	11/3/1	TR	Urbe/Brindisi

Aeronautica dell'Egeo

Gruppo	Squadriglie	Aircraft type	Number on strength	Duties	Base
72	25 only	Ro 37	9	AR	Coritza
Autonomo	161	Ro 43/Ro 44	1/8	DF, GA	Lero
Autonomo	163	CR 42/CR 32	9/7	DF	Marizza

5. First offensive on Malta, combined with the Luftwaffe
10 May 1941

ASIC

Gruppo	Squadriglie	Aircraft type	Number on strength	Duties	Base
6	79, 81, 88	MC 200		DF	Fontanarossa
17	71, 72, 80	MC 200		DF, AE	Trapani Milo
83	170, 184, 186	Z501/Z506	14/8	CE, AR, AS, ASR	Augusta
87	192, 193	SM 79		NB, DB	Sciacca
90	194, 195	SM 79		NB, DB	Sciacca
108	256, 257	SM 79		NB	(Sicily)
109	258, 259	SM 79		NB	(Sicily)
Autonomo	144	Z501/Z506		AS, AR, ASR	Stagnone
Autonomo	612	Z506C	5	ASR	Stagnone

ASAR

Gruppo	Squadriglie	Aircraft type	Number on strength	Duties	Base
Autonomo	613	SM 66C	5	ASR	Elmas
27	18, 52	SM 79		DB, AN	Villacidro

6. Campaign against Russia (Corpo di Spedizione Italiano in Russia) 29 July 1941

Cdo CSIR

Gruppo	Squadriglie	Aircraft type	Number on strength	Duties	Base
22	359, 362, 369, 371	MC 200	51	DF, AE	Tudora
61	34, 119, 128	Ca 311	32	AR	Tudora

7. Operation PEDESTAL (the biggest Malta Convoy battle) 11 August 1942

Aeronautica Sicilia

Gruppo	Squadriglie	Aircraft type	Number on strength	Duties	Base
2	150, 152, 358	Re 2001	10	AE, AN, AR	Castelvetrano
4	14, 15	SM 84	15	DB, AN, NB	Castelvetrano
7	76 only	CR 42/MC 200/MC 202	3/5/1	CE, AE	Pantelleria
16	169 only	MC 200	7	CE	Reggio Calabria
20	151, 352, 353	MC 202	6	AE, AR	Gela
25	8, 9	SM 84	7	DB, AN, NB	Castelvetrano
26	11, 13	Z1007	5?	NB	(Sicily)
29	62, 63	Z1007	8	DB, NB	Chinisia
30	55, 56	SM 79	10	AN, CE	Sciacca
32	57, 58	SM 79	6	AN	Boccadifalco
33	59, 60	Z1007	9	AN	Chinisia
83	170, 184	RS14	16	CE, AR, AS, ASR	Augusta
	186, 189	Z501/Z506	12/9	CE, AR, AS, ASR	Augusta
85	144	RS14/Ro43	2/1	CE, AR, ASR	Stagnone
	197	Z501/Z506	10/2	CE, AR, ASR	Stagnone
88	264, 265	BR 20	10	NB	Gerbini
102	209, 239	Ju 87R	15	IT	Castelvetrano
132	278, 281	SM 79sil	15	TB	Pantelleria
155	351, 360, 378	MC 202	21	AE, AR	Gela
Autonomo	173	CR 25	6	AS, CE	Boccadifalco
Autonomo	377	Re 2000	6	DF, AR	Pantelleria
Autonomo	612	Z506soc	5	ASR	Stagnone
	Sez Intercettori	CR 42	8	NF	Sciacca
Autonomo	Sez Fotografica	MC 202	3	AR	Reggio Calabria

Aeronautica Sardegna

Gruppo	Squadriglie	Aircraft type	Number on strength	Duties	Base
22	359, 362only	Re 2001	11	AE, AN	Elmas
24	354	CR 42/G 50	19/16	DF, AE, AS, CE	Elmas
51	212, 213	Z1007	7	AN, DB	Villacidro
65	28, 124	Ro 37/Ca 314		AN, AS	Alghero
89	228, 229	SM 84sil	13	TB	Villacidro
105	254, 255	SM 79sil	15	TB	Decimomannu
108	256, 257	SM 84sil	12	TB	Decimomannu
109	258, 259	SM 84sil	12	TB	Decimomannu
130	280, 283	SM 79sil	13	TB	Elmas
Autonomo	138	Z501/Ro 43	7/1	AR	Olbia
Autonomo	146	Z506	12	AN, AR, ASR	Elmas
Autonomo	188	Z501	3	AR, ASR	Elmas
Autonomo	287	Z506	7	AR, ASR	Elmas
Autonomo	613	SM 66C/Z506S	5/1	ASR	Elmas
	Sezione Intercettori	CR 42/G 50		NF	Cagliari

Squadra 5

Gruppo	Squadriglie	Aircraft type	Number on strength	Duties	Base
133	174, 175	SM 79sil	8	TB	Benghasi K3
Autonomo	614	Z506C	2	ASR	Caramanlis

8. Defence of the lines at El Alamein
20 October 1942

Squadra 5

Gruppo	Squadriglie	Aircraft type	Number on strength	Duties	Base
1 APC	12, 103, 104	Ca 309	15?	AR	Siwa/Misurata/Mellaha
8	92, 93, 94	MC 200	17	CE, DF	Bu Amud
9	73, 96, 97	MC 202	20	DF, AR, GA, AE	Fuka Sud
10	84, 90, 91	MC 202	19	DF	Fuka Sud
13	77, 78, 82	MC 200	19	DF	Bu Amud
18	83, 85, 95	MC 200	22	AR, DF, CE, GA	Abu Haggag
23	70, 74, 75	MC 202	20	GA, DF, AE	Abu Haggag
37	47, 48	SM 82	10	TR	Fuka
46	20, 21	CR 42AS	24	GA	Bu Amud
47	53, 54	CR 42AS	23	GA	(Cirenaica)
66	87, 131	Ca311	12	GA, CE, AR	Zuara
68	24, 33	Ca311/Ca312	12/5	AR	Misurata
86	190, 191	Z1007	8	AR, DB, CE	Barce
95	230, 231	Z1007	7	AR, DB, CE	Barce
101	208, 238	CR 42	22	CE	Derna
131	279, 284	SM 79sil	8	TB	Derna
133	174, 175	SM 79sil	8	TB	Benghazi K3
145	604, 610	SM 75/SM 82	2/10	TR	Fuka
146	603, 609	SM 82	21	TR	Fuka
147	601, 602	SM 82	17?	TR	Fuka
148	606 only	G12	10	TR	Tobruk
149	607, 608	S82		TR	Tobruk
150	363, 364, 365	MC 200/202	18/2	DF, CE, GA	Benghazi K3
158	236, 387, 388	CR 42	11	GA	Abu Nimeir
159	389, 390, 391	CR 42	11	GA	Abu Nimeir
160	393, 394, 375	CR 42/G 50	8/20	GA	Sorman
Batt av Sah	26, 99	Ca 309/SM 81/ SM 79/ CR 42	7/2/ 2/5	AR, DF	Hon
Autonomo	131	Ca 311		AR	(Egypt)
Autonomo	145	Z501/Z506	2/6	AR, ASR	Menelao
Autonomo	148	Z501	4	AR	Menelao
Autonomo	196	Z501	5	AR, ASR	Benghazi
Autonomo	600	Ca133S	8	TR (Ambulance)	Fuka Nord
Autonomo	614	Z506Ssoc	2/2	ASR	Caramanlis/Benghasi

Aeronautica Egeo

Gruppo	Squadriglie	Aircraft type	Number on strength	Duties	Base
82	139, 184	Z501	11	CE, AR	Prevesa, Greece
84	147, 185	Z501/Z506	6/5	CE	Suda Bay, Crete

9. Operation TORCH: The invasion of North West Africa by the Allies
7 November 1942

Squadra 4

Gruppo	Squadriglie	Aircraft type	Number on strength	Duties	Base
3	153, 154, 155	MC 200	20?	CE, AE	Lecce

Squadra 3

Gruppo	Squadriglie	Aircraft type	Number on strength	Duties	Base
28	10,19	Z1007		NB	Viterbo
33	59,60	Z1007		AN	Viterbo

ASIC

17	71,72,80	MC 202	33	GA AE AN DF	Pantelleria
37	47,48	SM 82	10	TR	Castelvetrano
56	222,223	SM 75/SM 82	6/6	TR	Castelvetrano
57	224,225	SM 81	11	TR	Castelvetrano
83	170,189	RS14/Z506	16/9	CE AR AS ASR	Augusta
132	278,281	SM 79sil	15	TB	Pantelleria
144	617,618	SM 82	14	TR	Castelvetrano
148	605,606	G12	13	TR	Castelvetrano

ASAR

22	357,358,359	Re 2001	23	AN GA AR	Monserrato
38	49,50	SM 84sil	10	TB	Alghero
50	210,211	Z1007	15	DB AN	Alghero
88	264,265	Z1007		NB	Milis
89	228,229	SM 84sil	17	TB	Alghero
105	254,255	SM 79sil	15	TB	Decimomannu
153	372,373.374	MC 202	24	AE DF	Decimomannu
Autonomo	274	P108B	8	NB	Decimomannu

10. Invasion of Sicily
9 July 1943

Squadra 2

158	236, 387, 388	G 50bis	37	GA	Osoppo

Squadra 3

56	222, 223	SM 83/SM 75bis/ SM 82	2/5/6	TR	Orvieto
148	605, 606	G12	28?	TR	Centocelle
159	389, 390, 391	G 50bis	35	GA	Pistoia
Autonomo	274	P108B	5	AN, NB	Guidonia
Ragr Bom	various	Z1007bis/ter	31	NB	Perugia San Egudio

Squadra 4

97	226, 227	Ro 57bis	15	DF, CE	Crotone

ASIC

9	73, 96, 97	MC 202/205	18/2	DF	Catania
10	84, 90, 91	MC 202/205	20	DF	Catania
16	167, 168, 169	MC 202	22	DF	Castelvetrano
21	356, 361, 386	MC 202	33?	DF	Chinisia
66	40, 87	Ca313/314		AR, AS	Gerbini
83	170, 186	RS14/Z506B/			
		Z506S/Z501/Ba 25	20/4/2/1/1	CE, AR, AS, ASR	Augusta
103	207, 237	Ju 87D-3	6	AN	Chinisia
150	363, 364, 365	Bf 109G	25	DF	Sciacca
153	372, 373, 374	MC 202	24	DF	Chinisia
157	163, 357, 371	MC 200	12	DF, CE	Reggio Calabria
161	162, 164, 371	MC 202/D.520	?/7	DF	Reggio Calabria
Autonomo	384	MC 200		DF	Reggio Calabria
Autonomo	7 Sez Soc	RS14	2	ASR	Siracusa

ASAR

Gruppo	Squadriglie	Aircraft type	Number on strength	Duties	Base
46	20, 21	CR 42	34	CE, GA	Capoterra
47	53, 54	CR 42	23?	GA	Oristano
65	28, 131	Ca313/314	5/19?	AR, AN, AS	Alghero
155	351, 360, 378	MC 202/205	20/12	DF	Monserrato
160	375, 393, 394	Re 2001/CR 42/G 50	23/6/2?	DF, AE, GA, CE	Olbia
Autonomo	146	RS14/Z506	1/6	AR, ASR	Ajaccio
Autonomo	188	Z501/Z506	1/6	AR, ASR	Elmas
Autonomo	287	Z506/RS14	5/5	AR, ASR	Alghero
Autonomo	5 Sez Soc	Z506	2	ASR	Elmas
Autonomo	6 Sez Soc	Z506	2	ASR	Ajaccio

11. The Regia Aeronautica at the Armistice
8 September 1943

Squadra 1

Gruppo	Squadriglie	Aircraft type	Number on strength	Duties	Base
2	152, 358	Re 2001/CR 42	6/11	DF, NF	Genova
3	153, 154, 155	Me109G	3	TG, DF	Torino Caselle
30	55, 56	Ca314	21	CE	Bresso
50	210, 211	Z1007	5	NB	Cameri
59	232, 233	Re 2001/CR 42/Do 217	11/3/2	NF	Venegono
60	234	Bf110/ Re 2001/ Do 217/CR 42	2/8/6/11	NF, DF	Venegono
60	235	see above	see above	NF, DF	Lonate Pozzolo
99	242, 243	SM 84	18	AN	Lonate Pozzolo
103	207, 237	Ju 87/Ba 88M	2/3	TG	Lonate Pozzolo
150	363, 364, 365	MC 202/CR 42/Bf 109G	1/2/2	DF, TG	Torino Caselle
151	366, 367, 368	G 55	1	TG	Torino Caselle
153	372, 373, 374	MC 202		TG	Torino Caselle
158	236, 387, 388	CR 42/G 50	4/13	TG	Lonate Pozzolo
159	389, 390, 391	G 50/Re 2002	8/10	GA	Lonate Pozzolo
	Sez Intercettori	CR 42	3	NF	Torino
	Sez Intercettori	CR 42	3	NF	Genova

Squadra 2

Gruppo	Squadriglie	Aircraft type	Number on strength	Duties	Base
6	79, 81, 88	MC 202/CR 42	4/2	DF	Ronchi
17	71, 72, 80	MC 205	2	TG	Ronchi
27	18, 52	Z1007	6	NB	Bologna
32	57, 58	Ca 314	4	TG	Jesi
33	59, 60	Z1007		TG	Jesi
95	230, 231	Z1007	4	NB	Bologna
107	262, 263	Z1007/Z1018	7/1	TG	Vicenza
	Sez Intercettori	CR 42	3	NF	Bologna
	Sez Intercettori	CR 42	3	NF	Verona

Squadra 3

Gruppo	Squadriglie	Aircraft type	Number on strength	Duties	Base
8	92, 93, 94	MC 200	24	DF, CE	Littoria
13	77, 78, 82	MC 202/205	17/4	DF, TG	Metato
18	83, 85, 95	MC 202/205/Bf 109/ SAI 207	16/6/11/1	DF, TG	Cerveteri
20	151, 352, 353	MC 202/205/G55	4/3/12	DF	Foligno
22	359, 362, 369	D.520/Re 2005/MC 202	8/7/22	DF	Capodichino
22	150	CR 42/Re 2001	4/6	DF	Capua
23	70, 74, 75	MC 202/MC 205	15/6	DF, TG	Cerveteri
24	354, 355, 370	MC 202/D.520	3/8	DF	Metato
29	62, 63	Ju 88D	16	TG	Viterbo
46	20, 21	CR 42	10	TG	Firenze

Gruppo	Squadriglie	Aircraft type	Number on strength	Duties	Base
47	53, 54	CR 42	16	TG	Firenze
51	212 ,213	Ju 88D	6	TG	Viterbo
104sil	252, 253	SM 79sil	8	TB	Siena
132sil	278, 281	SM 79sil	5	TB, TG	Littoria
161	162, 163, 164	SAI 207/ MC 202	4/2	DF	Castiglione del Lago
167	300, 303	CR 42/Re 2001/F5	8/14/6	NF	Littoria
Rag Bom	10, 19, 190, 191, 264,				
	265, 260, 261	Z1007bis/ter	54	NB	Perugia
Rag Sil	204, 205, 228, 229,				
	256, 257, 279, 284	SM 79sil	58	TB	Siena
Autonomo	172	Z1007/Ju 88	3/4	TG	Viterbo
Autonomo	274	P108B	4	NB	Foligno
Autonomo	310	MC 205	9	AR	Guidonia
	Sez Silurante	SM 79sil	0	TB	Capodichino

Squadra 4

Gruppo	Squadriglie	Aircraft type	Number on strength	Duties	Base
9	73, 96, 97	MC 202/205	8/22	DF	Gioia del Colle
10	84, 90, 91	MC205	8	DF	Castrovillari
21	356, 361, 386	MC 202	25	DF	Gioia del Colle
98	240, 241	SM 84	12	AN	Gioia del Colle
101	208, 238	Re 2002	11	AN, AR, DF	Manduria
102	209, 239	Re 2002	15	DF, GA, AN	Manduria
157	357, 371, 384	MC 200/CR 42	12/3	DF, CE	Grottaglie
	Sez Intercettori	CR 42	3	NF	Lecce

Aeronautica Sardegna

Gruppo	Squadriglie	Aircraft type	Number on strength	Duties	Base
121	206, 216	Ju 87D	12	AN, NB	Chilivani
155	351, 373, 374	MC 202/205	15/13	DF	Casa Zeppera
160	375, 393, 394	Re 2001	24	DF, AE, GA, CE	Olbia Venafiorita

Aeronautica Egeo

Gruppo	Squadriglie	Aircraft type	Number on strength	Duties	Base
87	192,193	Z1007	7	AR, AS, CE	Kalamaki
90	194,195	Z1007	13	AR	Marizza
154	395, 396	MC 202/CR 42/G 50	8/11/27	DF, NF, CE, AS, AR	Marizza
		Re 2000/Ro 43	4/28	AR	
	147	Z501/Z506	4/6	AR	Lero
	Sez Intercettori	CR 42	3	NF	Gadurra

Aeronautica Albania

Gruppo	Squadriglie	Aircraft type	Number on strength	Duties	Base
40	202, 203	BR 20	18	AG	Tirana
42	200, 201	BR 20	18	AG	Scjak
43	3,5	Ca 314	19	TG	Devoli
	376	CR 42/G 50	2/7	DF, GA	Tirana
	392	CR 42/G 50	11/4	CE, DF	Tirana

Aeronautica Grecia

Gruppo	Squadriglie	Aircraft type	Number on strength	Duties	Base
	385	MC 200/G 50/CR 42	16/3/5	CE	Araxos
	Sez Intercettori	CR 42	3	NF	Atene Tatoi

Cdo Av Slovenia Dalmazia

Gruppo	Squadriglie	Aircraft type	Number on strength	Duties	Base
	51	BR 20	8	AG, AR, DB	Mostar
	69	BR 20	6	AG, AR, DB	Scutari
	383	CR 42	22	CE	Zara
	Cdo Sq	MC 200/CR 42/G 50	4/6/4	NF, DF	Zara?

Regia Esercito

Gruppo	Squadriglie	Aircraft type	Number on strength	Duties	Base
5	33,128	Ca 311/Ca 313/Ca 314/BR 20/Ro 37	7/18/41/11/8	AG	Mostar, Zara

Gruppo	Squadriglie	Aircraft type	Number on strength	Duties	Base
61	25, 34	Ca 311/Ca 314/Ro 37	13/8/8	AS	Jesi
63	41, 113, 119	see 5gr	see 5gr	AG	Lubiana, Alture di Pola
64	122, 136	Ca 313	14	AR	Cuers, Hyeres
65	124, 131	Ca 313/Ca 314/Ro 37	23/12	AR, AN	Bastia, Ajaccio
68	39, 121	Ca 313/Ca 314	2/15	TG	Lavariano
69	103, 118	Ca 313/Ca314	1/18	AS, AR	Pontecagnano
70	114, 123	Ca 311/Ca 314	12/6	AR	Valona
71	38, 116	BR 20	23	TG	Venaria Reale
72	31, 35	Ca 311/Ca 313/BR 20	9/1/11	AS, AR	Larissa
73	24, 115	Ca 313/Ca 314	10/8	AG, AR	Scjak
76	30, 127	Ca 313	13	AR	Le Luc
Autonomo	36	Ca 314	5	AR	Lucca
Autonomo	137	Ca 313	9	AR	Albenga

Regia Marina

Gruppo	Squadriglie	Aircraft type	Number on strength	Duties	Base
Cdo Av Sardegna	138	Z506/RS14	3/5	AR	Portovecchio
Grecia	139	Z501	2	AR	Prevesa
Alto Tirreno	140	Z506/RS14	3/9	AR	Torre del Lago
Jonio e Basso Adriatico	141	Z501/Z506	1/2	AR, ASR	Brindisi
Jonio e Basso Adriatico	142	Z506	7	AR, CE, AS, ASR	Taranto
Alto Adriatico	143	Z506	2	AR, AS	Venezia
Basso Tirreno	144	Z501/Z506	6/6	AR, ASR, AS	Orbetello
Alto Tirreno	145	Z501/RS14	4/6	AR, ASR	Torre del Lago
Sardegna	146	Z506/RS14	5/1	AR, ASR	Ajaccio
Basso Tirreno	148	Z501/Z506/RS14	1/3/4	AR	Vigna di Valle
Alto Adriatico	149	Z501/Z506/RS14	10/5/4	AR, ASR	Kumbor
Alto Tirreno	171	Z501	6	AR, ASR	Tolone
Basso Tirreno	182	Z506	4	AR, ASR	Nisida
Alto Adriatico	183	Z501/Z506	6/6	AR, AS, ASR	Divulje
Alto Tirreno	187	Z501/Z506	11/1	AR, ASR	Cadimare
Jonio e Basso Adriatico	196	Z506	6	AR	Taranto
Sardegna	287	Z506/RS14	1/6	AR, ASR	Porto Conte
Jonio e Basso Adriatico	288	Z501/Z506	8/1	AR, ASR, CE	Taranto
	1 sez soc	Z506	1	ASR	Tolone
	2 sez soc	Z506	1	ASR	Cadimare
	3 sez soc	Z506	2	ASR	Orbetello
	4 sez soc	Z506	1	ASR	Nisida
	6 sez soc	Z506		ASR	Ajaccio
	9 sez soc	Z506		ASR	Brindisi
	10 sez soc	Z506	2	ASR	Prevesa
Aerei imbarcati GN	1 FFNN	G 50/Re 2003/Re 2000	2/1/4	AR	Cadimare
	2 FFNN	Ro 43	15	AR	Cadimare
	3 FFNN	Ro 43	12	AR	Cadimare

SAS

Gruppo	Squadriglie	Aircraft type	Number on strength	Duties	Base
56	222, 223	SM 82/SM 75	6/5	TR	Orvieto
57	224, 225	SM 82	10	TR	Orvieto
146	603, 609	SM 82	19	TR	Ferrara
149	607, 608	SM 82	20	TR	Ferrara
147	601, 602	SM 82	41	TR	Rimini
144	617, 618	SM 82	25	TR	Fano
148	605, 606	G12	12	TR	Fano

161 Left: *An IMAM Ro 43 from the cruiser* Armando Diaz. *It still wears the pre-war silver finish with a light grey overpaint to the rudder stripes. Location unknown*

162 Below: *A Reggiane Re 2000 'catapultabile' Series 3 (MM8282) on its transport trailer. It is finished in dark green and light grey. Just visible on the fin is the duck emblem of the unit. The strong point for attachment of the catapult launching strop can be seen on the fuselage just above the wing trailing edge. This machine was the second of a batch of ten to be built. 300 Re 2000s were ordered by Britain in January 1940...*

THE CARRIER *AQUILA*
The other *Eagle*, the other Royal Navy

In common with most Admiralties of the time, the Italian naval leaders still believed that the battleship was the major naval threat, and that land-based aircraft were sufficient to protect those areas of the Mediterranean where the Navy could not venture.

Italian naval experience with vessels capable of carrying aircraft was founded on the seaplane carrier *Giuseppe Miraglia* , a converted merchantman dating from 1927. For much of her career she was employed on desultory catapult experiments, this reflecting the somewhat ambivalent attitude of the Italian admirals toward naval aviation, most of whom, in common with many others of their kind, saw the primary role of aircraft as that of a scouting force for the big guns of the battleships. Despite this, factions in the Navy and in the Airforce began battling for control of this new weapon. The government could see other nations, such as Great Britain, Japan and the United States, beginning to make use of the carrier concept. Plans in the 1930s for a full-deck carrier were based upon another conversion, this time of the passenger liner, *Roma*.

After the massive costs of the Spanish Civil War, and the expeditions into Albania and Africa in the 1930s, the

government was short of ready funds. A modern Littorio-class battleship cost as much as the entire Air Force budget for 1933-34 (800 million lire). Consequently, in the absence of decisive action, work proceeded on the conversion with extreme slowness and there were still no firm plans to build a dedicated carrier when the country entered the war.

With the success of the British attack on Taranto in November 1940, and the defeat of the Navy during the Battle of Cape Matapan, in the spring of 1941, the government changed its mind. These events had highlighted the lack of co-operation between the Regia Marina and the Regia Aeronautica, at the expense of the former.

In July 1941 the *Roma* was sent to the shipyards at Genova for conversion work to begin on what was to become the carrier *Aquila* (Eagle). Over the next two years the 27,800 ton vessel, with a speed of 21 knots, was modified with a new deck, armour, weapons, and more powerful engines. Two Demag catapults, operated by compressed air and similar to those used in the German carrier *Graf Zeppelin*, were installed in the flight deck. They could each launch one aircraft every thirty seconds.

During 1942 the carrier suffered light damage from bombing raids. She was eventually sabotaged by her crew in the Genova shipyards before capture by the Germans in September 1943. After being bombed in 1944, and

163 Left: *Reggiane Re 2001 G under test at Perugia as a potential naval torpedo bomber. It has a lengthened tail wheel strut but no arrester hook*

164 Above: *The fine lines of* Aquila *are evident even in this fire-blackened and damaged condition in 1944*

attacked by human torpedoes in 1945, she was scuttled. Refloated in 1946 and sent to La Spezia for refitting, she was eventually broken up in 1952.

The carrier was to have been crewed by 1175 sailors and 245 airmen. Powered by 140,000 shp engines, with 8 boilers and 4 groups of turbines, she was intended to be capable of 30 knots maximum. Range was 4-5,500 nautical miles at 18 knots. Standard displacement was 23,500 tons, and 27,800 tons fully loaded. Length was 232.5 metres, ship width 30.05 metres, and deck width was 26.00 metres. The flight deck was partially armoured with 76mm plate.

Weaponry included six 135/45mm cannon, twelve 65/64mm AA cannon, and 82 20/65mm anti-aircraft guns. It was intended that ten aircraft would be anchored on the flight deck, twenty-six would be tied to the hangar deck, and fifteen more would be suspended from the hangar ceiling, thus saving space. This would mean fifty-one aircraft embarked altogether.

Several aircraft were investigated for carrier trials during 1942 and 1943. German instructors, who had worked on the *Graf Zeppelin*, arrived in March 1943 at Perugia to train potential carrier airmen and advise in the testing of suitable aircraft types. All flight tests, including braked deck landings, were land-based. Junkers Ju 87C and Arado 96B types were delivered by the Germans for trials, and the Italians supplied the SAIMAN 200, Fiat G 50bis, and Reggiane Re 2001. The Fiat was intended for deck-training, with the Reggiane as the standard carrier fighter.

The Germans considered the latter to have slightly better potential than its counterpart, the Messerschmitt Bf 109T. In the event the Fiats were not considered suitable, being under-powered, and only ten Re 2001s were converted for carrier use. They received a tail hook, RTG naval radio equipment, bombracks for 650kg of bombs, and two 12.7mm SAFAT guns on the cowling with 350rpg. A specifically naval version with wing folding was to have been developed. Trainee pilots were selected from 160 Gruppo C.T.

From November 1942 an additional carrier was planned. The passenger liner *Augustus* was readied for conversion to the escort carrier *Sparviero* (Hawk). Smaller and slower at 18 knots than the *Aquila*, work began to create a flight deck without an island. She kept much of her original structure, was to have had six 6 inch and four 4 inch guns, plus several AA guns. In the event, she was captured by the Germans the day after the Armistice before work was complete, and was sunk by them at the entrance to the port of Genova.

165 Below: A CMASA RS 14 Series 2 with maintenance personnel crawling all over it. What may be a Donald Duck insigne can be just made out on the fin which indicate ownership by 287ª Squadriglia and that the location is Cagliari-Elmas

ANTI-SHIPPING OPERATIONS
Aircraft, ships and heroes

Most of the combatant airforces of World War Two tended to highlight the successes of their fighter pilots, using their scores as morale boosters to the general public and armed forces alike. In Italy, however, equal publicity was given to the torpedo bomber crews whose names were as well known as the fighter pilots, if not more so.

Such was the success of these intrepid crews that the Germans sent their torpedo crews for training in Italy, for future use against both Mediterranean convoys as well as Arctic convoys. The Germans also used the potent Italian Whitehead (Fiume) torpedoes as standard. Thus even Luftwaffe torpedo successes in the Mediterranean could be attributed to Italian equipment.

The first experimental unit was formed in August 1940, and with minimal training was rushed straight into action with just five aircraft. The unit tested and developed tactical ideas in combat, and eventually became 278 Squadriglia. From this small nucleus and two further training units evolved several independent squadriglie, which by 1942 had expanded into several Gruppi. Such was the urgent need for this proven method of attack, that two whole Stormi were converted from level bombing to torpedo-bombing and put into action with very little training. As a result, one of them, 36 Stormo, was virtually annihilated in one day (27 September 1941). The Malta-bound supply convoy air battles were among the fiercest of the war, with, for example, the Italians losing 50 aircraft and 176 aircrew during the PEDESTAL

166 Above: The Savoia Marchetti SM 79, number '6' of Maggiore Vincenzo Dequal of the Reparto Sperimentale Aerosiluranti (278ª Squadriglia from 3 September 1940). Using this aircraft Capitano Massimiliano Erasi torpedoed the Royal Navy cruiser, HMS Liverpool, in the bows on the evening of 14 October 1940

convoy attacks alone. Success rates changed from 8 hits for every aircraft lost in 1941-42 to one hit for every 2.5 aircraft lost in 1943.

The main aircraft used were the SM 79 and SM 84, both equipped to carry two torpedoes, although it was found to be more efficient to carry just one, fitted slightly off-centre under the fuselage. Initially launching was by visual sight, but then a special viewfinder was developed which enhanced the chances of a successful strike. The crews did not like the SM 84 mainly due to its weak engines, and most units eventually re-equipped with 'Il Gobbo' (the Humpback) as the reliable SM 79 was nicknamed.

Italy's highest award, the *Medaglie d'Oro al Valor Militare*, (The Gold Medal for Military Valour)was granted to 29 torpedo crew members, all but three post-humously. The recipients are shown in the accompanying table.

Listed overleaf are the ships known to have been claimed sunk or damaged by the Regia Aeronautica, where most entries tally with the Royal Navy records. Locations often differ between reports, and due to a lack of records and the inherent difficulties in cross-referencing losses and claims, some claims have been omitted, while others have been included where probable. It is especially difficult if the unknown ships are not British or American. Torpedo hits have only been noted where they have been confirmed by sources such as the Royal Navy. It is interesting to note that only one warship, the destroyer, HMS *Quentin*, was sunk outright by Italian torpedo-bombers, but a significant number were put out of action when most needed.

The Aerosilurante Gold Medal Winners

Name	Rank	Position	Unit
Silvio Angelucci	Tenente	pilot	105 Gruppo
Domenico Baffigo	Capitano	naval observer	36 Stormo/279 Squadriglia
Riccardo Balagna	Sergente Maggiore	radio-operator	279 Squadriglia
Carlo Emanuelle Buscaglia	Maggiore	pilot	281Squadriglia
Vittorio Cannaviello	Tenente Colonello	pilot	2 NAS
Franco Cappa	Tenente	pilot	280 Squadriglia
Giuseppe Cimicchi *	Capitano	pilot	281 Squadriglia
Giorgio Compiani	Sergente Maggiore	pilot	253 Squadriglia
Pietro Dona Delle Rose	Sottotenente	pilot	283 Squadriglia
Francesco Di Bella *	Capitano	pilot	3 NAS
Massimiliano Erasi	Maggiore	pilot	284 Squadriglia
Giovanni Farina	Colonello	pilot	36 Stormo
Antonio Forni	Tenente	naval observer	283 Squadriglia
Aldo Forzinetti	Sottotenente	pilot	281 Squadriglia
Goffredo Gastaldi	Maggiore	pilot	259 Squadriglia
Giulio Cesare Graziani *	Tenente	pilot	130 Gruppo
Mario Ingrellini	Tenente	pilot	253 Squadriglia
Francesco Maiore	Aviere	photographer	132 Gruppo
Urbano Mancini	Capitano	pilot	105 Gruppo
Carlo Pfister	Sottotenente	pilot	132 Gruppo
Alfonso Rotolo	Capitano	pilot	257 Squadriglia
Luigi Rovelli	Tenente	pilot	281 Squadriglia
Riccardo Seidl	Colonello	pilot	109 Gruppo
Lelio Silva	Tenente	pilot	2 NAS
Vito Sinisi	Maresciallo	gunner	279 Squadriglia
Bartolomeo Tomasino	Capitano	pilot	36 Stormo
Mario Turba	Maggiore	pilot	109 Gruppo
Antonio Vellere	Sottotenente	pilot	130 Gruppo
Giusellino Verna	Capitano	pilot	36 Stormo
Achille Zezon	Sottotenente	pilot	

* survived

Allied Shipping Casualties

Date	Ship	Type	Flag	Location	Result	Responsible RA Unit
1940						
9 Jul	Eagle	carrier	RN		bombed near misses	high level SM 79s
9 Jul	Warspite	battleship	RN		bombed near misses	high level SM 79s
17 Jul	Havock	destroyer	RN		bombed near misses	high level SM 81s
17 Sep	Kent	cruiser	RN	north east of Sollum	torpedoed damaged	278 Sq
14 Oct	Liverpool	cruiser	RN	33°58"N 26°23"E	torpedoed damaged	278 Sq
13 Nov	?	merchant	?	32°5"N 28°45"E	torpedoed sunk	278 Sq
3 Dec	Glasgow	cruiser	RN	Suda Bay	torpedoed damaged	278Sq
1941						
24 Mar	Marie Maersk	tanker	?	south of Crete	damaged	34 Gr/281 Sq
2 Apr	Homefield	merchant	UK	south of Crete	bombed sunk	39 Stormo/34 Gruppo
4 Apr	Susanna	merchant	Greek	off Corfu	sunk	34 Gr
6 Apr	Viking	merchant	Greek	off Piraeus	sunk	34 Gr

Allied Shipping Casualties

Date	Ship	Type	Flag	Location	Result	Responsible RA Unit
18 Apr	British Science	merchant	UK	36°6"N 24°0"E	torpedoed sunk	281 Sq
21 Apr	British Lord	oiler	UK	33°56"N 24°18"E	torpedoed damaged	281 Sq
8 May	Rawnsley	motorship	RN?	34°55"N 25°46"E	torpedoed sunk	281 Sq
21 May	Juno	destroyer	RN	Caso Canal	sunk	30 Gr
27 May	Imperial	destroyer	RN	south of Crete	damaged	41 Gr
23 Jul	Fury	destroyer	RN	off Cap Bon	torpedoed damaged	278/280/283 Sq
23 Jul	Firedrake	destroyer	RN	off Cap Bon	torpedoed damaged	278/280/283 Sq
23 Jul	Wivern	destroyer	RN	off Cap Bon	torpedoed damaged	278/280/283 Sq
23 Jul	Manchester	cruiser	RN	37°46"N 8°10"E	torpedoed damaged	280/283 Sq
23 Jul	Fearless	destroyer	RN	37°46"N 8°10"E	torpedoed scuttled	280/283 Sq
24 Jul	Hoegh Hood	merchant	Norwegian	off Algeria	torpedoed damaged	278 Sq
3 Aug	Escaut	merchant	Belgian	off Port Suez	sunk	281 Sq
3 Aug	Desmoulea	merchant	UK	off Port Suez	torpedoed damaged	281 Sq
3 Aug	Alexandre Andre	merchant	Belgian	south of Port Suez	torpedoed damaged	281 Sq
11 Aug	Protector	net layer	UK	31°42"N 32°4"E	torpedoed damaged	281 Sq
20 Aug	Turbo	merchant	UK	32°08"N 31°57"E	torpedoed damaged	281 Sq
27 Aug	Phoebe	cruiser	RN	north of Bardia	torpedoed damaged	279 Sq
27 Sep	Nelson	battleship	RN	37°45"N 9°2"E	torpedoed damaged	257 Sq
27 Sep	Imperial Star	merchant	UK	37°31"N 10°46"E	scuttled	36 Stormo
24 Oct	Empire Guillemot	merchant	UK	west of La Galite	sunk	280/283 Sq
25 Oct	Latona	minelayer	RN	Tobruk	torpedoed damaged	279 Sq
14 Nov	Empire Pelican	merchant	UK	south of La Galite	sunk	130 Gr
15 Nov	Empire Defender	merchant	UK	south of La Galite	sunk	256 Sq
1 Dec	Jackal	destroyer	RN	north of Tobruk	torpedoed damaged	279 Sq
5 Dec	Chakdina	auxiliary	?	near Tobruk	torpedoed sunk	284 Sq
28 Dec	Volo	merchant	UK	32°10"N 25°10"E	torpedoed sunk	281 Sq
1942						
15 Jan	Frandale	destroyer	?	31°50"N 6°18"E	torpedoed damaged	205 Sq
19 Jan	?5000ton	merchant	?	31°50"N 27°0"E	torpedoed sunk	205 Sq
15 Feb	Jervis type	destroyer	RN	32°0"N 26°10"E	torpedoed damaged	205 Sq
22 Mar	?	destroyer	Greek	33°20"N 18°30"E	torpedoed damaged	130 Gr
20 Apr	?	merchant	?	31°56"N 31°12"E	torpedoed damaged	205 Sq
14 Jun	Birmingham	cruiser	RN	?	damaged	combined with Luftwaffe
14 Jun	Kentucky	merchant	?	?	torpedoed sunk	130 Gr/283 Sq
14 Jun	Burdwan	merchant	?	?	torpedoed sunk	130 Gr/283 Sq
14 Jun	Buthan	merchant	?	?	sunk	104 Gr
14 Jun	Liverpool	cruiser	RN	37°55"N 7°37"E	torpedoed damaged	252/253/3 NAS
14 Jun	Tanimbar	merchant	Dutch	36°58"N 7°30"E	sunk	130 Gr/283 Sq
15 Jun	Bedouin	destroyer	RN	36°12"N 11°38"E	torpedoed sunk while in tow	281 Sq
15 Jun	Nestor	destroyer	RAN	?	sunk	279 Sq
15 Jun	Malaya	battleship	RN		torpedoed damaged	132 Gr
15 Jun	Argus	carrier	RN		torpedoed damaged	132 Gr
30 Jun	Aircrest	merchant	UK	31°49"N 34°34"E	torpedoed sunk	205 Sq
4 Jul	?5000ton	merchant	?	31°40"N 32°10"E	torpedoed damaged	252 Sq
22 Jul	?10000ton	merchant	?	north east of Port Said	torpedoed sunk	205 Sq
12 Aug	Victorious	carrier	RN		hit by unexploded bomb	Re2001GVs of 22 Gruppo
12 Aug	Clan Ferguson	merchant	UK	north of Zembra Island	sunk	89/105/130/132 Gr/2 NAS
12 Aug	Brisbane Star	merchant	UK	Skerki Channel	sunk	3 NAS with Luftwaffe
12 Aug	Deucalion	merchant	UK	37°56"N 8°40"E	sunk	89/105/130/132 Gr/2 NAS
12 Aug	Foresight	destroyer	RN	37°45"N 9°0"E	torpedoed scuttled	89/105/130/132 Gr/2 NAS
13 Aug	Ohio	merchant	UK	Skerki Channel	torpedoed damaged	89/105/130/132 Gr/2 NAS
13 Aug	Empire Hope	merchant	UK		torpedoed damaged	89/105/130/132 Gr/2 NAS

Allied Shipping Casualties

Date	Ship	Type	Flag	Location	Result	Responsible RA Unit
14 Sep	Zulu	destroyer	RN	Tobruk	bombed sunk	MC200s of 82 Sq
25 Sep	Karlshamn	merchant	Swedish	Red Sea	damaged	
19 Oct	Scalaria	merchant	UK	Red Sea	torpedoed beached	
11 Nov	Awatea	merchant	US	Bougie	torpedoed sunk	278 Sq
11 Nov	Chatay	merchant	US	Bougie	torpedoed sunk	278 Sq
12 Nov	Leander type	cruiser	RN	Bougie	torpedoed damaged	130 Gr
12 Nov	?	merchant	?	Bougie	torpedoed damaged	132 Gr
18 Nov	Arethusa	cruiser	RN	33°36"N 20°44"E	torpedoed damaged	combined with Luftwaffe
23 Nov	Scythia	merchant	UK	off Algiers	damaged	280/283 Sq with Luftwaffe
24 Nov	Trentbank	merchant	UK	north of Cap Tenes	sunk	280 Sq with Luftwaffe
28 Nov	Selbo	merchant	Norwegian	off Cap Cavello	sunk	132 Gr with Luftwaffe
2 Dec	Quentin	destroyer	RN	37°32"N 8°32"E	torpedoed sunk	130 Gr
9 Dec	Marigold	corvette	RN	36°50"N 3°0"E	torpedoed sunk	105 Gr with Luftwaffe
9 Dec	Mascot	merchant	French	north east of Cap Bon	sunk	105 Gr with Luftwaffe
22 Dec	Cameronia	merchant	UK	37°3"N 5°24"E	torpedoed sunk	130 Gr

1943

Date	Ship	Type	Flag	Location	Result	Responsible RA Unit
7 Jan	Ville de Strasbourg	merchant	French	off Algiers	torpedoed damaged	combined with Luftwaffe
7 Jan	Benalbanach	merchant	UK		sunk	combined with Luftwaffe
7 Jan	Akabahra	merchant	Norwegian	37°7"N 4°38"E	sunk	combined with Luftwaffe
7 Jan	William Wirt	merchant	USA		damaged	combined with Luftwaffe
8 Jan	Acute	minesweeper	RN	off Bone	torpedoed damaged	combined with Luftwaffe
20 Jan	Walt Whitman	merchant	USA	36°55"N 3°7"E	damaged	combined with Luftwaffe
21 Jan	Ocean Rider	merchant	UK	west of Cap Caxine	damaged	combined with Luftwaffe
29 Jan	Avonvale	destroyer	RN	north of Bougie	torpedoed damaged	130/132/105 Gr withLuft.
6 Feb	Fort Babine	merchant	UK	36°15"N 0°15"E	damaged	combined with Luftwaffe
6 Feb	Louisburg	corvette	Canada	north east of Oran	torpedoed sunk	combined with Luftwaffe
21 Mar	Windsor Castle	merchant	UK	37°28"N1°10"E	sunk	combined with Luftwaffe
22 Mar	Garonne	merchant	Norwegian	Oran Bay	torpedoed damaged	105 Gr
26 Mar	Prins Willem III	merchant	Dutch	37°0"N 2°14"E	sunk	89/105 Gr
27 Mar	Empire Rowan	merchant	UK	37°16"N 6°54"E	beached	89/105 Gr
19 May	British Trust	merchant	UK	32°40"N 19°53"E	torpedoed sunk	89 Gr
9 Jun	Stureborg	merchant	Swedish	north of Alexandria	sunk	combined with Luftwaffe
16 Jun	?10000ton	merchant	?	off Algiers	torpedoed damaged	89 Gr
20 Jun	?5000ton	merchant	?	near Capo de Garde	torpedoed damaged	RSA
20 Jun	?10000ton	merchant	?	near Capo de Garde	torpedoed sunk	RSA
9 Jul	?15000ton	merchant	?	east of Capo de Fer	torpedoed damaged	RSA
10 Jul	?10000ton	merchant	?	north of Capo de Garde	torpedoed damaged	130 Gr
16 Jul	Indomitable	carrier	RN	near Capo Passero	torpedoed damaged	130 Gr/ RSA
24 Jul	?15000ton	merchant	?	off Sicily	torpedoed sunk	RSA
10 Aug	?6000ton	merchant	?	bay of Sicily	torpedoed damaged	RSA
16 Aug	Empire Kestrel	merchant	UK	west of Capo Bougaroni	torpedoed sunk	132 Gr

167: *The fin and rudder of a CMASA RS 14 Series 2 adorned with the Donald Duck emblem of the 287ª Squadriglia R.M. At least two similar other machines can be seen in the background, along with a CRDA Cant Z.506B. The RS 14s are from the 146ª Squadriglia R.M. which indicates that the location is Cagliari-Elmas, Sardinia, in summer 1941 when both Squadriglie were based there. In the absence of radar or Ultra decrypts, the precursor to many Italian bombing raids or torpedo strikes was reconnaissance by aircraft such as these*

168: *A familiar destination for many Italian airmen between 1940 and 1943 was Valletta, Malta, and its harbours. Here Ju 87s have hit naval stores on Manoel Island*

169: *Such raids were not without losses. Here SM 79 195-6 of the 195ª Squadriglia goes down in flames over Valletta Grand Harbour on 10 July 1940. Shot down by F/O Eric Taylor of 261 Squadron RAF in a Hurricane, the whole crew of* Sottotenente *Felice Filippi, Sergente Maggiore Muatori, 1° Aviere Serafini and Aviere Scelto Ottavini were all killed*

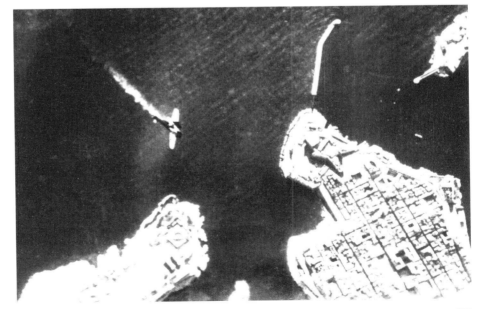

170: *Armourers readying one of the lethal Whitehead Fiume torpedoes which constituted the striking power of the RA torpedo-bombers. 450mm in diameter, 5.46 metres long and with a weight of 876 kg, it was a formidable weapon*

171: *A typical scene at an Aerosilurante base. A torpedo being loaded under a Savoia Marchetti SM 79 while a crewman looks on. The oil dripping from the engine probably did little for the life of the tyre*

172: *Taken from the co-pilot's seat of an SM 79 this shows how close the bomber formations flew on their way to the target*

173: *Taken during one of the attacks on the 'Pedestal' convoy of August 1942, this shows SM 79Sil torpedo bombers of one of the ten Squadriglie which took part in the action in action*

174: *Two views taken by a very cool photographer aboard one of the ships of the taking part in 'Operation Pedestal' of a Savoia Marchetti SM 79 maneouvring to launch its torpedo. These were very low level attacks*

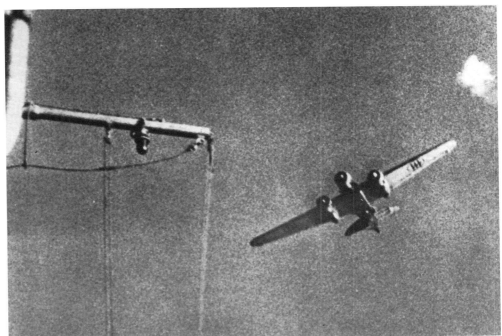

175: *In this view it can be seen that the SM 79 is an early model still with the underfuselage gondola for the bomb aimer. When the aircraft was being used as a torpedo bomber he was redundant as it was the pilot who aimed the aircraft*

176: *Tentatively identified as the British freighter* Empire Guillemot *which was caught and sunk by torpedo bombers in the Mediterranean on 24 October 1941 while travelling alone, the vessel seen here is being overflown by an SM 79. The aircraft which claimed the freighter were, in fact, SM 84s from 256ᵃ and 258ᵃ Squadriglie, so this is probably another, still unidentified, ship*

177 Left: *This is believed to be the Royal Navy destroyer HMS* Bedouin *sinking on 15 June 1943 after being torpedoed by an SM 79Sil (MM 23942) of 281ᵃ Squadriglia flown by Sottotenente Martino Aichner. The ship had previously been seriously damaged by gunfire from two Italian cruisers, but still managed to shoot down the bomber before sinking. 209 of her crew—and the Italian airmen—were rescued*

178 Below: *Junkers Ju 87R-1s from 97° Gruppo returning from a strike against Malta—note the empty under-fuselage bomb crutches hanging free*

179 Right: *The wooden SM 79 floated well. This one from 34° (sic) Stormo B.T. was photographed by a Saro London of 202 Squadron on 21 July 1940 after the bomber had ditched some 35 miles off the coast following a raid on Malta. The crew were picked up by their own side*

180 Below: *An unidentified Savoia Marchetti SM 84 shows off its leaner lines compared to the SM 79. Note the strange projecting windscreens and the counter weight to the Scotti 12.7mm gun in the Delta E turret. The roller blind to the waist position is of interest*

181 Right: *An all-green SM 84 being serviced on a Sicilian airfield*

182 Overleaf top: *Mechanics working on the Piaggio P.XI bis RC.40 engines of an SM 84. There appears to be a loose panel or flapping camouflage net under the wing. This aircraft is finished in dark green with yellow engine cowlings*

183 Overleaf below: *An SM 84 with a three-tone camouflage scheme. Note the white stripes on the propeller blades and the fuel dump pipe (?) at the wing root*

AIRMEN
Training and ranks

In the early stages of the war Italian airmen were generally well-trained, fighter pilots in particular excelling in aerobatics and the general handling of their aircraft. This led to a tendency for them to become involved in dogfights, where the good manoeuvrability of their aircraft came to the fore. Unfortunately for Italian pilots, this ability was often of little use against opponents whose faster aircraft and newer tactics allowed them to carry out single-pass diving attacks, hitting the Italians hard with their heavier firepower, before making a high-speed dive and escape. To a degree there is also the question of national tememperament. Like most young pilots of the time, Italians viewed flying as a great adventure. A natural excitability tended to counter true aggression, although when flying a competent aircraft the Italian pilot was as good as any combatant. For example, RAF fighter ace and later test pilot, Neville Duke (28 kills), commented in his book, *Test Pilot* , that the Italian fighter pilots he came across usually fought well—in particular those flying the MC 202. Australian ace Clive 'Killer' Caldwell, who fought German, Italian, and Japanese opponents, declared after the war that the MC 202 was "one of the best and most underrated fighters". Italian pilots in East Africa

184 Above: The crew of a Breda 88 demonstrate their cramped accommodation. Note the guard rail to prevent the gunner shooting his own aircraft. Location may be Guidonia in summer 1940, as just visible in the background is a French Aéronavale Loire-Nieuport LN 411 dive bomber which was tested there after force-landing on Sardinia in June

were regarded as particularly tenacious, as well as being extremely chivalrous. The crews of SM 79s, Macchis, and Messerschmitts could be notably dangerous.

The Regia Aeronautica lost over 5,700 casualties during the war, together with nearly 10,000 taken prisoner. They claimed 4,586 aircraft shot down or destroyed on the ground, but lost 5,200 in return. Even with the overclaiming typical of all combatants, this is a reasonable achievement, given the deficiencies in equipment and organisation which bedevilled the Italian airmen.

Italian aircrew came from a background where the majority of the population were peasants or workers, the national income was a quarter of that of France or Britain, and the people were generally less healthy and less educated than their contemporaries in other countries. Arguably, by the outbreak of war, even Russian soldiers were more familiar with modern technology than the average Italian. In society there was a great void between the upper classes and the rest, and this spilled over into the command structures and operational efficiency. There were also, and to some extent still are, great differences in skills and attitudes between the industrialised north of Italy and the predominantly agricultural south. Added to this was widespread corruption in industry and lethargy in command, and the failure by the high command, led by *Il Duce*, to plan for a longer term war. Despite all this, there was never a shortage of eager volunteers, and even the Germans were impressed by the ability of young aircrew to quickly adapt to new equipment and aircraft. Some evidence for this comes from the Luftwaffe who began training Italian pilots to fly both the Messerschmitt Me 163 and Me 262. When well equipped and well led the crews of the Regia Aeronautica were competent foes.

Training

It has to be said that, in general, the Italian pilot was not well served by the system intended to teach him his craft. While aircraft handling skills (in clear weather) were well covered, the necessary training in tactics which enable a pilot to become more than an aerial chauffeur, was mostly unstructured, being left largely to individual units. This led to wide variations in tactical skills and made co-ordinated operational planning more difficult than it should have been.

After completing his initial military training, the new recruit faced basic flight training. For the prospective fighter pilot, for example, this consisted of around 30 hours on the Breda 25, followed by 25 hours on the Ro 41 biplane fighter trainer, depending on the individual ability of the recruit. These aircraft were supplemented by the Avia FL3 and SAIMAN 202 from October 1940. A certificate was issued after nine months. Progress was then made to advanced training, which consisted of over 50 hours on obsolete fighters such as the Fiat CR 30 and CR 32, and 10 hours of aerobatics on the Caproni 164. By the middle of 1941 instrument training was introduced, with 5 hours on the SAIMAN 202. The following year the course was extended by 20 hours, and CR 42s, Nardi FN 305s, G 50s, and MC 200s were added as they became available. The latter two types were only released when it became almost impossible to use them on the front line, and then they were mostly war-weary machines. Finally, the crews were passed to the operational units for their last stage of training. This was in the hands of the unit leaders who expected them to complete over 30 to 50 hours of aerobatics, and an intensive series of simulated combat situations (Finta Caccia). There was no common training on tactics—this was left to unit leaders and depended upon their operational experience. Gunnery training was brief in the extreme, with a short excursion to strafe targets on the ground, and a flight or two to shoot at free floating balloons! Deflection shooting was not covered. The first time pilots fired their guns at a target was often in their first combat. Even with the later extended training periods, the Italian pilot only flew just over half the required time for Allied pilots before joining operations. Like the Germans, the aircrew flew for long periods with little or no leave.

Despite this, there were very few occasions that caused them not to enter combat. Poor supply organisation and the resulting low serviceability of aircraft and ground systems, frequently frustrated efforts to carry out operations as often as was required. Shortage of spares was so bad, even by 1941, that, for example, it prompted several demands from the RA commander in Sicily to his units to ensure that delays on take-off be reduced from over one hour to the officially permitted twenty minutes, and that unserviceable aircraft be worked on urgently instead of being left unattended. One assumes that the ground crew would have complied, had they had the necessary components. This situation caused a severe lack of success in operations against the Malta convoys, even with good initial planning. Even so, morale remained relatively high right through to the surrender, despite the periodic retreats.

One of the most important factors in their lack of tactical success was the poor co-operation between the German and Italian high commands. There was never a standard system for both Axis partners, in control or communications. Signal codes and such items as weather reports, where obtainable, were not shared, indeed were often kept secret from each other. Distrust and a 'superior' attitude by the Germans resulted in a typically Italian response of excessive administration which slowed down the resolution of even minor problems.

In combat, however, German bomber crews were often pleased to see Italian fighter escorts, as they would usually defend the bombers—against all odds if necessary. Co-operation at ground level in the lower ranks, between the fighting airmen of both countries, was generally quite good. After all, they lived and died under the same conditions, be it Russia, Africa, or Sicily. Italian officers and NCOs, however, were segregated in much the same way as in the RAF, which sometimes caused a lack of cohesion and aloofness in crew procedures.

As mentioned earlier, there was never a shortage of trainee aircrew, although lack of fuel and first-line trainers meant a slow and diminishing flow of replacements. There are many comments recorded on the keenness of these inadequately trained young men, many as young as eighteen years old, but there was always a problem in giving them a proper initiation into combat with the limited number of aircraft available. For example, on 14 May 1943, 160 Gruppo had 39 pilots available, but only five operational Re 2001s.

Accustomed to the the generally fine weather over the Mediterranean, Africa and Spain, the RA neglected navigational and instrument training, particularly for fighter pilots. The result was obvious over England in 1940, when those who did not get lost in bad weather were badly mauled by the RAF. On the other hand, maritime and desert navigation skills were quite good, especially with the experienced colonial crews. As with the RAF, the most innovative crews came to form the backbone of the bomber arm, following their bombing experiments in the 1920s and 1930s in colonial territories.

Lack of radio communications was a major handicap, and one of the great failures of planning by the Italian high command and industry. Initially, most aircraft had no radio and when they did start to receive them—in late 1940 and early 1941— the slow-timing beacons and receiver/transmitter interference were never completely cured. This was especially disastrous when trying to intercept raids on the home territories, day or night. Lack of resources and finance was the root cause of this, despite the inventive minds of the best Italian engineers.

From mid-1942, with German assistance and newer equipment, the Italians became more aggressive, even in the retreat following the Alamein battles. Naturally, when the Allies were pressing in on their homeland they responded with vigour within their limited means, especially when equipped with the new generation fighters. Despite heavy losses on the ground thanks to enemy superiority in numbers and poor warning systems, the Allied tide was temporarily stemmed on occasions.

To most combatant countries the main hero of the air force was the fighter pilot. In Italy, however, just as famous as the fighter pilots, if not more so, were the heroes from the torpedo-bomber units. These flew with skill and nerve through ever- increasing defences. Among the most celebrated were *Maggiore* Carlo Buscaglia, *Generale* Guilio Graziani, and *Colonello* Giovanni Farina. Only three out of the 29 top medal winners from the Aerosilurante survived the war. Their achievements rank with the best of the equivalent combatant arms from any other nation in the war. In over two years (April 1941 to June 1943) they sank or badly damaged at least 44 major merchant and warships, plus an unknown quantity in co-operation with German aircraft. They were also very successful against coastal units.

Although officially all victory claims were allotted to the parent unit (a similar system was operated by the Hungarians) individual pilots and crews would still keep their own records. Thus, scores can be occasionally found painted on aircraft in the fashion followed by other nations.

Ranks

The Regia Aeronautica rank structure was generally similar to the RAF, with most aircrew made up of Officers and NCOs. Pilots could be of any rank, based on their experience and qualifications. The other crew members were known as *specialisti* —specialists. Promotion was slow, even in depleted units. In an echo of the nineteenth century, or perhaps just symptomatic of Mussolini's Italy, some commissions were bought. Others were earned in the field.

The table below gives a comparable chart of the aircrew ranks of the major competing air forces involved with or against the Italians. Each nation's system had its own idiosyncracies. In particular, the level of responsibility for personnel and equipment given to individual ranks could vary widely, so this table can only be an approximation of the 'similar' ranks.

RA	RAF	LUFTWAFFE	USAAF	SAAF	ARMÉE DE L'AIR	YUGOSLAV JRKV	GREEK EVA	RUSSIAN VVS
Colonnello	Group Captain	Oberst	Colonel	Colonel	Colonel	Pukovnik	Sminarchos	Polkovnik
Tenente Colonnello	Wing Commander	Oberstleutnant	Lieutenant Colonel	Lieutenant Colonel	Lieutenant Colonel	Podpukovnik	Antisminarchos	Podpolkovnik
Maggiore	Squadron Leader	Major	Major	Major	Commandant	Major	Episminagos	Major
1ª Capitano	Flight Lieutenant	Hauptmann	Captain	Captain	Capitaine	Kapetan I Klase	Sminagos	Kapitan
Capitano						Kapetan II Klase		
1ª Tenente	Flying Officer	Oberleutnant	1st Lieutenant	Lieutenant	Lieutenant	Porucnik	Yposminargos	Starshiy Leytenant
Tenente						Leytenant		
Sottotenente	Pilot Officer	Leutnant	2nd Lieutenant	2nd Lieutenant	Sous Lieutenant	Podporucnik	Anthyposminarchos	Mladshiy Leytenant
Aiutante di Battaglia					Adjudant Chef		Archisminias	
Maresciallo Maggiore	Warrant Officer		Chief Warrant Officer		Adjudant			
Maresciallo Capo								
Maresciallo Ordinaire		Stabsfeldwebel	Warrant Officer					Starshina
Sergent Maggiore	Flight Sergeant	Oberfeldwebel	Master Sergeant		Sergent Chef	Narednik vodnik	Episminias	
		Feldwebel	1st Sergeant			Narednik		Starshiy Serzhant
Sergent	Sergeant	Unterfeldwebel	Technical Sergeant	Air Sergeant		Podnarednik	Sminias	Serzhant
			Staff Sergeant					Mladshiy Serzhant
Primo Aviere	Leading Aircraftman		Sergeant					
		Unteroffizier				Kaplar		Yefreytor
		Hauptgefreiter						
	Aircraftman 1st Class	Obergefreiter						
		Gefreiter						
Aviere	Aircraftman 2nd Class	Flieger				Redov	Sminitis	Krasnoarmeyets

185: Pilots gather around a hangar full of Breda 25s at the training school at Falconara. Large numbers of these aircraft served for both primary and basic training (such as it was) in the largely unstructured syllabus utilised by the Regia Aeronautica. Up to a hundred may have been used at Falconara alone. The ones seen here have dispensed with the Townend rings to their engines

186: A lineup of IMAM Ro 41s from the Scuolo 2° Periodo (intermediate flying training school) at Perugia. The Ro 41, originally conceived as a fighter to compete with the Fiat CR 32, served as the standard advanced and fighter trainer for virtually all pilots of the Regia Aeronautica. It was customary for training aircraft to carry an abbreviation of the name of the base from which the school operated in large letters on the fuelage. Here 'PER'. Individual aircraft within the school were given numbers

187: As in all air forces, war-weary and obsolescent types were pressed into service as advanced trainers. This is an IMAM Ro 37bis belonging to a Gruppo Complementare (operational training unit) and used for refresher or supplementary specialist training

188: *The Caproni Ca 310 and its variants was the aircraft of choice for the bomber schools, but many were sent to operaional observation and light bomber squadrons. This Ca 311 is serving its intended purpose with the Scuola Osservazione Aerea at Cerveteri. It may have served previously with an operational squadron as there are the vestiges of a red(?) number on the rear fuselage*

189: *Some kind of ceremony involving Caproni Ca 316 floatplanes of the Scuola Osservazione Marittima at Orbetello. Intended for use as a catapult launched reconnaissance machine for the Italian navy, only fourteen were built. Most seem to have ended up at Orbetello in 1942-1943. Of interest is the Heinkel He 115 floatplane of the Luftwaffe in the far background*

190: *It was rare to find capable operational types in use with Italian trainig schools, but here is a CRDA Cant Z.506B with the Scuola Osservazione Maritima at Pola. Finish is still the pre-war silver with a red lightning flash with the addition of the white rudder cross introduced in late 1940 and the abbreviated school name*

191 Above: *Seen at Istres in February 1943, this ex-French Dewoitine D.520 has been partly repainted in Italian colours, probably for use as an advanced fighter trainer, as indicated by the white bands. In view of the RA's dire shortage of aircraft, however, several Gruppi used them operationally as fighters.*

192 Left: *Another Dewoitine D.520 at Istres in February 1943. The aircraft has received a quick coat of paint over the Vichy French red and yellow stripes on the nose and tail, and white training bands.*

193 Left: *The unit signwriter putting the finishing touches to a rare personal marking on the nose of a Macchi MC 202. 'Go, Banana' was the aircraft of ace Maggiore Eunio Tarantola of the 151ᵃ Squadriglia, 20° Gruppo, 51° Stormo and refers to his pre-war occupation as an importer of bananas. The aircraft is finished in the standard Macchi D3 'smoke rings' pattern using Nocciola Chiaro 4 and Verde Oliva Scuro 2*

FIGHTER ACES
The top scorers

Through most of the war the Regia Aeronautica high command frowned upon individual achievements, preferring to note successes as joint results by the unit— "a result from the combined action of many other pilots". The idea was to prevent loss of morale by less able pilots and crews. Individual pilots were allowed to note their claims in their personal logbooks but the claims were officially credited to their units. By March 1943, because of the changing fortunes in the air war and a desperate need to encourage the surviving aircrews, officialdom had changed its mind, and actively encouraged individual claims; even offering a bonus scheme for successes. 5,000 Lire was awarded for a single or twin engined aircraft shot down; 15,000 Lire for a four engined aircraft; 150,000 Lire for a merchant vessel sunk and 250,000 Lire for a warship sunk. All claims had to be witnessed.

In total, men of the Regia Aeronautica were awarded 85 Gold Medals (*Medaglio d'Oro*), 1838 Silver Medals (*Medaglia d'Argento*), 2059 Bronze Medals (*Medaglia di Bronzo*), and 1809 War Crosses (*Le Croci di Guerra*). The Gold Medal was awarded only for exceptional bravery and was highly prized.

The top scoring fighter aces, as far as is known, for the period 10 June 1940 to 8 September 1943 are listed as follows, courtesy of Gregory Alegi and Giovanni Massimello. This list is by no means definitive, but it is the most complete published to date, although logbooks are being recovered currently which will probably alter the rankings. For example, Adriano Visconti had previously been listed as the third highest scorer with 19 RA kills plus 7 ANR. His recently discovered logbooks, however, show only 6 and 4 respectively.

---

194 Above: Tenente *Marchi Vicino of the 72ª Squadriglia, 17° Gruppo, 1° Stormo, admires his new Macchi MC 205 Veltro, most likely in Sicily in January-February 1943. The aircraft is clearly brand new. The first operations the unit undertook after conversion training were escort missions in support of the forces evacuating from Tunisia*

195 Page 218: CRDA Cant Z.1007bis of the 95° Gruppo in cose formation. The yellow engine cowlings are Balkan theatre markings and probably indicate that the date is early summer 1941. This was when the Gruppo was converting to the Z.1007 while operating briefly over Greece and Crete

Name	Rank	Score	Unit	History
Martinoli, Teresio	Sergent Maggiore	22+1 with the Co-Bel*	10 Gr	KIFA 25 August 19 44
Lucchini, Franco	Capitano	21+5 in Spain	10 Gr	SDK 5 July 1943
Ferrulli, Leonardo	Sottotenente	21+1 in Spain	10 Gr	SDK 5 July 1943≠≠
Bordoni-Bisleri, Franco	Tenente	19	18 Gr	
Visintini, Mario	Capitano	16+1 in Spain	412 Sq	KIFA 11 February 1941
Gorrini, Luigi	Maresciallo	15+4 with the ANR**	18 Gr	WIA June 1944
Baron, Luigi	Sergent Maggiore	12	412 Sq	
Giannella, Luigi	Tenente	12	10 Gr	
Ruspoli di Poggio Suasa, Carlo Maurizio	Maggiore	11	10 Gr	
Solari di Briona, Giorgio	Tenente	11	18 Gr	
Solaro, Claudio	Capitano	10 + 1 in Spain	23 Gr	
Malvezzi, Fernando	Capitano	10	9 Gr	
Reiner, Guilio	Capitano	10	9 Gr	
Magnaghi, Carlo	Maresciallo	9+2 with the ANR	7 Gr	
Veronesi, Mario	Sergent Maggiore	9+2 with the ANR	10 Gr	
Tarantola, Ennio	Maresciallo	9+1 in Spain,+1 with ANR	20 Gr	SDW April 1944
Annoni, Emanuele	Capitano	9	9 Gr	
Barcaro, Giovanni	Tenente	9	9 Gr	
Omiccioli, Walter	Sergent Maggiore	9	7 Gr	
Benati, Amedeo	Maresciallo	8+2 with the ANR	6 Gr	
Torresi, Guilio	Capitano	8+2 with the ANR	13 Gr	
Stabile, Natalino	Sottotenente	8+1 with the ANR	6 Gr	
Mazzitelli, Orfeo	Tenente	8	22 Gr	
Soffritti, Aroldo	Maresciallo	8	412 Sq	Captured 26 April 1941
Valtancoli, Tito	Capitano	8	7 Gr	
Roberto, Giuseppe	Capitano	7+3 with the ANR	16 Gr	
Bonet, Giovanni	Capitano	7+1 with the ANR	2 Gr	
Camaioni, Antonio	Sottotenente	7+1 with the ANR	150 Gr	
Biagini, Bruno	Sergent	7	9 Gr	
Canella, Carlo	Tenente	7	412 Sq	
Canfora, Antonio	Tenente	7	9 Gr	
Daffara, Vittorino	Tenente	7	9 Gr	
Filippi, Luigi	Maggiore	7	23 Gr	
Foschini, Ettore	Tenente Colonello	7	21 Gr	
Gaucci, Roberto	Maresciallo	7	155 Gr	
Guarnaccia, Filippo	Sergent Maggiore	7	7 Gr	
Lombardo Schiappacasse, Enzo	Tenente	7	7 Gr	
Mandolini, Orlando	Tenente	7	10 Gr	
Niclot Doglio, Furio	Maggiore	7	20 Gr	SDK 27 July 1942
Nioi, Clizio	Capitano	7	17 Gr	
Oblach, Giuseppe	Tenente	7	9 Gr	
Piccolomini Clementini Adami, Ranieri	Capitano	7	10 Gr	
Salvatore, Massimo	Sergent Maggiore	7	10 Gr	
Savini, Angelo	Maresciallo	7	10 Gr	
Serafini, Ferruccio	Sergente	7	155 Gr	SDK 22 July 1943
Vanzan, Virgilio	Tenente	7	10 Gr	
Visconti, Adriano	Maggiore	6+4 with the ANR	7 Gr	Killed by partisans 29 April 1945
Filippi, Fausto	Tenente	6+2 with the ANR	150 Gr	
Bartolozzi, Osvaldo	Tenente	6	167 Gr	
Bassi, Livio	Tenente	6	154 Gr	SDW 20 February 1941
Bonfatti, Piero	Tenente	6	9 Gr	
Buvoli, Aldo	Maresciallo	6	155 Gr	SDC 23 June 1942
Celentano, Agostino	Sottotenente	6	2 Gr	
Di Bert, Cesare	Sergent Maggiore	6	2 Gr	
Mecatti, Mario	Tenente	6	10 Gr	

Name	Rank	Score	Unit	History
Montcrumici, Amleto	Sergent Maggiore	6	10 Gr	
Perdoni, Luciano	Sergent Maggiore	6	10 Gr	
Querci, Alvaro	Sottotenente	6	9 Gr	
Scarpetta, Pier Giuseppe	Maggiore	6	2 Gr	
Veronese, Alberto	Tenente	6	410 Sq	SDW 23 February 1941
Forlani, Dino	Maresciallo	5+2 with the ANR	6 Gr	
Fibbia, Guido	Maresciallo	5+1 with the ANR	18 Gr	
Biagini, Lucio	Sergent	5	22 Gr	
Bianchi, Manfredo	Sergent	5	154 Gr	
Bianchi, Pietro	Maresciallo	5	20 Gr	
Bladelli, Alessandro	Maresciallo	5	10 Gr	
Buogo, Egidio	Sergent Maggiore	5	12 Gr	
Chiarini, Guglielmo	Capitano	5	151 Gr	
Damiani, Rinaldo	Maresciallo	5	9 Gr	
Facchini, Domenico	Sergent Maggiore	5	2 Gr	
Ferazzani, Giuseppe	Tenente	5	10 Gr	
Fissore, Giuliano	Tenente	5	160 Gr	
Frigerio, Iacopo	Tenente	5	9 Gr	
Giardina, Antonio	Sergent Maggiore	5	412 Sq	
Giudice, Eber	Capitano	5	161 Gr	
Graffer, Giorgio	Capitano	5	150 Gr	SDK 28 November 1940
Guerci, Mario	Sergent Maggiore	5	9 Gr	
Longhi, Felice	Maresciallo	5	18 Gr	
Mariotti, Luigi	Maggiore	5	8 Gr	
Maurer, Sergio	Capitano	5	7 Gr	
Minguzzi, Vittorio	Maggiore	5	22 Gr	
Miotto, Elio	Sottotenente	5	10 Gr	
Ocarso, Dante	Capitano	5	6 Gr	
Omiccioli, Enzo	Sergent Maggiore	5	412 Sq	SDK 3 February 1941
Palazzeschi, Antonio	Tenente	5	6 Gr	
Pecchiari, Francesco	Sergent Maggiore	5	20 Gr	
Petrosellini, Costantino	Tenente	5	8 Gr	
Pinna, Mario	Capitano	5	23 Gr	
Pocek, Giorgio	Tenente	5	2 Gr	
Roveda, Riccardo	Maggiore	5	20 Gr	
Seganti, Carlo	Tenente	5	2 Gr	
Simionato, Olindo	Maresciallo	5	2 Gr	
Squarcia, Vittorio	Tenente	5	9 Gr	
Sterzi, Annibale	Capitano	5	2 Gr	
Torchio, Luigi	Tenente	5	377 Sq	
Tugnoli, Giorgio	Maggiore	5	23 Gr	
Zemella, Celso	Sergent Maggiore	5	23 Gr	
Cenni, Giuseppe	Tenente	2+7 in Spain	5 St	SDK 3 September 1943
Bonzano, Mario	Maggiore	2+15 in Spain	20 Gr	Final score unknown
Ricci, Corrado	Capitano	2+12 in Spain	410 Sq	
Mottet, Giuseppe	Maresciallo	2+4 in Spain	413 Sq	
Botto, Ernesto	Maggiore	1+7 in Spain	9 Gr	Final score unknown

* Co-Belligerent Italian Air Force, post-armistice   KIA: Killed in Action   SDK: Shot down, killed

** The ANR was the Fascist air arm of the post-armistice Italian Forces   WIA: Wounded in action   SDW: Shot down, wounded

KIFA: Killed in flying accident   SDC: Shot down, captured

AIRCRAFT TYPES
Thunderbolts, Hawks and Herons

Listed below are brief details on all the types used by the Regia Aeronautica in the period covered. More detailed specifications can be found in other publications. Readers are referred to the bibliography. Details of weapons, engines, and equipment can be found in the appropriate charts elsewhere in this book. Until the introduction of German-designed liquid-cooled engines, most aircraft suffered from underpowering and poor armament. Handling and controls were mostly well-harmonised, although not all pilots were unanimous in this, some even expressing reservations about the MC 200. Workmanship and build quality was almost always of a high order, possibly too good for what were, after all, expendable war machines.

F = Fighter, B = Bomber, T = Transport, G = Ground Attack or Assault Plane, S = Flying boat or seaplane. R = Reconnaissance.

Type	First Flown or used	No. built	Role	Crew	Engine	Performance				Notes
						Speed at Height (mph/feet)	Service Ceiling (feet)	Range (miles)	Climb (min to height in feet)	
Ambrosini										
SAI 207	1940	16	F	1	1	398	39,370	528	7'33 to 19,680	Lightweight fighter. Good performance.
Breda										
Ba 44	Jun 1934	11	T	2	2	140	15,580	335		Biplane, similar to DH Dragon.
Ba 65	Sep 1935	201	G	1	1	267	27,230	342		Slow and hard to fly. Also two-seat version.
Ba 88 *Lince* - Lynx	Oct 1936	149	G	1	2	304	26,240	1019	7'30 to 9,840	Difficult to maintain.

Type	First Flown	No. built or used	Role	Crew	Engine	Performance				Notes
						Speed at Height (mph/feet)	Service Ceiling (feet)	Range (miles)	Climb (min to height in feet)	
Cansa										
FC 20bis	Apr 1941	12	F	2	2	292	22,750	715		Difficult to fly.
Cant										
Z501 Gabbiano - Seagull	Feb 1934	453	S	5	1	171 at 8,200		1,490	16' to 13,120	Flying boat - Long range but slow.
Z506 Airone - Heron	Aug 1935	324	S	5	3	227	26,240	1242	14' to 13,120	Floatplane - used for bombing, but at best for recon. and ASR duties.
Z1007bis Alcione - Kingfisher	Mar 1937	561	B	5	3	280 at 15,000	26,500	1242		Main bomber from 1941. Popular with crews.
Z1018 Leone - Lion	Oct 1939	17	B	4	2	323	23,785	1367	3'10 to 6,560	Similar performance to US B-25 Mitchell.
Caproni										
Ca 111	Feb 1932	154	T	3	1	180	21,976	807	5'22 to 3,280	Often used as 'hack' aircraft in combat units.
Ca 133	Dec 1934	417	B	3	3	166	18,050	838		Bomber-transport. Main bomber in AOI.
Ca 164			T	2	1	144	13,776	329		Liaison and training aircraft. Highly manouevrable.
Ca 309 Ghibli - Desert Wind	Aug 1936	243	B	2	2	155	14,760	417	17'30 9,840	Colonial light bomber. Efficient but vulnerable.
Ca 310 Libeccio - Southwest Wind	Feb 1937	256	B	3	2	218	22,960	745	6'40 to 6,560	Uprated version of Ca 309.
Ca 311	Apr 1939	320	B	3	2	217		800		Replaced Ro 37 in army co-operation role.
Ca 313	Aug 1939	122	B	3	2	268 at 16,400	29,035	795		Sturdy but plagued by engine and system problems. Disliked.
Ca 314	Mar 1941	407	B	3	2	253 at 16,400	27,070	665		Multi-role and better armed than Ca313.
Caproni Vizzola										
F5	Feb 1939	13	F	1	1	317 at 9,840	31,170	621	6'30 to 21,325	Home defence only.
F6M	Sep 1941	2	F	1	1	353 at 16,400	34,450	590	5'30 to 19,685	Uprated F5, too late for full production. Home defence.
CMASA										
RS 14B	May 1939	186	S	5	2	242 at 15,400	16,400	1553		Recon floatplane. Good range. Used on coastal, A/S and ASR roles.
Dewoitine										
D.520	Oct 1938	47	F	1	1	326				Ex-Vichy French fighter with useful armament.
Dornier										
Do 217J	1941	12	F	2	2	320				Worn German nightfighters, most without radar.

Type	First Flown	No. built or used	Role	Crew	Engine	Performance				Notes
						Speed at Height (mph/feet)	Service Ceiling (feet)	Range (miles)	Climb (min to height in feet)	
Fiat										
BR 20	Feb 1936	514	B	5	2	267	22,140	1242		Relegated to night bombing by mid-1941.
CR 25bis	Jul 1937	12	F	2	2	286 at 18,200	26,575	1305	7' to 13,120	Easy to maintain. Mainly convoy escort role.
CR 32	Apr 1933	1053	F	1	1	221 at 9,840	24,764	484	5'10 to 9,840	Close support and nightfighter until 1941.
CR 42 *Falco* - Falcon	May 1938	1553	F	1	1	267 at 13,120	33,456	481	3'53 to 9,840	Sturdy biplane. Ground attack and nightfighter from 1942.
G 12T	May 1941	104	T	4 + 22	3	242 at 16,400	27,880	1428		High altitude cargo and troop transport with good range.
G 50 *Freccia* - Arrow	Feb 1937	782	F	1	1	293	32,480	621		Low performance. Used as fighter-bomber from 1941.
G 55 *Centauro* - Centaur	Apr 1942	105	F	1	1	385 at 22,960	42,640	745	7'12 to 19,680	Good manouevrability, equal to opponents.
Junkers										
Ju 87R-2 *Picchiatello* - Little Woodpecker	1939	110	B	2	1	237				German import used successfully.
Ju 87D-3 *Picchiatello*	1942	49	B	2	1	248				German import over-whelmed by odds.
Ju 88A-4	1940	50	B	4	2	292				Worn out ex-Luftwaffe machines
Lioré et Olivier										
LeO 451	Jan 1937	27	B	4	2	285				Worn out examples from Vichy France.
Macchi										
MC 200 *Saetta* - Lightning	Dec 1937	1153	F	1	1	314 at 15,744	29,200	540	5'52 to 16,400	Slow but good dive and manouevrability.
MC 202 *Folgore* - Thunderbolt	Aug 1940	1106	F	1	1	370 at 16,400	37,730	475	5'55 to 19,680	Potent but outclassed by 1943. Very successful design.
MC 205V *Veltro* - Greyhound	Apr 1942	250	F	1	1	399 at 23,620	36,090	646	7'6 to 22,960	Interim model. Equal to Spitfire and Mustang
MC 205N *Orione* - Orion	Nov 1942	2	F	1	1	390 at 22,960	36,910	612	9'48 to 26,240	Contender with G 55 and Re 2005 in the Series 5 types intended to create a modern fighter force.

Type	First Flown	No. built or used	Role	Crew	Engine	Performance				Notes
						Speed at Height (mph/feet)	Service Ceiling (feet)	Range (miles)	Climb (min to height in feet)	
Meridionali										
Ro 37	Nov 1933	619	R	2	1	205 at 16,400	23,616	696	9'20 to 13,120	Army co-operation biplane. Balkans only after late 1942.
Ro 41	Jun 1934	743	F	1	1	202 at 16,400	25,580	350	6'20 to 13,120	Fighter-trainer biplane, inferior to CR32.
Ro 43	Nov 1934	194	R	2	1	186 at 8,200	21,648	495	11' to 13,120	Coastal and catapult recon floatplane.
Ro 44	Oct 1936	35	F	1	1	189 at 8,200	22,960	745	8'40 to 13,120	Floatplane fighter. Single-seat version of Ro 43.
Ro 57bis	1939	201	F	1	2	311 at 16,400	25,590	745	9'30 to 19,680	Slow and average manouevrability.
Ro 63	Jun 1940	6	T	3	1	130		560		Inspired by Fiesler Storch. Reached units in 1943.
Messerchmitt										
Bf 109G	1941	80	F	1	1	387				German import used successfully in Sicily and Italy.
Bf 110C	1939	3	F	2	2	349				Worn nightfighter examples from Germany with no radar.
Nardi										
FN 305	Feb 1935	345	T	2	1	211	22,960	621	13' to 13,120	Liaison aircraft. Anti-partisan duties from late 1942.
Piaggio										
P108B	Nov 1939	24	B	6	4	267 at 13,780	27,880	2484	30' to 16,400	Only operational Italian heavy strategic bomber.
Reggiane										
Re 2000 *Falco I* - Falcon I	May 1939	28	F	1	1	329	36,736	522	6'10 to 19,680	Inspired by US P-35, but lost major contract to MC 200.
Re 2001 *Falco II* - Falcon II	Jul 1940	243	F	1	1	337 at 16,400	39,200	646	12'10 26,240	Used in ground attack, escort and nightfighter roles.
Re 2002 *Ariete* - Ram	Oct 1940	201	G	1	1	329 at 18,045	34,450	683	8'48 to 19,680	Re 2000 uprated as fighter-bomber, appeared in 1943 but overwhelmed.
Re 2005 *Sagittario* - Archer	May 1942	36	F	1	1	390 at 22,800	39,360	786	6'33 to 19,680	Excellent fighter, highly rated by Germans.
Savoia Marchetti										
SM 73	Jul 1934	50	T	4	3	205 at 13,120	24,272	994	33' to 19,680	Civil transport command-eered for the Libyan front.
SM 74	Nov 1934	3	T	4	4	205	22,960		8'55 to 9,840	Commandeered from Ala Littoria.

Type	First Flown	No. built or used	Role	Crew	Engine	Performance				Notes
						Speed at Height (mph/feet)	Service Ceiling (feet)	Range (miles)	Climb (min to height in feet)	
SM 75 *Canguro* - Kangaroo	Nov 1937	94	T	4	3	229 at 10,070	22,960	1416	18' to 13,120	Slow transport. Later versions received a dorsal turret.
SM 79 *Sparviero* - Sparrowhawk	Oct 1934	1217	B	6	3	267 at 13,120	21,320	1180	19'45 16,400	Easy to fly and maintain. Standard level bomber and torpedo-bomber.
SM 81 *Pipistrello* - Bat	Feb 1935	535	B	6	3	214	22,960	1242	12' to 9,840	Military version of SM 73. Main bombing role in AOI, then transport.
SM 82 *Marsupiale* - Marsupial	Oct 1939	721	T	4	3	200	20,230	2484		Larger version of SM 75. Excellent load range/ capability. Used as recon-bomber-transport.
SM 83	Nov 1937	45	T	4	3	276	27,552	1242	13'30 13,120	Civil version of SM 79.
SM 84	Jun 1940	309	B	5	3	266	29,512	1130		Less manouevrable successor to SM 79.
SM 85	Dec 1938	36	B	1	2	228	19,190		13'19 13,120	Unsuccessful dive-bomber, quickly withdrawn.

196: Italian bombs had a style all their own—the use of reinforcing straps, fluted fin fairings and heavy rivets made them all look old-fashioned compared to those of the other protagonists. It would be interesting to know how the ballistic behaviour was effected by these features. The Italians also seem to have had a much wider range of small calibre bombs of odd weights. Those seen here are probably 100kg GP type, although it is difficult to be sure as Italian bombs seem to be light for their size

AIRCRAFT EQUIPMENT
Guns, sights, bombs and radios

Italian 7.7mm and 12.7mm Breda SAFAT machine guns were generally efficient and reliable, using a mix of solid, incendiary and tracer bullets. The 12.7mm gun outranged the machine guns of their opponents with a close punch as good as the US 0.5". Wing structure problems, however, due to the gas-operated firing mechanism, led to the guns being situated on top of the engine cowling. This obviously inhibited the number of guns which could be carried, consequently weight of fire was a problem which beset most of the early war Italian fighters. Some fighters were manufactured with ammunition counters in the cockpit. The FM62 gun camera was also installed in fighters from 1940.

The San Giorgio reflector sight was introduced in 1937, developed through Types A, B, and C. Due to it being unreliable in the early stages many pilots retained their Chretien telescopic or OMI ring and bead sights for a while as a backup. Both types of sights could be seen on some fighters as late as 1943.

Regia Aeronautica aircraft were late in acquiring radios; the Allocchio Bacchini B30 transmitter/receiver only coming into use from 1940/41, followed by the TBR30 in late 1941. As explained elsewhere static interference and slow response times prevented them becoming as efficient as the German or Allied equipment. Even the latter suffered in the mountainous regions of Italy and the Balkans throughout the war.

In the absence of suitable domestic cannon, the desperate need to increase the weight of fire to counter increasingly heavily-armoured Allied aircraft led to a reliance on German imports of the excellent MG151, and the French cannon-armed D520 fighters. Operational trials were also carried out by fighters with air-to-air bombing over Sicily.

Multi-seat aircraft used either Breda SAFAT or Scotti Isotta-Fraschini machine guns, both 7.7mm and 12.7mm. The latter company's guns when fitted to gun rings and turrets were more prone to jams and faults. Both Breda and Caproni-Lanciani made rings and turrets for multi-seated aircraft, but they were rarely effective against determined attacks.

Initially the bomber crews were encouraged to carry a multitude of smaller bombs (15, 20, 36, 40, 50, 100, or 160 kg). The idea was that the more bombs, the more likely a hit on the target—an acknowledgment of the indifferent

197 Above: Armourers working in a Sicilian bomb dump attend to the fusing of what appears to be a 250kg high explosive type. The elegant fluted fins were something of an Italian trademark. Official instructions were very specific about which bombs were to be used on types of targets

capabilities of contemporary bombsights and training. Later, a mix of light (2 to 100kg) and heavy (250 or 500kg) bombs was used. Heavier bombs such as the 800kg could only be used on shorter missions due to the lack of power of most aircraft engines, and consequent load-carrying ability of the aircraft.

For anti-submarine work the RA mostly used 160kg depth-bombs and 70kg depth-charges. The most potent anti-shipping weapon was the 800kg Whitehead or 930kg Fiume torpedo. These could be launched at 300kmh, at 40 to 120 metres altitude during a dive of between 10°-35°, at a range of 3,000 to 160 metres. Running depth of the torpedo was 2-10 metres at 40 knots.

In 1942 a new weapon was introduced as a diversion during torpedo attacks. This was the motorised 'FF' bomb which was dropped by parachute into the water, and via a motorised propeller automatically began circling in a radius of about 15km. They had little success.

Another innovation by the Italians in 1942 was a series of experiments with radio controlled aircraft as guided bombs, using war-weary aircraft. Unfortunately, the early trials were unsuccessful although showing promise. On 12 August 1942 *Maresciallo* Mario Badii took off from Villacidro in an SM 79 loaded with 1,000kg of explosives. He bailed out on reaching altitude, and the aircraft was guided by a Z1007bis, aboard which was *Generale* Ferdinando Raffaelli who had invented this system. After 200km, however, a fault developed in the radio-equipment, and instead of attacking the ships in the PEDESTAL convoy, the aircraft flew on to crash in the mountains near Constantine, Algeria.

Specifications for the main guns used

Company	Calibre	Weight	Feed	Rpm	Mv	Notes
Breda SAFAT	7.7mm	12.5kg	Belt	900	730ms	
Breda SAFAT	12.7mm	28kg	Belt	700	760ms	
IF Scotti	7.7mm			1300	725ms	
IF Scotti	12.7mm			800	740ms	
Mauser	20mm	42kg	Belt	630	790ms	German MG151. Each belt had multiples of 50 rounds.
Breda?90/53	102mm	1500kg	Drum		700ms	Used in Piaggio 108A anti-shipping bomber. 12 round drums.

Turrets

Type	Weapon	Vertical Traverse °	Horizontal Traverse °	Example Aircraft
A	1x7.7	+90/-?	90	Z501
D	2x7.7	+90/-15	360	SM 82
E	2x7.7	0 /-90	360	P108T, Z506B, Z1007, Ca 313/4, SM 84, RS 14
G	1x12.7	0 /-90	360	P108B
H	1x7.7	+85/-38	90	BR 20
L	1x7.7	+90/-70	80	Ro 43
M	1x12.7	+90/-12	360	BR 20
V	1x12.7	+80/-12	360	Z1007
Z2	2x12.7	+85/-10	360	P108A

Regia Aeronautica Aircraft Equipment

					FIGHTERS					
Aircraft Type	Gun Calibre (mm)	Gun Type	No.	Rpg	Position	Gun sight	Bomb load (kg)	Radio	Camera	Notes
CR 32qtr	12.7	SAFAT	2	350	engine cowling	San Giorgio telescope				
CR 32bis	7.7	SAFAT	2		engine cowling	San Giorgio telescope				
Ba 65	12.7		2	350	wings					
	7.7		2	500	wings					
	7.7		1		Breda L dorsal turret		1,000			
Ba 88	12.7		3		nose					
	7.7		1		dorsal		1,000			
Ba 88M	12.7		4		nose					
Ro 44	12.7	SAFAT	2		engine cowling					
G 50	12.7	SAFAT	2	300	engine cowling	San Giorgio Type A		ARC 1		
G 50bis	12.7	SAFAT	2		engine cowling	San Giorgio	160	B30		
MC 200	12.7		2	370	engine cowling	San Giorgio	400[1]	ARC 1 B30[1]		[1]later series
CR 42	12.7		2	400	engine cowling		200[2]	ARC 1[1] IMCA[1]		[1] commanders only [2]later series
CV F 5	12.7	SAFAT	2	350	engine cowling			ARC 1		
Re 2000	12.7		2	300	engine cowling	San Giorgio Type A	200[1]			[1]series 3
CR 25bis	12.7	SAFAT	2	400	nose					
	12.7	SAFAT	1	400	dorsal turret		300			
Ro 57	12.7	SAFAT	2		nose					
Ro 57bis	20		2		nose		500			
Re 2001	12.7	SAFAT	2	350	engine cowling					
	7.7	SAFAT	2	600	wings		250[1]			[1]later series
Re 2001 CN	12.7/20	SAFAT	2	350	engine cowling					
	20		2		wings					
MC 202 Series 1 to 5	12.7		2	360	engine cowling					
MC 202 Series 6 on	12.7		2		engine cowling					
	7.7		2		wings		150		Avia RB20-75/30	
Re 2002	12.7	SAFAT	2	450	engine cowling					
	7.7	SAFAT	2	290	wings	San Giorgio	640	B30		
FC 20bis	37 or 54	Breda M39	1	42	nose					
	12.7	SAFAT	2	250	nose					
	12.7	SAFAT	1	500	Scotti dorsal turret		252			
SAI 403	20	MG151	2	200	wings					
MC 205V Series 1	12.7	SAFAT	2	400	engine cowling					
	7.7	SAFAT	2	500	wings	San Giorgio	320	B30 BG42		
MC 205V Series 3	12.7/20	SAFAT	2	400	engine cowling					
		MG151	2	200	wings	San Giorgio	320	B30 BG42		
MC 205N1	12.7	SAFAT	2		engine cowling					
	20	MG151	1		nose					
	12.7	SAFAT	2		wings	San Giorgio		B30 BG42		
MC 205N2	12.7	SAFAT	2		engine cowling					
	20	MG151	1		nose					
	20	MG151	2		wings	San Giorgio		As above		

Regia Aeronautica Aircraft Equipment

FIGHTERS

Aircraft Type	Gun Calibre (mm)	Gun Type	No.	Rpg	Position	Gun sight	Bomb load (kg)	Radio	Camera	Notes
G 55 Series 0	12.7	SAFAT	2	300	engine cowling					
	20	MG151	1	250	nose					
	12.7	SAFAT	2	300	wings	San Giorgio		B30 BG42		
G 55 Series 1	12.7	SAFAT	2	300	engine cowling					
	20	MG151	1	250	nose					
	20	MG151	2	200	wings	San Giorgio		B30 BG42		
Re2005	12.7	SAFAT	2	350	engine cowling					
	20	MG151	1	150	nose					
	20	MG151	2	200	wings	San Giorgio	930	B30 BG42		
Do 217J	20		4		nose					
	7.9		4		nose					
Bf 110C	20		2		nose					
	7.9		4		nose					
	7.9		1		dorsal position					
Bf 109G-2										
Bf 109G-6	13	MG131	2	300	engine cowling					
	20	MG151	1	150	nose					
	20	MG151	2	120	underwings					
Bf 109G-14										
Bf 109K	13	MG131	2		engine cowling					
	30	MK108	1		nose					
D.520	20	HS404	1	60	nose					
	7.5	MAC34	4	675	wings					

BOMBERS

Aircraft Type	Gun Calibre (mm)	Gun Type	No.	Rpg	Position	Bombsights	Bomb load (kg)	Radio	Camera	Notes
SM 81	7.7	SAFAT	2	500	Breda dorsal turret					
	7.7	Lewis	1	500	port waist					
SM 79	7.7	Lewis	1	500	starboard waist		2,000			
	12.7	SAFAT	1	350	forward gondola					
	12.7	SAFAT	1		dorsal position					
	12.7	SAFAT	1	350	ventral position					
	7.7		1		either waist	Jozza	1,250	TelefunkenP63N		Extra waist gun added in 1941
SM 79bis	12.7	SAFAT	1	350	forward gondola					
	12.7	SAFAT	1	350	dorsal position					
	12.7	SAFAT	1		port waist					
	12.7	SAFAT	1		starboard waist	Jozza	1,250			
BR 20	7.7	SAFAT	1	500	Type H nose turret	Jozza U3A	1,600			
	7.7	SAFAT	1	500	Type DR dorsal trt					
	7.7	SAFAT	1	500	ventral position					
BR 20M	7.7	SAFAT	1	500	Type H nose turret					First 100 had
	12.7	SAFAT	1	350	TypeMI dorsal trt					2 x 7.7mm in

Regia Aeronautica Aircraft Equipment

Aircraft Type	Gun Calibre (mm)	Gun Type	No.	Rpg	Position	Bombsights	Bomb load (kg)	Radio	Camera	Notes
					BOMBERS					
BR 20M	7.7	SAFAT	1	500	ventral position	Jozza U3A	1,600			DR dorsal turret
BR 20bis	7.7	SAFAT	1	500	nose turret					
	12.7	SAFAT	1	350	Breda V dorsal trt					
	7.7	SAFAT	1	500	ventral position	Jozza				
SM 75	12.7		1		Delta E dorsal trt					
SM 82	12.7	Scotti	1	350	Delta dorsal turret					
	7.7	SAFAT	1	860	undernose position					
	7.7	SAFAT	1	860	port waist					
	7.7	SAFAT	1	860	starboard waist	Jozza U3	4,000	AR8 RA350-2 P63N AGR90		
G 12	7.7		1		port waist					
	7.7		1		starboard waist					
Ca133	7.7	Lewis	1	470	nose					
	7.7	Lewis	1	470	dorsal position					
	7.7	Lewis	1	470	port waist					
	7.7	Lewis	1	470	starboard waist	Jozza G3U2	300	AR5 RA350-1 P63N	AGR61 AL30 APR3	
SM 84	12.7	Scotti	1	350	Delta E dorsal turret					
	12.7	Scotti	1	350	ventral position					
	12.7	Scotti	1	350	port waist					
	12.7	Scotti	1	350	starboard waist	Jozza U3	1,000	AR8 RA320ter RGM37 A40 intercom B30 R/T	AGR90 APR87	
Z1018	12.7	SAFAT	1	350	nose					
	12.7	Scotti	1	350	Delta F dorsal turret					
	12.7	Scotti	1	350	ventral position					
	7.7	SAFAT	1	500	port waist					
	7.7	SAFAT	1	500	starboard waist		2,000			
P108B	12.7		2	300	Breda Z2 wing turret					
	12.7		2	300	Breda Z2 wing turre					
	7.7		1	450	Breda G ventral turret					
	7.7		1	400	port waist					
	7.7		1	400	starboard waist	Jozza U3	3,500	AR18/24 RA100 MGR37	AGR90	
P108A	102		1	50	undernose					
Ba 201	12.7	SAFAT	2	350	nose		500			
Ju 87R-2	7.92	MG17	2		wings					
	7.92	MG15	1		dorsal position		500			
Ju 87D-3	7.92	MG17	2		wings					
	7.92	MG81Z	2		dorsal position		1,800			
Ju 88A-4	13	MG131	1		nose					
	7.9	MG81	1		nose					
	13	MG131	1		dorsal position					
	7.9	MG81	2		ventral position	BZG2 ?	2,000			

Regia Aeronautica Aircraft Equipment

					BOMBERS					
Aircraft Type	Gun Calibre (mm)	Gun Type	No.	Rpg	Position	Bombsights	Bomb load (kg)	Radio	Camera	Notes
Ro 37	7.7		1	500	engine cowling					
	7.7		1	500	dorsal position		180	AR5		
Ro 43	7.7	SAFAT	1	500	engine cowling			AR4		
	7.7	SAFAT	1	500	dorsal position			A-200/1		
Z501/Asso 750	7.7	Lewis	1	470	Vickers dorsal turret					
	7.7	Lewis	1	470	S82 dorsal turret	Jozza	500	AR5 AR350-1		
Z501/AssoXI	7.7	SAFAT	1	500	Breda A2 dorsal trt					
	7.7	SAFAT	1	500	Breda A3 dorsal trt	Jozza	640	As above		
Z506B	12.7	Scotti	1	350	Delta E dorsal trt					
	7.7	SAFAT	1	500	ventral position					
	7.7	SAFAT	1	500	port waist					
	7.7	SAFAT	1	500	starboard waist	Jozza U3A	1,100	AR8 RA350-2 P63N	AGR61 APR3	
SM 85	7.7	SAFAT	1	500	nose		800	ARC 1		
Ca 309	7.7	SAFAT	2	500	nose					
	7.7	Lewis	1	500	either waist		336			
Ca 310B	7.7		2	500						
	7.7		1	500			400			
Ca 311	7.7		1	500	nose					
	7.7		1	500	dorsal turret					
	7.7		1	500	ventral position		400			
Ca 314A	12.7	Scotti	2	300	wings					
	12.7	Scotti	1	300	Delta E dorsal trt					
	7.7	SAFAT	1	500	ventral position		320*			*1,000 on Ca314B
Ca 314C	12.7	SAFAT	4	300	wings					
	12.7	Scotti	1	350	Delta E dorsal trt					
	7.7	Scotti	1	500	ventral position		1,280			
RS 14B	12.7	Scotti	1	350	Delta E dorsal trt					
	7.7	SAFAT	1	500	port waist					
	7.7	SAFAT	1	500	starboard waist	Biggio V3	400	AR8 RA350-1 RGM37	AGR90	
Z1007bis	12.7	SAFAT	1	350	Breda V dorsal trt					
	12.7	Scotti	1	350	ventral position					
	7.7	SAFAT	1	500	port waist					
	7.7	SAFAT	1	500	starboard waist		1,200	AR8 RA320ter M37S A40 TRC30		Some early series had Delta E dorsal turret. Z1007ter had 12.7mm waist guns.

198: Sweating ground crew load up 50kg bombs by hand under the wings of a Fiat CR 42. The impression is that the RA was very labour intensive with few mechanical aids, such as fuel bowsers or purpose-designed bomb trollies, for the long-suffering ground crews. Turnaround times between sorties must have suffered and compounded the other problems afflicting the force

199: Armourers checking a bomb bay full of 50kg weapons in the belly of a Cant Z.1007. The Cant could accommodate up to twelve of these or a wide variety of other calibres of ordnance. Part of the reason was that it had been designed as a bomber from the outset, unlike the Savoia Marchetti types

200: The success of the Aerosilurante units seems to have tempted the RA to experiment with hanging torpedoes from all kinds of aircraft. This is the Caproni Ca 314RA (Ricognizione-Aerosilurante). As the type's performance was marginal at best, it is highly unlikely that the combination was ever tried in anger. This one is probably being used by a training school

201: *Captured in East Africa by South African forces, this Caproni Ca 111 of 66ª Squadriglia was put on display in South Africa to help the war effort. The 'colonial' finish of overall ivory with red stripes to assist location in the event of a forced landing in the bush is clearly evident*

202: *This crashed Fiat CR 32 also demonstrates an unusual style of anti-camouflage. Seen pre-war in Libya, the CR 32 did not normally sport such bold markings. The fighter is finished in overall aluminium with the usual red/white/green tail stripes, but also has red/white/red (or green?) flashes on the wings. No other details are known*

RA CAMOUFLAGE
Colours for all seasons—except winter

To describe the history and variations of camouflage used by this airforce in detail would require yet a further book, to add to the several good works already published (see Bibliography). As this book is, however, essentially an operational history and reference, camouflage schemes are summarised in tabular format. For examples of the colours and patterns refer to the illustrations included in this book.

Italian experience in the Spanish Civil War led to the intensive use of mottled paint schemes of varying densities and combinations of greens, browns and yellows on the aircraft uppersurfaces. With the outbreak of World War II there was a sudden need for a much wider range of colours and patterns in order to cope with the many and varied colours of the different terrain to be found in northern Italy, the East African bush, the Libyan deserts and the Channel coast. From 1941 the conditions on the Russian Front gave yet another set of variables.

Apart from the difficulties of deciding upon the colours and patterns to be used, the RA had another problem in as

far as many of its aircraft were of mainly wood and fabric construction, thus requiring paints of a very different composition to those to be used on metal airframes. This led to a long study by the D.S.S.E (Direzione Superiore Studi Esperienze) at Guidonia which eventually presented the results of its research in 1941.

The outcome of the D.S.S.E's research was a standardisation on three uppersurface colours, namely Green 1090/96, Brown 1091/1095 and Yellow 1092/1097. These were the 'standard basic camouflage colours'. There was also a fourth camouflage colour, specifically intended for use in desert environments. This was 'Nocciola Chiaro' (Light Hazel). These colours were then intended to be applied in one of three patterns to aircraft mainly operating over land:

The 'Continental' scheme used a green base, either as a solid colour, or with various oversprays of yellow and brown.

The 'Mediterranean' scheme used combinations of colours in various mottles.

The 'African' scheme used a base of Nocciola Chiaro with, optionally, light mottles of green.

203 Above: A Macchi MC 200 fighter-bomber of the 356a Squadriglia ready for an attack on Russian cavalry near Stalino in 1942. The aircraft wears yellow Eastern Front markings, as well as the white wing triangles adopted only by the Italians. Note the number on the wheel door

Natural metal finishes were banned.

In early 1943 the loss of the African territories led to another revision and a simplification of camouflage. Nocciola Chiaro was declared obsolete and the standard finish was to be the basic overall green Continental scheme. This could then be field-modified with the application of various mottles in brown or yellow depending upon the aircraft's ultimate destination. At the same time, all aircraft mainly flying over water were to be finished in an overall dark blue-grey, with undersurfaces of all aircraft to be a light blue-grey ('ash blue-grey'). These were the essential finishes in use until the Armistice of September.

Foreign aircraft such as the Ju 87, Ju 88, Do 217, Bf 110, D.520 and Fizir were mostly left in their original colour schemes with Italian national insignia and markings painted over the original finishes. Exceptions

were the Bf 109 which added Grigio Azzuro Chiaro, and the Fi 156 Storch which used Verde Mimetico 2 and Grigio Mimetico in the Balkans, and yellow with green splotches in the desert.

Needless to say, the schemes promulgated led to many variations, depending upon manufacturer and painter. Italian paints varied in their pigment, and different factories produced different shades of the same colour. Thus, there was a great variety, and due to poor supplies the same units often had aircraft with different finishes in the same flights. Local supplies sometimes supplemented the official schemes. Consequently, the varieties of finish are endless, making for a very picturesque air force, and a nightmare for the researcher.

The colours listed below are from top surfaces in order of predominance to lastly the undersurface. The numbers next to the colours indicate factory variants of each shade.

204: The first Fiat G 50 prototype (MM334) in 1937 displays the hard-edged transverse bands type of camouflage more usually associated with bombers and the Fiat CR 32. It was, as far as is known, the only one of the type to be finished in this way

205: Much of the early development work on camouflage was begun in Spain with the Aviazione Legionaria. This is an IMAM Ro 37bis wearing a field-applied striped finish which did not find general favour. Most machines had versions of the mottle patterns which were to become standard for the Regia Aeronautica in World War II

SCHEME	COLOURS	PATTERN	PERIOD	AIRCRAFT
Bands, metropolitan territories				
		diagonal wavy bands merging into one another		
A3	Giallo Mimetico 3			
	Verde Mimetico 3			
	Marrone Mimetico 53193			
	Grigio Mimetico			
		yellow, green , and brown slightly wavy bands, with yellow repeated every second band. Grey undersurface	1940-41	SM 79, SM 82
A3A	Giallo Mimetico 3			
	Verde Mimetico 53192			
	Marrone Mimetico 53193			
		variation on above	1940-41	SM 79, SM 82
A4	Giallo Mimetico 3			
	Verde Mimetico 3			
	Marrone Mimetico 53193			
		yellow, green, brown, green, yellow, green, brown, green etc	1940-41	SM 79, SM 82
A5	Giallo Mimetico 3			
	Verde Mimetico 53192			
	Marrone Mimetico 53193			
		yellow, green, brown bands blending into each other	1940	Z1007bis
Multi-coloured splotches, metropolitan areas				
		hard edged irregular triangles		
B1	Giallo Mimetico 3			
	Verde Mimetico 3			
	Bruno Mimetico			
	Alluminio or Grigio Mimetico			
		yellow, green, dark brown irregular triangular pattern with light metallic grey or grey undersurfaces	1940	Ba 64, Ba 65
B2	Giallo Mimetico 3			
	Verde Mimetico 53192			
	Verde Mimetico 3			
	Marrone Mimetico 2			
	Alluminio or Grigio Mimetico			
		smaller triangles than above, with both light and dark green shades included	1940	Ba 64, Ba 65
Mottled	most common patterns in the period irregular shaped splotches on solid background			
C1	Giallo Mimetico 1-2-3-4			
	Verde Mimetico 2-3-53192			
	Marrone Mimetico 1-2-53193 or Bruno Mimetico			
	Grigio Mimetico			
		green, and brown or dark brown separate splotches on yellow base with grey undersurfaces	1940-41	CR 32, CR 42, G 50, Ro 37, SM79
C1A	Giallo Mimetico 1-3			
	Marrone Mimetico 1-2			
	Verde Mimetico 3-53192			
	Grigio Mimetico or Alluminio			
		variation on above—more graphic separate splotches	1940-41	CR 42, Ca 311
C1B	Giallo Mimetico 1-3			
	Marrone Mimetico 1-2-53193			
	Verde Mimetico 3			
	Grigio Mimetico			
		variation on above—more elongated separate splotches	1940-43	CR 25, G 12, SM 82

SCHEME	COLOURS	PATTERN	PERIOD	AIRCRAFT
C1C	Giallo Verde			
	Marrone			
	Grigio Mimetico			
		blended green/brown splotches on yellow base with grey undersurfaces	1941-42	MC 200
C2	Giallo Mimetico 3-4			
	Verde Mimetico 1-2-3-53192			
	Grigio Mimetico			
		green splotches on yellow base with grey undersurfaces	1940-43	CR 32, CR 42, BR 20, FN 305, G 50, Ca 311, SM 79, SM 79sil, SM 84sil, MC 200, MC 202, SM 81, Ca 310
C2A	Giallo Mimetico 3-4			
	Verde Mimetico 1-2-3-53192			
	Grigio Mimetico			
		smaller splotch variant of above	1940-43	SM79, SM 81, Ca 310, Ca 311
C2B	Giallo Mimetico 3-4			
	Verde Mimetico 1-2-3-53192			
	Grigio Mimetico			
		more spaced out splotch variant of C2	1941-43	MC 200, MC 202
C3	Verde Mimetico 53192			
	Verde Mimetico 2-3			
	Grigio Mimetico			
		Darker green shade splotches over lighter green base with grey undersurfaces	1940-43	CR 42, BR 20, G 50, SM 79, Ba 65, Ba 88
C3A	Verde Mimetico 53192			
	Verde Mimetico 3			
	Grigio Mimetico			
		hazier elongated variant of above	1940-42	G 50
C3B	Verde Mimetico 53192			
	Verde Mimetico 3			
	Grigio Mimetico			
		smaller splotch variant of C3	1940-43	SM 79
C4	Verde Mimetico 53192			
	Verde Mimetico 2			
	Grigio Mimetico			
		worm like pattern of darker green over lighter green with grey undersurfaces	1940-42	MC 200
C5	Verde Mimetico 2-3			
	Giallo Mimetico 3-4			
	Grigio Mimetico			
		yellow splotches over dark green base with grey undersurfaces	1940-43	SM 79, Ca133, Ba 88, SM 81, Re 2000—also probably Z1007bis, Ca 311, CR 42
C6	Bruno Mimetico			
	Verde Mimetico 3			
	Grigio Mimetico			
		spaced green splotches over dark brown base with grey undersurfaces	1940-43	Ca 133, Ba 88
C7	Verde Mimetico 53192			
	Bruno Mimetico			
	Grigio Mimetico or Alluminio			
		spaced dark brown splotches over green base with grey or light metallic grey undersurfaces	1940-1	Ba 88

SCHEME	COLOURS	PATTERN	PERIOD	AIRCRAFT
C8	Verde Mimetico 2 Giallo Mimetico 4 Bruno Mimetico Grigio Mimetico			
		dark brown splotches with yellow surrounds over green base with grey undersurfaces	1941-43	MC 200, MC 202
C9	Giallo Mimetico 2 Verde Mimetico 2 or 3 Verde Mimetico 1 or 53192 Grigio Azzurro Chiaro 1			
		dark green and light green splotches over yellow base with light grey blue undersurfaces	1941-43	SM 79sil
C10	Giallo Mimetico 2 or 3 Verde Mimetico 2 Bruno Mimetico or Marrone Mimetico 53193 Grigio Mimetico			
		brown splotches and yellow splotches over dark green base with grey undersurfaces	1940-42	P108
C10A	Giallo Mimetico 3 Verde Mimetico 3 Marrone Mimetico 53193 Grigio Mimetico			
		brown splotches mingled with dark green spinach over yellow base with grey undersurfaces	1940-42	Z1007bis
C10B	Giallo Mimetico 3 or 4 Verde Mimetico 3 or 53192 Marrone Mimetico 2 or 53193 or Bruno Mimetico Grigio Mimetico			
		elongated brown or dark brown splotches mingled with green spinach over yellow base with grey undersurfaces	1940-42	Ro 37, SM 79, SM 82, SM 84
C11	Giallo Mimetico 3 Verde Mimetico 3 Grigio Mimetico			
		green spinach pattern over yellow base with grey undersurfaces	1942	Z1007bis
C11A	Giallo Mimetico 4 Verde Mimetico 2 Grigio Mimetico			
		yellow splotches surrounded with light green over dark green base with grey undersurfaces	1942	MC 200

Colonial or desert

SCHEME	COLOURS	PATTERN	PERIOD	AIRCRAFT
D1	Verde Oliva Scuro 2 Nocciola Chiaro 4 Grigio Azzurio Chiaro 1			
		light brown splotches over green base with light grey blue undersurfaces	1941-43	MC 200, MC 202
D1A	Verde Oliva Scuro 2 Nocciola Chiaro 4 Grigio Azzurio Chiaro 1			
		variant of above—larger splotches more spaced out	1941-43	G 50, G 55, CR 42
D1B	Verde Oliva Scuro 2 Nocciola Chiaro 4 Grigio Azzurio Chiaro 1			
		spinach type variant of D1	1942-43	MC 200

SCHEME	COLOURS	PATTERN	PERIOD	AIRCRAFT
D2	Nocciola Chiaro 4			
	Verde Oliva Scuro 2			
	Grigio Azzurio Chiaro 1			
		green splotches over light brown base with light grey blue undersurfaces	1942-43	MC 200, MC 202, Ba 65, Ba 88
D2A	Nocciola Chiaro 4			
	Verde Oliva Scuro 2			
	Grigio Azzurio Chiaro 1			
		spinach type variant of above	1942-43	MC 200, MC 202
D2B	Giallo Mimetico 3 or Nocciola Chiaro 4			
	Verde Mimetico 2 o3 or Verde Oliva Scuro 2			
	Grigio Mimetico or Grigio Azzuro Chiaro 1			
		green or dark olive green spaced out splotches over grey or light brown base with grey or light grey blue undersurfaces	1942-43	MC 202
D2C	Nocciola Chiaro 4			
	Verde Oliva Scuro 2			
	Grigio Azzurio Chiaro 1			
		dark olive green spinach over light brown base with light grey blue undersurfaces	1942-43	MC 202
D3	Nocciola Chiaro 4			
	Verde Oliva Scuro 2			
	Grigio Azzurio Chiaro 1			
		dark olive green irregular circles over light brown base with light grey blue undersurfaces	1942-43	MC 200, MC 202, MC 205, CR 42
Unofficial				
E1	Giallo Mimetico 2			
	Verde Mimetico 1			
	Marrone Mimetico 2			
		bands of alternating green then brown spinach over yellow base	1940	SM 81
E2	Grigio Azzuro Chiaro 1			
	Azzuro 11			
		light grey blue splotches over azure base	1941-43	SM 84
E3	Giallo Mimetico 1 or 2			
	Verde Mimetico 1 or 3			
	Marrone Mimetico 1 or Bruno Mimetico			
	Grigio Mimetico			
		green and brown or dark brown 'worms' over yellow base with grey undersurfaces	1940-42	CR 32
E4	Giallo Mimetico 2			
	Verde Mimetico 3			
	Marrone Mimetico 2			
	Grigio Mimetico			
		variant of above with worms overlapping in thick patterns	1940-42	CR 32
E5	Giallo Mimetico 3			
	Verde Mimetico 3 or 53192			
	Marrone Mimetico 2 or Bruno Mimetico			
	Grigio Mimetico			
		variant of E3 with worms running diagonally to each other	1940-43	Ca164
E6	Giallo Mimetico 3			
	Marrone Mimetico 53193			
	Verde Mimetico 2 Grigio Mimetico			
		green patches surrounded by brown over yellow base with grey undersurfaces	1940-43	SM 75

SCHEME	COLOURS	PATTERN	PERIOD	AIRCRAFT
E7	Giallo Mimetico 3			
	Verde Mimetico 2			
	Grigio Mimetico			
		green and yellow diagonal bands with grey undersurfaces	1940-43	Ca 309
E8	Verde Oliva Scuro 2			
	Grigio Azzuro Chiaro 1			
	Grigio Azzuro Chiaro 1			
		dark olive green spinach over light grey blue base with light grey blue undersurfaces	1940-43	SM 79
Single colour defensive		**most common late war period**		
F1	Verde Oliva Scuro 2			
	Grigio Azzuro Chiaro 1			
		dark olive green with light grey blue undersurfaces	1941-43	Z1007bis, SM 79, SM 84, SM 81, SM 82, SAI207, Re 2001, Re 2002, Re 2005, P108, MC 200, MC 202, Ro 37bis, Ca 311, Ca 313, Ca 314, BR 20, CR 42, G 12, G 55
F2	Grigio Azzuro Scuro 3			
	Grigio Azzuro Chiaro 1			
		dark grey blue with light grey blue undersurfaces	1941-43	all naval aircraft from 1941: RS14B, Ro 43, Z501, Z506
F3	Grigio Azzuro Chiaro 1			
		light grey blue	1940-43	all trainers, torpedo aircraft, carrier fighters, S200, S202, SM 79, SM 84, Re 2000, Re 2001
F4	Nero Opaco			
		matt black	1941-43	all night aircraft, CR 42, Z1007bis Re 2001, P108, BR 20, SM 82,
High visibility single colour—mainly non-operational aircraft				
G1	Bianco Avorio 5			
		ivory white	1940-41	colonial aircraft, trainers, and transports
G2	Alluminio			
		light metallic grey	1940-41	naval aircraft up to 1941
G3	Bianco Neve 6			
		snow white	1940-43	all ambulance and rescue aircraft
	Cachi Avorio Chiaro			
		light khaki or ivory white	1940-41	most East African aircraft, eventually recamouflaged with C/D/F patterns by 1941

206 *Left:* This SM 79 of the Aviazione Legionaria shows a field-applied mottle over the Giallo Mimetico portion of the original scheme, which was obviously felt to need toning down

207 *Below:* A formation of SM 79s from the 192ᵃ and 193ᵃ Squadriglie, 87° Gruppo, 30° Stormo, in flight over Yugoslavia display a wide range of camouflage patterns—each one is different

208 *Left:* This Fiat CR 32 displays no unit markings, but has had the rudder stripes only recently overpainted. The camouflage appears to be a very finely applied CI type. Date and location unknown

209 Above: *This Macchi MC 200 of the 373ª Squadriglia in North Africa in 1941 is marked with the pennant of a General of an Air Brigade. This could indicate that it was used as a personal aircraft by Generale Ferdinando Raffaelli*

210 Right: *Fiat G 50bis, MM5944, wears an elegantly applied three-tone pattern which was non-standard on the type, probably applied when it was reconditioned at the manufacturers*

211 Right: *Another view (see photo 157) of the Fiat CR 42 of the 95ª Squadriglia soon after it forcelanded at Orfordness on 11 November 1940. The factory-applied camouflage pattern is very like that used on the CR 42s exported to Sweden. Colours are Giallo Mimetico, Verde Mimetico and Marrone Mimetico with Grigio Mimetico undersides*

212: *One of the first 242 Macchi MC 200s to be produced, with a sliding canopy, this is a machine of the 72ª Squadriglia, probably in winter 1939-1940. The very closely applied mottle is typical of the early MC 200s*

213 Left: *A Caproni Ca 309 of one of the Colonial Patrols displays a typical early desert pattern of the C2 type. Colurs are simple green blotches on yellow ochre*

214 Below: *A pair of Cant Z.1007bis from the 63ª Squadriglia, 29° Gruppo, 9° Stormo in 1941 display the 'polycyclic' C10 type pattern so typical of the type. Colours are Giallo Mimetico 3, Verde Mimetico 3 and Marrone Mimetico 53193. The three tones are clearly visible on MM23350, the nearest machine*

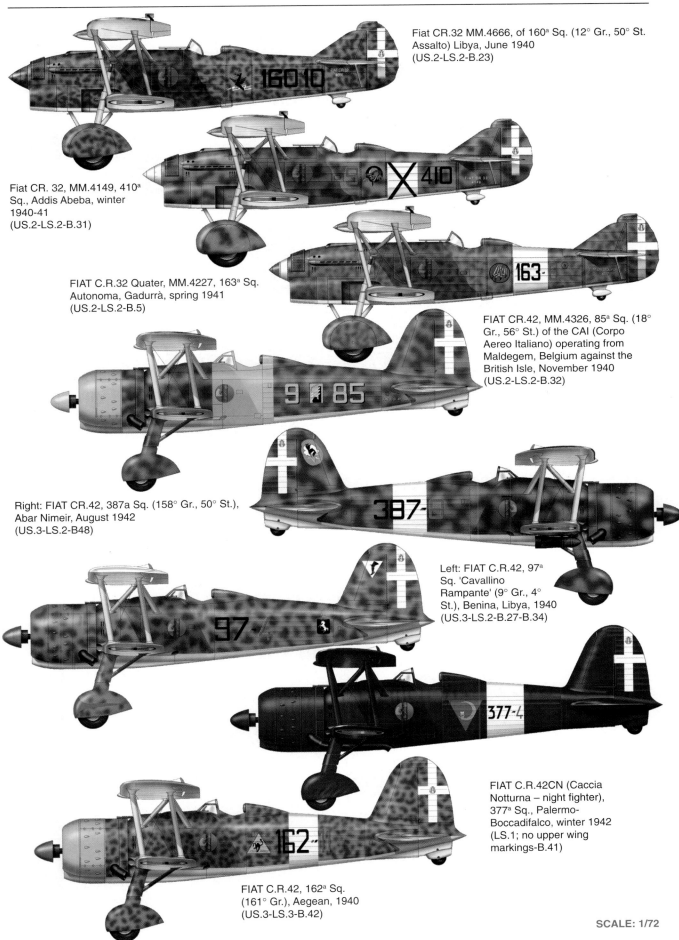

Fiat CR.32 MM.4666, of 160ª Sq. (12° Gr., 50° St. Assalto) Libya, June 1940 (US.2-LS.2-B.23)

Fiat CR. 32, MM.4149, 410ª Sq., Addis Abeba, winter 1940-41 (US.2-LS.2-B.31)

FIAT C.R.32 Quater, MM.4227, 163ª Sq. Autonoma, Gadurrà, spring 1941 (US.2-LS.2-B.5)

FIAT CR.42, MM.4326, 85ª Sq. (18° Gr., 56° St.) of the CAI (Corpo Aereo Italiano) operating from Maldegem, Belgium against the British Isle, November 1940 (US.2-LS.2-B.32)

Right: FIAT CR.42, 387a Sq. (158° Gr., 50° St.), Abar Nimeir, August 1942 (US.3-LS.2-B48)

Left: FIAT C.R.42, 97ª Sq. 'Cavallino Rampante' (9° Gr., 4° St.), Benina, Libya, 1940 (US.3-LS.2-B.27-B.34)

FIAT C.R.42CN (Caccia Notturna – night fighter), 377ª Sq., Palermo-Boccadifalco, winter 1942 (LS.1; no upper wing markings-B.41)

FIAT C.R.42, 162ª Sq. (161° Gr.), Aegean, 1940 (US.3-LS.3-B.42)

SCALE: 1/72

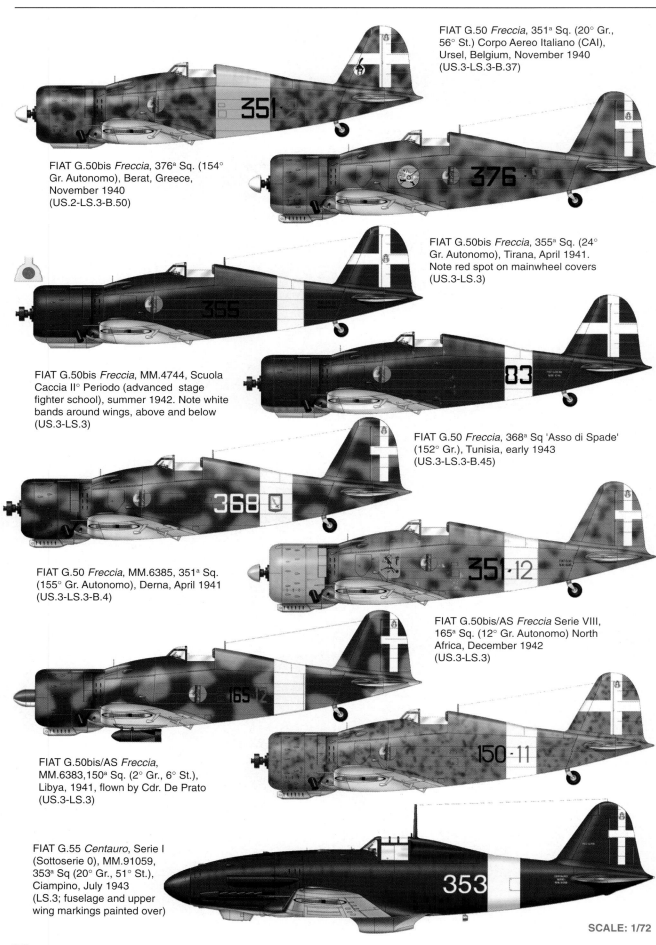

FIAT G.50 *Freccia*, 351ª Sq. (20° Gr., 56° St.) Corpo Aereo Italiano (CAI), Ursel, Belgium, November 1940 (US.3-LS.3-B.37)

FIAT G.50bis *Freccia*, 376ª Sq. (154° Gr. Autonomo), Berat, Greece, November 1940 (US.2-LS.3-B.50)

FIAT G.50bis *Freccia*, 355ª Sq. (24° Gr. Autonomo), Tirana, April 1941. Note red spot on mainwheel covers (US.3-LS.3)

FIAT G.50bis *Freccia*, MM.4744, Scuola Caccia II° Periodo (advanced stage fighter school), summer 1942. Note white bands around wings, above and below (US.3-LS.3)

FIAT G.50 *Freccia*, 368ª Sq 'Asso di Spade' (152° Gr.), Tunisia, early 1943 (US.3-LS.3-B.45)

FIAT G.50 *Freccia*, MM.6385, 351ª Sq. (155° Gr. Autonomo), Derna, April 1941 (US.3-LS.3-B.4)

FIAT G.50bis/AS *Freccia* Serie VIII, 165ª Sq. (12° Gr. Autonomo) North Africa, December 1942 (US.3-LS.3)

FIAT G.50bis/AS *Freccia*, MM.6383,150ª Sq. (2° Gr., 6° St.), Libya, 1941, flown by Cdr. De Prato (US.3-LS.3)

FIAT G.55 *Centauro*, Serie I (Sottoserie 0), MM.91059, 353ª Sq (20° Gr., 51° St.), Ciampino, July 1943 (LS.3; fuselage and upper wing markings painted over)

SCALE: 1/72

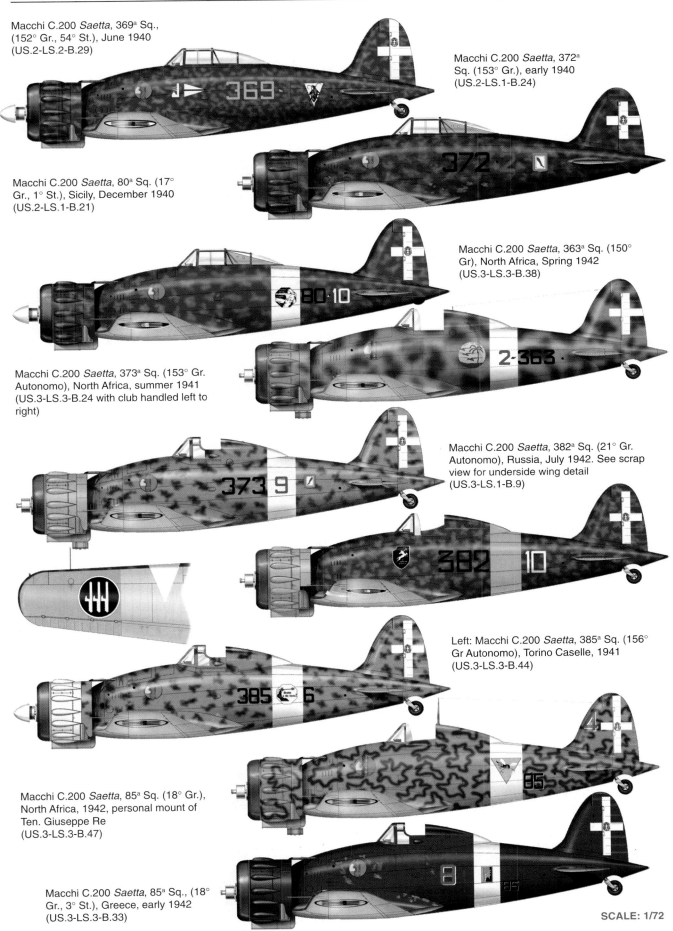

Macchi C.200 *Saetta*, 369ª Sq.,
(152° Gr., 54° St.), June 1940
(US.2-LS.2-B.29)

Macchi C.200 *Saetta*, 372ª
Sq. (153° Gr.), early 1940
(US.2-LS.1-B.24)

Macchi C.200 *Saetta*, 80ª Sq. (17°
Gr., 1° St.), Sicily, December 1940
(US.2-LS.1-B.21)

Macchi C.200 *Saetta*, 363ª Sq. (150°
Gr), North Africa, Spring 1942
(US.3-LS.3-B.38)

Macchi C.200 *Saetta*, 373ª Sq. (153° Gr.
Autonomo), North Africa, summer 1941
(US.3-LS.3-B.24 with club handled left to
right)

Macchi C.200 *Saetta*, 382ª Sq. (21° Gr.
Autonomo), Russia, July 1942. See scrap
view for underside wing detail
(US.3-LS.1-B.9)

Left: Macchi C.200 *Saetta*, 385ª Sq. (156°
Gr Autonomo), Torino Caselle, 1941
(US.3-LS.3-B.44)

Macchi C.200 *Saetta*, 85ª Sq. (18° Gr.),
North Africa, 1942, personal mount of
Ten. Giuseppe Re
(US.3-LS.3-B.47)

Macchi C.200 *Saetta*, 85ª Sq., (18°
Gr., 3° St.), Greece, early 1942
(US.3-LS.3-B.33)

SCALE: 1/72

243

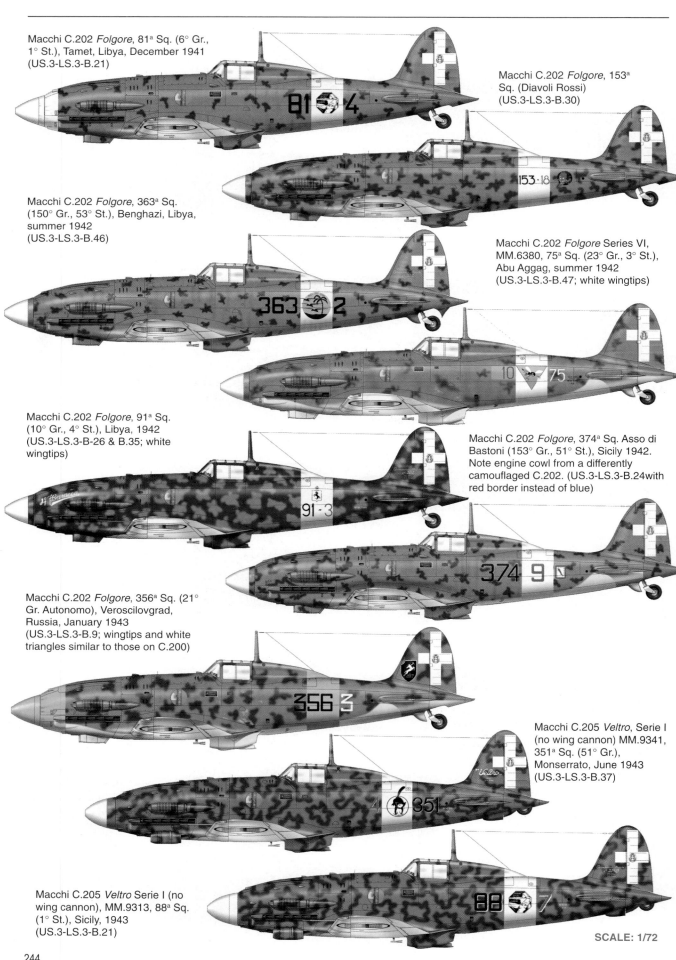

Macchi C.202 *Folgore*, 81ª Sq. (6° Gr., 1° St.), Tamet, Libya, December 1941 (US.3-LS.3-B.21)

Macchi C.202 *Folgore*, 153ª Sq. (Diavoli Rossi) (US.3-LS.3-B.30)

Macchi C.202 *Folgore*, 363ª Sq. (150° Gr., 53° St.), Benghazi, Libya, summer 1942 (US.3-LS.3-B.46)

Macchi C.202 *Folgore* Series VI, MM.6380, 75ª Sq. (23° Gr., 3° St.), Abu Aggag, summer 1942 (US.3-LS.3-B.47; white wingtips)

Macchi C.202 *Folgore*, 91ª Sq. (10° Gr., 4° St.), Libya, 1942 (US.3-LS.3-B-26 & B.35; white wingtips)

Macchi C.202 *Folgore*, 374ª Sq. Asso di Bastoni (153° Gr., 51° St.), Sicily 1942. Note engine cowl from a differently camouflaged C.202. (US.3-LS.3-B.24 with red border instead of blue)

Macchi C.202 *Folgore*, 356ª Sq. (21° Gr. Autonomo), Veroscilovgrad, Russia, January 1943 (US.3-LS.3-B.9; wingtips and white triangles similar to those on C.200)

Macchi C.205 *Veltro*, Serie I (no wing cannon) MM.9341, 351ª Sq. (51° Gr.), Monserrato, June 1943 (US.3-LS.3-B.37)

Macchi C.205 *Veltro* Serie I (no wing cannon), MM.9313, 88ª Sq. (1° St.), Sicily, 1943 (US.3-LS.3-B.21)

SCALE: 1/72

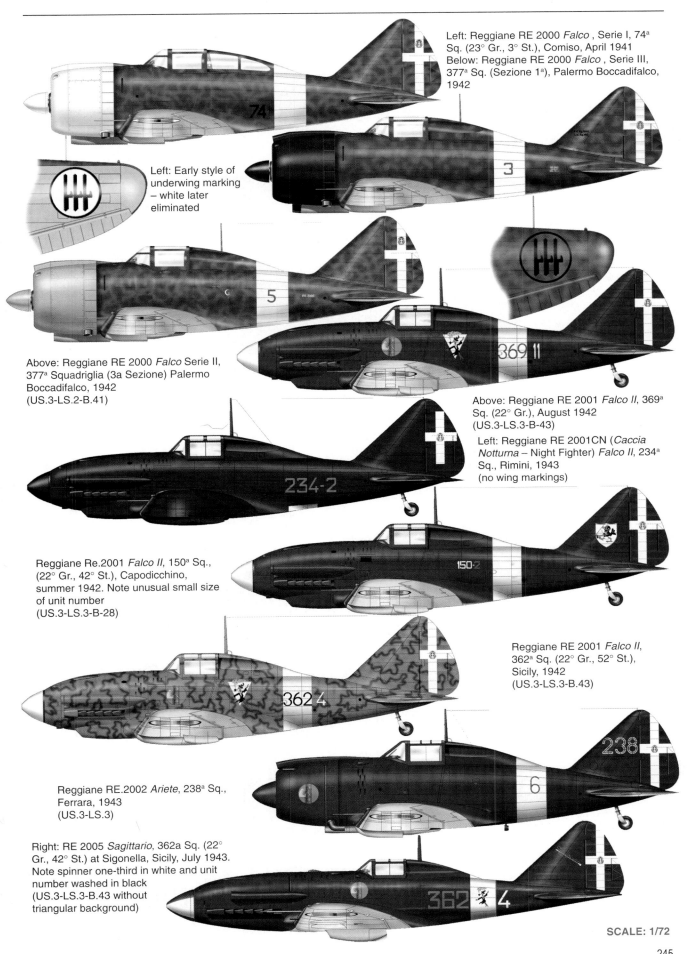

Left: Reggiane RE 2000 *Falco* , Serie I, 74ª Sq. (23° Gr., 3° St.), Comiso, April 1941
Below: Reggiane RE 2000 *Falco* , Serie III, 377ª Sq. (Sezione 1ª), Palermo Boccadifalco, 1942

Left: Early style of underwing marking – white later eliminated

Above: Reggiane RE 2000 *Falco* Serie II, 377ª Squadriglia (3a Sezione) Palermo Boccadifalco, 1942 (US.3-LS.2-B.41)

Above: Reggiane RE 2001 *Falco II*, 369ª Sq. (22° Gr.), August 1942 (US.3-LS.3-B-43)

Left: Reggiane RE 2001CN (*Caccia Notturna* – Night Fighter) *Falco II*, 234ª Sq., Rimini, 1943 (no wing markings)

Reggiane Re.2001 *Falco II*, 150ª Sq., (22° Gr., 42° St.), Capodicchino, summer 1942. Note unusual small size of unit number (US.3-LS.3-B-28)

Reggiane RE 2001 *Falco II*, 362ª Sq. (22° Gr., 52° St.), Sicily, 1942 (US.3-LS.3-B.43)

Reggiane RE.2002 *Ariete*, 238ª Sq., Ferrara, 1943 (US.3-LS.3)

Right: RE 2005 *Sagittario*, 362a Sq. (22° Gr., 42° St.) at Sigonella, Sicily, July 1943. Note spinner one-third in white and unit number washed in black (US.3-LS.3-B.43 without triangular background)

SCALE: 1/72

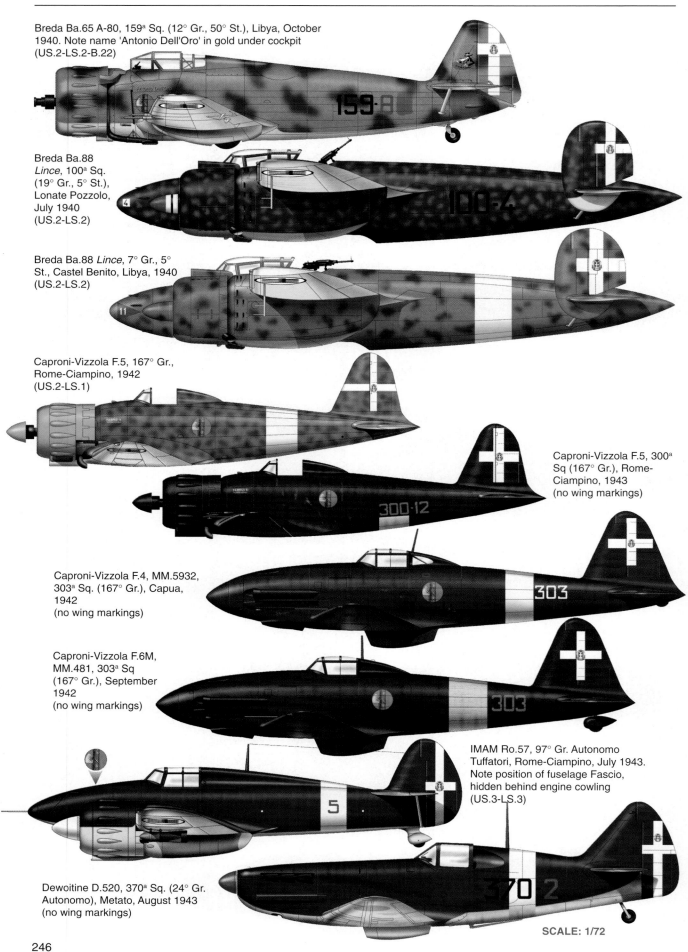

Breda Ba.65 A-80, 159ª Sq. (12° Gr., 50° St.), Libya, October 1940. Note name 'Antonio Dell'Oro' in gold under cockpit (US.2-LS.2-B.22)

Breda Ba.88 *Lince*, 100ª Sq. (19° Gr., 5° St.), Lonate Pozzolo, July 1940 (US.2-LS.2)

Breda Ba.88 *Lince*, 7° Gr., 5° St., Castel Benito, Libya, 1940 (US.2-LS.2)

Caproni-Vizzola F.5, 167° Gr., Rome-Ciampino, 1942 (US.2-LS.1)

Caproni-Vizzola F.5, 300ª Sq (167° Gr.), Rome-Ciampino, 1943 (no wing markings)

Caproni-Vizzola F.4, MM.5932, 303ª Sq. (167° Gr.), Capua, 1942 (no wing markings)

Caproni-Vizzola F.6M, MM.481, 303ª Sq (167° Gr.), September 1942 (no wing markings)

IMAM Ro.57, 97° Gr. Autonomo Tuffatori, Rome-Ciampino, July 1943. Note position of fuselage Fascio, hidden behind engine cowling (US.3-LS.3)

Dewoitine D.520, 370ª Sq. (24° Gr. Autonomo), Metato, August 1943 (no wing markings)

SCALE: 1/72

246

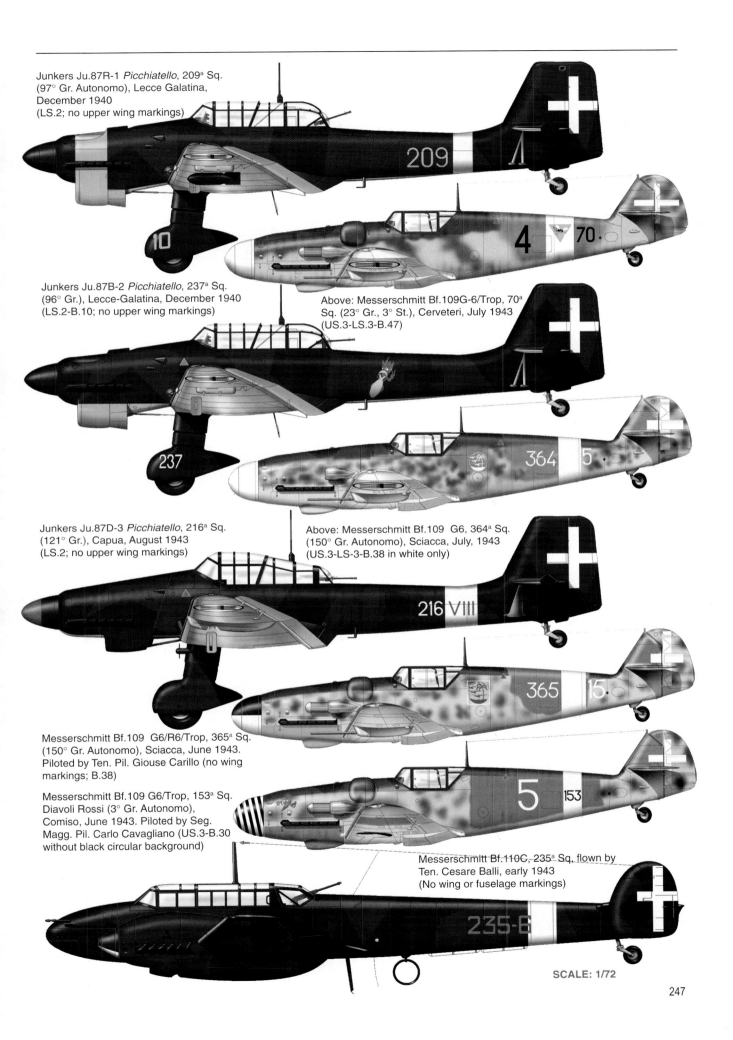

Junkers Ju.87R-1 *Picchiatello*, 209ᵃ Sq.
(97° Gr. Autonomo), Lecce Galatina,
December 1940
(LS.2; no upper wing markings)

Junkers Ju.87B-2 *Picchiatello*, 237ᵃ Sq.
(96° Gr.), Lecce-Galatina, December 1940
(LS.2-B.10; no upper wing markings)

Above: Messerschmitt Bf.109G-6/Trop, 70ᵃ
Sq. (23° Gr., 3° St.), Cerveteri, July 1943
(US.3-LS.3-B.47)

Junkers Ju.87D-3 *Picchiatello*, 216ᵃ Sq.
(121° Gr.), Capua, August 1943
(LS.2; no upper wing markings)

Above: Messerschmitt Bf.109 G6, 364ᵃ Sq.
(150° Gr. Autonomo), Sciacca, July, 1943
(US.3-LS-3-B.38 in white only)

Messerschmitt Bf.109 G6/R6/Trop, 365ᵃ Sq.
(150° Gr. Autonomo), Sciacca, June 1943.
Piloted by Ten. Pil. Giouse Carillo (no wing
markings; B.38)

Messerschmitt Bf.109 G6/Trop, 153ᵃ Sq.
Diavoli Rossi (3° Gr. Autonomo),
Comiso, June 1943. Piloted by Seg.
Magg. Pil. Carlo Cavagliano (US.3-B.30
without black circular background)

Messerschmitt Bf.110C, 235ᵃ Sq. flown by
Ten. Cesare Balli, early 1943
(No wing or fuselage markings)

SCALE: 1/72

247

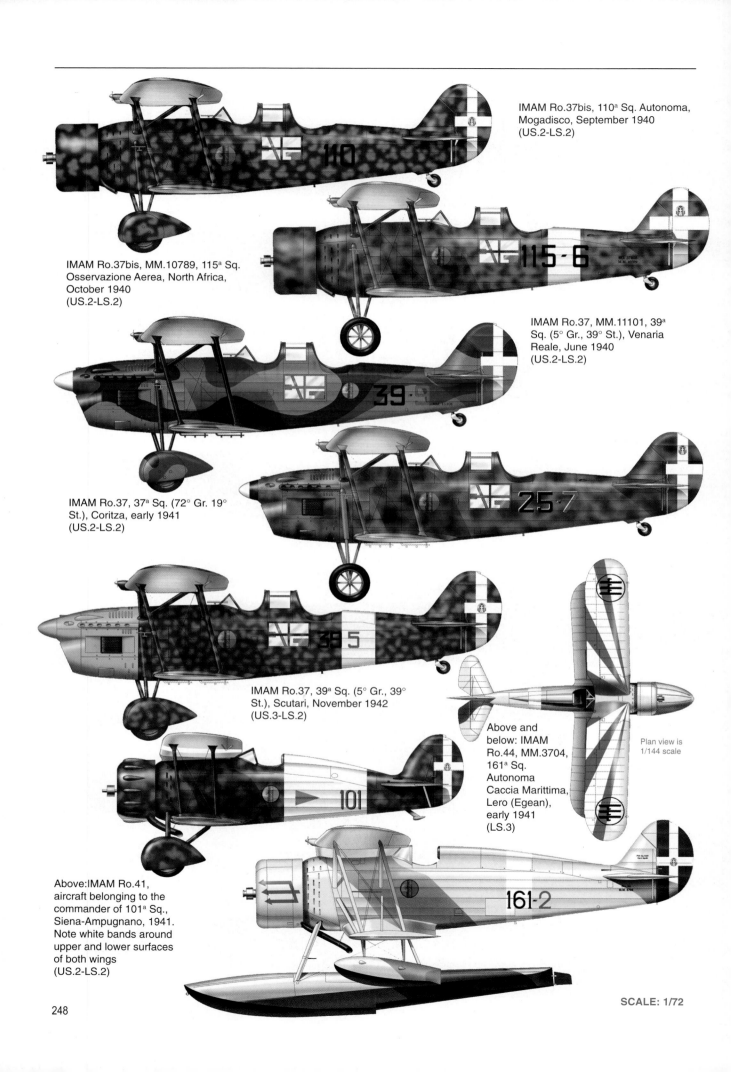

IMAM Ro.37bis, 110ᵃ Sq. Autonoma, Mogadisco, September 1940 (US.2-LS.2)

IMAM Ro.37bis, MM.10789, 115ᵃ Sq. Osservazione Aerea, North Africa, October 1940 (US.2-LS.2)

IMAM Ro.37, MM.11101, 39ᵃ Sq. (5° Gr., 39° St.), Venaria Reale, June 1940 (US.2-LS.2)

IMAM Ro.37, 37ᵃ Sq. (72° Gr. 19° St.), Coritza, early 1941 (US.2-LS.2)

IMAM Ro.37, 39ᵃ Sq. (5° Gr., 39° St.), Scutari, November 1942 (US.3-LS.2)

Above and below: IMAM Ro.44, MM.3704, 161ᵃ Sq. Autonoma Caccia Marittima, Lero (Egean), early 1941 (LS.3)

Plan view is 1/144 scale

Above: IMAM Ro.41, aircraft belonging to the commander of 101ᵃ Sq., Siena-Ampugnano, 1941. Note white bands around upper and lower surfaces of both wings (US.2-LS.2)

SCALE: 1/72

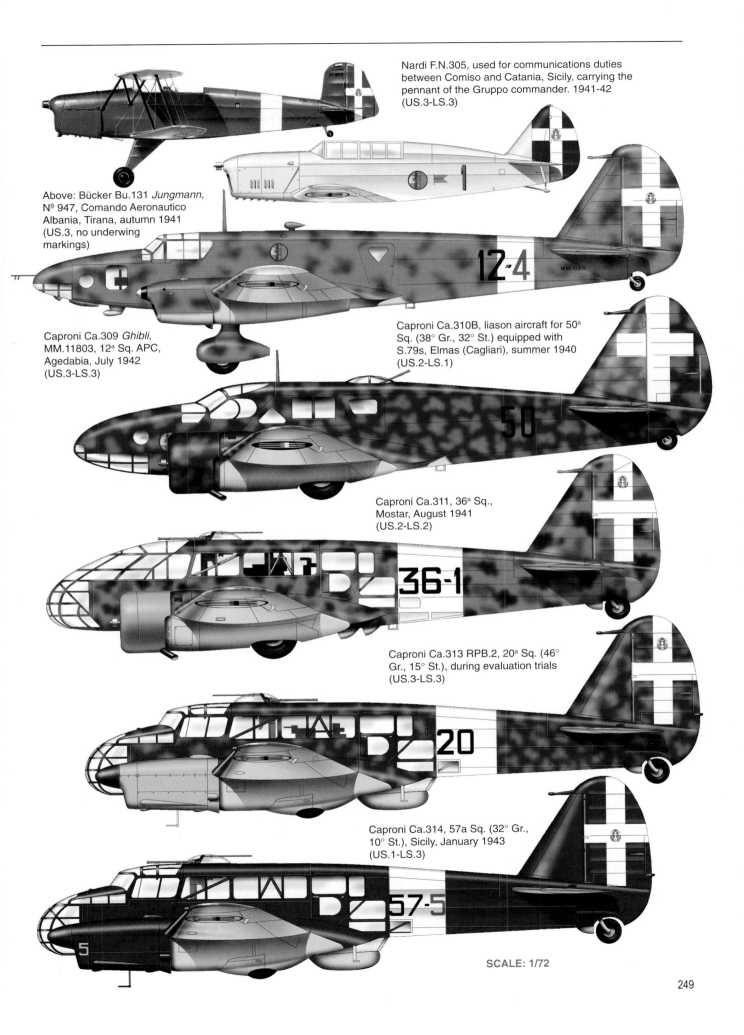

Nardi F.N.305, used for communications duties between Comiso and Catania, Sicily, carrying the pennant of the Gruppo commander. 1941-42 (US.3-LS.3)

Above: Bücker Bu.131 *Jungmann*, Nº 947, Comando Aeronautico Albania, Tirana, autumn 1941 (US.3, no underwing markings)

Caproni Ca.309 *Ghibli*, MM.11803, 12ª Sq. APC, Agedabia, July 1942 (US.3-LS.3)

Caproni Ca.310B, liason aircraft for 50ª Sq. (38° Gr., 32° St.) equipped with S.79s, Elmas (Cagliari), summer 1940 (US.2-LS.1)

Caproni Ca.311, 36ª Sq., Mostar, August 1941 (US.2-LS.2)

Caproni Ca.313 RPB.2, 20ª Sq. (46° Gr., 15° St.), during evaluation trials (US.3-LS.3)

Caproni Ca.314, 57a Sq. (32° Gr., 10° St.), Sicily, January 1943 (US.1-LS.3)

SCALE: 1/72

249

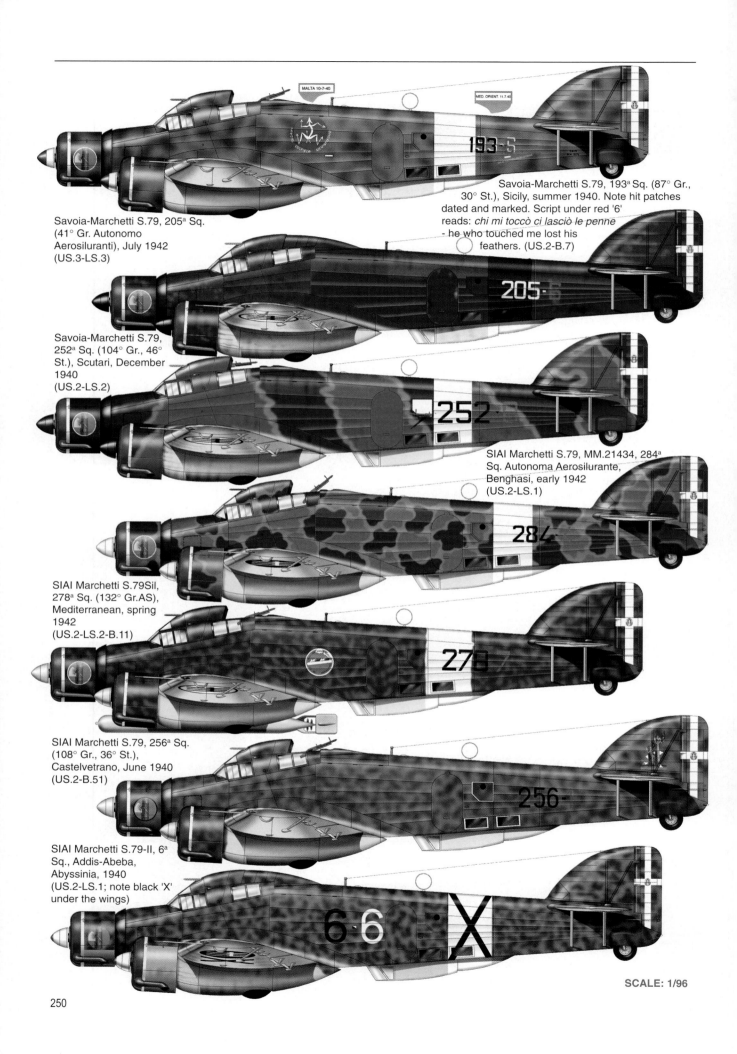

Savoia-Marchetti S.79, 193ª Sq. (87° Gr., 30° St.), Sicily, summer 1940. Note hit patches dated and marked. Script under red '6' reads: *chi mi toccò ci lasciò le penne* - he who touched me lost his feathers. (US.2-B.7)

Savoia-Marchetti S.79, 205ª Sq. (41° Gr. Autonomo Aerosiluranti), July 1942 (US.3-LS.3)

Savoia-Marchetti S.79, 252ª Sq. (104° Gr., 46° St.), Scutari, December 1940 (US.2-LS.2)

SIAI Marchetti S.79, MM.21434, 284ª Sq. Autonoma Aerosilurante, Benghasi, early 1942 (US.2-LS.1)

SIAI Marchetti S.79Sil, 278ª Sq. (132° Gr.AS), Mediterranean, spring 1942 (US.2-LS.2-B.11)

SIAI Marchetti S.79, 256ª Sq. (108° Gr., 36° St.), Castelvetrano, June 1940 (US.2-B.51)

SIAI Marchetti S.79-II, 6ª Sq., Addis-Abeba, Abyssinia, 1940 (US.2-LS.1; note black 'X' under the wings)

SCALE: 1/96

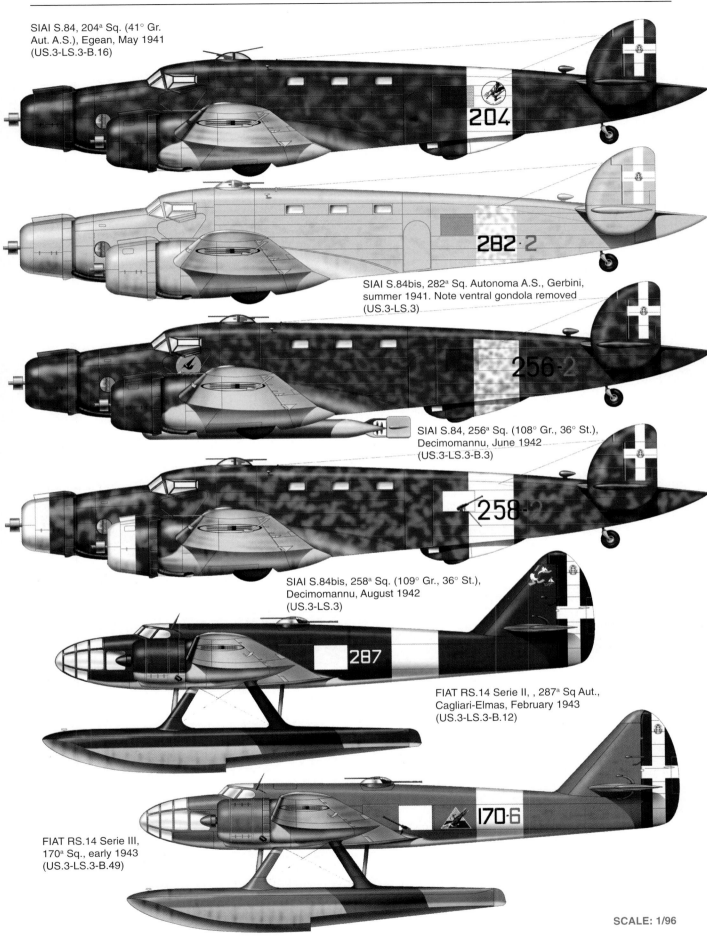

SIAI S.84, 204ª Sq. (41° Gr.
Aut. A.S.), Egean, May 1941
(US.3-LS.3-B.16)

SIAI S.84bis, 282ª Sq. Autonoma A.S., Gerbini,
summer 1941. Note ventral gondola removed
(US.3-LS.3)

SIAI S.84, 256ª Sq. (108° Gr., 36° St.),
Decimomannu, June 1942
(US.3-LS.3-B.3)

SIAI S.84bis, 258ª Sq. (109° Gr., 36° St.),
Decimomannu, August 1942
(US.3-LS.3)

FIAT RS.14 Serie II, , 287ª Sq Aut.,
Cagliari-Elmas, February 1943
(US.3-LS.3-B.12)

FIAT RS.14 Serie III,
170ª Sq., early 1943
(US.3-LS.3-B.49)

SCALE: 1/96

251

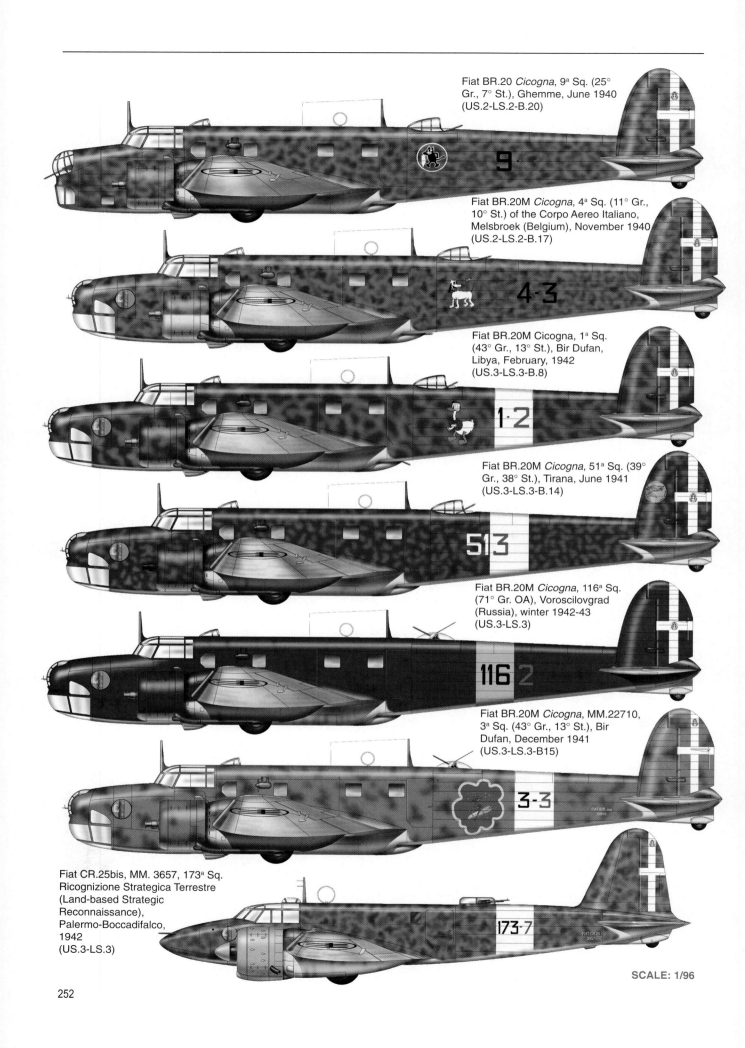

Fiat BR.20 *Cicogna*, 9ª Sq. (25°
Gr., 7° St.), Ghemme, June 1940
(US.2-LS.2-B.20)

Fiat BR.20M *Cicogna*, 4ª Sq. (11° Gr.,
10° St.) of the Corpo Aereo Italiano,
Melsbroek (Belgium), November 1940
(US.2-LS.2-B.17)

Fiat BR.20M Cicogna, 1ª Sq.
(43° Gr., 13° St.), Bir Dufan,
Libya, February, 1942
(US.3-LS.3-B.8)

Fiat BR.20M *Cicogna*, 51ª Sq. (39°
Gr., 38° St.), Tirana, June 1941
(US.3-LS.3-B.14)

Fiat BR.20M *Cicogna*, 116ª Sq.
(71° Gr. OA), Voroscilovgrad
(Russia), winter 1942-43
(US.3-LS.3)

Fiat BR.20M *Cicogna*, MM.22710,
3ª Sq. (43° Gr., 13° St.), Bir
Dufan, December 1941
(US.3-LS.3-B15)

Fiat CR.25bis, MM. 3657, 173ª Sq.
Ricognizione Strategica Terrestre
(Land-based Strategic
Reconnaissance),
Palermo-Boccadifalco,
1942
(US.3-LS.3)

SCALE: 1/96

252

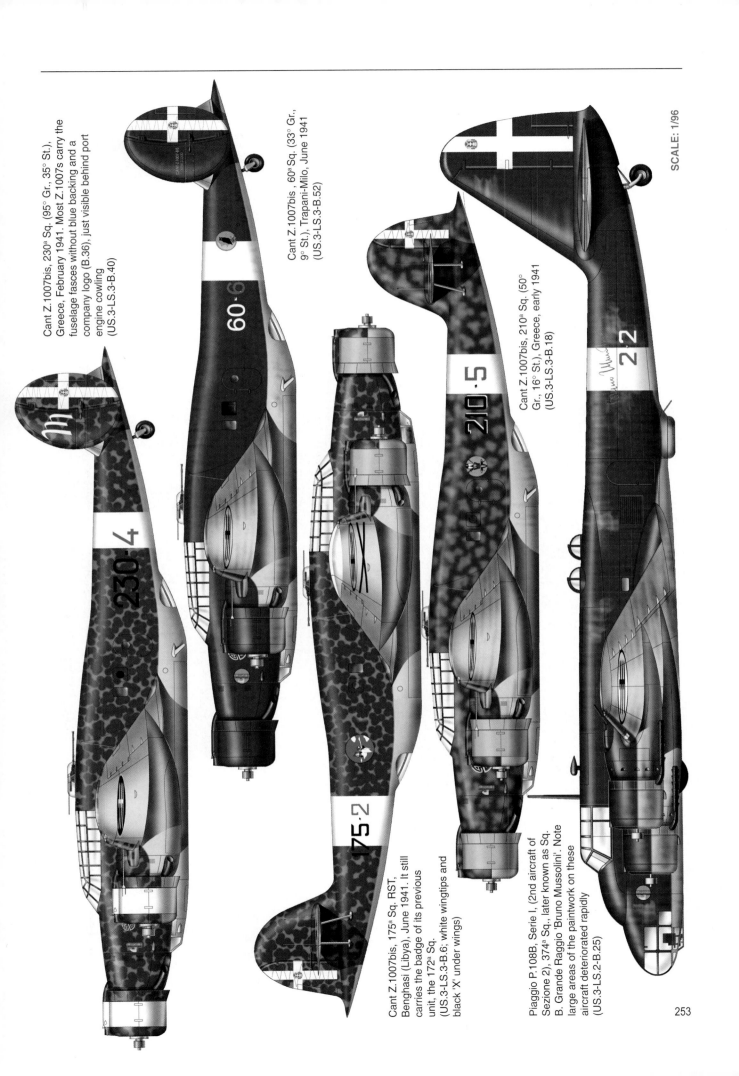

Cant Z.1007bis, 230ª Sq. (95° Gr., 35° St.),
Greece, February 1941. Most Z.1007s carry the
fuselage fasces without blue backing and a
company logo (B.36), just visible behind port
engine cowling
(US.3-LS.3-B.40)

Cant Z.1007bis , 60ª Sq. (33° Gr.,
9° St.), Trapani-Milo, June 1941
(US.3-LS.3-B.52)

Cant Z.1007bis, 210ª Sq. (50°
Gr., 16° St.), Greece, early 1941
(US.3-LS.3-B.18)

Cant Z.1007bis, 175ª Sq. RST,
Benghasi (Libya), June 1941. It still
carries the badge of its previous
unit, the 172ª Sq.
(US.3-LS.3-B.6; white wingtips and
black 'X' under wings)

Piaggio P.108B, Serie I, (2nd aircraft of
Sezione 2), 374ª Sq., later known as Sq.
B. Grande Raggio 'Bruno Mussolini'. Note
large areas of the paintwork on these
aircraft deteriorated rapidly
(US.3-LS.2-B.25)

SCALE: 1/96

253

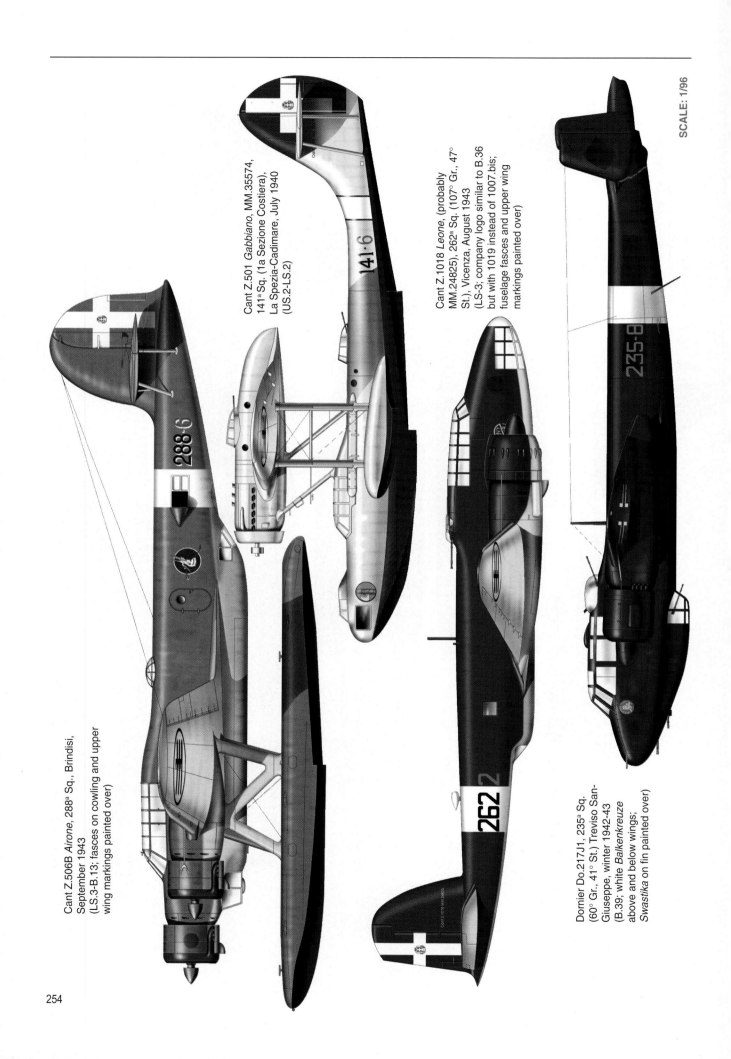

Cant Z.501 *Gabbiano*, MM.35574,
141ª Sq. (1a Sezione Costiera),
La Spezia-Cadimare, July 1940
(US.2-LS.2)

Cant Z.1018 *Leone*, (probably
MM.24825), 262ª Sq. (107° Gr., 47°
St.), Vicenza, August 1943
(LS.3; company logo similar to B.36
but with 1019 instead of 1007.bis;
fuselage fasces and upper wing
markings painted over)

Cant Z.506B *Airone*, 288ª Sq., Brindisi,
September 1943
(LS.3-B.13; fasces on cowling and upper
wing markings painted over)

Dornier Do.217J1, 235ª Sq.
(60° Gr., 41° St.) Treviso San-
Giuseppe, winter 1942-43
(B.39; white *Balkenkreuze*
above and below wings;
Swastika on fin painted over)

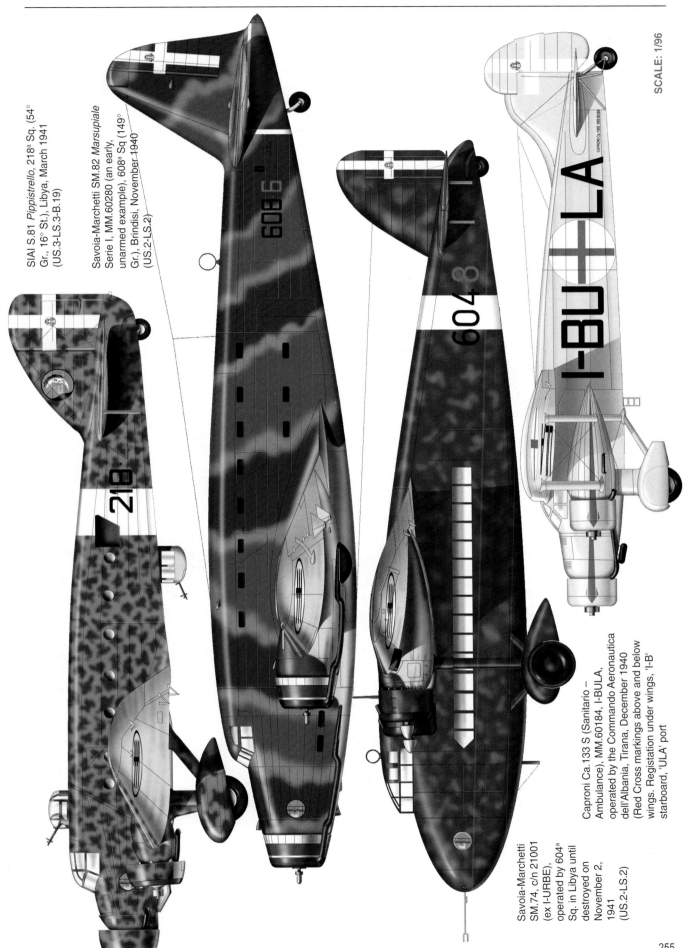

SIAI S.81 *Pippistrello*, 218ª Sq. (54° Gr., 16° St.), Libya, March 1941 (US.3-LS.3-B.19)

Savoia-Marchetti SM.82 *Marsupiale* Serie I, MM.60280 (an early, unarmed example), 608ª Sq (149° Gr.), Brindisi, November 1940 (US.2-LS.2)

Savoia-Marchetti SM.74, c/n 21001 (ex I-URBE), operated by 604ª Sq. in Libya until destroyed on November 2, 1941 (US.2-LS.2)

Caproni Ca.133 S (Sanitario – Ambulance), MM.60184, I-BULA, operated by the Commando Aeronautica dell'Albania, Tirana, December 1940 (Red Cross markings above and below wings. Registration under wings. 'I-B' starboard, 'ULA' port

B.1 B.2 B.3 B.4 B.5 B.6
B.7 B.8 B.9 B.10 B.11 B.12
B.13 B.14 B.15 B.16 B.17 B.18
B.19 B.20 B.21 B.22 B.23 B.24
B.25 B.26 B.27 B.28
B.29 B.30 B.31 B.32 B.33 B.34
B.35 B.36 B.37 B.38 B.39 B.40
B.41 B.42 B.43 B.44 B.45 B.46
B.47 B.48 B.49 B.50 B.51 B.52

WING MARKINGS

KEYED TO THE COLOUR PROFILES

GENERAL NOTE TO COLOUR PAGE CAPTIONS

The final line (within brackets) in each caption is keyed to the drawings above and the unit and personal emblems on page 256. Thus, for example: (US.1-LS.1-B.50) referes to the upper surfaces marking (US.1), the lower surface marking (LS.1) and the unit badge which apprears on the aircraft (B.50)

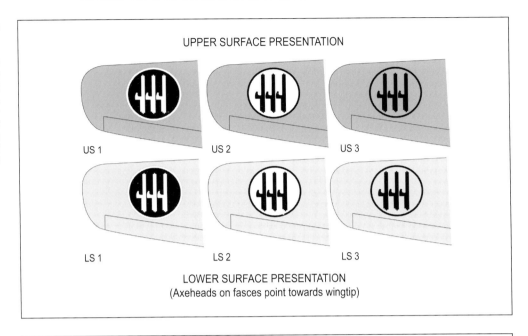

UPPER SURFACE PRESENTATION

US 1 US 2 US 3

LS 1 LS 2 LS 3

LOWER SURFACE PRESENTATION
(Axeheads on fasces point towards wingtip)

SOME FASCES STYLING VARIATIONS

Note that these markings, together with the fuselage fasces, were generally deleted or painted over after July 25, 1943

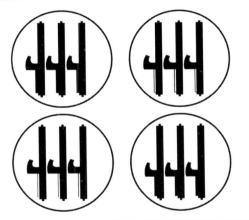

KEY TO UNIT BADGES

B1:	Fuselage fasces	B17:	4ª Squadriglia BT	B35:	10° Gruppo CT
B2:	Arms of House of Savoy on tail	B18:	210ª Squadriglia BT	B36:	CRDA Cant Z.1007 trademark
B3:	108° Gruppo Autonomo	B19:	54° Gruppo BT	B37:	51° Stormo CT
B4:	155° Gruppo CT	B20:	9ª Squadriglia BT	B38:	150° Gruppo Autonomo CT
B5:	163ª Squadriglia CT	B21:	1° Stormo CT	B39:	235ª Squadriglia BT
B6:	172ª Squadriglia RST	B22:	150ª Squadriglia Assalto	B40:	230ª Squadriglia BT
B7:	193ª squadriglia BT	B23:	160ª Squadriglia Assalto	B41:	377ª Squadriglia CN
B8:	1a Squadriglia BT	B24:	153° Gruppo Autonomo CT	B42:	162a Squadriglia CT
B9:	21° Gruppo Autonomo CT	B25:	374ª Squadriglia	B43:	22° Gruppo Autonomo CT
B10:	237ª Squadriglia BaT	B26:	4° Stormo CT	B44:	157° Gruppo Autonomo CT
B11:	278ª Squadriglia AS	B27:	9° Gruppo CT	B45:	152° Gruppo CT
B12:	287ª Squadriglia Autonomo RM	B28:	2° Gruppo Autonomo CT	B46:	150° Gruppo Autonomo CT
B13:	288ª Squadriglia RM	B29:	152° Gruppo CT	B47:	3° Stormo CT
B14:	51ª Squadriglia BT	B30:	6° Stormpo CT	B48:	96° Gruppo BaT
B15:	3ª Squadriglia BT	B31:	410ª Squadriglia CT	B49:	170ª Squadriglia Autonomo RM
B16:	41° Gruppo Autonomo AS	B32:	18° Gruppo CT	B50:	154° Gruppo Autonomo CT
		B33:	85ª Squadriglia CT	B51:	30° Stormo BT
		B34:	97ª Squadriglia CT	B52:	60ª Squadriglia BT

AIRCRAFT MARKINGS

From 1926 a single grey-brown fascio in a light blue circle, with black bordering, was applied on both sides of the forward fuselage or engine cowling. The fascio blade always faced vertically forwards or horizontally outwards. This symbol, consisting of an axe bound by ribbons to a bundle of rods, dated from ancient times and represented the power and authority of the imperial Roman state. It was adopted by Mussolini and his political party, hence the term 'Fascists'.

Originating from 1935 and Mussolini's consolidation of power, a new national insignia was introduced. This consisted of three black fasces on a white circle, bordered in black, and applied to the upperwings. A reverse white on black background was sometimes applied underwing. By 1942 the background colour was deleted to allow the camouflage to show through. Prior to this being officially adopted, some units had already overpainted the upper white circle for better concealment.

From June 1940 the rudder stripes (green, white red, green to front) were converted into a simple white cross on both sides, sometimes with the horizontal arm extending across the fin. The badge of the House of Savioa (introduced in 1930) was placed in or above the centre of the cross. For the first few weeks of combat, some units still retained the pre-war tricolour rudder markings (e.g. Z506Bs of 35 Stormo). Very few foreign aircraft wore the fascio or Savoia badge. Only Bf 109s and Fi 156s in this category used upper wing insignia.

Other markings were adopted as the conflict de-veloped. A broad white band was applied around the mid-fuselage from the autumn of 1940, although not widely used until early 1941, when the need for recognition between the Axis partners in the Mediterranean arose. Aircraft operating with the C.A.I. over Belgium and the English Channel during the Battle of Britain received yellow engine cowlings. This practice was also used in the Balkans and Russia. On the Eastern Front Italian aircraft also carried a yellow fuselage band in line with Luftwaffe custom. Yellow wingtips were added to aircraft in Russia from 1942, and fighters on this front also added one or two white triangles above and below each wing with the base aligned on the leading edge. Yellow could also be seen on the cowlings of aircraft in North Africa during 1941-1942. White spinners were used on fighters in Italy, with white extended to engine cowlings, particularly on bombers, in the Mediterranean. Aircraft in East Africa wore a black 'X' over the white fuselage band, also with a black cross under each wing inboard of the insignia. For night missions the fuselage bands and fin crosses were usually blacked out.

Units were referred to in Roman numerals until 1 January 1940, when all documentation was ordered to be written in Arabic numerals. For example, XII Gruppo became 12 Gruppo.

The squadriglia number was normally shown on both sides of the mid-fuselage, followed by a hyphen and the aircraft number (rarely higher than 15). Occasionally the squadriglia number would appear on the fin, such as on the Re 2002s of 101 Gruppo. The colour was nearly always black, although some aircraft with dark camouflage received white numbers. The aircraft number was mainly red, but black, white or yellow was used if paint stocks were limited. These numbers were occasionally repeated on undercarriage legs (fighters and assault planes) or the cockpit area (bombers). The hyphen usually matched the colour of the squadriglia number. For dark camouflage schemes the numbers were outlined in white or yellow. There was no set size for the numbers. Occasionally units used coloured cowlings, spinners, and bands instead of squadriglie numbers. 377 Sq for example, used red, white, and yellow cowlings on their Re 2000s in mid 1941. 6 Gruppo's MC 200s had a white tip on their tail in early 1941. 151 Gruppo had coloured stars on their MC 202s. Trainers used a three letter code, which indicated the location or role. This was usually an abbreviation of the home base, such as FAL, used on Breda 25s used at Falconara.

Unit commanders sometimes used personal aircraft with the Gruppo or Stormo number applied in Roman numerals (e.g. CLIII on an MC 202 of 153 Gruppo). The commander's pennant was also applied under the cockpit or on the rear fuselage. The colours of these varied, but were usually seen as a red horizontal stripe on a light blue standard, or black on white.

Company logos were also applied, mainly on bombers and transport aircraft.

Officially, individual markings and victory tallies were frowned upon. This is why tail fins or fuselages marked in the way the Germans or Allies celebrated their 'kills' are rarely seen. Honours were given to the unit, rather than the pilot or crew. It is difficult, even now, to ascertain individual claims unless the crews kept their own unofficial records. Research in the official communiques rarely reveals nominated airmen, unless the unit commander was involved.

215 Right: *A Macchi MC 202 of the 79ª Squadriglia, 6° Gruppo, 1° Stormo, in North Africa, late in 1941. Finished in the 'serir' mottle camou-flage, this is the aircraft of the squadron commander, as indicated by the blue and red pennant under the cockpit. The emblem is the famous archer of the 1° Stormo*

216 Right: *Trouble with the tailwheel of a Macchi MC 202 of 81ª Squadriglia, 6° Gruppo at Tamet, Tripoli-tania at the end of 1941*

217 Below: *Two Fiat G 50s of the 20° Gruppo, 56° Stormo, of the CAI at Ursel in Belgium showing the poor adhesive qualities of Italian paint in the depths of a northern winter. Machine in the background with the pennant is that of the 20° Gruppo's commander,* Maggiore *Mario Bonzano*

218: *An overall dark green Macchi MC 200 of the 95ª Squadriglia, 18° Gruppo. To judge by the background scenery, the location could be Greece early in 1942. Unusually, the aircraft has a name, 'Robur', written in small white letters forward of the windscreen*

219: *Pilots discussing tactics in front of a lineup of Macchi MC 200s of the 372ª Squadriglia, 153° Gruppo. Date and location unknown, but possibly early in the Balkan capaign on accunt of the yellow noses and the retention of the white discs to the wing fasces*

220: *The prototype Fiat G55, MM491, just before its first flight from Corso Francia, on 30 April 1942. It is finished in the so-called D1A 'lizard' camouflage adopted by Fiat which used Nocciola Chiaro 4 and Verde Oliva Scuro 2*

221: *A Luftwaffe pilot checks the route for the departing pilot of a Macchi MC 200 of an unidentified unit, somewhere in the Western Desert. The aircraft is finished in a classic D1 pattern of a dark green backround with brown spots, which seems entirely inappropriate for desert use. The difference in uniforms between the two pilots speaks volumes about their respective air forces*

222: *An anonymous Reggiane Re 2000, apparently brand new. The soft camouflage pattern appears to consist of green spots on a yellow ochre base. The nose band is yellow, that on the fuselage white. Date and location unknown*

223: *The pilot of a 162ª Squadriglia, 161° Gruppo, Fiat CR 42 boarding his machine, probably at Rodi Marizza in the Aegean. Date is summer 1941, shortly after they had formed for the task of shipping protection in the area. Camouflage is probably a C1 pattern using three uppersurface colours, combined with a yellow cowling and the usual white fuselage band*

224: *A mechanic helps the pilot of a 377ª Squadriglia Fiat CR 42CN with his straps. Given the job of both night and day interception over Sicily in autumn of 1942, the aircraft wears day camouflage and a badge with an obvious nocturnal theme*

225: *September 1943, and the pilots of an unidentified fighter Squadriglia have brought their Macchi MC 202s over to the Allied side. The unit and national insignia all appear to have been painted over, with the exception of the arms of the House of Savoy on the rudder. The fairly hard-edged blotches suggest that the aircraft is finished in the D2C pattern*

226: *One of the last distinctive markings to be applied on Italian aircraft was a black and white spiral spinner, inherited from their German allies. This one is on the nose of the Fiat G 55 (MM91150) which was taken back to Tangmere for examination at the end of the war*

227: *The red devil of the 6°
Stormo CT having his beard
pulled on the flank of a Fiat
CR 32. There are no other
clues to help identify the
aircraft further. Date and
location are unknown*

228: *Another unidentified
Fiat CR 32 in a very light
finish. It is believed that this
is not the usual silver, but
white, which was the colour
liberally used by training
aircraft. Presumably the
machine had been relegated
to advanced training with an
unidentifed school or
squadron, which could
explain this undignified
pose*

229: *Another odd marking
scheme, but with a unique
story behind it concerns this
Cant Z506B in RAF
markings. The crew of
MM45432 (once 139-13 of
139ª Squadriglia RST) rescued the crew of a Beaufort
torpedo bomber which had
been shot down off Greece
on 28 July 1942. Following
an overnight stay at the
Italian base, the same aircraft was being used to take
the prisoners to Taranto
when the RAF crew over-
powered the Italians and
hijacked the Cant to Malta.
It is seen here some time
later in RAF markings,
possibly in Egypt*

DEFEAT
Why the Regia Aeronautica lost

Ultimately, the Italian armed forces were defeated on the battlefield. Most of the reasons for this lie in the original ill-judged decision to enter the war when those forces, and the nation, were badly prepared and under-resourced for a war of more than a few weeks. With the benefit of hindsight it is clear that the collapse of the RA was only a matter of time once combat had been joined—the force simply had too many factors working against it for it to succeed in a conflict against major industrial nations.

Firstly, even at its peak in 1941-42, Italian aircraft production was only 1/50th of US production at its peak in 1944-1945. Most of those aircraft produced by Italian industry suffered from indifferent engines. Liquid-cooled types had only, on average, 40% of the power of similar British and US types. Radials were more reliable, but produced only about half the power of, say, the Pratt & Whitney R-2800. The effect of this upon aircraft design meant that large aircraft needed to be tri-motors, which in turn created even more drag and complexity and reduced capabilities even further.

As for armament, the most reliable Italian aircraft gun, the Breda SAFAT, was heavy and bulky, and consequently needed to be in the fuselage, which in turn reduced the number of guns which could be carried, thereby reducing

the weight of fire. This was a particular handicap for the fighter pilots when trying to shoot down modern well-armoured metal aircraft.

Much production effort was wasted on the unnecessary duplication of types, such as the 5 Series fighters, all of which were similar in capabilities. In 1941, Italy had as many prototypes under test as the Germans, who had an aeronautical industry some twenty times larger, and nearly as many projects under development as the US, which had fifty times the industrial capacity. As an example of what might have been achieved with more rigorous control of the industry, had the Italians earlier rationalised production and development in the excellent Macchi MC 202 fighter, there could have been large numbers available in Africa at the time of Rommel's advances. More significantly, by the time of the Sicily landings there could have been 500 or more available—instead of the 100 or so serviceable examples scattered throughout Italy. Much of the blame for this situation lies with various aircraft companies being allowed too much latitude to protect their vested interests.

230 Above: Allied troops inspecting the wreck of a Fiat CR 42, which has been extensively damaged by fire, somewhere in the desert. The white wingtip and background to the fasces marking suggest that it is during the early period of the war

There was another, less obvious, factor working against the Regia Aeronautica. In a country almost completely lacking in natural resources, particularly steel and oil, the need for foreign exchange meant that export orders for aircraft took priority, both before the war and even after it began. Among the customers for Italian aircraft were Sweden, Hungary, Yugoslavia and several countries in South America. Indeed, so great was this need that Count Caproni vainly tried to dissuade Mussolini from entering the war as the Caproni company had a large order for Ca 313s from the RAF!

The proliferation of types led to lack of spares keeping many aircraft on the ground for want of simple components. As an example, the nightmarish situation developed in North Africa where units with a complement on paper of 50 or 60 aircraft had only a dozen or so operable. Sand filters were a particular problem, compounded by the highly inefficent Italian support system. It is interesting to note that German aircraft never suffered from this particular problem to the degree that the the RA did. This is even more remarkable when one considers that most of the sand filters used by the Luftwaffe were made in Italy.

Logistics support was so bad that the Italian Chief of Staff, Count Ugo Cavallero, seriously suggested that ammunition and fuel be shipped to North Africa concealed in the lower hulls of hospital ships to avoid the Allied blockades.

Bad design planning was another self-inflicted wound for the RA. Bedazzled by the easy successes in Spain and Ethiopia, Italian planners responsible for future aircraft came up with specifications which were wholly insufficient in performance and capability. For example, at the time the Italians were introducing the new Fiat CR 42 in mid-1939, the RAF already had nearly 300 Spitfires and 400 Hurricanes in service. Each of these was capable of over 300 mph and carried eight guns. The Fiat was certainly highly agile, but could manage only 270 mph—if pushed—and had two guns. Total production reached 1,553—but not until June 1943.

As for bombers, despite the fact that Piaggio had four-engined prototypes under test in 1937, lengthy development times—and the cost—meant that the RA had to make do with lumbering bomber-transport types such as the SM 81 and Ca 133 for far too long. In contrast, the RAF had begun phasing out their equivalent Harrow and Bombay well before the war and replacing them by Wellingtons, Hampdens and Whitleys.

Yet, not all components of the RA were disasters waiting to happen. The often-overlooked reconnaissance units, especially the maritime units, did sterling work with their elderly flying boats and seaplanes. Indeed, the contribution of the OA units was vital to the Axis before the first battle at Alamein. Even so, these laudable efforts could not make up for the fact that not only were most aircraft of indifferent quality, the whole composition of the Regia Aeronautica was flawed. When Italy joined the war in June 1940, there were almost 1,000 serviceable aircraft to hand. About 40% of these were SM 79s. Perhaps in the country which fathered Giulio Douhet one should not be surprised at the preponderance of bomber types. Yet, typically, only 1,200 or so examples of the SM 79, the most numerous Italian bomber, were built; and that over ten years.

The crucial impact of the spares shortages can be seen in the way that as early as January 1941 only 28 SM 79s were available. This at a critical phase during the East African/Ethiopian campaigns.

The effect of all this upon operational units was nothing short of disastrous. In theory a fighter Gruppo consisted of two or three Squadrigli. Significantly, each of these was supposed to have a complement of only twelve aircraft. Compare this to the average US fighter squadron establishment which had a minimum of 18 aircraft (and could have as many as 30 by 1943), and the RAF which had a usual establishment of 16. With spares and replacement shortages it was not unusual for a Gruppo which, on paper, had 18-27 aircraft on strength to have only 50% serviceability.

RA strength was further dissipated in pointless expeditions such as those to the Channel in 1940 and Russia in 1941. In neither case had the Germans asked for help. In both cases the RA found again that its equipment was simply not up to the task asked of it.

This bad situation was exacerbated as the war progressed as many capable aircraft engineers were simply impressed by the Germans into working in Germany, leaving only semi-trained personnel available to the home industry and air force.

Throughout the war the RA was handicapped by poor communications. Not only did Italian industry fail to develop adequate radio, radar was effectively non-existent. The defence of Italy by night therefore depended on second-rate aircraft rejected for day use, and Luftwaffe hand-me-downs. Ultimately, the Italian war effort had to be shored up by the Germans, who were often in nearly as bad a situation as the Italians themselves.

Arguably, Italy had lost her war before it even began, thanks to the incompetence of its dictator and his delusions of Imperial grandeur. Short of equipment, short of training, short of aircraft and of time, the Italian airmen had little with which to do the job which their leadership had thrust upon them. Given these enormous disadvantages, all too often the only thing which the men of the Regia Aeronautica had in quantity equal to their opponents was courage alone.

231 Above: *Italian crafts-manship was of the highest order, but production methods were old-fashioned. These are IMAM Ro 37bis in the Capodichino plant before the war*

232 Left: *Heavy bombers were seen as the cutting edge by all the major air forces of the period, but the Piaggio P.108 was an expensive diversion for the Italians who could never afford enough of them to create a viable striking force*

233 Left: *With no clear strategic aims from their political masters, nor the means with which to carry them out, much of the RA's potential was frittered away in pointless campiagns of little more than propaganda value. A case in point are these Fiat BR 20Ms from 116ᵃ Squadriglia, 71° Gruppo of the CSIR, somewhere in Russia, probably Saporoshje, in winter 1942-1943. The numbers committed were far too small to have any real effect, although the units acquitted themselves well considering their equipment. Over 60% of the Italians sent to Russia were casualties*

234: *Another waste of Italian lives and equipment was the stay in Belgium by the CAI during the tail end of the Battle of Britain. The nonplussed Germans were polite allies, but really had little use for pilots who had had no bad weather flying training. It should have been obvious that even if little could be done in the short term about the equipment of the RA, then there was a desperate need for properly structured training. Those Italians fortunate enough to be trained by the Luftwaffe had their chances of survival greatly enhanced—and were more use as airmen. Here Fiat CR 42s of the 95ª Squadriglia fly close escort to one of the five Cant Z.1007s of the 172ª Squadriglia sent to the Channel. The aircraft with the white band is that of the Gruppo commander, Maggiore Ferruccio Vosilla*

235: *An RAF airman shows where the arms of Savoy have been removed by victorious pilots (from 257 Squadron RAF) from the Fiat BR 20M, 243-2, (MM 6976) of the 243ª Squadriglia, 99° Gruppo, 43° Stormo, which crashed in Tangham Forest on Armistice Day 1940. It had been shot down by Hurricanes from 46 and 257 Squadrons RAF. Two of Tenente Affriani's crew were killed, the other four were taken prisoner*

236: *Taken from the manufacturer's brochure, this picture shows the rear gunner/observer's position in the IMAM Ro 43 float-plane. Similar in concept and purpose to the Fairey Seafox, it reveals interesting structural details. Looking to the tail, there are two firing steps for use when operating the rear gun. In the centre is the A-200/1 radio transmitter and AR4 receiver, with the handwheel for the trailing aerial to the right. Top speed was quoted as 300kph at 2500m altitude, with a rider to the effect that there was a tolerance of 3% on performance either way*

237: *A view of the radio-operator in a Cant Z.1007 at his post. Dominating the picture are the ammunition feeds to the two waist guns. For some reason works drawings show the star-board version to be a 7.7mm Scotti, while that to port was of 12.7mm calibre. The Alcione was an excellent design, despite its tri-motor engine layout and wooden structure. This was its major handicap, as the aircraft burned easily*

238: *A less successful design was the Savoia Marchetti SM 84, essentially a rehash of the SM 79. It also had a wooden structure and serves to illustrate how Italian designers were handicapped by the materials available, but also hung on to outmoded concepts for too long*

239: *One of the unsung success stories of the Italian aviation industry was the Savoia Marchetti SM 82. With the ability to carry a dismantled Fiat CR 42 fighter in its capacious fuselage, it was the only means the RA had of resupplying its outposts in East Africa. The Germans, not easily impressed by their Allies' aircraft, commandeered almost half of the 720 examples built, a number of which served at Stalingrad. The Italian transport arm was, on balance, one of the most effective components of the Regia Aeronautica, despite fearful losses to Allied attacks*

240: *A ground crewman servicing the rear Breda SAFAT 7.7mm machine gun of an IMAM Ro 37bis. Although the training of aircrew left something to be desired, the ground crews were reasonably well served by their instruction. A major problem for the maintenance crews, however, was the very low amount of specialised ground support equipment and vehicles available. Consequently this led to inefficiency in re-arming and refuelling between sorties. It is clearly difficult to attain high sortie rates when, for instance, refuelling has to be done by hand pumps from fuel drums*

241: *Not all sections of the Regia Aeronautica were badly equipped. The long heritage of marine aviation in Italy meant that aircraft such as this Cant Z.506B were more than adequate for their ASR and reconnaissance tasks. Apart from the Cant Z.501, the Italians made little use of the flying boat concept generally favoured by other nations for large marine aircraft. Maintenance for the maritime squadrons was possibly simpler than for other arms as there was not the proliferation of types*

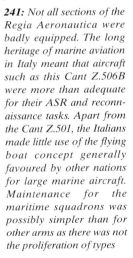

GLOSSARY AND ABBREVIATIONS

AALB: Aeronautica dell'Albania   Airforce Command Albania

AE: Aerial escort duties

AEGF: Aeronautica dell'Egeo   Airforce Command Aegean

AG: Anti-guerilla duties

AGRE: Aeronautica della Grecia   Airforce Command Greece

AN: Anti-naval duties

AOI: Africa Orientale Italiano   Italian East Africa

APRO: Aeronautica della Provence Airforce Command France

AR: Armed reconnaissance duties

A.S.: Aerosilurante   Torpedo bombing arm of RA

ASAR: Aeronautica della Sardegna Airforce Command Sardinia

ASIC: Aeronautica della Sicilia   Airforce Command Sicily

ASR: Air-sea rescue duties

Ass.: Assalto   Lit. assault—Close air support arm of RA

ATUN: Aeronautica della Tunisia   Airforce Command Tunisia

Aut.: Autonomo   Independent

AVRE: Aviazione Per il Regio Escercito   Air Arm of the Royal Italian Army

B.a.T.: Bombardamento a Tuffo   Dive bomber

BGR: Bombardamento a Grande Reggio   Long range bomber

bis: bis   Second model

B.M.: Bombardamento Marittima   Naval bomber

CAI: Corpo Aereo Italiano   Italian Air Corps

C.B.: Caccia Bombardamento   Fighter-bomber

Cdo: Commando   Command HQ

CE: Convoy escort duties

C.M.: Caccia Marittima   Naval fighter

C.N.: Caccia Notturna   Night fighter

Comb.: Combattimento   Combat or ground attack

CSIR: Corpo de Spedizione Italiano in Russia Italian Expeditionary Corps in Russia

C.T.: Caccia Terrestre   Land-based fighter

DB: Day bombing duties

DF: Day fighting duties

FF.NN: Forze Navali   Naval unit

GA: Ground attack duties

Int.: Intercettori   Point defence interceptor

IT: In transit

NB: Night bombing duties

NF: Night fighting duties

O.A.: Osservazione Aerea   Air Observation

qtr: qater   Fourth model

RA: Regia Aeronautica   Royal Air Force (Italian)

R.M.: Regia Marina   Royal Navy (Italian)

R.M.: Ricognizione Marittima   Naval reconnaissance

R.S.: Ricognizione Strategica   Strategic reconnaissance

R.S.M.: Ricognizione Strategica Marittima   Naval strategic reconnaissance

R.S.T.: Ricognizione Strategica Terrestre   Land-based strategic reconnaissance

SAS: Servizi Aerei Speciali   Air transport arm of RA

sil: Aerosilurante   Torpedo bombing arm

socc.: Soccorso   Rescue arm of RA

Sq.: Squadriglia   Squadron or flight

Sqa.: Squadra   Area Command

TB: Torpedo bombing duties

ter: ter   Third model

TG: Training duties

TR: Transport duties

ZAT: Zona Aerea Territoriale   Land Air Zones of Command

SOURCES

As many readers will already know, there are many gaps in the period under study. Records were destroyed or lost during the 'to and fro' battles in the Mediterranean area. Therefore, this book can by no means claim to be definitive, but only act as a guideline to future historians and present readers.

The primary source has been the Italian Airforce files held in the Imperial War Museum Department of Documents, along with volumes from the Department of Books. This has been backed up with correspondence from aircrew and fellow researchers, along with many hours spent deciphering the multitude of Italian publications produced since the war.

Fortunately, immediately after the war, the Italian Air Ministry provided the Allies with a résumé of its war history where records allowed. In the last twenty years there has been an increase in Italian interest in their history, with many excellent accounts by historians such as Nino Arena and Nicola Marizia, to name just two. The major English language contributor has been Christopher Shores who has produced some highly detailed and comprehensive campaign histories in this specialist field.

To help anyone who wishes to investigate this subject further, the following is a list of document references on the files found at the IWM. There were also several files I came across which were not catalogued until I summarised them with permission from the Department. Reference numbers are still to be allotted. Some of the files are sparse in their information, so be prepared to find more or less than you hope.

Not all the wartime files were found, and I understand that in the past these were possibly borrowed by researchers and institutions who failed to return them as requested. Most, if not all, archives are subject to this loss. It not only makes future studies more difficult, but is a very selfish approach to what are meant to be publicly available archives.

The IWM no longer lends out documents, quite rightly, because of the misappropriations. They do, however, have copying facilities if required. As a private individual, with no previous connections with these archives, I ask anyone, both new and experienced, to take due care when using these files. The paper is wartime issue and is now extremely fragile.

E2470	Command and squadron arrangements	Jan 1943
E2471	Ceding airfields to the Luftwaffe— Squadra 1, 2, 3, 5	Jan 1943
E2473	Tables of fighter strengths	Jan 1943
E2475	Air-sea co-operation and protection of convoys	May-Sept 1943
E2476	Collaboration between base defences and air and ground commands	Dec 1942
E2477	Setting up Italian-German W.T. system for aerial reconnaissance	June 1943
E2478	Ultra short wave network as above	March 1943
E2480	Daily reports of Fighter Group activities and movements	
E2481	Monthly reports on airfield organisation	April 1943
E2483	Airfield defence - AA Battery movements	June 1943
E2484	Italian-German fighter collaboration	Jan 1943
E2485	Monthly reports on fighter activity	Jan 1943
E2486	Reports on Allied air attacks	Sept 1943
E2487	Daily air situation reports	July 1943
E2489	Night fighter defence zones	Jan 1943
E2490	Telegrams ordering operations	June-Nov 1942
E2493	Silhouette album of Italian aircraft	1942
E2494	Defence of Malta	1941
E2495	Radar map installations	1943
E2497	Enrolment of recruits 1923-24	1943
E2499	Location of German and Italian radar installations	Jan 1943
E2500	Re 2001 versions	Jan 1943
E2501	Ground lighting for night landings	Dec 1942
E2502	W.T. network in Italy	Dec 1942
E2503	Radar installations	Jan 1943
E2504	Defence organisation of Squadra 1, 2, 4	Jan 1943
E2506	Enemy air activity	Sept 1943
E2509	Call up of 1923-24 recruits for base defence	May 1943
E2511	Pyrotechnics for naval targets	Jan 1943
E2512	Experiments with photoelectric cells against enemy aircraft	Mar 1943
E2514	As above, but for own aircraft and beacons	Jan 1943
E2516	Maps of radar installations	
E2517	RAF bombing of German towns	Mar 1943
E2518	Enemy air activity	Feb 1943
E2519	GEMA radio network	Sept 1942
E2521	Ground defence radar	1943
E2522	Files on D520, Do 217, Bf 110	
E2523	Radar installations Greece to Corsica	1943
E2524	Italian visit to German aircraft factories	June 1941
E2525	List of Junkers compressors sent to Italy	August 1940
E2526	Defence organisation of Italy	1943
E2527	Allied air activity	May-Sept 1943
E2528	Inventions and aircraft exchanged between Germany and Italy	Jan 1941

E2530	Statistics	1940-41
E2531	Operations	1940-Sept 1942
E2532	Operational orders—mostly for Malta	Sept-Nov 1941
E2533	Monthly reports on enemy aircraft destroyed from Sicily	July 1941
E2534	Occupation of Albania	April 1939
E2535	Weekly bulletins on Allied equipment, statistics	1943
E2536	Operations leading to capture of Sidi Barrani	Sept 1940
E2537	Maps showing where RAF aircraft shot down in Italy	
E2538	Reports on British parachute landings	Feb 1941
E2539	Organisation charts for Yugoslav campaign	April 1941
E2541	Squadron statistics	Aug 1940- March 1942
E2543	Plots of bomb damage at Livorno	
E2544	Daily and weekly bulletins on the Russian front	
E2545	Location of German units in Italy	
E2546	Daily bulletins on CAI activity in Belgium	4-23 Jan 1941
E2547	Italian signals regarding the Battle of Britain	1940
E2549	Ground defence of bases	1943
E2550	Daily and weekly squadron strengths	May-Sept 1943
E2553	Mobilisation plan	
E2554	Airfield construction in Libya	1940
E2560	Operational orders for Sicily	1941
E2561	File on British prisoners	Aug 1943
E2562	Lists of men and material transported	Dec 1940- Feb 1941
E2565	Inspection of Squadra	5 Sept 1940
E2567	Malta situation	June 1940- Oct 1942
E2568	Plan for the invasion of Malta	
E2569	Defensive plans	Aug 1943
E2570	Operations in North Africa	Oct 1942- Jan 1943
E3001	Operations in Squadra 5 area	Mar-July 1942
E3002	Statistics and encounters of the Italian navy	1940-43
E3003	Flights by Mussolini	1938-Sept 1943
E3007	Operations against Malta	1941
E3007A	Operations in Africa	Feb 1941- Jan 1942

BIBLIOGRAPHY

Campaign Histories

Garello G: *Regia Aeronautica e Armée de L'Air;* Bizarri 1975

Ghergo Emiliani & Vigna: *Balcani e Fronte Orientale;* Intergest 1974

Ghergo Emiliani & Vigna: *Periodo Prebellico e Fronti Occidentalli;* Intergest 1975

Ghergo Emiliani & Vigna: *Il Settore Mediterraneo;* Intergest 1976

Ghergo Emiliani & Vigna: *I Fronti Africani;* Albertelli 1979

Ghergo Emiliani & Vigna: *La Guerra in Italia;* Albertelli 1982

Gori C. & Borgiotti A: *La Guerra Aerea in Africa Settentrionale;* Stem Mucchi, two volumes

Malizia N.: *Ali Sulla Steppa;* Ateneo 1987 Santoro G.: *L'Aeronautica Italiana Nella Seconda;* Esse Milano 1957

Guerra Mondiale two volumes

Shores C.: *Pictorial History of the Mediterranean Air War Vol.3;* Ian Allen 1974

Shores C.: *Regia Aeronautica 1940-43;* Squadron/Signal 1976

Shores C.&Ring H.: *Fighters over the Desert;* Spearman 1969

Shores Ring & Hess: *Fighters over Tunisia;* Spearman 1975

Unit Histories

Circi M.: *30 Stormo A/S;* Bizzari 1974

Pesce G.: 101 Gruppo Tuffatori; Stem Mucchi 1975

Pesce G.: *Il Walzer del 102 Gruppo;* Stem Mucchi 1976

Pesce G.: *8 Gruppo Caccia;* Stem Mucchi 1974

Petillo A. & Merigo G.: *6 Stormo Caccia;* Stem Mucchi 1976

Unia C: *Storia del Aerosilurante Italiani;* Bizzari 1974

Aircraft Profiles

Abate R.: *Gli Aeroplani della Caproni Bergamasca 1920-1946;* Dell'Ateneo & Bizzari 1978

Apostolo G.: *Fiat CR 42;* La Bancarella Aeronautica 1995

Apostolo G.: *Macchi MC 202;* La Bancarella Aeronautica 1995

Arena N.: *La Luftflotte Italiana;* Aeronautiche Italiane 1978

Bonanni M.: *Caproni Ca 33 e Ca 314;* Editore D'Anna 1969

Garello G.: *Il Breda 65;* Ateneo 1980

Garello G.: *Il Piaggio P108;* Bizarri 1973

Gentilli R.: *SM 79 in Action;* Squadron/Signal 1986

Gentilli R.& Gorena L.: *Macchi 202 in Action;* Squadron/Signal 1980

Govi S.: *Il Caccia Re 2001;* Apostolo 1982

Malizia N.: *Il Fiat CR42;* Ateneo 1977

Malizia N.: *Il Reggiane 2000;* Ateneo 1978

Malizia N.: *Il Fiat CR32;* Ateneo 1981

Prato P.: *Caproni-Reggiane Fighters 1938-45;* Intyrama 1968

Sgarlato N.: *Italian Aircraft of World War Two;* Delta 1979

Thompson J.: *Italian Civil and Military Aircraft 1930-45;* Aero 1963

Valentini & D'Amico: *The Messerschmitt 109 in Italian Service;* Monogram 1985

Vergnano P.: *Fiat Fighters 1930-45;* Intyrama 1969

Various: *Dimensione Cielo* Volumes 1 to 11; Bizzari 1971

Various: *Le Macchine e La Storia;* Stem Mucchi 1976

Camouflage and Markings

Arena N.: *Italian Air Force Camouflage in World War II;* Mucchi 1983

Ghergo Emiliani & Vigna: *Colore e Insegne 1935-43;* Intergest 1974

Postiglioni U. & Degl'Innocenti A.: *Colori e Schemi Mimetici Della Regia Aeronautica 1935-1943;* GMT/CMPR/GAVS 1994

Magazine Articles

Aerofan

Air Enthusiast

Air International

Air Pictorial

Interconair Aviazione e Marina

Modelaid International

242 Left: This picture of Sergent Pilota *Mariotti, seated in the cockpit of his Macchi MC 200 of the 86a Squadriglia, 7° Gruppo, 54° Stormo, symbolises all the young men of the Regia Aeronautica who often had to make do with equipment and resources inferior to their opponents, but did their duty regardless*

243 Above: The calm before the storm. A Macchi MC 202 of the CO of the 151ª Squadriglia, 20° Gruppo, 51° Stormo CT, pictured at Foligno, Italy in August 1943. Finished in the standard factory-applied D3 camouflage scheme it wears the cat and mice badge of the Stormo, as well as a command chevron, somewhat after the style of the Luftwaffe*